D1520090

Intellectuals and Decolonization in France

Intellectuals
and
Decolonization
in France

BY PAUL CLAY SORUM

The University of North Carolina Press
Chapel Hill

Copyright © 1977 by
The University of North Carolina Press
All rights reserved
Manufactured in the United States of America
ISBN 0-8078-1295-1
Library of Congress Catalog Card Number 76-56186

Library of Congress Cataloging in Publication Data

Sorum, Paul Clay, 1943—
  Intellectuals and decolonization in France.

  Bibliography: p.
  Includes index.
  1. France—Colonies. 2. Intellectuals—France.
I. Title.
JV1818.S67   325'.344   76-56186
ISBN 0-8078-1295-1

For Christie

❧ Contents

∿ Tables

ᴄᴧ Preface

This book is a study of the writings of French intellectuals about the problems of decolonization after World War II. It is a discussion of their criticisms of France's colonial policies, of the alternative policies they suggested, of their reactions to the issues connected with decolonization, and, above all, of the arguments they used to justify their positions. It is a history of ideas and, as such, is based on two assumptions.

I assume that a person's ideas can and do have some influence on his actions, that these ideas can be and are in some circumstances altered by rational argument, and that, as a result, it is not impossible that ideas expressed by intellectuals might influence both the ideas and the actions of other people. I investigate concrete examples of intellectuals' efforts to exert such an influence. I do no more than speculate, however, about the nature and extent of the impact of these efforts. Although a study of impact would be fascinating and might be accomplished by means of interviews and polls, it is beyond the scope of this work.

I also assume that in the debate over decolonization the writings of intellectuals can be studied without a great deal of attention to their biographies. It cannot be denied that intellectuals, like other people, are subject to a variety of economic, social, and personal pressures and that these pressures are likely to influence their ideas. Nonetheless, as I will try to demonstrate in this book, it is at least plausible that the primary determinants of the intellectuals' public statements were intellectual: the cultural biases shared by educated Frenchmen, the ideological orientations associated with their particular religious and political affiliations, and the intellectual demands of membership in a professional community that defined itself in terms of an intense commitment to rational inquiry, free debate, and intellectual honesty. To answer such broader questions as why these intellectuals had certain political and religious affiliations and why they had chosen to be intellectuals would require an investigation of prosopography and of the social history of ideas. In this study I am concerned only with their positions on the issues of decolonization.

The primary difficulty encountered in making this study was the overwhelming amount of literature provoked by the problems of decolonization. To limit my inquiry to a manageable size, I focused (though not exclusively) on those intellectuals who protested against colonialist abuses in the overseas territories. In the writings of these "anticolonialists," more than in the writings of the outspoken defenders of empire, the nature and strength of the mental hindrances to decolonization are revealed. Even with this restriction, the field of research remained enormous. I chose to penetrate this mass of polemic in three ways.

The first method of research was to examine in detail the writings of ten anticolonialist intellectuals: Jean-Paul Sartre, Claude Bourdet, Jean-Marie Domenach, François Mauriac, Albert Camus, Jean-Jacques Servan-Schreiber, Raymond Aron, and, for the chapter on ethnocentrism, Léopold Sédar Senghor, Claude Lévi-Strauss, and Jacques Berque. As I began my investigations these names quickly assumed prominence. They were men of high intellectual standing who were actively involved in the debates over decolonization. They also expressed quite different points of view. They seemed to me to be the most eminent and representative sample of individuals.

The second, concurrent method of sampling the opinions of the intellectuals was to consider all the relevant articles in the prestigious non-Communist periodicals that regularly carried anticolonialist writings: the monthlies *Les Temps Modernes*, *Esprit*, *La Nef*, and *Preuves* and, secondarily and less completely, the daily *Combat* (until 1950) and the weeklies *France-Observateur* and *L'Express*.

I chose not to study a Communist periodical because the positions and arguments of the French Communist party on the issues of decolonization have been analyzed in considerable depth by other scholars. Both critics and party apologists agree on the essential aspects of the party's stands. As a result, I am able to discuss Communist positions extensively and with confidence on the basis largely of secondary sources. The intellectuals in the Communist party were not able to deviate very far from the official party line; this has been affirmed repeatedly by former Communists who objected to party policy. Moreover, after May 1947 the Communist party was excluded from the process of policy formation. From that point on the non-Communists alone determined France's policies. The electors and politicians whose opinions are important for an analysis of French decolonization, therefore, are the non-Communists. The significant intellectuals are those who had access to the non-Communist public.

The third method of research was to expand its scope by sending some probes outward: by investigating the writings of other, less well-known intellectuals who worked actively for colonial reform, such as Jean Rous, Charles-André Julien, Pierre-Henri Simon, Germaine Tillion, Francis Jeanson, Frantz Fanon, and Raymond Cartier; by examining a number of less important reviews; by sampling the literature defending the empire to learn the arguments that were advanced, the arguments that were refuted, and the personalities who were attacked; and by studying the retrospective assessments of French and foreign participants and observers and of other scholars.

Bias due to the selectivity of research might still remain. To this must be added the distortions introduced by the attempt to synthesize the product of this research. I discuss the debates over the issues of decolonization in an order intended to be both logical and historical, but as a result not quite either. Chapters 2 through 6 describe how the "humanist" intellectuals responded to the intellectual problems that were successively posed by the objective situation; chapter 7 focuses on the concurrent reactions of the "realists"; chapter 8 on the more general problem of ethnocentrism. The conclusion that independence for the colonial peoples was the best solution was reached only slowly and with difficulty. Since independence was demanded by much of the indigenous population and ultimately was granted by France, the principal question around which this study is organized is why the intellectuals found it so difficult, on intellectual grounds, to advocate and justify independence.

I have tried to appreciate and to present as fairly as possible the points of view of all the protagonists. In addition, as is, I believe, my right and duty, I have offered my own assessments of these points of view. In these assessments, my personal dislike of ethnocentrism, colonization, and warfare—sharpened by America's ordeal in Vietnam —may be all too evident. I am grateful for aid from a number of people.

Many of the protagonists of my book were willing to talk with me about their involvement in the debates over decolonization: Jeanson, Aron, Julien, Bourdet, Rous, Sartre, Domenach, Tillion, Lévi-Strauss, and Berque. Jeanson, Julien, and Tillion also offered me access to their own collections of writings on decolonization. Jean Suret-Canale, director of the Centre d'Études at de Recherches Marxistes, explained to me at considerable length the position of the Communist party. Alfred Grosser and Raoul Girardet, professors at the Institut d'Études Politiques, gave me words of caution near the beginning of my project, although I did not heed them.

Several persons have read my work and offered valuable suggestions. The book is an expansion and revision of the doctoral thesis that, with H. Stuart Hughes as my adviser and Stanley Hoffmann as my second reader, I completed in 1971 for the history department of Harvard University. Christina E. Sorum, David Harnett, Tony Smith, Tom Cassilly, C. H. Sorum, Richard Brace, Joan Brace, Édouard Morot-Sir, and Gordon Wright, in addition to Professors Hughes and Hoffmann, have examined the whole study in one of its versions. Several of the protagonists—Jeanson, Aron, Berque, and Tillion—were kind enough to read and comment on the part of my thesis devoted to them. Joseph Tulchin helped me to clarify my discussion of the role of intellectuals. Tom Reefe, Craig Williamson, and William Levine suggested numerous improvements in chapter 8.

I would also like to thank the people who have helped in research, editing, and typing: Bruce Brooks, Milton Ayala, Pauline Stinchfield, Pat Maynor, Linda Killen, and, most of all, Mrs. Jacob Kaplan.

The translation of a French quotation is mine if a French work is cited in the note and the official translator's if a translated work is cited. Only the author and title of a work are mentioned in the notes; full bibliographical information is supplied in the Bibliography.

Intellectuals and Decolonization in France

1 &. EMPIRE AND INTELLECTUALS

At the end of World War II the French people found themselves embroiled in a long and losing struggle to retain their colonial empire. French intellectuals were engaged in polemics over the nature and function of the intellectual in modern society. The aim of this book is to elucidate both the agony of decolonization and the role of the intellectual by studying these issues at their point of intersection: the involvement of the French intellectuals in the process of decolonization.

THE AGONY OF DECOLONIZATION

On 8 May 1945 the people of Paris crowded into the streets to celebrate the end of the war in Europe. On the same day in Algeria, Moslem nationalists joined the victory parades carrying banners calling for political liberation. In the town of Sétif, in a mountainous region of Algeria where the people suffered from famine, a policeman killed one of the demonstrators, and the celebration ended in the murder of twenty-one French citizens. This insurrection spread through the countryside but was quickly repressed by the French army, which killed thousands of Moslems in the area of Sétif in the following weeks. On the very day that one period of bloodshed ended another began: the battles of French decolonization.

Although the Algerian inhabitants did not forget Sétif, Algeria remained fairly quiet until 1954. But troubles immediately arose elsewhere in France's vast empire. In the Middle East, de Gaulle had in 1941 promised independence to France's League of Nations mandates, Syria and Lebanon, but had postponed putting this promise into effect. His attempt in May 1945 to send replacements for the small French garrisons there provoked an uprising of Arab nationalists spurred on by the British. The French resisted, even bombarding Damascus in early June. De Gaulle was forced by military weakness, however, to agree to quick evacuation of Syria and Lebanon. While these territories were not an important part of the empire, the circumstances of France's eviction were humiliating.

The loss of Syria and Lebanon was of minor significance, however, compared to contemporaneous events in French Indochina. On 9 March 1945, Japanese troops eliminated the colonial administration that had functioned throughout their occupation of Indochina. On 11 March, Emperor Bao Dai, under Japanese patronage, declared the independence of Vietnam. The popularity of Bao Dai, however, soon was overshadowed by that of the anti-Japanese resistance chief, the Communist Ho Chi Minh. After the surrender of Japan to the Allies, Bao Dai abdicated his throne and rallied to Ho Chi Minh, who in turn proclaimed the independence of the Democratic Republic of Vietnam on 2 September. But the French were unwilling to give up their sovereignty in Indochina and in December 1946 began an eight-year war. They set up Bao Dai again as a rival to Ho Chi Minh and tried to win popular support for him even at the cost of conceding, gradually and reluctantly, most of the independence he too demanded. But the rebels could not be defeated.

In 1947 conflicts erupted in other parts of the empire, most seriously in Madagascar, where a savage massacre of over a hundred European settlers provoked a repression that resulted in the deaths of tens of thousands of Malagasies. With order restored in Madagascar, attention in France was focused increasingly on the North African protectorates of Tunisia and Morocco. Faced with growing nationalist demands there, the French turned from a refusal to grant reforms to repression, culminating on 20 August 1953 in the deposition of the sultan of Morocco. In both territories the nationalists resorted to terrorism.

In 1954, Premier Pierre Mendès-France acted to resolve the conflicts in the colonies. He went to Geneva to negotiate an end to the war in Indochina and concluded on 20 July the accords that recognized the complete independence of North and South Vietnam, Cambodia, and Laos. He flew to Carthage on 31 July to proclaim the "internal autonomy" of Tunisia and thus reopened dialogue with the North African nationalists, although Morocco and Tunisia did not achieve independence until early 1956. Mendès-France also presided over the transfer to India of Pondichéry and the other French trading posts on the Indian coast.

Mendès-France was still in office when, on 1 November 1954, a small group of Algerian nationalists, the Front de Libération Nationale (FLN), began a new war. By 1956 a French army of over four hundred thousand men was stationed in Algeria, but the rebellion continued. The regime in Paris itself became a casualty of this rebellion. Faced with the uprising on 13 May 1958 of the French settlers and army in Algeria, the National Assembly of the Fourth Republic delegated its power to Charles de Gaulle.

De Gaulle presided over the end of the empire in Africa. The territories of sub-Saharan Africa and Madagascar had already received a more decentralized and democratic administration in June 1956. Under de Gaulle each of these states achieved a peaceful transition to independence by the end of 1960. In Algeria, however, the war with the FLN continued. Before he could end it, de Gaulle faced both an uprising of settlers in January 1960 and a rebellion of French army officers in April 1961. Finally, in a treaty signed at Évian on 18 March 1962, de Gaulle agreed to an independent Algeria under the control of the FLN.

On the eve of World War II, France had controlled a colonial empire second in size only to that of Britain, an empire over twenty times as large as the home country and containing one and a half times as many inhabitants. In 1962 only scattered remnants were left.

France was not the only European power to experience the disintegration of its empire after the war, but France was rivaled only by Portugal in the degree of suffering inflicted and experienced in the loss of its empire.

POLICY AND OPINION

The political leaders of the period after the Liberation must be held responsible for the long agony that accompanied the process of decolonization. Although they treated the colonial subjects with greater equality than before, making them French citizens and renaming the empire the "French Union," their constant aim was to maintain control over the empire. Their intransigence resulted from a particular political system and a deeply held set of beliefs.

France was governed by a cabinet of ministers that remained in power only as long as its policies were supported by a majority in the National Assembly.[1] This majority was difficult to establish and maintain. The strength of the parties that rejected the Republic—the Communists, the Gaullists (until the organized movement dissolved in the early 1950s), and later the Poujadists—meant that during most of the Fourth Republic one-third of the deputies refused to support all cabinets. Furthermore, the deputies who remained as potential supporters of the government were divided into a multiplicity of parties and factions with wide disagreements on important issues.

The governments of the Fourth Republic were, therefore, uneasy coalitions of diverse political groups. The deputies of each group proved ready to desert a coalition whenever they opposed a government policy; any such desertion was likely to bring down the government. Even if parliamentary leaders themselves were able to compromise in order to prolong the life of a cabinet, they were unable to control the votes of the rank-and-file deputies of their parties. The result was that any given cabinet usually survived only a few months. Yet, because of the unavailability of the votes on the extremes, each coalition had to include some of the members of its predecessors. The ministers of one cabinet were likely to be ministers in the next.

The consequence of this discontinuity in governments with the accompanying continuity of personnel was that governments found it difficult to undertake innovative policies. Creative and energetic measures were likely to offend a part of the majority, especially when some members of the coalition were identified with the policies of past governments. The colonial policy that least threatened the cohesion of the governing majority was to try to preserve the French presence overseas but to avoid as much as possible any specification of the means by which this goal might be achieved. This left the definition of means to local officials and the colonial interest groups and to the *faits accomplis* of the military.

The Communist party was the only one strongly opposed to empire, but, after its exclusion from parliamentary politics in May 1947, it could exert little influence on overseas policy. Thenceforth, in order to obtain a parliamentary majority, a government had to win the support of political groups that cherished France's imperial vocation. Foreign and colonial affairs became the special preserve of the imperially minded Christian democrats, the Mouvement Républicain Populaire

(MRP), which controlled the Ministry of Foreign Affairs from 1947 to 1954. The disintegration of the Gaullist movement after the elections of 1951 permitted the leaders of the center parties to seek the support of deputies who, as Gaullists, were outspoken imperialists. The Communists tried to reenter the government after the leftist victory in the elections of January 1956, but they were rebuffed by the Socialist premier Guy Mollet. To stay in power Mollet was forced to rely on the votes of rightist deputies who insisted on the continuation of a hard-line policy in Algeria.

The political system alone, however, does not explain the resistance to decolonization. Although the governments permitted overseas affairs to be regulated for the most part by the civilian and military officials on the spot who were devoted to preserving the status quo, the governments were willing to commit France to vigorous action against any overt threat to the empire—as is evidenced by the wars in Indochina and Algeria. Although the deputies were divided over the details of overseas policy, they were in agreement, with the partial exception of the Communists and a few others, over the basic aim—the maintenance of an imperial system. The instability of coalition government contributed to the incoherence and ineffectiveness of overseas policy, but the refusal to accord independence derives from a more profound source: the widespread belief in the value and legitimacy of the French empire.[2]

This belief in empire must be analyzed to determine whose ideas were responsible for the unfortunate pattern of overseas actions. As an initial hypothesis, it can be suggested that the French voters should receive the blame. During the Third Republic, following the government's conquest of empire, imperialist ideas spread among the French voters. By World War II belief in empire had been solidly implanted in the public mind and was reinforced by the role played by the colonies in the liberation of France from the Nazis. While during the Third Republic the governments had led the public on colonial affairs, there is reason to believe that during the Fourth Republic they followed it. The imperialist convictions of the electorate may have imposed an imperialist policy on the political leadership.

Opinion polls reveal that, when World War II ended, the French people were used to possessing an empire, expected that it would remain French, and wanted to keep it. In the words of one observer, while public opinion was "ready to accept any transformation, even a radical one, of the colonial system," it was "absolutely not disposed to allow the slightest attempt at secession."[3] Only in early 1947, when it was impossible to ignore the crises in the British and Dutch colonies as well as in the French, did large numbers of Frenchmen realize that the empire might be doomed. Even then, most continued to hope that France would be able to retain at least its African territories and, above all, Algeria (see table 1).

The polls also reveal that the segment of the electorate most opposed to empire voted for the Communist party, but these were a stable and isolated group with very little political influence. Not only were their deputies excluded from participation in policy formation, but the other parties made few efforts to appeal to them. The governing parties, even the Socialists, competed for the votes of people who, as one of their characteristics, tended to favor or at least to be ambivalent about empire (as exemplified in table 1).[4] The electoral threat to these parties came not from the Communists, but from the imperialist Gaullist and Poujadist movements. The governing parties would hardly undertake a policy of decolonization that might persuade their voters to join the anti-Republican surges.

Yet the electorate appears to have exerted little influence on actual overseas policy. On a concrete level the French people were mostly ignorant of and indifferent to the overseas territories. In the early Fourth Republic the turmoil overseas, even the war in Indochina, was overshadowed by the turmoil within France—food and fuel shortages, inflation, strikes, and political instability.[5] In the 1951 elections to the National Assembly the war in Indochina and the condition of the French Union were only minor issues. The French people apparently thought about the empire only when it was endangered, and even then they were unwilling to sacrifice heavily to retain it. The military effort in Indochina, for example, was never very popular (see table 2). No French government dared to test the limits of public tolerance of the war by sending draftees to fight there. The voters who were unenthusiastic about policy in Indochina did not, however, care enough about it to turn it into an electoral issue. Because of the general indifference, the deputies could ignore overseas matters or act on them without accountability. Not until 1953 did the public become seriously concerned about overseas problems, and this occurred in large part because the war in Indochina was held responsible for budgetary problems at home.[6] Only in the case of Algeria did the public give active support to

Table 1. Proposals for Policy in Tunisia

Responses to the question: In your opinion, what would it be necessary to do in Tunisia?

Percentage distribution of proposals, August 1954.

	Distribution among All Those Polled	Distribution among Those Who Indicated Party Affiliation					
		Communist	Socialist	MRP	Radical	Moderate	Gaullist
Accord complete independence	17%	50%	18%	9%	14%	9%	7%
Accord autonomy while safe-guarding French interests	15	11	20	17	19	16	22
Amend the current policy without changing the status of the country	14	14	15	20	11	19	15
Reestablish order without violence	4	3	2	4	4	4	10
Use force	11	2	12	16	14	19	16
Assimilate Tunisia to France	2	2	3	4	3	1	2
Other solutions	2	1	2	1	1	3	4
No response	35	17	28	29	34	29	24
	100%	100%	100%	100%	100%	100%	100%

Source: *Sondages* 16, no. 4 (1954): 12–14.

Table 2. Evolution of Public Opinion on Indochina

Responses to the question: What is it necessary to do in Indochina now, in your opinion?

Percentage distribution of opinions at five different dates.

	January 1947	July 1949	October 1950	May 1953	February 1954
Reestablish order, send reinforcements	37%	19%	27%	15%	7%
Call for aid from the United Nations or the Americans	—	—	8	6	1
Negotiate with the Vietminh	15	—	24	35	42
Stop the war and recognize the independence of Vietnam	22	38	—	—	—
Abandon Indochina, recall the troops	—	11	18	15	18
Either be more energetic or abandon it	—	2	3	4	2
Other solutions	5	5	—	2	1
No response	21	25	20	23	29
	100%	100%	100%	100%	100%

Source: *Sondages* 16, no. 4 (1954): 10.

the fight against colonial nationalism. Except for Algeria, therefore, the French electorate was only "passively imperialist."

More generally, the French public exerted little influence over the formulation of policy in any area. The French citizen participated very little in public affairs. His only regular function was to select the representatives—local and national—in whom sovereignty subsequently resided. He was more likely to vote than an American citizen, but the act of voting was "more expressive than instrumental"; it was a means more of registering his opinion, perhaps his protest, than of influencing public policy.[7] Parliamentary elections tended to be fought not over national problems, but over general political ideology or specific local concerns, and the electorate viewed its deputy as the defender of local interests rather than as the architect of a coherent national policy. Between elections the public did not expect, and was not expected, to influence national policy. The electoral system of the Fourth Republic —voting at the departmental level between lists of candidates drawn up by the parties—increased the distance between the voters and the policy makers.

Real political influence in France was concentrated in the small minority active in politics. The 5 percent of the electorate who claimed party membership were much more conscious of issues and doctrines than were American party members. Among these, the party workers (*militants*) were able to apply such effective pressure on their deputies that they have been held responsible for the peculiar divisiveness and ideological character of French politics. During the Algerian war Premier Mollet, for example, had to gear his policies to keep the support of the Socialist party congresses as well as of the National Assembly. One reason for the power of the *militants* in the Fourth Republic was that they usually decided a candidate's position on the party list in their department and, therefore, controlled his chances of being elected. If the important people in such areas as business and administration are added to the *militants* and the deputies, a political elite emerges composed of persons who were concerned about national policy and were in a position to influence its formulation.[8]

The evidence suggests, though it does not prove, that this elite was more imperialist than was the mass of the public. The polls indicate that people of higher income, education, and social status tended to be the strongest believers that the empire should be preserved. Moreover, not only government policies but also public statements of parties and politicians seem to have been more intransigent than the electorate demanded. The war in Indochina is a striking example. The governments continued the war even though for most of its duration the majority of the public that voted for the governing parties either opposed or refused to express an opinion on it. The underlying reason for the agony of decolonization, therefore, appears to have been the imperialist convictions of the small politically influential segment of the French public.[9]

It is difficult to understand why these educated and active people did not adjust their ideas concerning empire to permit a smoother process of decolonization and thereby to ease the agony for both the colonies and France. Reasons may be found in the ideas to which the elite was exposed in books, magazines, newspapers, and private discussions. The members of society who devote themselves to ideas and who mediate in, if not initiate, the process of ideological change are the intellectuals. This group and its social role must be examined to comprehend the persistence of the outmoded belief in empire.

THE ROLE OF THE INTELLECTUALS

The intellectual is the explorer of the sacred. He questions what man, society, and the universe are and ought to be. He investigates and illuminates the answers of other men to these basic questions. If he is dissatisfied with the answers, he criticizes them and offers alternatives. He judges men's particular notions and actions in light of fundamental ideas and values.

The intellectual is likely to be both attracted to and produced by professions—literature, teaching, the clergy, law, and scientific research —that involve a concern with the truth of men's beliefs and the morality of their actions. In expressing this concern, he is likely to be critical of the beliefs, institutions, and actions of the men of his society, attacking either the content of their ideas and values or the inevitable failure to act according to them. It is this concern, rather than his profession, that both defines him as an intellectual and gives him a potentially important role in society.[10]

As an individual grows up, he is taught a set of values, rules of conduct, and expectations about the world. This education serves a double function. First, it guides the individual in his actions and loyalties; it defines the acceptable, even conceivable, lines of conduct for him. It provides him with ideas that are characteristic of his society or of groups within it and thus gives him ideological grounds for social identifications. Second, this education is useful to society. In conjunction with the education given to other individuals, it creates ideological consensus and designates social roles, thus increasing the cohesion and harmony of the society.[11]

The social role of the intellectual is to examine his society's basic principles and their particular application. The basic values and beliefs may be found contradictory, false, contrary to the true interests of society or the individuals who compose it, or inferior to alternative values and beliefs. Because of changing circumstances and advances in knowledge, some of them may be found anachronistic and in need of replacement or restatement. Particular institutions, beliefs, and practices may be found inconsistent with and potentially destructive of the fundamental principles of the society. Even those beliefs not found wanting may be strengthened and reaffirmed by testing and questioning. For these reasons, although the intellectual's criticism may promote disorder or even social disintegration, it usually can be expected in time to prove beneficial to his society.

The major protagonists of this study are professional intellectuals —literary figures, journalists, professors—who shared the conception of the intellectual's role described above and acted accordingly. Refusing to restrict themselves to a narrow pursuit of their literary and scholarly specialties, they chose to reflect on and to write about the political and philosophical issues of their age and of their nation. They chose to be "engaged."

French intellectuals have a tradition of active involvement in the controversies of their day—Pascal of *Les Provinciales*, the *philosophes*, Hugo and Lamartine, the Dreyfusards. By the time of the Liberation in 1944, the French intellectuals had been politically sensitized by a decade of struggle against fascism, highlighted by the Spanish Civil War and, most of all, by the French Resistance. Most of the figures considered in this study fought against the Nazis and the Vichy regime, either in the interior Resistance or with the Free French. This experience convinced them to involve themselves as writers in the postwar struggle for liberty and social justice in France and in the world. As François Mauriac declared in defense of his intervention in politics, "Our generation has paid dearly for the knowledge that we are all engaged, that we are all embarked in the same tragic adventure, all in solidarity, all responsible, and that of all the partisan positions the refusal to take a side is without doubt the only one that can find no justification, neither before God nor before men."[12] Jean-Paul Sartre wanted imaginative literature to be written to promote human liberty, while those writers who insisted on the separation of literature from politics were willing as individuals to take public political stands.

The impact of intellectuals on the ideas and behavior of other people is a function, in part, of the status attributed to them and to their ideas. Their potential impact is great in France because both intellectuals and ideas are highly respected by the French and the areas of culture in which the intellectuals are the recognized specialists have enormous prestige. In the *lycées* the middle- and upper-class youth are imbued with the classics of French literature and philosophy. Political and military leaders, as well as writers and artists, seek in carefully written essays and memoirs to participate in this brilliant tradition and even aspire to gain admission to its official shrine, the Académie Française. Even among the lower classes the conviction is widespread that literature and art are the source of a large part of France's past and present glory. This prestige is utilized by newspaper editors who seek to grace their columns with the reflections of well-known literary figures and scholars and by political leaders who display their party intellectuals.[13]

Another reason for the respect for intellectuals and ideas is the important role of ideology in French politics. Deputies usually have received extensive education, and about half of them come from "intellectual" professions. The numerous parties and factions into which they are separated use ideology as a means of identifying and distinguishing themselves. The party members, especially the *militants*, insist that the deputies adhere to this ideology. Although politicians are suspicious of intellectuals in general, they need party intellectuals to help formulate doctrines.

Furthermore, the long tradition of intellectual engagement has familiarized the French people with, and given legitimacy to, the intellectuals' claim to be the public's secular "directors of conscience." The resulting power of the intellectuals is testified to by the shrill attacks of their opponents. Even if these attacks have disguised the true cause of problems by blaming the intellectuals, they suggest that many French people are willing to believe that intellectuals have a great deal of influence on opinion and policy.

Intellectuals in France, therefore, have a high status and are considered to have a great deal of influence. They have actual influence, however, only to the extent that they are able to change the ideas of other Frenchmen. Consequently, their real impact depends not only on their status but also on the channels of communication, the power of their particular messages, and the receptivity of the audience to these messages.

Intellectuals address both other intellectuals and a wider audience; their writings have a double aim of developing and clarifying ideas through interchange among themselves and of convincing the reading public of the validity of those ideas. The second aim may seem to be largely frustrated by the very limited circulations of the publications in which the writings of the intellectuals usually appear.[14] Yet the small group to which the initial impact of intellectuals is restricted is an important one. The people who read monthlies like *Preuves*, *La Nef*, *Esprit*, and *Les Temps Modernes*; weeklies like *L'Express* (before its transformation in 1963 to a popular news weekly) and *France-Observateur*; dailies like *Combat*, *Le Monde*, and *Le Figaro* are likely to be concerned about and active in politics. They include much of the segment of the French population that is or might be influential in policy formulation, especially those of the Left. The intellectuals' lack of direct access to the general public, therefore, is more than compensated for by their access to the policy makers and opinion leaders of France.[15]

The political elite, apparently distinguished from the general public by a stronger belief in empire, seems to have persisted in this belief throughout most of the period of decolonization. The impact of the intellectuals' messages on their audience does not appear, therefore, to have resulted in a significant shift of opinion in favor of granting independence to the colonies. Accordingly, this study is an examination of the content of these messages.

INTELLECTUALS AND EMPIRE

The attitudes concerning colonial empire of both intellectuals and nonintellectuals can be categorized on two levels: treatment and possession. The attitudes toward treatment of colonies are spread between the poles of "colonialism" and "anticolonialism." The first is the approval of the exploitation of colonies for the benefit of the home country. The second is the opposition to such exploitation and its related abuses and the insistence that the colonies must be administered in the interests of the indigenous population. The attitudes toward possession of colonies are spread between the poles of "imperialism" and "anti-imperialism." At the one extreme is not only the belief that empire is legitimate and beneficial to the home country and to the colonies, but also the willingness to fight in order to gain or retain colonies. At the other extreme is the belief that empire is illegitimate and that colonies should be granted independence.

The spread of attitudes toward treatment of colonies is illustrated by the responses to the question posed in 1946 in a French public opinion poll: "Should we administer our colonies above all for the profit of France, or above all for the profit of the indigenous populations?" Thirty-one percent replied for the profit of France, 25 percent for the profit of both France and the "natives," 28 percent for the profit of the natives, while 16 percent had no opinion.[16] The underlying assumption of the question, however, was imperialist: it was that France would continue to possess colonies and could choose to administer them in either a colonialist or an anticolonialist fashion.

Anticolonialism and anti-imperialism, therefore, must not be confused. The anticolonialist is interested in reforming the colonial system for the benefit of the colonial people, but not necessarily in ending the system. The anti-imperialist is opposed to the system itself. The anticolonialist is concerned primarily with economic and social issues, the anti-imperialist initially and primarily with political issues.[17]

Few postwar intellectuals, or politicians, were willing to advocate colonialist exploitation of the empire. One reason was the ascendancy of the Left at the Liberation; another was the increased criticism of colonialism by the Soviets and Americans and by colonial leaders. The intellectuals who wrote about overseas questions varied greatly, however, not only in the degree of their anticolonialism, but also in their attitudes toward the possession of empire. They can be separated, though awkwardly and without a clear boundary line, into two groups: the "imperialists" and the "anticolonialists."

Most of the imperialist intellectuals were also rightists. They justified empire in terms of the nationalist, elitist, and paternalist ideas that characterized the traditionalist and Bonapartist strains of the French Right. Two prominent examples were Thierry Maulnier and Jacques Soustelle. Maulnier was an essayist and dramatist of the traditionalist Right who had supported the Vichy regime. Soustelle, an anthropologist who was an expert on the Aztecs, had rallied instead to de Gaulle during the war and was a leading Gaullist politician during the Fourth Republic. Both men defended French sovereignty especially in Algeria; Soustelle, who served as governor general of Algeria in 1955, even turned against de Gaulle when the president of the Fifth Republic began the process of disengagement from Algeria.[18]

The writings of the other, larger group of intellectuals were primarily anticolonialist in theme. This group was composed mainly of leftists who, in accord with their overall vision of the world, expected the lower classes to suffer injustices at the hands of privileged groups and spoke out on behalf of the victims. They charged that French officials and businessmen, intellectuals like Soustelle and Maulnier, and the governments of the Fourth Republic were trying to continue the colonialist domination and exploitation of the overseas peoples.

Yet the "anticolonialists" too shied away from the anti-imperialist position. They too hesitated to declare that France should accord independence to its colonies. Consequently, they too must share in the responsibility for the continued efforts to preserve the empire. Indeed, the inability of the proponents of colonial reform to develop a convincing case for independence provides greatest insight into the ideological obstacles to decolonization, and therefore this study focuses on the anticolonialist intellectuals.

Certain of the more active and prestigious anticolonialists and certain of the periodicals in which they wrote will be mentioned repeatedly in the following chapters, and I will introduce them briefly here.

On the far Left were the various socialists, such as Claude Bourdet, Jean Rous, and the writers of *Les Temps Modernes* and *Esprit*. Disappointed by the failure of the Liberation, these men persistently criticized the Fourth Republic. As socialists, they were sympathetic to people in revolt against any form of capitalism. Although all were influenced by Marxism, their brands of socialism differed.

Bourdet, who edited the daily *Combat* (1947–50) and the weekly *L'Observateur* (renamed *France-Observateur* in 1954), was the Left's leading journalist. A hero of the Resistance, he continued to fight for the principles of socialist humanism that had inspired many of the non-Communist resisters. He also called for a neutralist French foreign policy during the Cold War. In the late 1940s and early 1950s he became the most vociferous of the critics of France's overseas policies.

Rous, who had been a companion of Trotsky in the 1930s, devoted himself even more quickly than Bourdet after the Liberation to support for revolutionary forces overseas. He has been described by other intellectuals as the one who saw "earliest and clearest" in colonial matters.[19] In addition to writing articles, primarily for the newspaper *Franc-Tireur*, Rous collaborated with a variety of colonial nationalists as secretary general of the Congress of Peoples against Imperialism.

The monthly review *Les Temps Modernes* was founded in 1945 by a group of intellectuals headed by the existential phenomenologists Jean-Paul Sartre and Maurice Merleau-Ponty. Committed to the extension of liberty to people of all classes, Merleau-Ponty and Sartre became allies of the Communist party and tried to elaborate an existentialist version of Marxism. Led by Merleau-Ponty and the surrealist poet and anthropologist Michel Leiris, the review supported the overseas struggles for liberation although not strongly until the early 1950s. The most active anticolonialist on the staff was the young Francis Jeanson, the managing editor of *Les Temps Modernes* from 1952 to 1956, who was a more militant Marxist than Sartre and Merleau-Ponty and had lived in North Africa.

The socialism and anticolonialism of *Esprit* had a quite different inspiration than the others. The review originated in 1932 in a study group in the home of the Catholic philosopher Jacques Maritain, and its editors—Emmanuel Mounier (1932–50), Albert Béguin (1950 –57), and Jean-Marie Domenach (since 1957)—were all devout Roman Catholics. Nonetheless, *Esprit* deliberately avoided church ties, and its general inspiration was not Catholic doctrine but the "personalist" philosophy of Mounier. Rebelling against the contrast he saw between the "established disorder" of bourgeois, nominally Christian society and the ideal Christian order, Mounier called for a "personalist revolution": a social transformation dedicated to the respect for and fulfillment of the human person in all his facets, especially to the reinfusion of spirituality and communitarian feeling into modern life. In the name of France's responsibility to create a "personalist" community of peoples, *Esprit* examined colonial problems both before and after the war in greater depth than did any other of the intellectuals' publications.

The writers of *Esprit* and other left-wing Catholics formed close alliances with the nonreligious intellectuals of the non-Communist far Left. The different individuals communicated with each other, signed joint manifestos, combined in short-lived groups for political action, and wrote in each other's publications. Rous, for example, wrote anticolonialist articles in *Les Temps Modernes* and *Esprit*, Bourdet in *Les Temps Modernes*, and Jeanson in *Esprit*.

The moderate leftists—including Albert Camus, François Mauriac, Jean-Jacques Servan-Schreiber, and Maurice Duverger—made up another loosely interconnected group of intellectuals. They were concerned with the liberties, rights, and welfare of the individual and advocated social justice but not socialism. They were, therefore, anti-Communist, criticizing many of the far leftists for their sympathy for the Soviet Union and the French Communist party. They were for the most part slower than those on the far Left to denounce the Fourth Republic and its overseas policies.

The weekly *L'Express*, founded by Servan-Schreiber in 1953, became the focal point of moderate leftist anticolonialism. Servan-Schreiber was a supporter of Pierre Mendès-France, the leader of the left wing of the Radical party, and the publication benefited from the surge in Mendès-France's popularity among France's electorate and intellectuals. Mauriac, the Catholic novelist who received the Nobel prize for literature in 1953, was a regular contributor, switching his column to *L'Express* from the conservative newspaper *Le Figaro*. The occasional contributors ranged from moderate to far leftists. They included Camus, who had edited *Combat* from 1944 to 1947 and who would receive the Nobel prize for literature in 1957; the economist and demographer Alfred Sauvy; Domenach; and Sartre.

The two other important political publications of the leftist intellectuals were the newspaper *Le Monde* and the review *La Nef*. These were politically more moderate than *L'Express* and more closely linked with official government circles. *Le Monde*, founded in 1944 by the liberal Catholic Hubert Beuve-Méry, became the most influential printed source of information and analysis for France's directing elites. Servan-Schreiber was one of its writers on foreign policy before he left to start *L'Express*.

La Nef was founded in 1944 as a monthly literary review, was transformed in December 1952 into a trimonthly periodical devoted to reflection on current issues, and was changed in December 1956 into a "monthly political review with large circulation." Its editor was Lucie Faure, whose husband, Edgar, was the leader of the moderate faction of the Radical party and a rival to Mendès-France. *La Nef* received frequent contributions from left-centrist politicians such as Faure and François Mitterrand and from the political scientist Maurice Duverger, a professor at the law school of the University of Paris, who also wrote for *Le Monde* and *L'Express*.

The differences between the moderate Left and the moderate or "liberal" Right, the heirs of the Orleanists of the nineteenth century, are difficult to pinpoint. Both stressed individual freedoms, but the latter put more emphasis on free enterprise (versus social welfare) and on social hierarchy and order. Liberal opposition to empire during the eighteenth and nineteenth centuries, founded on a calculation of the economic consequences of colonization, was revived by Raymond Aron in the mid-1950s. Aron, France's most brilliant and prolific social scientist, wrote briefly for *Les Temps Modernes* and subsequently for Camus's *Combat*. He soon allied himself with the Right, however, supporting the political movement launched in 1947 by de Gaulle and writing for *Le Figaro* as well as for the liberal monthly *Preuves*, which was founded in 1950 by the Congress for Cultural Freedom in order to fight communism.

The various leftist anticolonialists took largely "moralist" positions. They judged overseas policies according to their compatibility with basic moral values, in particular with the amorphous and sometimes contradictory set of values that, under the label of "humanism," stood for the interests of every individual (human rights, the integrity of the person, social justice).[20] At the same time many of these anticolonialists—especially Bourdet, Servan-Schreiber, and Duverger—criticized overseas policies from a "realist" point of view, as did Aron. They questioned the feasibility of the policies in achieving French aims, either in creating a stable French Union or, more generally, in furthering national interests.

The moralists and the realists focused on different sides of France's imperial ideology. The moralists were concerned with the claim that the French were fulfilling a civilizing mission in the interests of the colonial peoples; the realists with the claim that retention of empire was in the interests of the French people. Moralist criticism of France's colonial policies was more widespread, more passionate, and, at first, more influential than realist criticism. Accordingly, this book concentrates initially and at greater length on moralist criticism; it returns in the seventh chapter to deal with the realist arguments.

2 ⟪ THE HUMANIST EMPIRE

The French entered the period of decolonization with a widespread belief in the "humanist" nature of their imperial efforts. This initial good conscience about empire must be examined in order to appreciate the resistance to decolonization of France's people, politicians, and moralist intellectuals.

THE COLONIAL MISSION OF FRANCE

The French had acquired colonies, during the Third Republic as well as earlier, primarily as a means of demonstrating and augmenting the glory and power of the state. The motives for conquest were geopolitical—the strategic, demographic, economic, and symbolic value of the colonies—rather than humanitarian. At the same time an accessory idea was developed and spread that the French had a vocation and a mission to bring Christian and Western civilization to the overseas lands. This idea helped to legitimize an otherwise morally questionable venture and, therefore, was particularly attractive to moralist intellectuals. It was nourished and successively reinforced during France's colonial history by a variety of sources: the Catholic religion, Jacobin ideology, the celebration of Western science and industry, the doctrines of military and civilian administrators, the requirements of colonial development.[1]

Conquest of empire was, from the beginning, accompanied by an effort of Roman Catholic proselytism. The activity of French missions increased considerably in the nineteenth century, and during the anticlerical Third Republic the missionaries continued to aid and be aided by the political expansion of France. Even under the Catholic kings proselytism was only a secondary reason for colonization, but thousands of French men and women—two-thirds of all Catholic missionaries—were drawn overseas by a desire to spread their religion. Their appeals for support from the parishes of France helped to spread the idea of colonial mission. More generally, Christian charity was a constant and powerful motive for support of all efforts to improve the lives of the overseas peoples.

The enthusiasm of the Jacobins was a parallel source of modern French colonial zeal. The armies of the Old Regime had invaded foreign territories to subjugate and annex them; the armies of the French Revolution came, at least in theory, to liberate. The Jacobin leaders proclaimed that their soldiers were freeing Europe from the tyranny of kings and aristocrats, that they were spreading enlightenment, the Rights of Man, and popular sovereignty. The missionary ardor of the Jacobins outdid that of the Catholics they were trying to suppress in France.

Jacobin nationalism, a peculiar blend of Francocentrism and expansive generosity, was the final product of the age of neoclassicism —the age of Louis XIV and of the *philosophes*, of French political and cultural predominance, of the conviction that differences among men were superficial. Jacobin armed expansion was a political application of the pride of the neoclassical French in their "universalism": they believed that their civilization was based on a common human denominator, on the principles and values that were applicable, indeed best, for all men. Furthermore, the Jacobins and their descendants believed that France had a mission to spread this civilization not only to Europe but also to the whole world. As a naval officer wrote in 1864 to justify continuing the French occupation of Cochinchina, "This generous nation, whose opinion rules civilized Europe and whose ideas have conquered the world, has received from Providence a higher mission [than the extension of its commerce], that of the emancipation, of the call to enlightenment and liberty, of the races and peoples still the slaves of ignorance and despotism."[2] The Jacobin desire to spread French civilization contrasted with the exclusiveness of, for example, German nationalism, which was in large part a product of the Romantic era, a reaction against the theoretical universalism of French classicism and the applied universalism of the Napoleonic conquests.

The French republicans of the nineteenth and twentieth centuries continued to espouse Jacobin ideology. Consequently, in spite of hesitations at home and objections from experienced colonial administrators, the colonial policy of the French republics was dominated by the ideal of assimilating the overseas peoples into the French community. This policy of assimilation was applied on three levels: administrative, civic, and cultural. Administratively, the French tried to govern the colonies and to regulate their economies, even in the so-called "protectorates" of Tunisia and Morocco, as if they were parts of continental France. On the civic level, the republicans aimed to grant the colonial subjects the rights and duties of French citizenship. Accordingly, in 1848 the Second Republic abolished slavery and made citizens and voters of all residents of the colonies inherited from the Ancien Régime, and in 1946 the first Constituent Assembly of the Fourth Republic granted French citizenship to the residents of the more recently conquered territories (excluding the protectorates). Culturally, the French aspired to turn the overseas peoples into Frenchmen. The Catholic missionaries and the republicans established schools in which the French language was used and the young subjects learned about "our ancestors the Gauls." The attraction of this policy of assimilation was that it appeared to satisfy at the same time the desires both to dominate the colonial peoples and to liberate them: their absorption would be their liberation.

French Catholicism and Jacobin nationalism differed from other brands of Catholicism and nationalism in the intensity of their missionary zeal. This zeal expressed, as well as reinforced, a fundamental vision of France that underlies the divisions and conflicts that have clouded French history. As the Catholic leftist Jean-Marie Domenach has explained: "If you look back at the history of France since 1789, you will notice that most Frenchmen have agreed on one theme: that France was charged with an historical mission. For the French of the Right as for the French of the Left, France was a people set apart from the others, invested by God or by Reason or by the hopes of peoples with a special mission that consisted in bringing progress and enlightenment, in sacrificing itself for the other nations."[3]

The particular embodiments overseas of this vision of France were the military officers who were largely responsible for administering as well as conquering the colonies. Adding the ideals of military service and noblesse oblige to the Catholic and Jacobin traditions, they created within the army a sense of colonial mission that persisted through the end of empire. Officers like Thomas Robert Bugeaud in Algeria; Louis Faidherbe in Senegal; Joseph Gallieni in Senegal, Tonkin, and Madagascar; and, above all, Louis-Hubert Lyautey in Morocco, were celebrated at home as the heroes of colonization, the warriors who brought peace and progress. Their legends helped to popularize the idea of France's civilizing vocation.

Another major source of belief in France's overseas mission was the stunning progress of Western science and industry. Pride in this progress, however, had altered the civilizing ideal by the end of the nineteenth century. The colonial mission became a double project; the West not only must pacify and educate the backward peoples, but also develop, for the benefit of all mankind, the untapped resources of the world. Furthermore, the spread of the idea of social evolution indicated that the industrial civilization of the West was not only the most advanced stage of mankind but a natural goal of all societies. Yet the Western sense of technological superiority undermined the equalitarian, universalistic basis of the Catholic and Jacobin ideals, as well as of the evolutionist vision. Viewing alien cultures with scorn, French colonizers were able to assert that the overseas peoples were inferior not only in education, but in natural intellectual ability. This belief was further stimulated by the social theorists' belittling analyses of the newly colonized African peoples.[4] In the midst of such a climate of opinion, the French were not likely to have many qualms about colonial conquest. Their civilizing mission appeared to be a gratuitous expression of their humanitarian generosity. They believed that, unlike their European rivals, they were achieving an industrial civilization without losing sight of basic spiritual and moral values and, therefore, were especially suited to the role of colonial tutors.

The concept of mission was altered further and given a larger role within imperialist ideology by the changed set of circumstances after World War I. In the early Third Republic the champions of empire had been a minority; the overthrow of Jules Ferry as premier in 1884 had been precipitated by his colonial efforts in Tonkin. As more colonies had been conquered and as disputes over them had arisen with England and Germany, however, many French people had begun to prize their overseas possessions. After the war the idea that France was and ought to be an imperial power spread widely for many reasons: the large role of the colonial soldiers in World War I; the fascination with French engineering and military feats in Morocco;

the growth of a considerable commerce with the colonies; the beginning of African tourism; the increased concern of the daily and weekly press with colonial affairs; the use of colonial themes in French literature; the grandiose celebration in 1930 of the centennial of the conquest of Algeria; the astounding miniature empire erected on the outskirts of Paris for the Colonial Exposition of 1931, which received nearly thirty-four million visitors; and, above all, the increased time devoted to the empire in primary and secondary education. The insecurities of the period of economic depression and Nazi threat seemed to confirm the economic and military value of the colonies. By 1939, according to an opinion poll, half of the French people judged that the loss of a piece of the colonial empire would be as painful as the loss of a piece of France.[5]

Yet the era of exciting colonial conquest was over by World War I, even though fighting continued in Morocco. The French were willing to go to considerable expense to acquire colonies and to build up their defenses, but subsequently devoted very few private or public funds to the task of increasing their economic value. Arguments were needed, therefore, to encourage, in the interests of both the home country and the colonial peoples, the difficult and expensive work of development. World War I had made the French grateful for the important contributions of the colonies, including 205,000 colonial subjects killed in battle. The proponents of empire desired to turn this gratitude into concrete acts.

Paradoxically, while the ideology of empire seemed to be completing its conquest of the French public, new factors of the interwar period arose to erode the good conscience of the imperialists: the birth of modern nationalism among the colonial youth who studied in French schools and worked or fought in France; the appearance of the outspokenly anti-imperialist Communist party at home; and the new self-doubt in the West provoked by the slaughter of World War I, by a new appreciation of the worth of non-Western cultures (especially in art and religion), and later by the rise of fascism. Accordingly, in the early 1930s a number of Catholic and rationalist intellectuals reassessed the morality of colonization.

Both groups of ideologues came to similar conclusions. They argued that colonization was legitimized by the right of humanity to use for its well-being the material and moral riches of the whole world. They insisted, however, that the colonizer had to act in the primary interest of the colonial population and that his tutorship must end in emancipation, whether by integration into the home country or by independence. The projected end of colonization was a distant event: it would come gradually, take into account the rights of the colonizers, and lead to the fullest moral and material blossoming of the indigenous population. Unsure of their rights, colonial imperialists stressed their duties to the colonies, which, they hoped, would justify the continuation of their domination. Nevertheless, the development of this theory of legitimate colonization indicated that French imperial ideology was beginning to transcend a primarily French point of view. The spread of this attitude was accelerated by the increase in political strength of the Socialists, who came to power in 1936 as the leaders of the Popular Front and who consented to colonization only if it aimed to benefit the overseas peoples.[6]

The imperial moralists continued to be confident that France was preeminently capable of a truly humanist colonization. Yet another group of thinkers—anthropologists and colonial administrators—began to question the nature of the colonial vocation. Studying the conquered societies more carefully, they learned to appreciate the virtues of traditional cultures and to beware of the destructive effects of Westernization. Their conclusion that modernization had to be gradual and conservative, however, did not imply a rejection of colonization; indeed, it reinforced the view that colonial tutorship had to last a long time. Yet they viewed the colonial mission from a new and less arrogant perspective.[7]

The eminent colonial administrator Robert Delavignette even suggested in the mid-thirties that Europe, suffering from a crisis of its civilization, should learn from the African peasants the forgotten virtues of the community, the land, and the sacred. While continuing to insist that Africa needed the West, he launched the novel slogan, "Africa the salvation of Europe!" The aim of colonization, he argued, was not to assimilate the overseas peoples, as republican tradition demanded, but to create a community of different and symbiotic cultures. Addressing the Senegalese poet Léopold Sédar Senghor, Delavignette wrote: "For me humanism consists in our encounter and our mutual enrichment, and the colony exists morally only if it fosters that humanism which unites us."[8] The lessons of this new school of colonial humanism were only beginning to penetrate when France and the empire were engulfed in World War II.

World War II had a profound impact on the French view of empire. The Nazi occupation of the major portion of France left the empire as the nation's remaining source of prestige and power and made it the battleground of the rival Vichy and Free French governments. For Vichy possession of colonies was a key means of preserving some independence from the Nazis. For de Gaulle it was even more vital. The initial adhesion to de Gaulle's cause of French Equatorial Africa provided the indispensable means for his own personal success and, as he saw it, for the restoration of France's honor; it gave him the political and military base essential to win recognition from the English and Americans and to enable French forces to reenter the war. The role of the empire and of colonial troops in the eventual liberation of France was a concrete and stirring demonstration to the French people of the value of their empire.

The triumph of de Gaulle over all his rivals gave the colonies and France, gradually freed from Vichy and German control, government by a staunch imperialist. De Gaulle insisted in his speeches on the imperial vocation of France.[9] In dealing with the empire, he associated himself with the school of colonial humanism that had developed among the colonial administrators. In January 1944 he convoked the top administrators of Africa to meet at Brazzaville to prepare a plan for the economic and political development of the African territories. In his opening speech de Gaulle told the conference that France had to adopt a progressive overseas policy for three reasons:

> In the first place and very simply, because she is France, that is, the nation whose immortal genius is designated for initiatives that, by degrees, raise men toward the summits of dignity and fraternity where, some day, all will be able to unite. Next because, in the extremity to which a provisional defeat drove us, it is in these overseas lands, in which all the populations, in all parts of the world, have not for one single minute altered their fidelity, that she found her recourse and the base of departure for her liberation and because there is henceforth, from this fact, a definitive bond between the Home Country and the Empire. Finally, for the reason that, drawing from the drama the appropriate conclusions, France today is animated, in what concerns herself and in what concerns all those who are dependent on her, with an ardent and practical will for renewal.[10]

De Gaulle had a fourth reason for calling the Brazzaville conference. Indigenous elites around the empire were demanding political reforms, even independence. The most alarming situation was in North Africa where the collapse of the Vichy colonial regime after the Anglo-American disembarkment in November 1942 and the presence of the powerful and outspokenly anti-imperialist American forces stimulated nationalist ambitions. In Tunisia the recently enthroned bey was determined to reestablish the authority of his office. At the end of December 1942, with Tunisia occupied by German troops, he appointed a new ministry without, for the first time since the establishment of the protectorate, seeking the prior approval of the French resident general. In January 1943, French control of Morocco was challenged when President Franklin D. Roosevelt promised the sultan that America would aid Morocco's economic development. Various Moroccan nationalist groups, supported by the sultan, combined at the end of the year to form the new party of Istiqlal (Independence), and on 11 January 1944, to the joy of the city crowds, Istiqlal issued a declaration of Moroccan independence. Meanwhile, the Algerian leader Ferhat Abbas, previously a proponent of assimilation, issued a series of declarations, notably the "Manifesto of the Algerian People" on 10 February 1943, in which he condemned French colonialism and demanded "the recognition of the political autonomy of Algeria in its quality of sovereign nation."[11] The political agitation of Abbas and his followers contributed to the outbreak in May 1945 of the most serious Algerian insurrection since 1871.

The Free French were not willing to acquiesce in the disintegration of the French empire. When their troops entered Tunisia in May 1943, they immediately deposed the unruly bey, refused to cooperate with the nationalist leader Habib Bourguiba, even though after the defeat of 1940 he had preached fidelity to France and support for the Allies, and reorganized the Tunisian government to bring it more completely under French control. In Morocco the French authorities replied to Istiqlal's declaration of independence by arresting several nationalist leaders, thereby provoking bloody demonstrations in the cities. Only a military siege restored order in Fez. In Algeria the French savagely repressed the insurrection of May 1945, arrested Abbas and other nationalist leaders, and outlawed Abbas's party.

But de Gaulle did not want to base the empire on force. He hoped to win or to retain the voluntary allegiance of the colonial masses and elites by offering them social reforms and political participation. The expansion of the voting rights of Algerian Moslems by the decree of 7 March 1943 and the proposals of the Brazzaville conference to extend civil and political liberties and to introduce administrative and political decentralization were intended as signs to the indigenous peoples that France was beginning a new era of just and fraternal relations with them.

Many of the Brazzaville conference's egalitarian proposals were put into effect by the Gaullist government. These reforms, however, were mostly assimilationist in spirit and, in any case, were limited in impact by the government's clear insistence on continued French dominance. The conference declared: "The ends of the *oeuvre* of civilization accomplished by France in the colonies exclude any idea of autonomy, any possibility of evolution outside the French bloc of the Empire; the eventual, even distant, establishment of 'self-government' in the colonies is to be rejected." The greatest impact of the Brazzaville conference was not on the indigenous populations, but on the French. Impressed by the reforming spirit of Brazzaville, they assured themselves that the colonial peoples could not possibly want to separate from humanist France.[12]

The French felt that the colonial peoples' attachment to France was proved by their fidelity during the war as well as by their contributions to the war effort. As Raymond Aron, for example, wrote in the monthly *La France Libre* in London in January 1943, "The French empire has given since the armistice a dazzling proof of its solidity and of its fidelity: in unprecedented fashion, a beaten country, almost completely disarmed, maintained without difficulty, without trouble, despite an inevitable loss of prestige, the administration of vast territories some of which had been only recently conquered." In spite of the subsequent troubles in the liberated territories, the theme of wartime fidelity was repeated constantly by de Gaulle and his supporters and was picked up by the men of the interior Resistance after the Liberation.[13]

To be optimistic about the empire was easy at home, where most Frenchmen were ignorant of colonial realities and, in particular, of the depth of colonial discontent. The usual critics of colonial policy during the Third Republic, the leftist intellectuals and politicians, were themselves out of touch with colonial problems after a decade of preoccupation with the struggle against fascism; even the Communists, except during the two pariah years of the Nazi-Soviet pact, had stilled their attacks. During the Nazi occupation the isolated French were absorbed by their personal and national problems, unaware of the nationalist agitation and, as the Allied troops advanced, willing to believe Gaullist propaganda.[14]

The leaders of the Resistance gave very little thought to the empire in their plans for the future of France.[15] They and their followers were experiencing a revival of Jacobin nationalism. Domenach has recalled:

> We felt ourselves again in the skin of the soldiers of the Year II. We had evidently no kind of worry about the justice of our cause since we were fighting at the same time against the enemy of the nation and against the enemy of the human species, which was Hitlerian racism. Consequently our struggle was both a patriotic and a universalistic struggle. From this came the difficulty for the resisters at the Liberation to ascertain that in fact others experienced France as an oppressor. It was a mental conversion that was even more difficult to make to the extent that we were coming out of a war in which we thought that we had struggled in good faith for the liberty of our people. At bottom we were dreaming of a sort of prolongation of this national liberty in a somewhat utopian kind of community where France would associate herself with these other nations in order to lead them to their liberty in friendship with France.

As a result, the National Council of the Resistance called for "an extension of the political, social, and economic rights of the native and colonial populations," but did not question France's sovereignty over the empire.[16]

The new association envisioned by the colonial humanists and the neo-Jacobins of the Liberation was named the "French Union." Delavignette described it in an article in *Esprit* in July 1945 as the embodiment of a new conviction that "the home country and its colonies are to organize themselves in order to live *together*, in order to construct *together* the community in which peoples very different from each other will be able to serve *together* the same material and moral interests, and to work *together* for a better future." Soon, Delavignette proclaimed, they would all be "the natives of a same French Union." He defined this union further, in a utopian socialist vision, as the new power that would "give an augmented value to the riches of the earth" and "put them in the service of the workers, in the service of Man." When this ideal was realized, he prophesied, "It will be a new kind of life, and a profound modification in the structure of our consciousness. We will be linked in the current of everyday life to Moslems, to Buddhists, to animists. We are [so linked] already but without suspecting it. The Union will make us assume consciousness of new social contacts, of a new and complete human solidarity." This French Union would be the culmination of "the world-wide vocation of French humanism," of France's peculiar aptitude in "seeking and confronting Man in the yellow or the black man."[17]

Delavignette's lyrical conception of the French Union was not shared by most Frenchmen. Nonetheless, they joined quite sincerely in the more assimilationist vision of Pierre Cot, the reporter general of the Constitutional Committee of the first Constituent Assembly, who declared: "The colonial empire is dead. In its place we are setting up the French Union. France, enriched, ennobled, and expanded, will tomorrow possess a hundred million citizens and free men." In a poll taken in early 1946, when asked if in the new constitution it was necessary "to give to the populations of the French colonies the same rights as to French citizens," 63 percent said yes, only 22 percent no, while 15 percent gave no response.[18]

At the Liberation, therefore, the French had several reasons to view their overseas possessions with good conscience: pride in the colonial achievements of the Third Republic, belief in France's civilizing vocation, ignorance about colonial problems and nationalist demands, pride in the wartime fidelity of the overseas peoples, exaggeration of the "spirit of Brazzaville," and confidence in the good will of the new leaders emerging from the Resistance. This frame of mind led to further misinterpretations of the colonial situation. The men of the Liberation tended self-righteously to deny the validity of criticisms of France's overseas policy and to attribute ulterior motives and anti-French intentions to the critics. Attacks on the French Union were seen as attacks on the fundamental integrity of France and its new leaders.

THREATS FROM OUTSIDE

The daily press was the chief source of the public's information about events and conditions in the colonies. In the months after the Liberation the press not only illustrated but also helped to perpetuate the good conscience about empire. Forced to rely mostly on government communiqués and foreign news agencies, the newspapers gave an incomplete and distorted picture of the overseas situation. Outstanding examples are two newspapers read by the political and intellectual elites, *Combat* and *Le Monde*. They gave their readers the impression in 1945 that a loyal French empire was under attack from outside enemies.

The first threat was perceived in the conference of the Institute of Pacific Relations held in January 1945 at Hot Springs, Virginia. The representatives of the Allies adopted a resolution proposing the creation of an international committee to oversee the colonies; the French delegation vigorously opposed this resolution. In Paris official circles declared: "The conference of Brazzaville, in making the order of the day the principles of liberty and of progress in the colonies, remained faithful to the traditional policy of France while rejuvenating it. But France means to pursue this policy totally under her own responsibility and under the sanction solely of the confidence of the populations."[19]

Le Monde, which had taken over the presses of the Third Republic's prestigious and moderate *Le Temps*, supported the government's position. The paper, later to become critical of French overseas policy, asserted in response to the Hot Springs conference:

France, always in the avant-garde of human progress, does not need anyone to commend to her the natives of her empire. The latter have proved to her in the course of these years of war, in remaining faithful to her, that she had understood them and that she had known how to show herself "humane" toward all, in the widest and most elevated sense of the word, in having no racial prejudice, in not subjecting the people of color to a discrimination as painful as it would be unjust, in contrast to what sometimes occurs elsewhere, in educating them and in having them attain more and more to the administration of the affairs of their country.

Le Monde insisted also that de Gaulle had rectified any unjust aspects of the empire and that the overseas peoples obviously understood his intent.[20]

Combat, the famous Resistance journal, was more critical of the past than was *Le Monde*. From the standpoint of socialist humanism, Camus, its editor, and his colleagues insisted in their editorials on the Hot Springs conference that French colonization, like all colonization, had been a scandal and that France should be grateful for, not proud of, the wartime fidelity of the colonial peoples. To break with the French colonial tradition was essential, not to defend it as the French delegation at Hot Springs had done; the empire would survive only if based on principles of justice and equality. *Combat*, however, affirmed that this had already been done, that the Brazzaville conference had broken with the past. Accordingly, the paper argued against the international colonial administration: "There is no reason to believe, a priori, that an international committee must show itself more humane toward the natives than a reformed French administration."[21]

The Italians, Germans, and Japanese had coveted France's colonies before and during the war, but now the threat came from France's allies. De Gaulle and his colleagues were alarmed by Roosevelt's stress on the principle of self-determination and by the wartime machinations of the British and Americans in French territories. The reactions of Le Monde and Combat to the Hot Springs conference helped to spread these suspicions to the French public.

The writers of Le Monde were convinced that Britain and America had contrived a plot to dismantle the French empire for their own profit at the very moment when France was unable to defend it. When plans for an international commission for the colonial territories were revived at the San Francisco meeting that established the United Nations, Le Monde's correspondent declared: "The six international commissions proposed by England correspond too closely to the present necessities of 'world trade' for France not to understand that, under the banner of liberating the dependent peoples, we run the risk of placing them under the anonymous rod of economic trusts. . . . It seems that people want to outrun France before she has recovered enough lucidity and vigor. . . .and to place under international control those among her overseas territories that cannot be threatened directly."[22] Despite these forebodings, the United Nations finally adopted a very limited trusteeship system that, for France, applied merely to its League of Nations mandates, Togo and the Cameroons, but the French governments tried to avoid compliance.

The unfortunate corollary of the distrust of both former enemies and former allies was that, in spite of scattered warnings about the effect of World War II on indigenous elites, colonial nationalists tended even in anticolonialist circles to be discounted or viewed as foreign agents. This misunderstanding was evident in the reactions of Le Monde and Combat to the uprising in Algeria, to the confrontation with Britain in the Middle East, and to the troubles in Indochina.

The uprising at Sétif was, according to the official communiqué, "of Hitlerian inspiration," or, as the Communist daily L'Humanitè put it, the result of a "fascist plot." Le Monde's reporter returned from Algeria with a less crude, but similar account. The various "anti-French movements," he charged, had planned and triggered the series of attacks in which "nearly 300 Frenchmen were massacred in indescribable conditions of bestiality and sadism." These enemies of France were unjust since, in spite of some awkwardness, the French had "never had" and "would not know how to have any line of conduct other than the well-being of the peoples" whom they governed. These enemies were ungrateful as well, since they were among those whom the French had "tried to raise" to the level of Frenchmen. *Le Monde*'s reporter still advocated a policy of justice and well-being, if perhaps not assimilation, but he insisted that France must react vigorously to the uprising in order to show its resolution to the French Algerians, the faithful but disoriented Moslem masses, and the other nations.[23]

The articles of Camus in *Combat* were the most extensive and sensitive treatment of Algeria's troubles in the French press. He argued that their primary causes were not nationalist agitation, but social injustices and a severe famine. In the background, Camus realized, was a widespread disillusionment with French policy, but, although he discussed the demands for autonomy of Abbas and his supporters with unique sympathy, even he did not give an accurate picture of their commitment to a specifically Algerian nation. He contended that a policy of justice—a true application of assimilation—could still win the Algerian Moslems to France.[24] Neither Camus nor *Le Monde*'s reporter appeared to be aware of the brutality with which the uprising was repressed.

The problem of Algeria was submerged in the newspapers' concern with the traumatizing confrontation with Great Britain in the Middle East. During the war the rivalry of the British and the Free French in the Middle East nearly had led to armed conflict. To protect French interests from the British, de Gaulle had insisted on maintaining a French military presence in the virtually independent states of Syria and Lebanon. As the war ended, both *Combat* and *Le Monde* denounced the British maneuvers to replace the French. *Le Monde* asserted: "It would be impossible to find any serious divergences on fundamentals between France on the one hand and Syria and Lebanon on the other if third parties did not come to poison the situation at their pleasure."[25]

When troubles broke out at the end of May 1945, both *Combat* and *Le Monde* charged that the debarkation of French relief troops was only a pretext for anti-French demonstrations orchestrated by the British.

Combat eventually criticized the excessive attacks on the British, but *Le Monde* dismissed the announcement by an American news agency that there had been ten thousand victims of French repression in the Sétif region of Algeria, charging that this story was only part of the Anglo-American offensive to discredit France in the eyes of the Arabs of the Middle East. Public opinion was in accord with the newspapers, for 65 percent of the French people—and 74 percent of the Parisians—stated that England was responsible for the troubles in Syria, while only 3 percent cited France and only 2 percent cited Arab circles.[26]

Both papers soon noted that foreigners were at work in another colonial area, Indochina. The Americans refused to transport a French force to Indochina, arguing that they were not fighting in the Pacific to restore European colonies. The French, therefore, helplessly sat by as Chinese and British troops took over from the Japanese forces of occupation after Japan's surrender on 15 August 1945. *Le Monde* interpreted this situation as an indication both of an Anglo-American plot to exclude France from Indochina and of Chinese territorial designs. Meanwhile, although *Combat* had been printing the incisive articles of Colonel F. Bernard, a member of the French delegation at Hot Springs who had opposed the official French position and called for self-government in Indochina, the paper itself held a position more similar to that of *Le Monde*. Camus worried about American designs and hoped that Indochina would remain federated with France.[27]

On 2 September 1945, *Combat* wondered if Ho Chi Minh's new Republic of Vietnam, which had emerged from the Japanese occupation and apparently was placing itself under American protection, was not the beginning of another *"coup of Syria." Combat* believed that the new government was supported by only 5 percent of the people. A story on 6 September was headlined "In Indochina the Japanese pass their arms to Vietnam." On the eighth *Le Monde* reported that an intercepted Japanese telegram to Ho Chi Minh revealed that the Japanese were giving military supplies to the Vietnamese; *Le Monde* concluded, "This document proves, if there was any need for it, that the agitators who claim to struggle for the independence of Indochina are in reality nothing but agents in the pay of the Japanese and armed by them." In October, when asked who was responsible for the troubles in Indochina, 36 percent of the French public blamed the Japanese, 12 percent the British, 9 percent the Chinese, and 6 percent the Americans; only 5 percent blamed the Indochinese and 5 percent the French.[28]

The newspaper reports on colonial issues served, in the face of violent discontent in Algeria, the Middle East, and Indochina, to buttress the good conscience apparently shared by France's people and political leaders. On 21 October 1945 the voters chose a constituent assembly to design the institutions of the Fourth Republic. The constitution makers' treatment of the empire would further indicate that the political elite, in particular, was imbued with a profound confidence in the emerging French Union.

THREATS FROM WITHIN

The Constituent Assembly met on 6 November 1945 in an atmosphere of enthusiasm and optimism. The large majority, some 400 of the 586 deputies, was new to parliamentary politics. Most had been active in the Resistance; many only recently had returned from German prison camps. Most claimed to be leftists; the Socialists and Communists together had a small majority. They were, on the average, about ten years younger than prewar deputies.[29]

The deputies' reforming spirit, their sense of moral obligation toward the faithful overseas peoples, and their ignorance of colonial conditions prepared them to draft a liberal plan for the French Union that accorded with the wishes of most of the representatives of the colonial peoples. The preamble of the completed draft not only insisted on legal equality but also declared: "France forms with the overseas territories, on the one hand, and with the associated states, on the other hand, a union of free consent." The constitution planned "a system of counterbalancing legislatures within the French republic" that would ensure, in the short run, the unity of the French Union and its control by mainland France, but also would include territorial assemblies giving local power to the colonial voters. Moreover, as Senghor, the special reporter on the French Union articles, told the assembly, it was "a dynamic system" that left "the door open for the future, permitting the most diverse alterations and expansions while still preserving the harmony of the whole."[30]

The assembly could adopt such a plan because the French and overseas deputies shared the assumption that France and the colonies were and would continue to be linked by an underlying harmony of interests and aspirations. The Communist deputy from Martinique, the black poet Aimé Césaire, proclaimed that "the colonialist myth, this myth of the white man's burden, this myth of the colored man's inferiority" had been "renounced by the Fourth Republic" and replaced by "the revolutionary myth of liberty, equality, and fraternity."[31] But this first plan for the French Union was not instituted, for on 5 May 1946 the French people rejected the constitutional draft.

The provisions for the French Union were not the overt reason for the defeat of the constitution. During the referendum campaign they drew little criticism, and three-quarters of the deputies who had adopted the provisions were elected to draft the new constitution. Yet the second Constituent Assembly, which convened on 11 June 1946, adopted a far less liberal plan for the French Union. There were several reasons for this change.

The Socialists lost votes, while the Christian Democrats, the Mouvement Républicain Populaire (MRP), gained. Consequently, the balance in the assembly shifted toward the center, the MRP emerged as the largest party, and its leader, Georges Bidault, the former president of the National Council of the Resistance, became head of the government. Bidault was a firm believer in empire and was willing to use his governmental authority to force the assembly to provide for a French Union more clearly and permanently controlled by mainland France.

Furthermore, the colonial provisions of the first draft had alarmed many persons, especially Frenchmen overseas, who now applied pressure on the deputies. General de Gaulle himself, in his celebrated speech at Bayeux on 16 June 1946, called for a constitution that gave the president of France and the French Union much greater authority.[32] The governing partners—the Communists, the Socialists, and especially the MRP—feared that, unless de Gaulle's ideas were at least partly incorporated, the French people might vote down the constitution a second time and a powerful Gaullist party might arise, taking votes away from the MRP in particular.

Moreover, the colonial peoples were expressing their desires for independence more forcefully. The first Constituent Assembly had liberated Ferhat Abbas and legalized his party. Abbas and his comrades won eleven of the thirteen Moslem Algerian seats and, joined by the two Malagasy deputies who had been the sole colonial nationalists in the first Constituent Assembly, spoke out in the new assembly for the autonomy of the overseas territories. Ho Chi Minh and a

Vietminh delegation arrived in Paris at the end of June to negotiate with the Bidault government on the future of Vietnam, while at the same time the deputies were receiving letters from the French in Indochina complaining of Vietminh terrorism. A congress of the principal political movements of Tunisia proclaimed on 23 August 1946 the independence of their country. Three members of Istiqlal came to Paris to talk with French politicians and on 30 August held a press conference to call for Moroccan independence followed by close cooperation with France.

Faced with these developments, the deputies finally were compelled to take seriously the threat to the empire of colonial nationalism. The myth of a unity of desires was no longer tenable; the colonial peoples no longer could be trusted to stay with France. The only reward for the first Constituent Assembly's generosity had been the election of Abbas and his followers. Anxiety reached a peak with the success of the Intergroup of Native Deputies, led by Abbas and backed by the Communists and Socialists, in pushing through the Constitutional Committee a plan for a federal union based on the voluntary adhesion of self-governing states.

On 27 August the venerable Radical leader Édouard Herriot raised the cry of alarm. He warned that, if the provisions for the French Union in the new constitutional draft were adopted as proposed, either the colonial peoples would take advantage of the principle of free consent to secede or, with French citizenship extended to all, they would overwhelm France. On the same day, outside the assembly, de Gaulle too condemned the principle of free consent and declared: "The constitution should, on the contrary, affirm and impose the solidarity with France of all the overseas territories. It should, in particular, place beyond question the preeminent responsibility and, consequently, the rights of France in matters concerning the foreign policy of the entire French Union, the defense of all its territories, common communications, and economic matters of interest to the whole."[33] Prodded by the ministers, the assembly voted on 29 August to send the French Union provisions back to the Constitutional Committee. Bidault subsequently threatened resignation and the end of tripartite government and made a deal with the Communists to coerce the committee and the assembly to provide for a French Union dominated by France. Even though it appeared to conform to his ideas, de Gaulle condemned the new plan, along with the rest of the constitutional draft. Nonetheless, on 9 October the French voters, by a narrow plurality, adopted the new constitution.

The preamble to the constitution declared: "Faithful to its traditional mission, France intends to guide the peoples of whom it has taken charge to the liberty of administering themselves and of managing democratically their own affairs." The goal was self-administration rather than self-government, and the institutions of the French Union as actually defined in the body of the constitution were inegalitarian and authoritarian.

The "overseas departments"—Algeria and the "old colonies" of Martinique, Guadeloupe, Guiana, and Réunion—were to be integral parts of the French republic and, accordingly, administered by the minister of interior. Yet they were treated as separate from continental France in apportioning seats in the Assembly of the French Union, and the voting rights of Algerian Moslems were limited by the Algerian statute of 1947.

The "overseas territories"—French West Africa, French Equatorial Africa, Madagascar, the Pacific islands, Saint Pierre and Miquelon, Somali, and the trading posts in India—were defined as parts of the "one and indivisible" republic, but they were to be treated as colonies, different from and ruled by France. The indigenous residents of these territories were to send deputies to the National Assembly and to the Council of the Republic, but the local electoral procedures were designed to limit this right. They were also to elect representatives to territorial assemblies, but French residents were assured of disproportionate representation, and the assemblies would do no more than advise the governors. The indigenous residents were, in addition, to send representatives to the Assembly of the French Union, but half of this body's members would be elected in continental France, and its role would be only advisory. The "associated territories"—the United Nations trust territories of Togo and the Cameroons—were to be treated like overseas territories.

The "associated states"—the protectorates of Tunisia and Morocco and the states of Indochina united in an Indochinese Federation —were to be linked to France and its overseas territories by treaty. The real power belonged to the government of the French republic, which undertook the coordination of the defense of the union and "the direction of the policy appropriate to prepare and to assure this defense" and assumed responsibility for "the general conduct of the Union," that is, for all common questions such as foreign affairs, money, economy, and communications. The High Council of States, to which the associated states sent their representatives, could do no more than advise the French government and the National Assembly. The president of the French Union was the president of France.

Faced with the threat of dissociation, the second Constituent Assembly had reaffirmed its heritage of Jacobin centralism. As a result, the provisions of the French Union did not satisfy the growing political aspirations of the colonial peoples. Instead of learning to appreciate these aspirations, the French deputies had become embittered that persons for whom France had done so much and was planning to do much more were betraying France and joining its enemies. Abbas's final speech, criticizing French colonization, ended in a near riot.[34] The deputies had lost much of their optimism about the future of the French Union, but most had not abandoned their self-righteous stance.

The French Union was no sooner proclaimed than it was torn apart by the nationalist desires the second Constituent Assembly had tried to deny on paper. The violence that erupted in the overseas lands—particularly in Indochina and Madagascar—did not compel French leaders to treat these desires with greater respect. It had the opposite effect. The nationalists were viewed all the more as traitors to France, agents of foreign powers, and criminals. Before the French Union could demonstrate its virtues, the French government would have to impose it. The coercion that was applied earlier in the assembly chambers was used now on the battlefields and in the law courts.

When war broke out in Indochina at the end of December 1946, the interim head of the government, the Socialist leader Léon Blum, declared to the National Assembly:

> In our republican doctrine, colonial possession reaches its final goal and finds its true justification only on the day that it ceases, that is, on the day that the colonial people has been rendered fully capable of living emancipated, of governing itself. The recompense of the colonizing people is then to have aroused in the colonial people sentiments of gratitude and affection, to have created the penetration and solidarity of thought, culture, interests that permit both of them to unite freely. Once this crisis is surmounted, therefore, our aim will still remain the same. It is not a question of satisfying private interests; it is even less a question of going back on our principles and our commitments. It is a question of resuming with loyalty the interrupted *oeuvre*, that is, the organization of a free Vietnam in an Indochinese Union freely associated with the French Union. But before all else peaceful order, which

serves as the necessary basis for the execution of contracts, must be reestablished.[35]

With the assembly's approval, Blum sent reinforcements to restore this order.

The French people were confused by the events in Indochina and uncertain where to place blame, but only a minority chose to blame the French authorities in Saigon or in Paris. Consequently, although the outbreak of war turned the people's attention to their colonies, it did little to make them doubt the justice of France's overseas policies. They were unaware of the immense responsibility borne by the French because of the colonial administration's sabotage of the earlier agreements with Ho Chi Minh and, in particular, because of the bombardment of Haiphong by French planes and warships on 23 November.[36]

Even the liberal press reflected and stimulated an increased hostility toward the Vietminh. Although *Combat* had treated them with growing respect during 1946, Aron's editorial on 22 December gave them full responsibility for the war because of their attack on the French residents of Hanoi on the nineteenth. Aron supported Blum's decision to respond with force, as did Albert Ollivier, another *Combat* writer, who charged the Vietminh with bad faith and treason. On 5 January 1947 the main headline of *Combat* announced that "a military decision" was necessary (quoting the Socialist minister of overseas France), and the boldface subtitles in the story declared: "'Premeditation is demonstrated!'"; "the Vietminh alone guilty"; "serious losses of Frenchmen in the area of Hanoi." A story on the seventh was titled "Two hundred French civilians manhandled by the Vietnamese."

Even when the truth about the insurrection was revealed, the Vietminh remained discredited in the eyes of many by their attacks on the French and because their leadership was Communist. With the rise of Cold War passions in 1947, negotiation with Ho Chi Minh came to be seen as participation in the expansion of communism. The war in Indochina never was popular, but the governments were unable to end it by negotiations, as much of the public would have liked, because they would negotiate only with Vietnamese other than the "traitors" and Communists who were doing the fighting.[37]

Meanwhile, on the night of 29 March 1947, over a hundred Frenchmen in Madagascar were murdered by bands of Malagasies in a sudden and unexpected revolt. The insurrection continued through the summer, but French troops gradually isolated the rebellious areas and crushed all signs of dissidence. Thousands of Malagasies were killed by the troops or died of exposure after fleeing into the jungle. The insurrection was a stunning demonstration of the discontent among the Malagasies, but it was not likely to make the French public more sympathetic to Malagasy nationalism. The Malagasies had made the initial attack—for reasons unknown to the French public—and reputedly had massacred French residents in a barbaric fashion. Their actions were highly publicized, while the subsequent repression was not.

The French administration in Madagascar, encouraged by frantic colonists, decided to use the occasion to destroy the main political party, the nationalist Mouvement Démocratique de Rénovation Malgache (MDRM). The police claimed that a telegram sent a few days before the uprising to MDRM members by the three Malagasy deputies to the National Assembly—instructing them to "maintain absolute calm and coolness in face of maneuvers and provocations [of] all kinds destined to stir up troubles [among the] Malagasy population and to sabotage peaceful policy of the MDRM"—was in reality a disguised call to rebellion. To strengthen its case and to justify the arrest of the three deputies, who were protected by parliamentary immunity, the police used torture to collect accusations against the MDRM.

In spite of the intense opposition of the Communists, the National Assembly voted 342 to 195 to raise the immunity of the Malagasy deputies. Most of the public was unaware of this vote; of those who knew, few disapproved.[38] The assembly also was unwilling to aid the deputies by ordering their trial shifted from Madagascar, where the passions of the European residents would make a fair trial difficult, to France. One of the deputies subsequently was sentenced to life imprisonment, the other two to death, though their sentences were commuted to life imprisonment. The jails in Madagascar at this time held nearly six thousand political prisoners.

The internal threat to the French Union was demonstrated further, though more subtly, by the speech of the sultan of Morocco on 10 April 1947 at Tangiers. After a description of Morocco's brilliant future and of its attachment to Islam and to the Arab League, Sidi Mohammed omitted a final sentence of compliment to France. In reaction, as one scholar recalls, "the French press and opinion were shaken by a wind of disapproval, indeed of indignation."[39] The offended French government responded by appointing General Alphonse Juin as resident general and directing him to reassert French authority over the sultan, if necessary even by threatening to depose him.

The French Union was in danger of dissolution because of the action of the colonial nationalists. The governments of the Socialists Blum and Paul Ramadier had demonstrated that they, like succeeding governments, were willing to use force to preserve the union.

THE COMMUNIST POSITION

The power of the postwar vision of the French Union was demonstrated strikingly by the overseas policy of the French Communist party, which could have been expected to attack the French Union vigorously. It had been the foremost critic of the French empire between the two world wars. According to Leninist doctrine the liberation of the colonial peoples was desirable for two reasons: because they were unjustly exploited by the colonial powers and because their liberation would be a decisive blow against the capitalist system and its final stage, imperialism.

Colonial liberation, however, was viewed as only one aspect of the world struggle against the political and economic imperialism of capitalism. Consequently, Communist support of colonial nationalists at a particular time and place depended on the international situation. As one Communist intellectual explained, "Does this recognition of the right of peoples to self-determination and separation signify then that the proletariat ought, in every circumstance, to support *no matter what* national movement? No, the proletariat always keeps its right of evaluation and criticism. The essential criterion for the Communists is to know, 'in each particular and concrete case,' if the national movement under consideration aims at enfeebling or at reinforcing the system of imperialism."[40]

In the mid-thirties the primary concern of Western Communists became the fight against fascism. As a result, they discouraged colonial revolts, except during the period of the Nazi-Soviet pact, for they would weaken the Western democracies and would expose the colonies to the penetration of Germany, Italy, and Japan. After World War II the main enemy of Communists was not colonial Europe but the United States. The Communists feared that liberated French colonies would fall prey to American or British imperialism, an eventuality that would strengthen the forces of capitalist imperialism as well as hurt the former colonies. They worried about colonial nationalism all the more because most of the leaders were from the indigenous bourgeoisies. The French Communist party, therefore, joined more conservative Frenchmen in charging in 1945 that those who demanded independence from France were "the conscious or unconscious agents of another imperialism."[41] The Communists advised the colonial peoples not to exercise immediately their right to separate from France.

The Communist party in each country had to adjust its policy to the domestic situation. In France at the end of the war the Communist party was the largest and best-organized political force. For the first time in its history it had ministers in the French government. Its leaders believed that, by means of elections and infiltration and in alliance with the Socialists, they might be able to take control of the government. The party's strength had two moderating effects on its colonial policy.

First, the vision of coming to power stimulated the Communist version of France's civilizing mission. In 1920 the Communist International had asserted that backward countries, if guided by the proletarians of the advanced countries, could bypass the capitalist stage of development. Accordingly, the French Communists believed that the best way for France's colonies to achieve democracy and socialism—as well as to become part of the Communist bloc—was to remain closely united with the socialist France emerging from the Liberation. This conviction, of course, was reinforced by the threat to the overseas lands of Anglo-American capitalism. The Communists did not doubt that socialism, as defined by them, was the best future for all the peoples of the world.

Second, the party hesitated to jeopardize in any way its bid for power. The overseas lands were potential sources of Communist electoral strength if they remained linked to France. Moreover, working for unpopular colonial rebellion might alienate French voters, frighten the middle classes, and shatter the tripartite government. The efforts of the Communists during the Resistance had earned them the title of French patriots which they did not intend to sacrifice; they insisted on their concern for the preservation of French overseas interests. The party did not want to relinquish its present share of power even if its participation in French governments made it complicit with the acts of colonial repression in Algeria, Indochina, and Madagascar. The war in Indochina brought the contradiction to a point of crisis, for the Vietnamese nationalists were led by Communists. To preserve their coalition with the Socialists and the MRP, the Communist ministers voted in March 1947 for military credits for a war against fellow Communists, while the Communist deputies to the National Assembly merely abstained.

The French Communist party, therefore, instead of working for the dissolution of the French empire, strove to create, in the words of the party chief Maurice Thorez, a "free, confident, and fraternal union" of the colonial peoples and the people of France.[42] Even when the first Constituent Assembly's liberal plan for the French Union, which embodied the Communist vision, was replaced by the second Constituent Assembly's more authoritarian version, the French Communists supported the constitutional draft. They believed that the institutions of the French Union were still sufficiently elastic to permit "an evolution in the direction of liberty." Meanwhile, they argued, like many other Frenchmen, that, in face of the designs of the Anglo-American imperialists, France could "count on a deep attachment of the overseas population to maintain and reinforce the French Union."[43]

The situation changed in the summer of 1947. In May, Premier Ramadier expelled the Communist ministers from his cabinet after they had voted against the government policy on strikes at the Renault factories. As the Cold War rapidly intensified, both outside and inside France, the gulf between the Communists and the other parties became increasingly wide. Even though the nostalgia for government participation persisted, the Communists had little reason to avoid conflicts with other parties over the issues of decolonization. Indeed, abandoning its hope of wooing moderate voters, the party began a period of intransigent opposition to the Fourth Republic.

Yet the Communists did not begin an aggressive attack on the French Union. Their fear increased that liberated colonies, led by the bourgeois nationalists, quickly would fall under American domination. The Soviet Union preferred a feeble French imperialism to a strong American one, especially in strategic areas like North Africa. Furthermore, the French Communists were preoccupied with domestic conflicts and, like the Soviet Union, with the European theater of the Cold War. Even in the case of Indochina, where the Vietnamese nationalists could be trusted to choose the correct side in the Cold War, the Communists merely spoke out against the war, not undertaking an active campaign until international attention was focused on the war by the victory of the Chinese Communists in 1949 and the recognition of the Vietminh government by China and the Soviet Union in early 1950.

Most non-Communists paid even less attention to the French Union. The economic situation was critical. In the winter of 1947–48 the food and fuel shortages were as serious as during the German occupation. Prices continued to soar until 1949. Strikes engulfed France in the fall of 1947 and continued through 1948. The political institutions of the Fourth Republic, adopted in 1946 by the positive votes of only 36.5 percent of the electorate, were attacked by strong Communist and Gaullist forces. The political system was beset by the familiar problem of cabinet instability, and the governments lapsed into seeming immobility before France's immense difficulties. Forced to rely on Marshall Plan aid for economic recovery and on NATO for defense, France appeared to be no more than a pawn in the struggle between the United States and the Soviet Union. Meanwhile, for several years following the crises of 1947, a relative calm prevailed in the French Union. The war in Indochina persisted, but it was distant, its costs in men and money were quite low, and official reports said that it was almost over. The French Union seemed the least of France's problems. As *Les Temps Modernes* later charged, "indifference was the home country's form of colonialism."[44]

3 ↷ THE FAILURE OF THE FRENCH UNION

The unrest in the overseas lands was a clear sign that all was not well in the French Union. The few journalists and writers who examined the causes of this unrest reported that the French had committed and were continuing to commit injustices. Hoping to arouse the concern of politicians and the general public, they warned that, because of these injustices, the French Union was failing.

THE MOBILIZATION OF THE INTELLECTUALS

The anticolonialist intellectuals who tried to serve as the vanguard of French opinion became involved in the fate of the French Union, for the most part, only in response to dramatic overseas events. Three sets of events—the uprisings in Indochina and Madagascar in 1946–47, the crises in Tunisia and Morocco in the early 1950s, and the rebellion in Algeria that began in 1954—provoked increasingly larger outbursts of concern.

The Fourth Republic had hardly begun when a number of French intellectuals were forced by the troubles in the colonies to examine and reappraise the republic's overseas policy. The publication most dedicated to this task was Mounier's *Esprit*. In addition, *Les Temps Modernes*, directed by Sartre and Merleau-Ponty, supported the struggle of the Vietminh. *Chemins du Monde*, the organ of the association "Civilisation," devoted one of its issues in 1948 to the question "End of the Colonial Era?" The topic for 1948 of the annual study conference of the French Catholic Church, the Semaines Sociales de France, was "Overseas Peoples and Western Civilization."[1]

The intellectuals reacted to their new awareness of the problems of the French Union in various ways. Rous became a more active defender of colonial nationalism. Along with other Trotskyists in the French Socialist party, he had worked for colonial emancipation even before World War II. He tried after the war to continue this effort within the Socialist party, representing the left wing of the party on its committee of directors. In 1948, however, he resigned from the party in solidarity with a group of overseas deputies, helped to found the Congress of Peoples against Imperialism at a conference in Puteaux in June, and became its secretary general. The Congress of Peoples was the major organization supporting the nationalist movements in the French and English colonies, and its membership included most of the future leaders of decolonized Africa and Asia. It lobbied in support of the colonial nationalists in the United Nations and publicized their causes in the home countries.[2]

Colonel F. Bernard, in contrast, reacted with more discouragement than militancy. He was the expert on colonial questions for *Combat* and for the publications that emerged from the Catholic Resistance group Témoignage Chrétien, the weekly *Témoignage Chrétien* and the monthly *Cahiers du Monde Nouveau*. In his earlier articles he had severely criticized French policy—the recommendations of the Brazzaville conference, the French position at Hot Springs, the constitutional drafts, and French actions overseas—for failing to take into account the great variety of conditions in France's possessions, the colonial peoples' desires for self-government, and the inability of the French to impose their sovereignty by force. Yet he also had contended that the aim of French colonial policy was to help the overseas peoples, that continued association with these peoples was important for France, and that they in turn wanted to stay attached to, if not ruled by, France. By January 1948, however, Bernard was disillusioned. He charged in *Cahiers du Monde Nouveau* that, in Indochina at least, France's accomplishments had been decidedly negative and that its policy since the Liberation had been merely to reimpose French rule. Nevertheless, he clung to the hope that France would change its policy in order to create "an association of free peoples," that is, to "save the French Union," to "reconstruct the Empire."[3]

Paradoxically, a reaction against Bernard's condemnation of the French Union came in *Cahiers du Monde Nouveau* itself. Even though Bernard remained on its editorial board, in 1948 the journal's articles

attempted to restore pride in France's colonial *oeuvre*, reassuring the readers that the French Union was viable if sufficient energy were devoted to it and that the overseas peoples wanted to be associated with France. The troublemakers in Indochina, Madagascar, and North Africa were described as "a minority of traditional fanatics, systematic agitators, destroyers of any order that is not theirs."[4] Yet these articles continued, in the tradition of the humanist mission, to argue that France had to act in the interests of the colonial peoples.

Most of the intellectuals who spoke at the Semaine Sociale and wrote in *Esprit* and *Chemins du Monde* took a position between the two currents in *Cahiers du Monde Nouveau*. The consensus was that the French Union was in danger of failure but that it still could be transformed into a thriving French-led association of peoples. Many of the intellectuals, now sensitized to overseas problems, kept up their vigilance. Rous supported overseas nationalists regularly in the daily *Franc-Tireur*, often in *Esprit*, and occasionally in *Les Temps Modernes*. In *Combat*, Bourdet, who replaced Camus as editor in June 1947, was a persistent critic of French policy in Indochina, Madagascar, and North Africa. *Esprit* continued to analyze the overseas situation, to warn of future violence in North Africa, to propose the goal of a federation of peoples, and to plead for justice. Its issue of July 1949 was devoted to the topic "Last Chances of the French Union." In his introduction to the collection of articles, Domenach, the future editor of *Esprit*, contended that many people saw the constructing of the French Union as "the great moral and political task of the young generation." Yet the relative peace after 1947 (except in Indochina) made the French Union a less urgent concern for the intellectuals as well as for the politicians and the public. Camus, *Les Temps Modernes*, and the majority of intellectuals became preoccupied with the philosophical and political issues of the Cold War.[5]

In the early 1950s, however, crises developed in the protectorates of Tunisia and Morocco. In Tunisia three years of quiet ended in September 1949 with the return of the nationalist leader Bourguiba from his self-imposed exile in Cairo. Following a series of appearances around Tunisia, Bourguiba traveled to France in April 1950 to bring his demands to the French leaders and public. On 10 June the minister of foreign affairs, Robert Schuman, appointed a new resident general, Louis Périllier, and declared, "M. Périllier, in his new functions, will have the mission to understand and guide Tunisia toward the full

blooming of its riches and to lead it toward the independence that is the final objective for all the territories in the French Union. It is necessary, however, to accept the required delays, and, should this enterprise succeed, France in the course of its so lengthy history will have accomplished once again its civilizing mission."[6] Schuman's reference to independence, even if distant, was bold. But the French governments were willing to proceed with reforms only slowly and under pressure from the nationalists and the bey.

In December 1951, after parliamentary elections had returned a more conservative National Assembly, the new cabinet decided that the evolution toward self-government had to be stopped. Schuman wrote to remind the Tunisians of France's contributions to Tunisia and to insist on the "cosovereignty" of the French residents, speaking now of the goal merely "to lead the Tunisian people to manage public affairs in association with the French."[7] When the nationalists replied with a protest strike, the government sent a new resident general, Jean de Hautecloque, to implement a policy of force. Soon after his arrival in January 1952, de Hautecloque arrested Bourguiba and other nationalist leaders. When popular demonstrations resulted, he decreed a state of siege and sent the French army into populous districts to hunt for nationalists and their weapons. In March, after the bey's refusal to jettison his nationalist ministers, de Hautecloque arrested the ministers and forced the bey to accept a French-sponsored prime minister who had little support in the country. The bey appealed to the president of France, the Socialist Vincent Auriol, whose haughty response instructed the bey to cooperate with France. French-Tunisian relations were at an impasse.

In Morocco, meanwhile, the quiet that General Juin had established in 1947 ended when, in December 1950, Juin clashed with nationalist ministers over the Moroccan budget. He demanded that Sultan Mohammed ben Youssef renounce the nationalist party, Istiqlal, and threatened to depose him if he did not. Juin had the support of the chief of the Berber tribes of the South, El Glaoui, the pasha of Marrakesh. In February 1951 troops of Berber horsemen arrived at Fez and Rabat. The sultan capitulated to Juin, disavowing Istiqlal though continuing to refuse to sign decrees instituting the participation of French residents in local administration. The setback to Moroccan nationalism was only temporary. Under Juin's successor as resident general, General Augustin Guillaume, Istiqlal became more active. The situation

exploded when the Moroccans heard of the assassination on 5 December 1952 of the Tunisian union leader Ferhat Hached. The unions of Casablanca held sympathy strikes and meetings on the seventh and eighth that led to bloody clashes with French police and residents. The French authorities in Morocco, hoping to crush Istiqlal, arrested hundreds of party directors and activists. The "irremediable" act had taken place.[8]

French intellectuals, as well as the general public, could not remain indifferent to this turmoil in the protectorates. The leftist historian Charles-André Julien, former secretary general of the Popular Front's Haut-Comité Méditerranéen et de l'Afrique du Nord, wrote controversial letters to *Le Monde* in praise of Bourguiba in April 1950 and in defense of the sultan in March 1951. *Esprit* continued to publish its prophetic analyses. Rous described the crises in North Africa in *Franc-Tireur* as well as in *Esprit*. Bourdet was even more active. Owing in part to his radical opposition to French policy in Indochina and elsewhere in the French Union, he was expelled from *Combat* in early 1950 by the maneuvers of the main stockholder, a French Tunisian. But he had already undertaken to found a weekly of political commentary, *L'Observateur*, which he made into a major organ of anticolonialism. In *L'Observateur* in summer 1950 and later in *Les Temps Modernes*, which theretofore had paid little attention to North African problems, Bourdet began a systematic attack on French activities in North Africa, particularly in Morocco.[9]

In the final months of 1952 two important books criticizing North African policy were published, Rous's *Tunisie . . . Attention!* in October and Julien's *L'Afrique du Nord en marche* in November. In December violence occurred at Casablanca. Soon thereafter the United Nations General Assembly passed resolutions calling for more progressive policies in Tunisia and Morocco. The result of this conjunction of events was a storm of anticolonialist protest at home. The original critics of the far Left, whose anticolonialist position was part of a generally critical attitude toward French politics and society, were joined by moderates and even by rightists who rallied to the defense of the sultan. At the core of this alliance were the Catholic intellectuals, in particular Mauriac.

The Catholics were the most vital group to emerge from the earlier struggle against fascism. During the thirties Catholics such as Mauriac and Mounier had turned their acute senses of Christian morality against

the reactionary French Catholicism of the past, which was discrediting itself by its social hypocrisy, by its support of Franco, and finally by its collaboration with the Nazis. The subsequent energetic and conspicuous participation of Catholics in the Resistance—including Mounier, Domenach, Beuve-Méry, and Mauriac—had consecrated their reintegration into the republican community.

At the Liberation this increasingly influential Catholic opinion was more attached to the idea of empire than was general French opinion.[10] The weekly *Témoignage Chrétien*, on the far left of official Roman Catholic publications, and *Esprit* were in the forefront of postwar anticolonialism and even were willing to talk of independence. Mauriac was more representative of the mass of Catholic opinion, however, when he defended French colonization in his column in *Le Figaro* in 1947. Taking the same self-righteous stance as that of *Le Monde* (itself edited by a Catholic, Beuve-Méry) in 1945, Mauriac argued, in response to an editorial in *Les Temps Modernes*, that past and present abuses were only the occasional betrayals of a colonial vocation that had to be reaffirmed, not relinquished.[11] By the end of 1952, however —after repeatedly defending the government's Indochina policy—Mauriac could no longer tolerate the continuation of these betrayals, especially by leaders who belonged to the MRP, the Catholic party that had emerged from the Resistance.

Liberal Catholics like Mauriac, who had opposed the Vietminh, were attracted to the North African nationalists because most of them were not only anti-Communist but devout Moslems. Mauriac felt both a spiritual affinity with and a paternalistic affection for the young North African nationalists, especially the Moroccans, whom he met in France. He was deeply moved by the suffering of the Moslem masses and enraged by the hypocrisy of their oppressors. His sensitivity to the victimization of the weak is suggested by his novel *Le Sagouin*, published in 1951, the story of a retarded boy who is rejected and driven to suicide by the adults who ought to care for him.

Just as Mauriac arrived in Stockholm to receive the Nobel Prize for literature, he learned of the killing of Moroccans demonstrating in sympathy for Hached. He seems to have interpreted this coincidence as a divine sign. In January 1953 he began a vigorous campaign on behalf of the Moroccan nationalists and the sultan in his columns in *Le Figaro* and in the monthly *La Table Ronde*, in articles in *Témoignage Chrétien*, in his preface to *Justice pour le Maroc* by the radical Catholic jour-

nalist Robert Barrat in late 1953, and, beginning in November 1953, in his column in the new weekly *L'Express*. With savage and deadly wit he attacked the French leaders responsible for the overseas crimes of the Fourth Republic. His enormous prestige as a great writer and a Catholic moralist gave his criticisms more weight than those of any other intellectual. Accordingly, he was a prime enemy of the defenders of French interests in North Africa. Meanwhile, Mauriac made contacts with both Moroccan students and French politicians, hoping that a new unity of Islam and Christianity could emerge from the crisis.[12]

Mauriac was joined by other Catholic intellectuals. In January 1953 the Centre Catholique des Intellectuels Français held a debate on the problems of North Africa that, according to Julien, "provoked in numerous believers a crisis of conscience in conformity with the richest traditions of Christianity." Mauriac helped to found and became president of the Comité France-Maghreb, which was one of the most influential of the many similar pressure groups of intellectuals formed in response to the issues of decolonization. Meeting in the offices of *Esprit* and including a large number of eminent Catholic and non-Catholic intellectuals such as Domenach, Senghor, Delavignette, Julien, Rous, and Camus, it tried to mobilize all opponents of a policy of force. Its members gathered information, talked with political leaders, and released statements to the press.[13]

The focus of this activity was the fate of the sultan of Morocco. After the arrests of nationalists in December 1952, colonialist circles in Morocco saw Mohammed ben Youssef as the last obstacle to a peaceful acceptance of French control. The deposition of the sultan was discussed openly in France as well as in Morocco, and preparations were made in Morocco by El Glaoui and other enemies of the sultan, in collaboration with the French administration. With Mauriac as intermediary, rightist intellectuals joined the leftists in defense of the sultan; *Le Figaro* fought on the side of *L'Observateur*, *Témoignage Chrétien*, *Esprit*, and *Les Temps Modernes*.[14]

La Nef published in March 1953 the analyses of the situations in Tunisia and Morocco by a distinguished group of scholars, journalists, and politicians. These articles demonstrated that the crises were capturing the attention of France's political as well as intellectual elite, but the cries of alarm were to no avail. The National Assembly was unwilling to examine the question of Morocco, leaving policy in the hands of the cabinet and overseas administration. The minister of foreign affairs, who was in charge of Morocco, was now Bidault, a persistent defender of France's empire. Under pressure from the French residents in Morocco and from El Glaoui and his forces, the council of ministers agreed on 20 August 1953 to the immediate deposition and exile of Mohammed ben Youssef. Mohammed's replacement was more cooperative; indeed, he was willing to give up his executive and legislative powers. Nonetheless, the maneuver failed. The new sultan had little authority over the populace. The nationalist movement turned to terrorism, and the French of Morocco replied with counterterrorism. Nor was the policy of force successful in Tunisia, where there was no cooperation with the French and increasing terrorism in the cities and guerrilla warfare in the countryside. The impasse in both protectorates was reflected in a great uncertainty among the French public, as well as among the politicians, over the policy to pursue.[15]

The Moroccan crisis stirred up more excitement in France than did the Tunisian crisis. The deposition of the sultan was condemned by such defenders of order and tradition as the Count of Paris, as well as by leftists and progressive Catholics.[16] It was easier to find a way out of the Tunisian impasse because the acts of repression had not been as drastic; the French had not again deposed the bey. In July 1954, therefore, Premier Mendès-France was able to begin the transformation to Tunisia's "internal autonomy." In Morocco, however, in spite of the continued efforts of the Comité France-Maghreb and of a less publicized intellectual pressure group, the Centre d'Études et de Documentation, the French governments were not willing to arrange the return of Mohammed until the summer of 1955, when Faure was premier.[17] In March 1956 the independence of both Morocco and Tunisia was declared officially.

The rise of concern for the North African protectorates was paralleled by an increase in consciousness of the war in Indochina. With the victory of the Communists in China in 1949 and the outbreak of war in Korea in June 1950, the Indochinese conflict came to be viewed by many as part of the worldwide struggle against the expansion of communism. In spite of the support given to the Vietminh by their Chinese neighbors, the French chances for victory appeared better than before because of American financial aid. In 1950 the French became anxious to win the war.[18]

The French public long had tolerated the war because the military and civil authorities had withheld accurate information from the press, claiming that the end of the war was near. Yet American aid to the military campaigns in Indochina failed to produce victory. Meanwhile, their efforts to make the former emperor Bao Dai into a moderate rival to Ho Chi Minh forced the French gradually to concede full independence to the anti-Communist nationalists, who in October 1953 threatened that Vietnam would not participate in the French Union. Furthermore, in return for American aid, which by 1954 was paying three-fourths of the war costs, the French had to give up considerable control in Indochina to the Americans. Thus the enthusiasm of 1950 turned out to be only a temporary reversal of the rising curve of sentiment to negotiate with the Vietminh or simply to abandon Indochina. The segment of the public that insisted on winning the war, with or without the aid of United Nations forces, diminished from 35 percent in October 1950, to 21 percent in May 1953, to 8 percent in February 1954.[19]

The desire to end the war in Indochina was reinforced by increased antiwar activity among the intellectuals. In January 1949, *Franc-Tireur* began a campaign against tortures and massacres by French troops in Indochina that was continued briefly in *Témoignage Chrétien*, *Les Temps Modernes*, and *Esprit*. In January 1950 a military and political scandal, the "Generals' Affair," developed out of the discovery that both the Vietminh and pro-French Vietnamese had obtained copies of a secret report on the Indochinese situation written by the chief of the general staff, General Georges Revers. Despite government efforts to quash the scandal, it was revealed that Revers, to advance his career, had been utilizing a certain political intriguer, trafficker, and double agent who had leaked the report. The affair and its implications were discussed extensively in the leftist press. The regime was shaken by the scandal, but the war continued.[20]

In late 1949 the Communist party began to increase its own opposition to the war through a series of strikes and demonstrations to obstruct the transport of men and materials to Indochina, to impair the recruitment of troops for Indochina, and to encourage mass action in favor of negotiation. On 25 January 1950 a number of work stoppages took place during the "national day against the dirty war."

The Communist efforts stimulated the leftist intellectuals. A group of them joined with the Communists in late 1951 to appeal for the pardon of Henri Martin, a Communist sailor who had been given a heavy prison sentence for urging fellow sailors to refuse to go to

Indochina. In addition to signing petitions, they held a large meeting in October 1952 in which Sartre and Domenach, among others, participated. Sartre composed the extensive commentary to *L'Affaire Henri Martin*, a collection of the letters of Martin and of supporting texts, including a poem by Jacques Prévert, a short story by Vercors, and essays by Domenach, Jeanson, and Leiris. While its major aim was to vindicate Martin by showing the injustice of the military court's decision, the book, which appeared in July 1953 (after Martin had been pardoned), also attacked the Indochinese war itself.

The founding of *L'Observateur* in 1950 and that of the more moderate but still antiwar *L'Express* in 1953 meant the appearance of two influential weeklies that were outspokenly critical of French policy in Indochina. Both constantly pointed to the precariousness of the French military position and to the various profiteering scandals connected with the war. The problem of insufficient accurate information on the war finally was remedied when in mid-1952 the first important studies of the war were published: *Histoire du Viêt-Nam de 1940 à 1952* by the journalist and historian Philippe Devillers and *Viêt-Nam, sociologie d'une guerre* by Paul Mus, France's most respected scholar of Indochina and a professor at the Collège de France. Both books pointed out France's many errors and recommended negotiation with the Vietminh. In November 1953 even the vigorously anti-Communist *Le Figaro* carried an article advising the French government to accept the offer of negotiations that Ho Chi Minh had just made.[21]

In 1954 the war in Indochina became the primary concern of the government and of the public. France, Britain, and the United States had agreed in December 1953 to include the Indochinese question in an international conference on Korea that opened at Geneva in April 1954. Meanwhile, in March the Vietminh laid siege to the French fortress of Dien Bien Phu. The agony endured by the French garrison was reported prominently by the French press; after a valiant struggle, the surviving troops surrendered on 7 May. In June the government of Joseph Laniel, unable to make progress in negotiations at Geneva, was overthrown by the assembly and replaced by that of Mendès-France. Acting as his own minister of foreign affairs, Mendès-France supplanted Bidault at Geneva and, with the approbation of a weary French public, succeeded on 21 July 1954 in ending the war.[22]

The crises in Tunisia, Morocco, and Indochina forced many intellectuals to reevaluate the French Union as a whole. For example, at the end of 1953 the Centre Catholique des Intellectuels Français studied "Colonization and Christian Conscience," and in June 1955, *La Nef*'s issue was devoted to the topic "Where Is the French Union Going?"[23]

A particular offshoot of the new attention given to the French Union was a renewal of concern for the fate of the Malagasy deputies who had been convicted of inciting the uprising of 1947. The irregularities of their trial—including the execution of the principal witness a few days before its opening and the claim of other witnesses that their earlier confessions had been extracted by torture—had created a scandal in France in 1948, but the verdicts had been upheld by the Cour de Cassation. In February 1953 the Socialist Daniel Mayer, president of the Ligue des Droits de l'Homme, and Jacques Duclos, a leader of the Communist party, tried without success to convince the National Assembly to vote an amnesty for the Malagasy political prisoners. In January 1954 a Comité pour l'Amnestie aux Condamnés Politiques d'Outre-mer was formed to work for the liberation of both North African and Malagasy political prisoners. Its president was Louis Massignon, professor of Islamic studies at the Collège de France, and its members included Julien, Bourdet, Rous, Mauriac, and Pierre Stibbe, who had been a defense lawyer at the trial of the Malagasy deputies. Mauriac pleaded on behalf of the overseas prisoners in his column in *L'Express*; Stibbe wrote an eloquent appeal for *Justice pour les Malgaches*, with a preface by Bourdet; Julien presented the multiple arguments for amnesty for the Malagasies to the Assembly of the French Union. Massignon's committee revived the question in the National Assembly in June 1955, and the following year the remaining Malagasy prisoners finally were released, though the former deputies were not able to return to Madagascar until 1960, on the occasion of its independence.[24]

In 1953, Catholic moralists had joined with leftist opponents of the government in attacking France's overseas policies, an alliance symbolized by Mauriac's decision in 1954 to abandon his column in *Le Figaro* in order to devote himself to his "Bloc-Notes" in *L'Express*. The awakening of the intellectuals had preceded, and surely contributed to, that of the politicians and of the public.[25] Overseas violence, however, had been much more influential than the actions of the intellectuals in arousing public opinion in 1953 and 1954 and forcing the political leaders to cooperate with the colonial nationslists.

The termination of the war in Indochina and the grant of independence to Morocco and Tunisia did not end the violence in the French Union. On 1 November 1954 an insurrection began in Algeria, which, as described in chapter 5, was to become the major preoccupation of the intellectuals as well as of the politicians and public.

INJUSTICES IN THE FRENCH UNION

The anticolonialist intellectuals not only helped to bring the problems of the French Union to the attention of France's leaders and people, but, more important, suggested ways to conceptualize these problems. It is necessary, therefore, to examine the content of their writings.

The intellectuals who lost their illusions about the French Union most quickly were, as has been seen, the leftists and the moralists. Heirs of a long tradition of sensitivity to colonial abuses, they realized that the Liberation vision had not materialized and that the Fourth Republic, like its predecessors, was acting unjustly in the overseas lands. In their writings they tried to force their readers—other intellectuals, the political elite, the general public—to share their indignation at this betrayal of France's "humanist" ideals. Their anticolonialist campaigns involved attacks on three kinds of injustices: social and economic ills, denial of basic rights, and repression.

The French were proud of the benefits of their pacifying and modernizing *oeuvre* in the empire. The unrest in the first years of the Fourth Republic did not change their minds. The humanist critics, however, pointed to the underside of the *oeuvre*: they exposed the social and economic injustices that the French tolerated or even produced. They condemned the misery of those who lived in the countryside and in the *bidonvilles* ("tin can towns") that sprang up next to the French colonial cities. Population growth canceled out the already insufficient French efforts to combat misery. In the words of the novelist Jules Roy, the French, "incapable of making them live," had only "prevented them from dying."[26]

The sufferings of the colonial peoples seemed even more odious because they were the basis of the enrichment of others. Already sensitive to the exploitation of the European proletariat, the humanist intellectuals, especially those with socialist convictions, attacked the even greater exploitation of the underpaid and powerless indigenous population for the benefit of French interests as well as for the benefit of French-supported local "feudalities." Most did not charge that the French economy as a whole profited from this exploitation, only particular capitalists and colonists. Indeed, the scandals that erupted over profiteering from overseas ventures, especially over the traffic in the overvalued Indochinese piaster, showed that the home country as well was being exploited.

Increasingly the French critics became aware that those subjected to colonial rule suffered not only greater exploitation than did the European proletariat, but also a more profound violence. The integration of the colonial people into the economic system of the Europeans, along with the partial introduction of reified aspects of European culture, was destroying their traditional way of life without creating a viable replacement. Their personal identities were under more direct attack as well: they either were subjected to racism or were asked to shed their original identities through assimilation. The Marxist concept of "alienation" thereby received new and deeper levels of meaning when applied to the transformation of the lives of the colonial peoples.[27] By the mid-1950s attacks on the injustices of misery and exploitation were presented mostly in this broader perspective of cultural dessication, social disintegration, and dehumanization—of what the anthropologist Germaine Tillion called *"clochardisation"* (the creation of tramps).[28]

In response to the popular belief that the French were spreading the Rights of Man and the Citizen to the rest of the world, the critics pointed to a second injustice: the actual denial of these rights—in particular, judicial and political rights—in the colonies. Judicial rights, the protective side of French law, traditionally had been defended with vigor by French intellectuals. The leftist intellectuals were obsessed with the Dreyfus Affair, in particular, as a symbolic episode of their predecessors' heroic engagement and stunning victory. Invoking the memory of Dreyfus, they repeatedly denounced the irregularities of colonial judicial proceedings—especially the trial of the Malagasy deputies, labeled a "Dreyfus Affair against a whole people"—which deprived the indigenous population of protection against the oppression of the French administration and of local powers.[29]

The denial of political rights was a more delicate question. The political means of expressing opinion and exerting power—voting, public assembly, political and trade union organization—were guaranteed to the residents of the French Union by the constitution of the Fourth Republic, but were greatly restricted in practice. Regardless of how much political autonomy the various intellectuals urged for the territories of the French Union, all insisted that France must export democracy. The critics agreed in general that democracy should be established gradually in territories as yet unused to it, but, in the name of human rights and of the French mission, this civic education must be provided more quickly than the Fourth Republic was doing.

Establishment of democratic reforms was resisted by the vast French colonial bureaucracy and by the privileged groups whose reign reform endangered. The most striking example was the fate of the Algerian statute voted by the National Assembly in 1947. Like other overseas territories, Algeria continued the electoral system established in 1944 of two "colleges," one grouping the Europeans and the small number of Moslems given full political rights, the other the mass of the Moslem population. European domination, already guaranteed by Algeria's subordination to the home country, was preserved on the regional level by allotting half the seats in the Algerian assembly to the first college in spite of its minority status. Nonetheless, since the arrangement meant a significant gain in potential political power for the Moslems, the statute was considered too dangerous by the French settlers and administration in Algeria. To avoid the threat of reformist or separatist Moslem representatives, the administration resorted to widespread and blatant fixing of the 1948 elections to the Algerian assembly and of later elections as well. Denouncing these and other antidemocratic acts, some French intellectuals, as well as colonial leaders, became aware that extension of political rights was the crucial question—that the economic and social injustices they attacked were the consequence of the monopolization of political power by the privileged groups.[30]

The third injustice, repression, arose from the other two. Discontent, combined with increasing political self-consciousness, resulted in political agitation and violence. To preserve the status quo, or at least to attempt to ensure the protection of French interests in a new regime, the local administrations, European residents, and French governments resorted to violent acts of repression.

The initial opponents of the war of reconquest in Indochina

reminded their readers of Nazi actions in France.[31] Yet the war itself provoked little further criticism on moral grounds, with the exception of the outburst in 1949 against the use of torture. Leaving moralism to the supporters of the war, especially to the anti-Communists, the opponents stressed instead the futility of the French policy. It was in the campaign to rectify the apparent judicial injustice to Martin, rather than in a campaign to end the war, that leftist moralists like Sartre joined with the Communists. War-bred corruption—the repeated piaster scandals and, above all, the murky "Generals' Affair" —rather than the destruction caused by the war created great stirs in the press. In the same way, criticisms of French actions in Madagascar centered on the judicial irregularities rather than on the suppression of the rebellion.

The intellectuals were, however, becoming less tolerant of colonial repression. The harsh measures taken against Tunisian and Moroccan nationalists in the early 1950s—in particular, the killings at Casablanca and the exile of the sultan—crystallized the increasing humanist disillusionment with the French Union. Some of the methods used during the Algerian war to repress the revolutionary movement, especially the use of torture to obtain information, were to be attacked so vehemently by French intellectuals that this kind of injustice would become a major issue of French politics.

THE FAILURE OF REFORMISM

The attacks on overseas injustices increased not only in volume but also in severity during the first decade after World War II. As they became conscious of these injustices, the anticolonialists called for reforms to end them, but by the 1950s they became aware that their efforts had failed. Stimulated in addition by the rising demands of the colonial leaders, the anticolonialist movement tended to become more radical and to seek the lessons of its previous failures. The evolution is illustrated by the contrast between Camus's analysis of Algeria in 1945 and Bourdet's analyses of North Africa in the early 1950s.

Camus was a French Algerian who had grown up in poverty in a suburb of Algiers and had developed, perhaps as a result of his poverty, a profound, sensuous love of Algeria—of its sun, its sea, its starry nights—as well as a lasting affection and sympathy for the ordinary Frenchmen of Algeria. After the Liberation, caught up in fame and in the ideological struggles of the Cold War, Camus was both celebrated and attacked as a defender of an abstract justice transcending history. Fundamentally, or at least initially, however, his acute sense of justice arose from concrete, passionate, and intimate —even if ahistorical—experience: it was a product of his intense enjoyment of physical living, of his pagan love of the beauty of the natural world.[32]

Injustice, for Camus, was deprivation of life, either by death or by loss of lucidity while alive. Short of death, injustice was the crushing of what Camus felt was essential in man's humanity: his ability to rise above the hostility of his surroundings and to enjoy the beauty of the world and the pleasures of living. The misery the Moslems suffered prevented them from experiencing the joys of living. As early as 1939, Camus exposed the injustice of this misery in a series of articles on the famine in Kabylia in the independent left-wing newspaper *Alger-Républicain*.[33]

During the occupation, Camus became associated with the underground movement Combat and aided his friend Pascal Pia in editing its newspaper, *Combat*, in the last months of clandestine activity, soon becoming editor-in-chief. Already more sensitive than most intellectuals to colonial injustice because of his background, Camus returned to Algeria at the end of April 1945 to report on the causes of Moslem unrest. In contrast to *Le Monde*'s correspondent, who insisted that the instigators of the Sétif revolt were "anti-French" agitators, Camus argued that the primary cause, though not the sole one, was the fact that the majority of Algerians was experiencing famine—a famine produced by a bad harvest at a time when the war had used up all reserve stocks, a famine that threatened to become even worse because a drought would make the current year's harvest even smaller. In pleading for immediate relief measures, Camus asked his readers, "Do people understand that in this country where the sky and the earth invite happiness millions of men are suffering from hunger?"[34]

The special gravity of the famine, wrote Camus, came from the conviction of the Algerians not only that their hunger was unjust in effect (as an outrage to human life and dignity), but that it was unjust in cause—that it was a result of human exploitation as well as of natural disaster. Camus shared this view. In 1939 he had charged that exploitation alone was the cause of the scandalously low salaries paid to the Kabyle workers; similarly, in 1945 he condemned the inequalities in food distribution—the larger rations given to the Europeans and to the favorites of the caids.

In 1939 he had outlined specific reforms—better education, regulation of salaries and prices, public works, mechanization of farming, and even organized emigration to colonize the underpopulated south of France—all aimed at ending both the misery and the exploitation. In 1945, however, aware of the necessity to restore confidence in France among the Moslems, Camus focused on a broader problem: the political malaise that was independent of, and ultimately more serious than, the immediate economic crisis.

Camus charged that France had failed to institute the democracy it had promised, which the Moslems had expected to be the means of social and economic conquests. He warned that the Algerian people apparently had lost their faith in the democracy of which they had been given a caricature and that only a major political reform could renew this faith. In 1939 he had demanded the decentralization and democratization of local administration in Kabylia. In 1945 he called for the extension of full metropolitan political rights to many more Moslems in order to prove to them that France desired "to export to Algeria the democratic regime" enjoyed by the French.[35]

Camus's appeals were eloquent. Like subsequent demands of other moderates for overseas reforms, however, they were ineffectual. Camus's position was flawed. He believed that the French, both on the continent and in Algeria, would be willing, voluntarily and for essentially moral reasons, to make reforms in order to give the Moslem population greater equality and justice. He lamented but nonetheless underestimated the hostility and suspicion between the Moslem and European communities that was to hinder the instituting of the reforms he wanted. The French in Algeria were in fact unwilling to permit the export of democracy.

Furthermore, Camus believed that the Algerians would be won over by and remain satisfied with political and social reforms. Apparently forgetting his own recent participation in the French Resistance, he contended that peoples generally aspired "for political rights only to begin and to complete their social conquests."[36] Interpreting Abbas's "Manifesto of the Algerian People" as a reaction to the French failure to apply the advertised policy of assimilation, he concluded that honest measures of assimilation could regain the Algerians' allegiance. He underestimated the seriousness of the demands of Abbas's party for an Algerian republic and did not realize that, even if the French had been willing to assimilate the Moslems socially and politically, it was probably too late to stop the rise of Algerian nationalism.

In the years following the Liberation the anticolonialist intellectuals had to face the fact that their efforts to correct injustices in the French Union had little impact. The National Assembly enacted few reforms, governments took few actions to end abuses, and even these few often were sabotaged overseas or at least turned to the benefit of the European settlers and their allies. Moreover, the French political leaders were willing to instigate or to acquiesce in acts of repression in an effort to protect the interests of France or of French citizens. The intellectuals blamed the failure of the Fourth Republic to establish a just overseas policy on a coalition of, on the one hand, the settlers and the colonial administration, sometimes allied with privileged local figures such as El Glaoui, and, on the other hand, the capitalists at home who had economic interests in the French Union.

The colonial administrations and settlers of all the French empire except Equatorial Africa, Cameroon, and the Pacific islands had been loyal to the Vichy government—to the point of fighting against the Gaullists at Dakar, in the Near East, and to a certain extent in North Africa. The Resistance men who had crossed to Algeria after the Allied invasion of North Africa had been dismayed at the Vichy atmosphere that still prevailed there. After the Liberation the new leaders of France continued to regard the French colonial residents with suspicion. The anticolonialists charged that the deeds and beliefs, especially the racism, of the colonial circles not only were responsible for overseas troubles but also demonstrated that these people were not truly Frenchmen.[37] In this way the anticolonialists cleared themselves, as well as most other Frenchmen of the home country, of direct complicity with overseas injustices.

The settlers and administrators did have certain important allies in France: the large number of capitalist enterprises, such as the Banque d'Indochine and the Banque de Paris et des Pays-Bas, that had important investments in the colonies. In the early 1950s the anticolonialists denounced the economic interests in North Africa, in particular, and charged that war profiteers were financing a campaign in the National Assembly to continue the war in Indochina. Schuman, who had ceased to be the minister of foreign affairs only a few weeks earlier, testified to the power over colonial policy of this combination of French and colonial groups in a celebrated article at the beginning of *La Nef*'s issue of March 1953 on Tunisia and Morocco.[38] The most penetrating analysis of this power, however, was made by Bourdet.

Bourdet had been one of the leaders of the French Resistance— second in command of Combat, organizer of the infiltration of the Vichy administrations, representative of Combat on the National Council of the Resistance, and editor of *Combat* until his capture by the Nazis on 25 March 1944. After his return from Buchenwald at the end of the war, he became vice-president of the Consultative Assembly of de Gaulle's provisional government and briefly was director of French radio. Eventually he turned to journalism, editing a short-lived weekly, *Octobre*, before taking over *Combat* again when Camus resigned. A militant socialist, Bourdet was much more critical than Camus had been of the exploitation of the overseas peoples by French interests and by French-protected local "feudalities." After the disillusionments of the first years of the Fourth Republic, he was also more aware of the power of these interests to resist reforms.

Bourdet tried in the early 1950s to explain why the colonial interests were so strong. He argued in his articles on North Africa in *L'Observateur* and *Les Temps Modernes* that each big agriculturist, industrialist, trader, and financier in the Maghreb was intent on preserving an economic and social status quo that generated "fabulous profits," but could be maintained only as long as "a political establishment supported by French rifles, machine guns, tanks, and planes" prevented any serious development of social demands.[39] These economic interests, he continued, were tightly linked and easily able to control the local French administration. The official representatives of the French of North Africa always defended the large interests, for the poor Frenchmen always voted the same way as the wealthy ones because they too were, and felt themselves to be, the beneficiaries of the colonial system. The administrators were quickly integrated into French colonial society and came to share its racist prejudices and its caste sentiment. In addition, economic interests received support from the Moslem chiefs who shared in the profits of French exploitation, especially from those like El Glaoui who were associated directly with some of the capitalist enterprises.

Against this bloc of local interests, explained Bourdet, a lone reformer, even a governor general, usually could do nothing, especially since the Moslems he might want to help had little legal means of expressing their support. All the reformer could do was to cause such a violent reaction in colonial circles that either he or his liberal attitude would be swept away. Nonetheless, an energetic governor might force changes if he were supported in Paris. As a result, Bourdet continued, colonial interests had built a further line of defense in the home country. This indispensable complement of local control was the colonial lobby, the trump card that gave colonial interests the ability to make French governments disavow liberal administrators and accept *faits accomplis* of colonial repression.

The power of the colonial lobby came from a number of sources: the parliamentary representatives from North Africa, who belonged to a variety of parties but who also were organized as a bloc; the wide network of personal contacts in the closely interrelated worlds of business and administration, especially important because, according to Bourdet, almost all big French financial and industrial companies had business interests in North Africa; a vast treasury to use for propaganda and bribes; the absence of opposition from a strong group representing the interests of the indigenous population, especially since the limited popular representation was falsified by fixed colonial elections; and the ignorance of and lack of interest in colonial matters of the public and even of most politicians, on whose "infantile emotions" the colonial lobby could play when necessary.[40]

The crucial question for the reformists, therefore, was how to break the power of the colonial interests. Bourdet suggested that if the people who were subjected to oppression and exploitation were given a greater means of political and social expression in their own lands and in France, they would be able to combat their enemies. Justice would be instituted because of pressure from below.[41] This was precisely the type of reform, however, that the colonial system was successful in preventing or sabotaging. Understandably, the colonial interests feared that the people would use this power to attack them and to gain more power.

Most reformers hoped that the French government in Paris would gain enough strength and resolve to overcome the pressure of the colonial lobby. The North African drama seemed, in Julien's words, to have resulted "less from the gravity of the situation than from the incapacity of the governments to conceive of a total plan and to require its application." Unable, however, to convince the leaders or to arouse public opinion sufficiently to force government action—even to destroy the public pride in France's overseas accomplishments—many anticolonialists began to see the solution in a change of leaders or of regimes. They did not arrive at the seemingly logical conclusion that a reign of justice was incompatible with, and prevented by, the maintenance of French control and that the only way to break the power of colonial interests was to grant independence.[42]

In fact, in the decade after the war few French anticolonialist intellectuals called for the independence of any French colonies except, in some cases, for that of Vietnam. As late as 1953, for example, none of the Frenchmen writing in *La Nef*'s issue on the protectorates proposed complete, much less immediate, independence. Most anticolonialists continued to work for the reform of the French Union. The charge of the Trotskyist sociologist Claude Lefort in 1947 remained apt: "The anticolonialists of the extreme Left are for the colonial movements, but they are for them 'conditionally.' Emancipation, they say, 'must' accommodate itself to the French Union." The Communist Césaire, for example, who charged, especially in his eloquent and savage pamphlet *Discours sur le colonialisme* (1950), that colonization was a radical evil that had dehumanized both the Europeans and the colonial peoples, did not use his position as mayor of Fort-de-France and deputy to the National Assembly to lead a movement for Antillean independence. Even Rous, insisting that the independence he favored had to be followed by "interdependence," wrote of transforming the French Union into "a democratic confederation of peoples."[43]

Some anticolonialists, such as Bourdet, may have refrained from speaking of independence for tactical reasons. As their opponents charged, they may have worked for measures that would favor the movements for independence while trying not to scare the French by invoking the desired goal. As Domenach has explained, "To speak immediately of independence was to reinforce the enormous opposition that we had against us, for I assure you that it is easy enough to be anticolonialist in 1970, but in 1947 I had extremely violent altercations with many people who now call themselves anticolonialists and who thought that in Indochina or Madagascar the French had brought liberty, happiness."[44] Most anticolonialist intellectuals, however, including Domenach, appear to have wanted to avoid, not to facilitate, the complete independence of the French colonies. How can this stance be explained?

By the early 1950s the French Union clearly was a failure. Subverted by "colonialist" interests, while the French at home remained indifferent, it was unable to attract the emerging indigenous elites. Nonetheless, as before the war, the intellectuals who criticized colonialist abuses continued, for the most part, to believe in France's overseas vocation.[45] Believing that the injustices were incidental rather than essential to France's presence, they tried to arouse among the French a greater awareness of and dedication to their humanist mission.

At the core of the exponents of France's mission were the Catholic intellectuals. The tenets of the morality of colonization expounded in the early 1930s were reaffirmed—by many of the same ideologues, in particular the sociology professor and journalist Joseph Folliet—at the 1948 conference of the Semaines Sociales de France on "Overseas Peoples and Western Civilization" and again at the 1953 debate of the Centre Catholique des Intellectuels Français on "Colonization and Christian Conscience." The regulating principle of Catholic doctrine on colonization was the well-being of the human community as a whole. As Folliet explained, in the absence of a world government it was up to the colonial powers—provisionally in the forefront of human development—to act in the interests of the whole community and, in particular, to communicate "the surplus of their spiritual riches" without stifling the other civilizations.[46]

The Catholic intellectuals stressed that colonization was only provisional: "to colonize is to educate, but to educate is to emancipate."[47] But the goal of emancipation was limited in two ways. It could occur only after the fulfillment of the overseas mission, that is, after the colonial peoples had reached maturity. It also had to serve the basic aim of the historical development of humanity, which was to unite rather than to separate the peoples of the world. Folliet suggested that the colonial empires, if transformed into federal associations rather than allowed to disintegrate, would be excellent bases of departure toward the ideal human community. By 1953, however, he realized that his vision could be transformed into reality only by a rededication of the colonial powers to the humanist mission.

Folliet's vision of the goal of colonization was shared by Catholics even on the far Left, such as the men of *Esprit*. They were enthusiastic about the French Union at the beginning of the Fourth Republic, interpreting the idea in a federalist sense, imagining a "friendly cohabitation" of internally autonomous peoples led by a paternal France. In face of the reality of overseas troubles, Mounier charged in April 1947: "When the tutors of provisionally inferior classes or peoples cease to consider themselves as educators, that is, as emancipators, in order to maintain indefinitely the privileges and the facilities of the tutelage, . . . they have the wars that they deserve and reap the hates that they have sowed." He added in the introduction to his book on *L'Éveil de l'Afrique noire* (1947): "Imagine a father who has failed in the education of his children, but to whom a kind of last chance gives a late-born son, and the possibility of not making with him the errors that he can no longer remedy with the others. Such is Black Africa for us. Will we understand in time?"[48]

Throughout the Fourth Republic the writers of *Esprit* insisted, in Domenach's words: "It is necessary to organize the French Union like an astral system, which, formed of stars having each its own movement, yet displaces itself in space in solidarity—not like a pyramid to build or a farm rent to exploit." As Domenach has recalled, "The particular mission of France for us was to make an alliance with the Third World and to give the example of a decolonization that would be completed by an entente. We hoped to be able to jump over the conflicts of decolonization, to jump over the tremors, the childhood diseases of independence, and to arrive at the place that we are approaching at this moment, that is, at an entente and a cooperation."[49] As a result, the intellectuals of *Esprit* refrained from speaking of independence.

The idea of France's mission was shared by the Catholics who wrote for *Témoignage Chrétien*, *Cahiers du Monde Nouveau*, and *Le Monde* and was vigorously reaffirmed by Mauriac and other Catholics in the early 1950s. The missionary spirit pervaded the whole debate over decolonization, even reaching the Marxists. In the name of international proletarian solidarity and of the revolutionary alliance of the European proletariat and the colonial peoples, Marxists believed that the European socialists had the duty to aid, instruct, protect, and fight alongside the overseas peoples. Both Communists and Socialists felt a responsibility to ensure that political liberation was accompanied by social liberation.[50]

The colonial leaders were growing impatient with France's affirmation of its mission, having experienced its hypocrisy. In reply to

Mauriac's defense in 1947 of French colonization, Merleau-Ponty reported in *Les Temps Modernes*: "A Vietnamese said to us: your system functions beautifully. You have your colonialists. And among your administrators, writers, and journalists, you have many men of good will. The former act, the latter speak and are the former's moral guarantee. Thus principles are saved—and colonization remains in fact just what it has always been." A new fervor for independence was spreading throughout all the territories subjected to European colonial rule—a fervor that would have doomed even a just French Union. In addition, the emerging nations were beginning to organize themselves in opposition to the great powers, as indicated by the conference of Asian and African nations at Bandung, Indonesia, in April 1955. In Césaire's words, "a billion five hundred million men met in a city of Asia to proclaim solemnly that Europe no longer had a vocation to direct the world unilaterally."[51]

In spite of the affection and respect for France exhibited by most colonial leaders, therefore, they began to demand independence. When the intellectuals who believed in France's responsibility for the peoples it had conquered were faced with these demands, they hesitated. They were unable to support an independence they feared would be a disaster for the indigenous peoples.

4 &MISGIVINGS OVER INDEPENDENCE

The humanist intellectuals found the failure of the French Union a negative reason to favor independence for the colonial peoples. They demanded positive reasons as well.

THE RIGHT OF SELF-DETERMINATION

The chief argument of the colonial nationalists for independence was a people's right of self-determination. They could expect the French intellectuals to be sensitive to this argument and to utilize it themselves, for it touched on the essence of Western democratic theory. The principles of popular sovereignty and, accordingly, of a people's right to choose their own government had constituted the ideological basis of the American and French revolutions. The right of self-determination had been asserted repeatedly in the twentieth century as a fundamental tenet of international politics—in Wilson's Fourteen Points, in the Versailles treaty, in the Atlantic Charter, in the charter of the United Nations—and it had been reaffirmed in practice in the struggles of the Free French and the Resistance. As Domenach declared in *Esprit*: "The right to independence is a consequence of the right of peoples to self-determination, [a principle] of which France made itself the historical promoter. To oppose it would be to oppose our very tradition, our reason to be heard in the world."[1]

Nonetheless, even those French intellectuals most sympathetic to colonial nationalism seldom appealed to the right of self-determination during the controversies over the French Union. When a writer cited the principle, it was usually not central to his case, but when the idea of self-determination was central to a writer's case, he often did not state the principle explicitly. The French anticolonialist intellectuals, unlike the colonial nationalists, apparently did not see in this principle a strong argument in favor of granting independence to the overseas people.[2]

The groups that used the argument of the right of self-determination most often in reference to the French colonies were, in addition to the colonial nationalists, the Anglo-Americans and the Communists. Most Frenchmen distrusted both groups. Britain's self-interested promotion of colonial nationalism had been demonstrated, the French believed, in the Middle East at the end of the war. In the same way, the French were convinced that the Americans spoke of the right to independence because they had discovered "in the needs of big business the necessity of emancipating the peoples subjected to colonial rule and of making profitable markets of them."[3] The Communists referred to this principle more often than did any other French political group because Lenin had insisted that the right to independence was a truth that had to become a reality before it could be transcended in an international Communist order. Anti-Communists responded by pointing to Soviet oppression of minorities in the USSR and to its colonial system in Eastern Europe and by arguing that the ultimate goal of the Communists was the absorption of all nations into the Soviet system. The right of self-determination was discredited, therefore, by its association with the desire of foreigners to despoil France of its colonies. By their own neglect of the principle, however, the anticolonialist intellectuals furthered this association.

A more important reason why most French intellectuals did not use this argument was that it seemed to ignore the concrete issues surrounding the political futures of the French colonies. Those on the far Left objected to the abstract moralism of the argument, the moderates questioned its applicability to the French possessions, and all worried about what would happen if the principle actually were put into practice.

The attitude of the far leftist intellectuals is illustrated by their reactions to the outbreak of war in Indochina. The weekly *Octobre* and the monthlies *Les Temps Modernes* and *Esprit* were almost alone in supporting the cause of the Vietminh. They pointed out that Indochina was the home of the Indochinese people, that the bloodshed demonstrated that these people regarded the French as an occupying power and wanted to end the occupation, and that the French troops were, therefore, playing in Indochina "the role of the Wehrmacht in France." The three periodicals refrained from going beyond their appreciation of the facts of the situation. As Merleau-Ponty explained in *Les Temps Modernes*, "In the Indochinese affair we have not opposed colonization with arguments of principle such as the equality of men or their right to self-determination. We have made the very concrete observation that after eighty years we remain badly tolerated occupying authorities' in Indochina, that we have failed, and that a military solution would confirm this."[4]

These leftist intellectuals avoided abstract moralism for several reasons. They were strongly influenced by Marxism or by the Christian "personalism" of Mounier. Both Marxists and personalists constantly attacked the formalism of bourgeois rights, charging that these rights gave a deceptive liberal veneer to the materialist, alienating, exploitive capitalist order. They believed that granting bourgeois rights or invoking abstract principles could be a means of hiding injustice or of avoiding the complicated issues posed by any specific situation. Furthermore, as former combatants in the Resistance, they found repugnant the sort of vapid moralizing—both ineffectual and hypocritical—that had not stopped Hitler during the 1930s and, under Philippe Pétain, had even helped to cover the spread of Nazism.[5]

The intellectuals' neglect of the argument of self-determination requires more explanation, however, for it was shunned in reference to later overseas problems and by intellectuals, including the writers of *Esprit*, who appealed to other, though perhaps less abstract, moral principles. For example, it was not mentioned in any of the articles by Frenchmen in *La Nef*'s issue on Tunisia and Morocco in 1953 or in its issue on the French Union in 1955, and it was cited only occasionally in *Preuves*, the monthly organ in France of the anti-Communist Congress for Cultural Freedom.

Many of the moderate critics of overseas abuses were inhibited in bringing up the right of national self-determination because of its questionable applicability to the various French possessions. The argument of self-determination presumably was not relevant to the Indochinese territories, Tunisia, and Morocco because their independence was not denied in theory. Except for Cochinchina, all were defined as protectorates; according to the treaties, this protection was to be only temporary. The issues were instead under what conditions, to whom, and when independence was to be granted. Claiming that they, as the protectors and tutors, alone were able to answer such questions, the French used these issues as means to deny independence in practice.

France's policy in Indochina was to keep an "independent" Vietnam (as well as Cambodia and Laos) within the French Union and, after the break with Ho Chi Minh, to grant independence to Vietnamese nationalists who were more cooperative than the Vietminh. On 6 March 1946 the French representative signed an accord with Ho Chi Minh, recognizing the Republic of Vietnam as "a free State having its government, its parliament, its army, and its finances, forming part of the Indochinese Federation and of the French Union." When war with the Vietminh broke out, Premier Paul Ramadier declared in his investiture speech on 21 January 1947 that France would not refuse to admit "the independence of Vietnam in the framework of the French Union and of the Indochinese Federation," but that first France had to find representatives of the Vietnamese people who would "speak the language of reason." On 5 June 1948 the French representatives signed with General Xuan, the head of the provisional government of the former emperor Bao Dai, a declaration recognizing the independence of Vietnam with "no other limits" than those imposed by "its membership in the French Union."[6]

The French also tried to impose limiting conditions on Tunisian and Moroccan independence. They tried, without success, to convince the bey of Tunisia and the sultan of Morocco not only to agree to make their countries "associated states" of the French Union, but to admit that the French residents had a right of cosovereignty because of their contributions to the development of the protectorates. The French authorities tried to avoid dealing with the Tunisian and Moroccan nationalists, claiming that they did not represent their peoples. But the nationalists won a great deal of respect and sympathy from French intellectuals, for whom the key issue was not the validity of the colonial representatives; rather it was whether the time had arrived for independence—whether the protected peoples had reached maturity and the international situation was favorable. Most contended that the time had not yet arrived.

The argument based on the right of national self-determination was held to be inapplicable to Algeria for quite different reasons. Algeria was defined as an integral part of France. The French had entered Algeria in 1830 and had transformed the land; their achievements, they believed, gave them a title of ownership. Since Algeria never had been a nation, the indigenous people had no national traditions and were to be liberated as individuals by their assimilation into France. The political scientist Bertrand de Jouvenel made an analogy by telling an American audience to imagine that the state of Mississippi tried to secede from the Union. American citizens would react, he said, the same way the French reacted to the outbreak of the Algerian revolt in 1954. Minister of Interior François Mitterrand declared, "It is necessary to distinguish between nationalist movements which can occur in the protectorates and uprisings of citizens in French territories. Negotiations with the enemies of the homeland cannot be allowed. In this case, the only negotiation is war."[7]

The status of the overseas territories in sub-Saharan Africa, Madagascar, and elsewhere was ambiguous. The constitution seemed to define them both as part of the French Republic and as not part of it. Even if the territories were considered as potentially separate states, until the mid-1950s most of the French judged the indigenous peoples much too immature even to discuss granting them independence.

Many French intellectuals, therefore, believed that the principle of self-determination was not relevant to France's particular overseas problems. Those who did think it relevant hesitated to use it because they believed that agreement on the level of abstract morality might serve only to ease French consciences and to camouflage the persistence of colonial oppression. Almost all had serious misgivings about the practical consequences of applying this principle. They feared the effects of granting independence not only on France but on the international scene and, above all, on the colonial peoples. They worried about the threat of the new imperialisms, the immaturity of the colonial peoples, and the plight of the economically undeveloped lands. They feared that the right to independence might be used as an excuse or a disguise for abandoning colonial peoples whose needs were a burden to France.

THE NEW IMPERIALIST THREATS

World War II exhausted the old nations of Europe and opened, in Domenach's words, an "era of great international aggregates."[8] In this new world France's continued association with its colonies seemed important for humanist as well as nationalist reasons.

Preservation of the imperial bonds seemed to provide a hope of avoiding a new world war. The postwar conflict between the two ideological blocs, each centered on a semicontinent, threatened to erupt in a war in which Europe would be a mere battlefield. Some intellectuals dreamed that France and its former colonies could form the nucleus of a worldwide "Third Force" to act as a buffer between the two antagonists of the Cold War. The disintegration of the French empire would make the former colonies into prizes in the Cold War and, therefore, would endanger peace by aggravating the rivalry between the United States and the Soviet Union. The internationalization of the war in Indochina in 1950 appeared to confirm this fear but also to demonstrate that French efforts to preserve the empire actually endangered world peace.

More important, the humanist intellectuals worried about the danger to the colonial peoples of the various new imperialisms. The right of self-determination not only was an abstraction, but in the postwar world it seemed a mirage as well. The formal independence of a weak country would be meaningless since the country would have to seek the aid of, or be unable to resist the penetration of, a new imperialist power, which would be unfortunate because the new imperialism probably would treat it in an even less humanist fashion than had France. Consequently, Joseph Rovan in *Esprit* appealed to the colonial nationalists in 1945: "In no way do we misunderstand the ambitions of the foreigners who lie in wait for our colonies and who are certainly not inspired by disinterested love of the colonial people. . . . We immediately ask the young Syrian, African, Indochinese nationalists that they not forget that outside of a great supracontinental federation a small country is today the impotent toy of the great powers." Ten years later the world situation still looked just as dangerous. As Duverger asserted in *La Nef*, "In the present-day world, in which small nations are reduced to the position of satellites, it is not a question of knowing if Tunisia, Morocco, Madagascar, French Black Africa will or will not be totally independent nations, but if they will be dependents (more or less) of France or of the United States or of a third robber."[9]

The imperialist forces that worried the intellectuals the most were American capitalism, communism, and Pan-Arabism. The greatest threat to the French possessions appeared, especially to leftists, to come from the Americans. *Esprit*'s special issue of July 1949 on "Last Chances of the French Union" is a good example of this concern. It was published soon after President Harry S. Truman's declaration that the American government would encourage the investment of American private capital in colonial regions as a counterpart to Marshall Plan aid. Alarmed by this statement, *Esprit*'s contributors made the menace of Anglo-American capitalism the major theme of the issue. They stressed that the colonial peoples would suffer greatly outside the French Union because capitalism, interested only in its own profits, would not promote social and cultural development that might endanger profits based on a low standard of living and a rigorous work schedule. The failure of the French Union, therefore, would halt the "evolution" leading the colonial peoples to democracy; it would mean "the end of all the democratic hopes of the nations who would have wanted to associate themselves with our destiny."[10] Bourdet tried, as early as 1946, to point out that the colonial peoples would be more likely to turn to the Americans for aid if the French refused to satisfy their political ambitions.[11] But, when independent, would they be able to resist the penetration of American capitalism even if they wanted to?

The threat of communism and Pan-Arabism differed from that of American capitalism. It was more specific geographically: communism was the main worry in Indochina; Pan-Arabism, in North Africa. Penetration was primarily by ideological rather than by economic means. Furthermore, the nationalist leaders themselves were charged with spreading the ideology and even with taking orders from Moscow or Cairo. The prospective leaders of the liberated colony, therefore, were not the victims or the dupes of the new oppression, but its deliberate agents. The Communist and Pan-Arab imperialisms would control France's former colonies directly rather than indirectly.

Decolonization in Asia was greatly complicated for France, while much less for England, by the Cold War. The French government did not make anticommunism into a primary reason to fight in Indochina until 1950. From the beginning, however, the fact that Ho Chi Minh was a Communist and that the Vietnamese Communists dominated the Vietminh provided sufficient reason that the French governments did not seek negotiations with the Vietminh and that anti-Communist intellectuals like Camus, Mauriac, and Aron refrained from attacking the war.[12]

Leftwing supporters of Ho Chi Minh like Bourdet and Rous, as well as East Asian experts like Mus and Devillers, argued in reply that Ho Chi Minh himself wanted reconciliation with France in order to protect Vietnam from Soviet and Chinese domination. They implied that the best way to save Vietnam from a new imperialism was to come to terms with the Vietminh before they were forced into total dependence on the Soviets and the Chinese. Even *Preuves* came to this conclusion by summer 1953.[13] The Geneva settlement in 1954, however, confirmed the Cold War fears of the humanist intellectuals, for Vietnam was in effect divided between the rival imperialisms while France retired to Africa.

The intellectuals feared that the North Africans would be seduced not by communism but by Islam and by the Pan-Arab ideology, first of the Arab League and subsequently of Gamal Abdel Nasser. *Esprit*, for example, worried that the "nominal independence" of Algeria would mask "an oppressive regime and retrograde customs."[14] The defenders of North African nationalism replied that the French-educated elites, even the Algerian terrorists, were profoundly imbued with French culture, respected France, and were aware that they needed to remain associated with France after independence. They argued, as in the case of Vietnam, that it was French intransigence that was turning the nationalists to foreigners for support. Yet, bonds with France might not be as strong as the ideological attraction of the Arab world. The general French public believed the French governments' repeated statements that Egypt was encouraging and supplying the Algerian rebels.[15]

The threat of Pan-Arabism appeared even more serious because of its association with other imperialisms. The Arab League, founded in 1945, appeared to the French to be allied with English imperialism. In 1952, however, Nasser and Mohammed Naguib threw out the pro-English King Farouk of Egypt, and in 1954, Nasser emerged as the leader of Egypt and of a more militant and socially revolutionary brand of Pan-Arabism. As a result, and with the Indochinese case in mind, the French began to associate Pan-Arabism with the Soviet menace. Echoing the conviction not only of French army officers but also of much of the public, Camus contended that, in Algeria, France was defending the free world against international communism:

The claims for Algerian national independence must be seen in part as one of the manifestations of this new Arab imperialism in which Egypt, overestimating its strength, aims to take the lead and which, for the moment, Russia is using for its anti-Western strategy. The Russian strategy, which can be read on every map of the globe, consists in calling for the *status quo* in Europe (in other words, the recognition of its own colonial system) and in fomenting trouble in the Middle East and Africa to encircle Europe on the south. The happiness and freedom of the Arab populations are of little account in the whole affair.

Soustelle, who had been governor general in Algeria in 1955, went one step further by arguing in 1957 that an independent Algeria would be "Pan-Arab, Communist, or American, perhaps the three things simultaneously by means of partition or successively."[16]

Most of the intellectuals, therefore, believed that membership in the French Union—in contrast to total independence—was necessary to protect the weak overseas peoples from domination by the selfish new imperialisms. One intellectual, after condemning colonialist abuses, put the issue thus: "There are several ways to liberate a galley slave. One of them consists in telling him one fine day: 'Go, you are free!' detaching his irons and throwing him overboard, in the open seas, in the middle of the sharks. Is that what we should do? We know well enough who the sharks are that circle our imperial galley. Are we, under the pretext of 'liberation,' going to abandon to them the destiny of the overseas populations, at the risk of delivering the latter to an even worse exploitation than that which they suffered under our rule?"[17] This position, however, had three flaws. First, it was not clear that resistance to decolonization was the most effective method of opposing the spread of other imperialisms, particularly of communism. Second, the obsession with the division of the world into two blocs helped to prevent many Frenchmen from fully appreciating the non-Western destiny of the Asian and African peoples, their search for political and economic forms of their own, and their ability to achieve a political autonomy outside the two blocs. Third, the humanist anxiety about other imperialisms was unlikely to be dispelled in the near future, but was a nearly permanent argument against independence that could be utilized for selfish as well as altruistic motives. The humanist intellectuals were giving support to the French imperialists.[18]

A change in attitude did take place in the mid-1950s, however, at least among the intellectuals. As Cold War tensions eased and the Bandung conference demonstrated that the peoples of the "Third World" could organize to protect their interests, preoccupation with other imperialisms lessened. The intellectuals shifted their attention from the external situation to the internal problems of the overseas lands: the immaturity of their peoples and the backwardness of their economies.

The danger of oppression from outside began to seem only an exacerbating factor in the internal crises that newly liberated colonies appeared destined to suffer.

THE IMMATURITY OF THE OVERSEAS PEOPLES

Most humanist intellectuals believed that the overseas peoples were not sufficiently mature for independence. The motives and capabilities of the nationalist leaders were often questioned, but the indigenous masses were the greatest cause for worry. They were manifestly unprepared to cope with the democratic politics that the French intellectuals conceived as the goal of colonial political development and were ill-adapted to the modern economy that the intellectuals believed necessary to conquer misery and win economic independence. A defender of the French-educated elite of, for example, Tunisia could at the same time castigate the ordinary people: "Eternally underfed, eternally exploited but offering itself to exploitation, this mass has never been anything but a negative element, ready to destroy the civilizations that have succeeded each other on its soil, without any desire of transforming the huts of stone or sheet-iron that is uses as shelter."[19]

The most original and widely discussed analysis of this supposed immaturity of the colonial peoples was O. Mannoni's *Psychologie de la colonisation*, a psychoanalytically oriented study of colonization in Madagascar published in 1950. As a philosophy professor in Madagascar and as the chief of its information service, Mannoni had become interested in anthropological research. While in Paris for holidays, he had begun psychoanalysis to solve personal problems and subsequently had trained to become an analyst himself. *Psychologie de la colonisation* was written soon thereafter in collaboration with France's leading psychoanalytic theorist, Jacques Lacan.[20]

The colonial situation in Madagascar, wrote Mannoni, had been created by the encounter of two peoples with different personality types: the Malagasies, whose personality structure was characterized by a "dependence complex," and the Europeans, who, in growing to adulthood, had overcome dependence and assumed the risks of individual autonomy. The European settlers and the Malagasy people had established a symbiotic relationship that was psychologically satisfying for each group because each was sheltered from feelings of insecurity—the Malagasies from the fear of abandonment that haunted the dependent personality and the Europeans from the fear of individual inferiority that plagued the autonomous individual. But this easy security was psychologically crippling. Mannoni believed that the goal of human development, for all men, was the achievement of an independent and responsible personality—the successful completion of the evolution undertaken by the Europeans. The Europeans who lived in Madagascar were stunted because their victory over inferiority was artificial, requiring no effort and no psychological growth. The Malagasies were protected from the need for autonomous behavior by their dependence on the Europeans.

The colonial system as described by Mannoni had to be changed— and was changing—but he warned against a sudden liberation of the indigenous population that might involve only a shift in objects of dependence from European settlers to nationalist leaders which would result in little psychological progress. Moreover, as the Malagasy insurrection of 1947 had demonstrated, a people who lost confidence in or felt abandoned by their protectors could turn against them with a regressive ferocity. In short, he argued, immediate self-government would be a bad solution because the Malagasies (and the settlers as well) would not be able to adjust psychologically to this drastic change. An evolution of the Malagasy personality structure was a prerequisite for independence.

Though the Malagasies currently were incapable of democracy because they had "very little sense of responsibility," Mannoni hoped that the gradual introduction of democratic politics would liberate the Malagasies psychologically. Arguing that politics was "the only genuinely collective psychotherapy," he called for a revival of the traditional village councils as a first stage in "the painful apprenticeship to freedom." When the Malagasies learned to be self-sufficient, they would be ready not only for democratic politics, but also for economic progress. They would be capable psychologically of adopting the experimental attitude of Western science and of relying on positive action and technical skill to overcome obstacles.[21]

Mannoni's study was one of the first French efforts to analyze the overseas peoples in terms of their interactions with the Europeans in the "colonial situation." His stress on the psychological dimension of the overseas problems and on the necessity of a psychological transformation before independence was a unique contribution. For this very reason, however, the French intellectuals treated Mannoni's analysis as inadequate. Suspicious of Freudian theory and highly influenced by the Marxist contention that personality was a function of social structure, they preferred to stress the economic and social dimensions of the colonial situation.[22]

Mannoni was severely criticized as a defender of the colonial regime because of his contention that the colonial peoples, at least the Malagasies, were psychologically suited to colonial domination. The most passionate attacks came from black intellectuals. Césaire charged that the theory of the dependence complex was only a disguised form of the old racist story: "The Negroes-Are-Big-Children." Mannoni, he suggested, justified colonialism by denying that the Malagasies even wanted liberty, much less were capable of dealing with it. Alioune Diop, the Senegalese editor of the review *Présence Africaine*, argued that the Malagasies' alleged substitution of the European colonizers who exploited them for their revered ancestors was both illogical and contrary to experience in Africa. Césaire and Diop, therefore, doubted that the Malagasies or other colonial peoples felt the dependence that Mannoni claimed.[23]

Frantz Fanon, a young psychiatrist from Martinique who later became a major ideologue of revolution in the Third World, focused his attack on the supposed origin of this relation to the Europeans. Mannoni had written that, because of a "need for dependence," the coming of the Europeans "was unconsciously expected—even desired—by the future subject peoples." Fanon noted that the hospitality shown to the first Europeans could also be explained "in terms of humanity, of good will, of courtesy." Complaining that Mannoni had ignored the violence that had accompanied colonization, he argued that the so-called dependence complex of the Malagasies and other colonial peoples was more likely to have been a product of colonial subjection than its antecedent.[24]

Fanon, Diop, and Césaire thus implied that what Mannoni called dependence actually was submission to colonial violence and that this type of behavior would disappear along with the colonial rule that caused it. Even if they agreed in refuting Mannoni's case, however, most of the intellectuals were not satisfied that the colonial peoples would be able to cope with independence. They continued to agree with Mannoni that modern politics and economics required self-reliant individuals who would be produced only by education, social reform, and gradual apprenticeship in political responsibility, and, like Mannoni, they continued to see peoples as individuals who must develop according to a common pattern. Treating the demands for independence as a "crisis of adolescence," they hoped that the colonial peoples would understand that emancipation should, in their own interests, await their full "maturity."[25] *Esprit* devoted its June 1957 issue to a depressing analysis of "the childhood diseases of independence" from which the newly liberated countries suffered.

The French intellectuals were committed to two kinds of liberty: individual and collective. During World War II the Free French and the Resistance had been able to struggle for both at the same time. The Mouvements Unis de la Résistance had declared: "The loss of National Liberty is identical to the loss of Individual Liberty." In the case of the colonies, however, the two kinds of liberty appeared to be in conflict: independence was, because of the immaturity of the colonial peoples, likely to lead to their subjection to local tyrants and to misery. Was the loss of individual freedoms worth the gain of independence? In spite of their own sacrifices for the sake of France's independence, the French intellectuals were unable to place collective liberty above individual liberty. In accord with the individualist bias of Western culture, all French political groups hesitated to support colonial nationalism when the liberation of the individual seemed more likely to take place under French control. Furthermore, the doctrinaire Marxist position was that genuine liberation would occur only when the proletariat was in power. Consequently, the Communists and some Socialists hesitated to abandon the colonial peoples to the rule of the local bourgeoisies.[26]

The independence of the colonies would, in addition, establish new centers of fervent nationalism. The masses were likely to be stirred by their leaders to nationalist, indeed xenophobic, passions that would endanger world peace, impede international cooperation, and lead to a waste of scarce resources on efforts to increase national prestige. After a century and a half of increasingly destructive nationalist wars and in a world that was becoming increasingly interconnected, nationalism appeared to many French intellectuals as harmful and anachronistic. It was a "childhood disease" from which the European nations had suffered earlier and which the French wished to prevent in the overseas lands.[27]

Furthermore, the formal independence of the overseas peoples promised to be empty of content. Because of their immaturity, they would be unable both to resist domination by a new imperialism and to cope with their most serious problem, their economic underdevelopment. By retarding their evolution toward technical, economic, social, and even political modernization, formal independence would retard the achievement of real independence.

Most of the anticolonialist intellectuals, therefore, by disapproving of premature independence for the colonial peoples, unavoidably gave further temporary support to the imperialist cause. Their arguments could be used to defend the position that the safest and most genuine liberation of the indigenous populations was by means of their assimilation into, or at least association with, France.

THE TRAGEDY OF UNDERDEVELOPMENT

The French always had been well aware of the economic backwardness of the colonial peoples, and part of their mission had been to ameliorate it. Domenach, for example, declared in *Esprit* in February 1948 that "the progressive emancipation of the colonial peoples" was conceivable only if "linked to the improvement of their living standard and of their national equipment." The French initially saw the problem as merely a retardation of economic growth that could be overcome by wise advice and large injections of capital. In the early 1950s, however, French economists and sociologists, following the lead of their American and British counterparts, became aware of the extreme complexity of the problem. They realized that "underdeveloped" countries were different from developed ones not only in degree but also in nature. The overseas economies could be modernized only as part of a transformation of their whole society and culture.[28]

The calamity that the underdeveloped countries were experiencing—the deepening misery resulting from the conjunction of economic stagnation and demographic explosion—was becoming more evident and more alarming. It was revealed to the wider public by the economic plight of newly independent states like India. By the mid-fifties, at the time of the Algerian war, the problem of underdevelopment had replaced the threat of outside imperialisms as the obsession of France's humanist intellectuals. The most celebrated study of underdevelopment was Germaine Tillion's *L'Algérie en 1957*.

Tillion was an expert on the people who lived in the Aurès mountains of Algeria. She had studied them closely during the 1930s but did not visit them again until 1955, when she returned to Algeria as adviser to her fellow anthropologist, Governor General Soustelle. A cataclysmic social transformation had occurred in the Aurès during her absence. "These men who, fifteen years ago, lived soberly but decently, and in conditions nearly identical for all, were now divided into two unequal groups: in the less numerous the comfort, it is true, was greater than before, but in the other no one knew any longer how he would eat between December and June."[29] This deterioration in way of life, Tillion explained, had been provoked, ironically, by the humanitarian efforts of France in Algeria.

The success of the French in preventing diseases and in distributing food in time of famine (such as in 1945) had resulted in a rise of population. With more mouths to feed, the people of the Aurès had cultivated old land more intensely and had cleared new land. As a result, the soil was worn out from overuse; the wells were dry because the forests had been destroyed, and rainwater ran off without being absorbed. The consequence was that food supplies had decreased.

These people had been caught up in the European money economy and had fallen into constant debt; they had been further demoralized by their awareness of the superiority of European mechanization. Their traditional way of life thus had been destroyed. Even reforms such as the campaign against illiteracy had hurt them by aiding in the destruction of their archaic civilization without substituting a new one. According to Tillion, the mass of the population of the Aurès had been turned into *clochards*—underemployed, impoverished tramps, deprived of energy and hope for the future. The population was given a choice only between "dismal abandon" or "unconditional revolt."[30]

Tillion's book was a radical condemnation of French achievements —but not of the French mission in Algeria. It was an appeal for a gigantic effort to modernize Algeria, not for the granting of independence. Although the French had been the agents of *clochardisation*, their presence, Tillion asserted, had not been its essential cause. She argued that three-fourths of humanity was facing the same danger of being trapped in a noncivilization of permanent misery and that the cause of this worldwide crisis was the contact of the mechanical civilization of the West with the archaic civilizations of the rest of the world —an unavoidable contact only speeded up by colonization. These archaic societies had countered a high death rate by developing collective sentiments and teachings favoring a high birth rate. They subsequently had been unable to cope with the sudden drop in the death rate, which was the most important result of the spread of Western civilization, whether through colonization or not.

As political subjection had not caused *clochardisation*, independence was not likely to remedy it and, Tillion insisted, the granting of independence to Algeria would actually prevent a solution. Since limited reforms merely caused further social disintegration, she argued, the only hope of salvation for Algeria was a total social mutation—the rapid construction of a modern society, involving, above all, the development in each individual of an entirely new "ideal of existence." But such a mutation could result only from a swift, generalized, and massive increase both of resources (especially of food) and of education, and the archaic society could not begin to afford these measures. Vast aid from outside was essential.

For this reason, Tillion asserted, Algeria was lucky to have its special relationship with France. Without the four hundred thousand jobs for Algerian workers in France, without the participation of the French Algerians in the local economy, without French financial aid, Algeria would be helpless against *clochardisation*. Nor would any other country be willing or able to help Algeria as much as France did. Salvation was possible through enormous French effort, which, Tillion believed, did not exceed France's means. She advised the FLN that the French people might agree to a program of massive aid if Algeria were federated to France, but warned that they never would consent to the necessary financial sacrifices if all political bonds were broken. Independence thus seemed to be contrary to the interest of the Algerians.

Tillion's book had a great impact. It shook the confidence of the FLN leaders and was cited repeatedly by opponents of Algerian independence. Camus, for example, had argued in 1956 that Algeria must resist the call of Pan-Islamism because Western technical civilization alone, despite its drawbacks, would be able to "give a decent life to the underdeveloped countries." In 1958 he was able to refer to *L'Algérie en 1957* for support and to argue more precisely that "a purely Arab Algeria could not achieve the economic independence" without which political independence would be only "a deception."[31]

As Tillion herself suggested, her conclusions coud be applied to Madagascar and sub-Saharan Africa as well, as Merleau-Ponty did after a visit to Madagascar in late 1957. He had supported Vietnamese independence in 1946 in spite of his awareness of the danger of other imperialisms, but, in consideration of the plight of underdeveloped areas, he now opposed the immediate emancipation of Madagascar, sub-Saharan Africa, and Algeria. Independence, he contended, must await economic development.[32]

This argument, even more than the humanist arguments of the threat of other imperialisms and the immaturity of the people, could be utilized by Frenchmen whose primary aim was to preserve the empire. The defenders of French control of Algeria, in particular, insisted on France's responsibility for the welfare of the Algerian people. Soustelle asserted that it was "evident" that Algeria could "live only by industrializing" and could "industrialize only with the aid of France." He warned that autonomy would reduce the Algerians to "a bestial misery." The Catholic professor and lawyer Michel Massenet charged that the "beautiful souls" who proposed independence actually were defending only "the right of peoples to make themselves die of starvation." The French army developed a passionate conviction in the civilizing mission of France. Like the colonial army in the past, its task of pacification in Algeria gave it the responsibility to care for the Moslem population, to improve its way of life, and to win its confidence and loyalty.[33] The civilian and military ideologues of *Algérie française* envisioned a prosperous and egalitarian Algeria "integrated" into France while retaining an Algerian "personality." They maintained an uneasy alliance, however, with the large number of French Algerians who wanted France to do no more than preserve the status quo. It is difficult to draw the line between the desire to help the Algerian people and the desire to protect colonialist privileges.[34]

This appropriation of the humanist arguments by defenders of empire was proof of the bankruptcy of French missionary humanism before the question of independence. In 1946, Bourdet, no doubt remembering the paternalism of the Vichy regime, had attacked in reference to Indochina "this suspect paternalism" that sought, or claimed to seek, "to make people happy in spite of themselves." When Soustelle unveiled his program of reforms in July 1955, Bourdet declared that the fundamental political conflict in the modern world was no longer "between tyranny and democracy," but rather "between democracy and paternalism."[35] In the period of decolonization, humanism had become the final refuge of colonialism.

Fanon justly charged, therefore, that the "technocratic paternalism" of most French anticolonialists, including the Communists, had a "neo-colonialist character." He asserted in December 1957, in a series of articles in the FLN newspaper that were greatly debated by French leftists, that the leftists were utilizing a "terrorism of necessity" in order to "maintain Algeria eternally in a stage of a minor and protected state."[36] But, after all, how could the anticolonialists counsel the French to grant an independence that would mean abandonment to underdevelopment?

THE COLONIAL SYSTEM

The humanist intellectuals assumed that under French control injustices did not have to be intolerable and that progress toward political and economic development could be made. Spurred by the Algerian rebellion, however, some intellectuals on the far Left began unreservedly to denounce French control. The most elaborate and thorough attack on French colonization was launched by Sartre. Although *Les Temps Modernes* had been among the first to condemn the war in Indochina and although the review had printed numerous articles on colonial problems, Sartre as its editor had remained quite uninvolved in these questions until 1952.[37] Even then his involvement had been a consequence of his concern with social and political conditions at home rather than overseas. Sartre was originally a proponent of the liberty of the isolated individual. After the experience of the Resistance, in the atmosphere of the Cold War, and under the guidance of Merleau-Ponty, he shifted his commitment to revolutionary socialism. He decided to devote himself to the cause of the French proletariat and, as a result, to form a practical alliance with the French Communist party. His first concrete act of alliance was to join in the party's campaign to free Henri Martin. He also was shifting his philosophical orientation from individualistic existentialism to Marxism and his theoretical interests from ontology to sociology and history. His analyses of French colonialism were important steps in the project of integrating Marxist sociology into his existentialism.

Sartre's first and most important contribution was an essay on Algeria in *Les Temps Modernes* in March-April 1956 titled "Colonialism Is a System." His aim was to refute what he called the "neo-colonialist mystification": the idea that colonialism could be reformed, that, more precisely, the Algerian problem was an economic, social, and psychological one that could be solved without touching the political realm (that is, without giving political control to the Moslems). Drawing on the insights of Bourdet, Jeanson, and others, he insisted that colonialism was an integrated whole that had to be accepted or rejected as a whole. In his subsequent writings on Algerian problems, he refined and developed this initial analysis of the colonial system.[38]

According to Sartre, France, after conquering Algeria, did not at first know how to use its new possession. Finally, during the Second Empire, French capitalists decided to use the colony as a market for their manufactured goods, and around this fundamental project the system of colonialism in Algeria was built. Since the indigenous Algerians had no money with which to buy industrial products, the mother country created a purchasing power by sending settlers. In order to maintain a trade balance, these settlers had to sell as well as to buy; their logical function was to sell food and raw materials to the home country. The good lands, however, were already cultivated by the Algerians. As a result, charged Sartre, the "so-called 'development'" was founded on "a despoiling of the inhabitants": the history of Algeria was "the progressive concentration of European landed property at the expense of Algerian property."[39]

The whole colonial system was organized without concern for the interests and needs of the indigenous population, whose only function was to work to produce food and raw materials for the French market. The Algerians were not even the customers of the colonizers, for the colonist had to export in order to pay for his imports: he produced for the French market. For example, former wheat land was turned over to the production of wine, while the Moslems, who were forbidden by Islamic law to drink, went hungry.

Adapting Marxist categories, Sartre argued that the colonial system in Algeria was based not only on the exclusion but also on the "superexploitation" of the indigenous population. At home the profits of the capitalists were, according to Marx, derived from the exploitation of the proletariat, that is, from the appropriation by the capitalists of the value, in excess of wages and other costs, that was created by the labor of the workers. In Algeria, the settlers were able to exploit the Moslem workers to a much greater degree, that is, to pay them drastically low wages. By this means they were able to make sufficiently high profits on their exports (such as wine) to France to enable the

European community in Algeria to enjoy a standard of living comparable to that in France. Without cheap Moslem labor, Sartre implied,
the colonial economy would not be viable from the settlers' point of
view.

When the colonial system was threatened, the French of Algeria
—landowners, shopkeepers, workers—rose to its defense. They opposed any reform that would threaten the system of Moslem exclusion
and superexploitation on which the livelihood of the whole French
community was based. Either the assimilation of the Moslems or the
creation of a Moslem-controlled state would mean the destruction of
the colonial economy and of their way of life; as a result, the French
Algerians had sabotaged the first and would, as Sartre predicted, revolt to prevent the second.

Sartre concluded that the profits of colonial capitalism and the
prosperity of the settlers depended on the continued misery and sub-
jugation of the indigenous people. He replied to the colonial reformers: "Yes, the fellah is dying of hunger; yes, he lacks everything,
land, work, and education; yes, diseases crush him; yes, the present
state in Algeria is comparable to the worst miseries of the Far East. And
yet it is impossible to begin with economic transformations because the
misery and the despair of the Algerians are the direct and necessary
effect of colonialism and because they will never be suppressed as long
as colonialism continues."[40] The only solution Sartre offered to the
problem of injustices in Algeria, or in any colony, was the total abolition of the system. This meant independence.

Sartre's line of reasoning was too doctrinaire to convince non-
Marxists. Even if his explanation of the settlers' resistance to reforms
was persuasive, it was not clear that their fundamental motives were
economic. Nor was it clear that French capitalism as a whole profited
enough from Algerian colonialism to insist on preserving the colonial
system, or that the French governments were following such dictates
from the capitalists; consequently, the resistance of the settlers to the
improvement of the Moslems' condition might be overcome without
abandoning French sovereignty.[41] Moreover, no matter how convincing, Sartre's arguments did not relieve the anxiety of the humanist
intellectuals when they thought of the economic problems that newly
liberated colonies would face. They could not be enthusiastic about
independence until persuaded that independence was a positive step
toward development.

Sartre's analysis of the colonial system fit into an emerging body of opinion that independence was a prerequisite to political maturation and economic development. This position had been asserted by Rous as early as 1950. Witnessing the emancipation of India, Indonesia, and Libya, and refusing to see only their difficulties, he had called for the independence of Madagascar as well (which he had not done two years earlier), arguing:

It is true that peoples undergo unequal development, as do individuals. But the essential means of hastening or of favoring this maturation has become political independence. In a few months India has learned more than in a hundred years of colonial rule. In the same way that an individual cannot be confined under the pretext of teaching him how to live, likewise colonialist internment has revealed itself as unfit for producing evolution. . . .

Yes, political independence is indeed the antechamber leading toward cultural and economic development, toward prosperity, and toward more happiness. It is not sufficient, but it is the necessary stage, the now indispensable stage.[42]

Few had been willing to agree with Rous in 1950, and even he believed that independence should be followed by association with France. But by the mid-fifties, when French intellectuals had learned to appreciate the depth and complexity of the problems of development as well as the strength of colonial nationalism, Rous's position began to gain favor.

Duverger's change of mind was symptomatic. In 1953 and 1955 he had opposed independence because it would lead to domination by a new imperialism and because it would profit only a small group of former subjects who would exploit the masses in the place of the colonists. He had argued that nationalism was a retrogressive and outmoded passion. In March 1957, however, he distinguished in *Le Monde* between two stages of nationalism: before and after independence. While continuing to attack the latter as reactionary, he insisted now that the nationalism of a dependent people was "liberating and 'progressive'":

The collective liberty of one nation in relation to the others is one of the conditions of the individual liberty of its members. In the short term, it is possible that the independence of a new state will mean for its citizens a greater administrative disorder, a lowering of the standard of living, indeed a curtailing of individual liberties—that is, a regression. In spite of everything, this independence creates the conditions of a long-term progression. However generous paternalism might be, it always constitutes an alienation. The youthful crises of originality bring great damages; they are, however, preferable to maintenance in infancy.[43]

Duverger's new position seemed reasonable for political, but not for economic, development. Apprenticeship in self-government might well be an invaluable educational tool, in spite of and perhaps because of the ensuing political and administrative disorder. In the meantime, however, the economic crisis would be untended and would grow more severe and more difficult to handle, the suffering of the people would become vastly greater, and the young government would have to face this catastrophic situation without help. In face of the tragic economic plight of the underdeveloped countries, how could independence be asserted as a means of progress?

The anticolonialists were offered a possible way out of their quandary over independence by the elaboration in the mid-fifties of a series of arguments to explain why independence was a prerequisite to economic as well as to political development. A variety of economists and other thinkers joined Sartre and Rous in contending that France's control impeded, if not prevented, economic development and that control by the colonial peoples themselves, in contrast, would stimulate it. The debate encompassed the whole Third World, but focused on Algeria.

France's efforts to develop the overseas economies were limited, it was widely agreed, by the fact that both public and private expenditures tended, quite naturally, to be made primarily in the interests of the French economy at home and of the French residents overseas. The major state projects—such as the construction of roads and dams—benefited the French-controlled sector of the economy, but had relatively little effect on the traditional economy by which the masses continued to live. French businessmen, for their part, chose not to build factories overseas, even though industrialization was a vital means of creating jobs to absorb the legions of unemployed or underemployed workers.

Sartre, like the Communists, blamed the lack of industry on the capitalist design to have colonies as sources of raw materials and as markets for manufactured goods, not as competitors. He attacked the very notion of "underdevelopment" because it hid the fact that the colonial power had prevented this development. Aron, a defender of the capitalist system, pointed instead to the dictates of economic rationality. French private capital was not invested overseas, specifically in Algeria, because it was economically more rational to build in France, where previous industrialization had prepared the terrain, by training workers for example, and where the investments would not be endangered by future decolonization. At the same time, Aron noted, local attempts to industrialize were paralyzed by the common market between France and the overseas lands. Sartre and Aron agreed, therefore, that little industrial development was likely to take place overseas as long as France retained control.[44]

Economic development under French control also was hindered by the inability of the French to bring about the necessary changes in the attitudes and practices of the colonial peoples. Economists had learned that the introduction of outside capital had little positive effect until the cultural and social preconditions for growth had been created. The French were trying to modernize ideas and behavior by means of education, but this was a slow process and still, even after many years of colonization, was restricted to a minority of the population. Meanwhile, to win the battle against misery, the people would quickly have to accept certain privations, regulations, and changes in custom—in particular, the imposition of Malthusian practices to check population growth. As Alfred Sauvy, the director of the Institut National d'Études Démographiques, and other experts pointed out, such measures, if introduced by the French, would be resented and resisted by the colonial peoples and condemned by world opinion.[45]

The cost of developing France's possessions—especially without private investment and against the resistance of the local population—was staggering. Aron argued that the efforts to modernize the economy and raise the standard of living in Algeria alone, much less in sub-Saharan Africa, would strain French resources to the utmost. The necessary sacrifices surely would be unacceptable to the French people. In the case of Algeria, the war ended any hope of development under French control: the money that might have been invested in Algeria was needed instead to fight the war, and efforts of construction were precarious at best under war conditions. As a result, Aron suggested, it would be wiser to agree to independence, continue to aid the former colonies, and hope that the Americans would take up the part of the burden that France could not bear. The calculations of other economists, however, suggested that not even the Americans, not all the rich countries, could afford to give the capital sufficient to end the poverty of the underdeveloped countries.[46]

The only way out of the impasse appeared to be to impassion and mobilize the population for development projects—to provoke an internal transformation that would reduce the need for outside capital.[47] But the French were not likely to be able to arouse any such enthusiasm and dedication. Sauvy and others concluded that it could be done only by a national government of the overseas people themselves. Delavignette, by this time an honorary governor general of overseas France, suggested in 1959 that the idea of self-help had resulted from the use of economic planning in France after World War II:

Planning means discipline and, in the case of Africa as well as in the case of Madagascar, discipline means austerity. In order to participate actively in this discipline, in order to make planning the spring of its development, a people must be free. The joining of the people and the plan is indispensable, and it comes by way of the liberty of the people and by way of the decolonization of the plan; without this, any exterior public power that would elaborate and apply the plan, were it moved by the best intentions, were it guided by a civilizing aim, would be suspect, intolerable, and ineffective. . . . No true development, no good planning without autonomy.

Bourdet, too, picked up this theme and argued in December 1958: "The passage from a primitive economy and a tribal mentality to those of a modern country requires, even with important outside financial aid, a mental revolution, sacrifices, a general *élan* that never were, and never will be, able to be aroused by a foreign government, however 'good' it might be. In order to mobilize the necessary reserves of energy that exist in these peoples, a national power is necessary."[48]

A newly independent government, therefore, could direct the economy in the interests of the indigenous people. It could impose painful but needed reforms, such as the Tunisian president Habib Bourguiba's prohibition of polygamy. It could stimulate and utilize the powerful ideological forces of nationalism, anti-imperialism, and even xenophobia—so distasteful to French moralists—to unite the people and redirect their emotions and energies toward the goal of a modern nation.[49] It could rely on new, creative forces within the colonial people that presumably would be liberated or even formed in the process of national emancipation.

The most influential source of optimism about the liberated peoples was the study by the novelist and sociologist Albert Memmi,

Portrait du colonisé, which was published in whole by *Esprit* and in part by *La Nef* in April 1957, prior to its publication as a book. Based on his own experience as a Jew in Tunisia, Memmi described the extreme depersonalization suffered by the people subjected to colonial rule. Arguing that colonial revolt was a mass attempt at self-rediscovery, he implied that national liberation would mean the birth of a revitalized people, at least in the case of those peoples, like the Algerians, who had remolded themselves in the fires of colonial revolt.[50]

Memmi's position was shared by Fanon, who had been assigned to an Algerian hospital in 1953 to practice psychiatry and in 1956 had joined the rebels. Replying in *L'An cinq de la révolution algérienne* (1959) to the arguments of Mannoni as well as those of Tillion, he asserted that "Algerian man and Algerian society" had, by revolting against the French, "stripped themselves of the mental sedimentation and of the emotional and intellectual handicaps" that had resulted from "130 years of oppression." The revolutionary struggle was the birth of "a new kind of Algerian man" and the reassertion of man's "capacity to progress." Pessimism about colonial independence was unwarranted: "Once the body of the nation begins to live again in a coherent and dynamic way, everything becomes possible."[51]

By 1959 the conviction that independence was a prerequisite for economic development had spread widely, as indicated in the conference of the Semaines Sociales de France devoted to the topic "The Rise of Peoples in the Human Community." Delavignette asserted in his speech that recently "good minds and even noble hearts" had considered that "a tutelage, a colonization was indispensable for African development" (and he had been one of these), but that now it seemed normal to believe that a country needed to be free before it could be developed. Pierre-Henri Teitgen, a former minister of overseas France, concluded: "The old formula of social Catholicism, 'to colonize is to educate, to educate is to set free,' revolutionary in its time, contained in truth a kind of contradiction: if to colonize is supposed to be to develop and set free, it is clear today that it is necessary to decolonize first in order to be in the position to develop and set free."[52]

Yet how could the humanist intellectuals truly agree with Rous that independence was "the means, the condition of all evolution"? Even if they admitted that development under French control was impossible, they were likely to remain unconvinced, in spite of Memmi's study, that the indigenous leaders could do much better. They had no assurance that the new government would make good use of the potentialities released by independence; it seemed likely that, encouraged by unscrupulous foreigners, it would instead squander its resources. The initial enthusiasm of the people would dissipate before the hardships and disillusionments of the struggle for development. In light of the problems encountered by the first European colonies to be freed, it was hard not to agree with Merleau-Ponty's reply to the optimism of men like Sartre and Memmi: "If we stick to what is observable, nothing justifies our saying that immediate and unconditional independence would be the relieving of a worn-out imperialism by a nation ripe for living by itself. It would be more of a draft drawn on the unknown, a challenge to destiny."[53]

Moreover, the financial data cited by Tillion made the future of an emancipated colony, especially that of Algeria, appear absolutely dismal. Even if the new government was ideal and the people were full of energy, the country would need a vast amount of outside capital. Consequently, many intellectuals responded to emancipation or its imminent prospect by attempting to arouse in the French a revised overseas mission. Experts in the economic problems of the Third World warned that a worldwide famine was coming unless the developed countries provided massive aid. The main theme of the Semaines Sociales of 1959 was the moral duty of giving such assistance. As Tillion and Aron pointed out, however, the French were unlikely to make sacrifices for a territory that had rejected them.[54] It could be replied that the French economy still would need workers from overseas and that the young countries would receive aid as a part of the struggle of "peaceful coexistence" between the capitalists and the Communists. But these sources of money probably would not be sufficient to combat the poverty and permit economic development.

Most French intellectuals, therefore, could not banish the suspicion that the best interests of the African peoples might be to remain under French control, in spite of its impediments, so that the French taxpayers would pay a large part of the bills. Even Aron, who stressed how little France could afford to pay, agreed with Tillion that the breaking of all links with France would be a catastrophe for Algeria and sub-Saharan Africa. Consequently, he hoped for a solution short of complete independence, though one that would give them autonomous economies. Faced with the tragedy of underdevelopment, Aron, like the humanist intellectuals of the Left, was unable to ignore Tillion's charge that, just as antislavery had been the alibi of colonization in the nineteenth century, anticolonialism was becoming the alibi of abandonment to *clochardisation*.[55]

The idea that independence was a prerequisite for economic as well as political development became widely accepted only when most of France's colonies were already on the verge of achieving independence. The idea was probably in large part a means of ideological rationalization—an attempt to find a humanist justification for an evolution that was inexorable. If most intellectuals never were able truly to overcome their misgivings about independence, the claim that independence was the threshold of progress enabled them to orient their thoughts toward the inevitable future. The popularization of this idea, to the extent that it occurred, enabled the French people to see decolonization in a more positive light.

THE POLITICS OF INDEPENDENCE

The principle of self-determination was not invoked by most French intellectuals because it seemed to ignore the real welfare of the colonial peoples. For this very reason, however, it offered them a way out of the dilemma of paternalism; transcending economic and social issues, it gave a reason to support the nationalists' political demands in spite of humanist misgivings. Its usefulness was illustrated by the few Frenchmen who did appeal to the right of self-determination: the Catholic hierarchy; Rous; the president of the Fifth Republic, Charles de Gaulle; and the Communists.

The Roman Catholic church had a universal vocation. Although its religious influence had spread in alliance with European colonization, it had both doctrinal and institutional reasons to be sympathetic to colonial demands. It was committed to the principle of the equality of human souls and was devoted to the propagation of Christianity among the overseas peoples and to the establishment of churches that would remain when European rule ended. In the era of decolonization, the Roman Catholics wanted to dissociate their religion and their church from European colonization.[56]

The French Catholic hierarchy was mostly silent on colonial questions until November 1953, when the apostolic vicars of Madagascar issued an eloquent statement in support of colonial liberation:

The church wishes ardently that both men and peoples progress toward more well-being and increasingly assume their responsibilities. The greatness of man comes from the fact that he is free and responsible, and political liberty is one of these fundamental liberties and responsibilities. Not to enjoy it is proof of an unfinished evolution and can be only temporary. Accordingly the church, like natural law, recognizes the liberty of peoples to govern themselves. . . .

In conclusion, we recognize the legitimacy of the aspiration to independence as well as of all constructive effort to arrive at it.

Subsequently, others in the Catholic hierarchy in Africa spoke out to affirm the validity of the desire for independence. In the second half of 1955, Catholic lay organizations in France were among the first to apply this principle to Algeria: "It would be impossible to deny, from a moral and Christian point of view, the legitimacy of the aspirations to independence of the Algerian people. . . . We cannot allow people to condemn as morally bad the aspirations to independence and even a political action undertaken in favor of independence, provided that this action conforms to the principles of justice and charity."[57]

Unlike most of the anticolonialist intellectuals, the Catholic bishops spoke to a large audience. The church's teachings had to remain on the abstract level of moral principles because the church did not want to mix in partisan politics. Yet such an assertion of principle helped Catholics to put the complex particular issues of decolonization into a larger moral perspective. The church's concurrent stress on France's humanist responsibilities for the overseas peoples confused the moral lesson, but its reaffirmation of the right of self-determination enabled, even if it did not force, some Catholics to transcend their paternalism and to support independence even while doubting its wisdom.[58]

A more concrete, though far less noted, application of the right of self-determination to the particular problems facing France was made by Rous. As a former colleague of Trotsky, he was used to insisting on adherence to principles in opposition to the Stalinists' appeal to the requirements of the concrete situation. It is not surprising that the most outspoken supporters of colonial nationalism in the late Third Republic and early Fourth Republic were Trotskyist sympathizers like Rous, Daniel Guérin, and Claude Lefort; they spoke of world revolution, international proletarian solidarity, and the right of self-determination, while the French Communists were worrying about the various effects of immediate independence. As Rous had been a former participant in the Resistance and the secretary general of the Congress of

Peoples against Imperialism, he had experienced the influences of the various sources of the argument for self-determination—the spirit of 1789, Leninist doctrine, Anglo-American rhetoric (for he was allied with English anticolonialists in the Congress of Peoples), and the appeals of the colonial nationalists. The fundamental aim of the Congress of Peoples, he wrote, was "to struggle for the right to independence and the right of each people to determine freely its own fate." He declared in La Nef in 1951 that this theme had to be reintegrated into French political ideology: "It is necessary to remake the mind of the public, through training and education in all forms, by reexplaining that the principles of the independence of peoples are no more than contributions of bourgeois liberalism and that democrats, even very moderate ones, cannot deny them without denying their own tradition."[59]

In *Tunisie . . . Attention!* Rous showed how the principle of popular sovereignty proclaimed by France in the Revolution should be applied to the two major issues in the Tunisian problem. First, he charged that the contention of the French of Tunisia that they had a right to cosovereignty with the Tunisians was undemocratic. Although their efforts gave them a right to participate in Tunisian institutions, this right was applicable, he insisted, only if they agreed to become Tunisian citizens, to submit themselves to the authority of the Tunisian state, and to participate as equals in the formation of Tunisian policy. Second, he responded to the French claim that the Tunisian people were too immature for self-government by arguing that the real issues were who was to judge when the Tunisians were ready and by what standards. Since each people should have the right to decide its own future, the crucial factor was the expression of national sentiment. He reminded his readers that this criterion of a nation, "the collective will," was a French principle. Thus, although Rous praised the Tunisians for their maturity, he concluded that France had to give them back their sovereignty not because of their maturity, but because of their clear will for autonomy.[60]

The defenders of France's continued presence in the overseas territories argued that France had contracted the obligation to help the overseas peoples and could not break this contract.[61] The implication of Rous's case was that, in accordance with the principle of popular sovereignty, the colonial peoples themselves could decide to break the contract and relieve France of its obligations. The colonial peoples, not the French—the tutored, not the tutors—were to decide when the mission was fulfilled and the time for liberation had come. The criterion must be not the colonial peoples' state of "development," but their will for independence.

Even if Rous's line of reasoning was accepted, however, a practical obstacle remained: the problem of deciding when this will for independence had emerged. More particularly, it was necessary to judge whether the colonial nationalists represented the people, that is, whether the mass of the population wanted independence and supported the leaders who claimed to express their wishes. These subsidiary questions were debated hotly in France. The answers to them regarding every possession remained unclear for a long time.

The political attitudes of the Algerian people were the subject of especially lively debate. The defenders of French control insisted that the Algerian people were not nationalist. In reply to them, and particularly to the minister of interior, Julien asserted in *Témoignage Chrétien* as early as 12 November 1954, only twelve days after the outbreak of the rebellion: "Mr. Mitterrand is wrong to affirm that there is not to be any Algerian nationalism. Nationalism is the compressed form of patriotism. From the moment that frontiers exist it is impossible to prevent aspirations to liberty and equality from assuming a national form. Eight million natives cannot indefinitely abandon their fate to a million non-Moslems who consider them as enemies or as second-class citizens." Julien's lesson should have been obvious after the rapid postwar growth of nationalist movements in European colonies around the world. Its validity was confirmed by the spread of the rebellion. In September 1955 a group of the Moslem deputies to French and Algerian assemblies declared that the "immense majority of the population" had been won over by "the Algerian national idea."[62]

The French intellectuals, beginning with the far leftists, were impressed by the nationalist fervor demonstrated by the rebellion. Francis and Colette Jeanson explained and defended the cause of the FLN in their book *L'Algérie hors la loi*, published at the end of 1955. Contributors to *Esprit*, *France-Observateur* (which had changed its name from *L'Observateur* in April 1954), *Les Temps Modernes*, and *L'Express* began at this time to argue that the growth of the rebellion indicated the profound complicity of the masses and that, even if an Algerian nation had not existed in the past, it was evidently being created by the insurrection. This opinion was echoed, along with opposing views, in

Preuves, and was spread to other moderate intellectuals. *La Nef* stated it in December 1956, as did Aron in 1957. In a letter to Aron in November 1957, published in *Preuves* in May 1958, Tillion asserted that by the end of 1956 the near totality of Moslem society had been solidly and effectively organized by the FLN into a clandestine state.[63]

Their awareness of the spread of Algerian nationalism was accompanied by, and was surely the major cause of, the French anticolonialist intellectuals' gradual transformation from opposition to support for independence. In November 1955, *Les Temps Modernes* demanded only the recognition of the Algerian people's "power of administering itself," although it already implied independence by referring to the rebels as "the Resistance" and predicting the same future for Algeria as for Vietnam, Tunisia, and Morocco; in spring 1956 it openly called for independence. In autumn 1955, Bourdet argued only for autonomy, as did Gilles Martinet, the coeditor of *France-Observateur*; by summer 1957, Bourdet was clearly advocating independence. *Esprit* argued in 1955 for a "federalist" tie between France and Algeria and in 1956 for a "national existence," but began in March 1957 to talk of independence while still hoping for an Algerian state "associated" with France.[64]

The majority of the French people continued to doubt that the Algerians wanted independence. This doubt was increased by the apparent improvement in the military situation from 1957 on, by the much-publicized fraternization of Moslems and Europeans in the forum of Algiers on 16 May 1958 during the settler and army revolt that brought down the Fourth Republic, and by the huge Moslem vote in favor of de Gaulle's constitution. The proponents of French control were able to argue that the great majority of the Algerian people wished to be part of France, though of a France in which they finally would be treated with respect, and that they cooperated with the FLN only out of fear of reprisals. When polled in September 1957, only 24 percent of the French public said that the majority of the Moslem population approved of the rebels, and by February 1959 this figure had fallen to 20 percent.[65] A striking demonstration of nationalist sentiment did not occur until December 1960, when, to impress de Gaulle, who was touring Algeria after promising an "Algerian Algeria," the Moslems of Algiers paraded in mass in favor of independence and the FLN.

Meanwhile, the intellectuals who supported Algerian independence based their decisions more often on the realist argument that the spread of nationalism meant the impossibility of winning the Algerians to France than on the principle of the right of national self-determination. Yet Algeria was a clear instance of the potential value of such an affirmation of principle.

The French governments defended their prosecution of the war by insisting on their democratic intentions. Proposing that the rebels lay down their arms and permit the Algerian people to elect representatives to discuss the future, they claimed that the government, not the rebels, wished to discover and respond to the will of the Algerian people. They refused, however, to admit the legitimacy of the future for which the rebels were fighting; they refused to concede that the Algerians had a right to be independent. Their actions and statements, therefore, indicated that they would abide by the will of the people only if independence was not chosen. In addition, considering the falsification of past elections, the FLN hardly could agree to entrust its cause to further elections. It believed that the Moslem population, whose allegiance it was winning, but on whom it could not yet wholly rely, would view a cease-fire as the defeat of the nationalist cause.

From the beginning the FLN refused to discuss a cease-fire until a French government would admit the right to independence. By 1956 it was demanding that the French agree to actual independence before it would negotiate; the talks would deal with the conditions of this independence. In all likelihood, however, it still would have accepted a declaration of principle. The best way the French intellectuals who were sympathetic to Algerian nationalism could both counter the hypocrisy of the French governments and stimulate the spirit of conciliation on both sides was, as Bourdet realized, "to popularize ever more in France the idea of the right of the Algerians to national independence." Even Bourdet, however, made no other references to this right.[66]

The position of moderates like Mauriac and Servan-Schreiber, who called repeatedly for negotiations to end the war without mentioning the right to independence, was particularly futile. On the one hand, negotiations with the FLN meant the implicit recognition of the possibility of independence, especially since both Moslem and French opinion would interpret them this way. On the other hand, the FLN would never negotiate without the prior admission of this right. The writers of L'Express earned the enmity of both camps without making a positive contribution to finding a solution.

When Charles de Gaulle came to power in 1958, he made the right of self-determination a part of official policy. The constitution of the Fifth Republic gave the overseas territories, except Algeria, the right to acquire independence. In a poll in February 1959, 73 percent of the French expressed their approval.[67] Guinea exercised its right of secession immediately by rejecting the new constitution in the referendum of 28 September 1958. Within two years the other territories had chosen to become independent.

De Gaulle announced on 16 September 1959 that the principle of self-determination would be applied to Algeria as well. Two and a half years more were needed to decide how to apply the principle, for the more particular issues still needed resolution: the time and nature of the referendum and elections by which the Algerian people would express their will, the role of the FLN in negotiations and in the future government of Algeria, and the place of the European population in the new state. But the essential point had been admitted: the Algerians would be permitted to choose independence. On 8 January 1961, 75 percent of the voters in France and Algeria—55 percent of the registered electorate—approved the policy of Algerian self-determination. The journalist and historian of decolonization Jean Lacouture drew the lesson in his biographical sketch of Abbas in 1961: "The history of the life of Mr. Ferhat Abbas, like that of contemporary France, proves only one thing, and General de Gaulle has understood it better than many others: it is that peoples need dignity and that one of the attributes of this dignity is membership in a national group recognized as such. It shows also that by contesting this right, if they clearly lay claim to it, you condemn yourself to cruel disappointments."[68]

In de Gaulle's speeches the right of self-determination became a respectable argument for decolonization, a useful rationalization for the colonial independence that, de Gaulle realized, no longer could be avoided.[69] But it became respectable only at the price of many years of bitter conflict.

If the anticolonialist intellectuals as a whole had stressed the right of self-determination in their writings, the cost of decolonization might have been reduced. The intellectuals might have been better able to retain the confidence of the colonial nationalists, and they would have helped to prepare the French public to accept independence. The most sound humanist position on colonial independence, therefore, may have been that taken by the French Communist party, which insisted that the colonial peoples had a right to independence and added that they would be wise, because of the danger of, above all, American imperialism, to wait until they were stronger before exercising this right.[70] Had they been more confident that the French truly intended to free the colonies, the colonial nationalists might have been willing to take more heed of the warnings of the humanist intellectuals. More important, repeating to themselves that all peoples had the right to independence, the French might have been more willing to free their colonies and, therefore, to deal with the nationalists. Decolonization might have occurred with less pain, and cooperation after independence with greater ease.

5 &TERROR IN ALGERIA

The Algerian war was the climax of the agony of French decolonization. France was torn apart by the disputes over the future status of Algeria. The intellectuals were tormented by the moral dilemmas Algeria presented.

THE WAR AND FRENCH OPINION

Algeria was quiet in 1954. The old nationalist movements were inactive. The administration had succeeded in falsifying the elections to the Algerian Assembly so as to get most of its candidates elected in 1948, 1951, and 1954. On the night of 31 October—1 November 1954, the calm suddenly was broken by terrorist attacks in various parts of the country. The hitherto unknown Front de Libération Nationale announced that it was beginning a war for the independence of Algeria. Premier Mendès-France, who recently had ended the war in Indochina and promised internal autonomy to Tunisia, immediately sent military reinforcements to hunt down the rebels. He declared to the National Assembly that, unlike Tunisia, Algeria was a part of France ("l'Algérie, c'est la France") and that France never would compromise with "sedition" or permit "secession." Like succeeding premiers, Mendès-France aimed to keep the loyalty of the indigenous population by means of economic and social reforms.

At first the French saw the war as part of the turmoil throughout North Africa. Tunisia was racked by terrorism until the Mendès-France government reached an agreement with the Tunisian leaders in November. Morocco was the scene of even greater violence in 1955. North Africa was cited as France's most important current problem by 24 percent of the public in September 1954 and by 27 percent (more than any other problem) in January 1955.[1] The French did not yet know, however, that the scattered acts of terrorism in Algeria were the beginning of a major insurrection.

On 20 August 1955 the seriousness of the revolution was suddenly revealed to the concerned populations—the European settlers (the "French" of Algeria); the Berbers and Arabs, almost all Moslems; and the mainland French. In commemoration of the second anniversary of the deposition of the sultan of Morocco, groups of Algerian Moslems, stirred up and joined by FLN fighters, attacked the European population in the area of Philippeville and Constantine, the same area that had erupted ten years earlier. The Faure government responded by extending the length of military service of current draftees beyond the normal eighteen months and by recalling fifty thousand reservists for service in Algeria. In Morocco violence broke out on 20 August, but the restoration of Mohammed ben Youssef to his throne in November brought a return to calm. The General Assembly of the United Nations discussed the Algerian question during the fall, but it decided not to offer any recommendations to Faure.

In December 1955 about the same number of French people as earlier—25 percent—saw North Africa as France's most serious problem, but now they referred primarily to Algeria. During the December electoral campaign, Algeria was the biggest concern of the press both in Paris and in the provinces, yet it did not dominate the electoral propaganda of the competing parties. The voters gave a slight victory to the "Republican Front" of Mendès-France's followers and the Socialists in the election of 2 January 1956, but did not thereby indicate a favored Algerian policy.[2]

In 1956 the Algerian war became the preoccupation of France's government and public. On 6 February the newly installed head of government, the Socialist party chief Mollet, visited Algiers and was met by a European population violently hostile to his plan to discuss Algeria's future with representatives of the Moslem people and, in particular, to his appointment of General Georges Catroux, who had just negotiated the return of the sultan of Morocco, as minister resident in Algeria. Mollet, stunned that ordinary working people as well as wealthy colonists would hate him, replaced Catroux with the Socialist Robert Lacoste and aimed at the impossible goal of pleasing both the Europeans and the Moslems of Algeria. His peace plan of cease-fire, free elections, and negotiations with the elected representatives was, in any case, an illusion. Since Mollet insisted that Algeria had to remain tied to France, the FLN could only see his plan as a means of avoiding independence.

Consequently, Mollet's search for peace meant an intensified military effort to suppress the rebellion. On 12 March 1956 the National Assembly voted overwhelmingly to give the government special— nearly unlimited—powers in Algeria. In April the government decided to recall thousands of reservists for Algeria and to station new conscripts there. The army in Algeria was increased from two hundred thousand in March to over four hundred thousand in August. Mollet also undertook secret discussions with the FLN, but they were not fruitful and were terminated by the army's capture, in violation of international law, of a Moroccan plane carrying Ahmed Ben Bella and four other FLN leaders to a conference with Mohammed V and Bourguiba in Tunis. Meanwhile, in retaliation for Nasser's support of the FLN and nationalization of the Suez Canal, the French government was preparing to join the British in an attack on the canal, in conjunction with an Israeli invasion of Egypt. The French-English invasion, begun in early November, was very popular in France, but was a humiliating failure because of Soviet and American opposition.[3]

Press coverage of the war in Algeria greatly increased in early 1956. The amount of the front page devoted to Algerian news jumped in *Le Monde* from an average of 4.1 percent in 1955 to 15.5 percent in 1956; in the Communist daily *L'Humanité* from 4.3 percent in 1955 to 14.1 percent in 1956; and in *France-Soir*, the daily with the largest circulation in France, from 2.0 percent in 1955 to 11.4 percent in 1956. From February through May 1956 these newspapers paid greater attention to Algeria than at any other time through at least the middle of 1961. The portion of the French public that judged Algeria as France's greatest problem soared to 63 percent in April and remained at 60 percent in July. Moreover, the massive use of draftees made the war in Algeria, unlike that in Indochina, an intense personal problem for the male youths of France and their families.[4]

The French leaders were deeply committed to the retention of Algeria. The Faure and Mollet governments supported the plan of "integration" elaborated in 1955 by the current governor general, Soustelle. Integration was an updated version of assimilation. The special personality of Algeria was to be recognized on the cultural and juridical levels, but the "province" was to be assimilated into the French Republic on the financial, administrative, and political levels. The French army adopted and fought for Soustelle's plan, and gradually even the European settlers in Algeria rallied to it, agreeing to its egalitarian aspects because of its insistence on the sovereignty of the French Assembly.

After the fall of Mollet's government in May 1957, however, the National Assembly decided to draft a statute to supersede both the old statute of 1947 and the program of integration. The law that was passed in February 1958 was an attempt to prevent autonomy by fragmenting Algeria into five territories, each with limited powers of self-administration and with institutions designed to protect the interests of the European minority. After two years a weak Algerian federation could be created based upon these territories, but "without being able to infringe upon the autonomy of the territory." The machinery was so heavy and complex and the plan was so little to the liking of either the settlers or the Algerian nationalists that it is doubtful that the political leaders expected it to provide a solution. The Fourth Republic fell before the scheme had a chance.

The intransigence of the ministers and the National Assembly was backed by the congresses of the parties that combined to govern the Fourth Republic. The Socialist party, not to mention the Radicals and the MRP, continued to oppose independence into the Fifth Republic. Even the Communist party, though it had described Algeria as a "nation in formation" as early as 1939 and had insisted from the beginning that the rebellion had resulted "essentially from the rejection by the French governments of the national demands of the immense majority of the Algerians," did not decide until February 1957 that the Algerian nation actually had been constituted.[5]

The positions of France's leaders were in accord with, and were probably reflected in, the opinions of the people. The war produced a gradual shift away from a defense of the status quo. When asked if they would accept looser ties with the home country than Algeria's current status as French departments, the French began in 1957 to favor the change (see table 3). But this choice did not usually mean independence. When asked in July 1957 to pick among three solutions for Algeria, 36 percent wanted an ensemble of ordinary departments; 34 percent, internal autonomy within the French Republic; and only 18 percent, complete independence (described by the pollsters, however,

Table 3. Opinion on the Ties between Algeria and France

Responses to the question: In your opinion, is it necessary that Algeria keep its status as French departments, or would you accept a different link between Algeria and continental France?

Percentage distribution at five different dates.

	October 1955	February 1956	April 1956	March 1957	September 1957
French departments	47%	49%	40%	34%	36%
A less tight link	26	25	33	35	40
No response	27	26	27	31	24
	100%	100%	100%	100%	100%

Source: *Sondages* 19, no. 2 (1957): 41.

as "completely abandoning Algeria"), with 12 percent giving no opinion. In September 1957, 34 percent stated that the demand of "certain Algerians" for independence was "justified," 47 percent said it was not justified, and 19 percent did not respond. Of those who found it justified, less than half believed that complete independence ought to be the result. The pollsters concluded that only 11 percent of the French people clearly favored Algerian independence.[6]

The segment that wanted to grant independence scarcely increased as the war continued. De Gaulle was able to rally the French public to his hope for an autonomous Algeria linked to France. Asked in February 1960 which of the three possible futures for Algeria outlined by de Gaulle was "the best from the point of view of the interest of the home country," 48 percent indicated autonomy ("the government of the Algerians by themselves in close union with France"), 27 percent "complete Frenchization," and only 6 percent "secession," while 19 percent did not reply.[7]

In light of their failures to prevent the loss of other territories, however, the French tended to doubt that they would succeed in retaining Algeria,[8] and they were less willing than were the governments to use every means to do so. When asked to choose between the two extremes of negotiations with the rebels to accord independence and the use of all possible military means to crush the rebellion, at least as many people chose independence as chose a military solution (see table 4). The explanation may be that the public was less eager than the political leaders to take actions that would require personal sacrifices.

The figures on French public opinion do not reveal the complete picture until broken down according to political affiliation. Table 5 shows the responses of the sympathizers of each party to two questions asked in 1957. The gulf between the Communist sympathizers and the others was enormous. The voters of the governing parties, even the Socialists, were opposed to Algerian independence. It is not surprising, therefore, that the war reached its height in 1956 with a Socialist premier and a Socialist minister resident in Algeria. Yet the public's favorable reactions to the end of the war in Indochina, to the return of the sultan of Morocco, and to the eventual end of the war in Algeria suggest that the voters would have forgiven the negotiators of independence in return for the lifting of the burden.[9]

Table 4. Opinion on the Choice in Algeria between War and Independence

Responses to the question: If it should be absolutely necessary to choose between the following two extreme solutions, which one would you prefer: to give total independence to Algeria, or to try by all possible military means to crush the rebellion?

Percentage distributions at three different dates.

	April 1956	July 1956	July 1957
Give total independence	39%	45%	38%
Crush the rebellion	39	23	36
Other responses	—	12	—
No response	22	20	26
	100%	100%	100%

Source: *Sondages* 19, no. 2 (1957): 44.

Table 5. Opinion on Algerian Independence according to Political Preference

Responses to two questions: a) Certain Algerians ask for the independence of Algeria. Do you consider that this demand is justified? (Asked in September 1957.) b) If it should be absolutely necessary to choose between the following two extreme solutions, which one would you prefer: to give total independence to Algeria, or to try by all possible means to crush the rebellion? (Asked in July 1957.)

Percentage distributions within each group of declared party supporters.

	Demand for Independence		Of the Two Extremes	
	Is Justified	Is not Justified	Give Independence	Crush the Rebellion
Communist	88%	7%	89%	2%
Socialist	34	51	31	48
Radical	30	54	43	41
MRP	27	60	35	41
Independent, Moderate	21	61	19	58
Gaullist, Poujadist	23	60	—	—
Undetermined	31	42	39	28

Note: The totals of each column for each question do not add up to 100%. The difference is presumably the percentage of each group that gave no response.

Source: *Sondages* 19, no. 2 (1957): 42, 44, 46–47.

The French political leaders and people felt a passionate attachment to Algeria for a number of reasons. First, many were convinced that France had to make a stand against decolonization. In a two-year period France had lost Indochina, the trading posts in India, and the protectorates of Morocco and Tunisia. If Algeria were lost, so presumably would be sub-Saharan Africa, and France would be reduced to the status of a second-rate, purely European power. Second, Algeria, just across the Mediterranean, was juridically and sentimentally a part of

France. The country had been built, the French believed, by the French soldiers and settlers who had come to an anarchic wasteland, and, in turn, it had played an important role in the liberation of France from the Nazis. Third, a million non-Moslems, whose ancestors had come from various parts of Europe, lived alongside the eight million Moslems. Called the "French" of Algeria even though the Moslems too were defined in the constitution as French citizens, they were viewed in the home country as compatriots who deserved the special protection of France. Fourth, in contrast to the nationalists with whom the French were used to dealing, at least in Africa, the FLN appeared barbaric and fanatical. It was painful to imagine an Algeria ruled by such men. Fifth, the fight with the FLN for the hearts of the Moslems gave a large number of Frenchmen, particularly in the army, a paternalistic sense of responsibility for their well-being. Sixth, the oil and gas that were discovered in the Sahara in 1956, though they did not arouse great enthusiasm in France, did promise to offset the financial burden of possessing Algeria and raising the living standard of its people.[10]

The special importance of Algeria is underlined by the contrast between the agonizing war in Algeria and the peaceful transition in sub-Saharan Africa and Madagascar. Without arousing great outcry in France, French political leaders were able to satisfy the expanding political demands of the local elites by moving from decentralization under the *loi cadre* of 1956 to internal autonomy within the new Community of the Fifth Republic to independence in 1960. These territories did not have known economic importance, large European populations, or strong sentimental ties to France, nor did France get involved in a war there that, once started, it hated to lose. Meanwhile, the war in Algeria no doubt facilitated the southern transition by focusing French attention and energies north of the Sahara.

The French intellectuals were greatly concerned with the present troubles and future condition of Algeria. The anticolonialists wrote articles, spoke in meetings, signed petitions, marched in demonstrations, and formed committees. They lamented the war, sought to defend various individuals from injustices, and called for negotiations to reach a just solution in Algeria. But their proposals for a just solution were no bolder than those of the politicians. The only prominent intellectuals who spoke for independence by 1957 were the far leftists—the writers of *Les Temps Modernes*, *France-Observateur*, and *Esprit*, but not those of *L'Express*—the Islamic scholar Jacques Berque and the liberal pragmatist Aron.

The activity of the intellectuals, both in criticizing and in defending the French efforts in Algeria, reached a peak in mid-1957. In the summer three of the most important books appeared: Tillion's *L'Algérie en 1957*, Memmi's *Portrait du colonisé, précédé du portrait du colonisateur*, and Aron's *La Tragédie algérienne*. In the spring the moralists started the most energetic effort made by intellectuals during the whole period of decolonization. They condemned the methods of war that the French army was using, rather than the aim of the war in Algeria.

THE CAMPAIGN AGAINST FRENCH ATROCITIES

The Nazis had taught the French intellectuals to what depths of evil men could descend. The postwar controversy over the Soviet labor camps had further sensitized them to totalitarian methods. When they protested against repression in the French Union, they inevitably compared these abuses to the crimes perpetrated by the Nazis or by the Soviets. Until the Algerian war, however, the anticolonialists, even the Communists, could blame such repression on the Germans in the Foreign Legion, the former collaborators in the expeditionary corps, or the Senegalese troops, as well as on the "Vichyist" elements in the colonies or on the colonial interests. They could continue to believe that Frenchmen, who came from the country of humanism, would not on the whole act as the Germans had done.

By 1957 this illusion was no longer possible. The army in Algeria, composed of young Frenchmen, was committing atrocities reminiscent of Nazi actions in France. For former participants in the Resistance like Domenach, this realization, which was in itself "extremely traumatizing," was even more painful because the leaders responsible for the repression in Algeria included former comrades of the Resistance.[11]

Bourdet had denounced judicial irregularities in Algeria, including the torturing of Moslem suspects by the police, in an article in *L'Observateur* in 1951 entitled "Is There an Algerian Gestapo?" He returned to this theme in January 1955 with a story exposing "Your Gestapo of Algeria"; at the same time Mauriac described in *L'Express* the tortures being perpetrated against some Moslems. At the end of

1955, in an attempt to embarrass the Faure government during the electoral campaign, *L'Express* printed photographs of the summary execution of a Moslem by a policeman in Algeria. For the most part, however, these injustices were still methods of the police alone—of "professionals of violence."[12] The complexion of the problem changed greatly with the arrival of the young conscripts, who came to take over the policing of the Moslem population.

In April 1956, *Le Monde* printed a blistering article by the historian and theologian Henri Marrou charging that in Algeria the French had grouped suspects into "concentration camps," had installed "veritable laboratories of torture," and had reverted to the barbaric principle of collective responsibility in their repression of the insurrection. The French government sent policemen to search Marrou's home, and the minister of national defense haughtily denied his charges. In September 1956 a report that the police had tortured several French Algerian Communists provoked another round of protest, and in October the National Assembly decided to send a commission to Algeria to report on the scandal. In general, however, the anticolonialists concentrated their energies on calls for negotiations to end the war.[13]

In January 1957 the tenth division of paratroopers under General Jacques Massu was given full police powers in Algiers in order to destroy the FLN cells that had been conducting a terrorist campaign in the city. Systematic torture of suspects was a key weapon of the paratroopers in the "battle of Algiers," and news of this widespread use of torture soon spread to the mainland. The many reservists who had been mobilized the previous summer were returning from Algeria with grisly firsthand stories about the conduct of the French army. Meanwhile, anticolonialists like Domenach who had hesitated to print reports of French atrocities because they did not want to hurt Mollet's peace efforts had grown totally disillusioned with the Republican Front government, although they did not comment until the United Nations, which was debating the Algerian question, decided not to intervene.[14]

Near the end of February 1957, *Témoignage Chrétien* published a pamphlet containing the letters of a young Catholic reservist, Jean Muller, who had been killed in an ambush in Algeria in October 1956. He told of summary executions, of punitive operations against the population, and of tortures. The "Dossier Jean Muller," the first in a series of testimonies by reservists, reached only a small public; nonetheless, it troubled Catholic circles and prepared the terrain for the sudden and vast outpouring of moral protest against pacification methods, especially by Catholics, that began in the second week of March.[15]

The first key document was Servan-Schreiber's *Lieutenant en Algérie*, the fictionalized account of his experiences in Algeria as a mobilized reserve officer, which appeared initially in weekly installments in *L'Express*. The first installment, of 8 March 1957, described the senseless murder of an Arab by a French soldier in the middle of the Arab section of a village. The second key document was the pamphlet *Contre la torture* by Pierre-Henri Simon, the Catholic literary critic, novelist, and essayist. Simon not only analyzed and condemned the resurgence of torture in Western civilization, but presented a series of testimonies of tortures inflicted by policemen and soldiers, of collective reprisals against the Moslem population, and of summary executions of prisoners.

Le Monde publicized Simon's pamphlet—and made its own entrance into the campaign against pacification methods—with a front-page note on 13 March by Beuve-Méry entitled "Are We 'Hitler's Vanquished'?" The Assembly of the Cardinals and Archbishops of France published a statement insisting that all those whose "mission" was "to protect persons and goods" had "the obligation to respect human dignity and make it respected and to avoid rigorously all excesses contrary to natural law and to the law of God." Condemning the crimes committed by both sides—but in context those of the French especially—the assembly concluded as had Marrou earlier: "In the present crisis, all and each must remember that it is never permitted to put to the service of a cause, even good, means intrinsically evil."[16] As in the storm over the North African protectorates in 1953, liberal Catholics had joined with non-Catholic leftists in a campaign against overseas injustices.

The government and the defenders of *Algérie française* attempted to check the rise of protest. On 15 March the Ministry of National Defense denounced the "campaign of systematic vilification against the action led by the army," insisted that the reports were exaggerated, accused the protesters of encouraging indirectly the Algerian rebels, and announced that it was opening judicial proceedings against those who were attacking and demoralizing the army. Servan-Schreiber was the principal object of the ministry's revenge, and at the end of the month Georges Montaron, the editor of *Témoignage Chrétien*, also was indicted. Charges against the two ultimately were dropped. At the same time, the parliamentary delegation sent to Algeria in October 1956 to investigate the alleged torture of French Algerian Communists submitted an ambiguous report in which eight of the nine members of the commission stated that nothing in their inquest could lead them to conclude that the Communists had been tortured. On 21 March, Soustelle denounced in the National Assembly "the four greats of French counter-propaganda": *Le Monde*, *L'Express*, *France-Observateur*, and *Témoignage Chrétien*.[17]

Such actions only provoked more protest. Duverger charged in *Le Monde* on 22 March that the report of the parliamentary commission was "bursting with bad faith." On the same day *Le Monde* printed an open letter to President René Coty protesting the methods of pacification. The letter had been delivered to Coty, along with a dossier of testimonies, by Marrou and several others and was signed by 357 persons, including the Catholic intellectuals Folliet, Massignon, Mauriac, and the philosopher Paul Ricoeur. Folliet wrote a longer open letter to Premier Mollet in *Témoignage Chrétien*, explaining why torture and summary executions were unjustifiable. A week later descriptions of the atrocities witnessed by Catholic reservists were published in a brochure *Des Rappelés témoignent* by the Comité de Résistance Spirituelle. The members of the committee, which had been founded in January 1957, included Domenach, Marrou, Massignon, Mauriac, Ricoeur, Simon, Julien, the dissident Socialist leader André Philip, and the jurist René Capitant. The committee pointed out that Frenchmen were committing what had been defined as "war crimes" since World War II.[18]

A more spectacular gesture came from Capitant, the distinguished law professor who had directed the North African branch of Combat during the Resistance and who had served as minister of national education under de Gaulle. In protest against the suspicious "suicide" of his former student Ali Boumendjel, who fell from a window during his interrogation by paratroopers in Algiers, Capitant suspended his course at the faculty of law in Paris and declared to the minister of national education: "Dismiss me, if you want, if you can. I will welcome with satisfaction everything that will contribute to publicize my protest against facts that are liable to dishonor France if it remains passive before them."[19] The government suspended his pay.

MRP and Socialist deputies inquired in the National Assembly on 26 March about Boumendjel and other reported atrocities. The next day Mollet denounced the use of torture even in response to attacks on innocent people, insisted that a government composed not only of members of the Resistance but also of former prisoners of concentration camps could never want to use torture, and asserted that in the few cases that had occurred sanctions had been applied.

Up to this point the campaign against the methods of pacification had been an affair of Parisian intellectuals, whose motives and whose grasp of the true situation in Algeria easily could be questioned. On 29 March, however, *Le Monde* splashed on its front page the news that General Paris de Bollardière, a Catholic and one of the first officers who had joined de Gaulle in London in 1940, had asked to be relieved of his command of one of the sectors of Algeria. As his colleague Colonel Roger Barberot explained in July in his wide-selling book *Malaventure en Algérie*, Bollardière's essential complaint was that the top military and civilian commanders were confining the army to a purely military role unsuited for a war in which the hearts of the Moslem population were the essential prize. But Bollardière permitted Beuve-Méry to use his resignation for the more limited purpose of the campaign against the atrocities of pacification—to prove that war chiefs as well as intellectuals could refuse to sacrifice moral values to expediency.

Bollardière also sent a letter to Servan-Schreiber, who had served under his command in Algeria, and permitted him to print it in *L'Express* on the same day that the story appeared in *Le Monde*. Expressing his approval of the publication of the notorious *Lieutenant en Algérie*, Bollardière wrote: "I think that it was highly desirable that after having lived our action and shared our efforts, you did your job as a journalist in underlining to public opinion the dramatic aspects of the revolutionary war we face and the frightful danger for us to lose sight, under the fallacious pretext of immediate efficaciousness, of the moral values that alone have made up to now the greatness of our civilization and of our army."[20] Since he did not seek the approval of his superiors for this letter—which the minister of national defense, who was prosecuting Servan-Schreiber, would not have given—Bollardière was guilty of insubordination and was given a punishment of sixty days in military prison.

The case of General de Bollardière was only the most dramatic of the signs that the campaign was spreading. The April issue of *Esprit* contained a damning article by a returning reservist. *France-Observateur* printed on 4 April a letter that the dean of the faculty of law at Algiers had written to the minister of national defense, in which he related that he had witnessed the summary execution of a Moslem by a paratrooper. On the same date a delegation of MRP members presented Mollet with information on more alleged immoral acts in Algeria. The next day the leftist bureau of the Union Nationale des Étudiants de France, which represented some two-fifths of France's university students, protested the abuses and added: "Faithful to the traditional teaching of the French University, founded on respect for law and for the human person, we would be unable to tolerate the pursuit of the Algerian war in such conditions. If it should be true that the Algerian war cannot be pursued by other means, it is this war itself that it would be necessary to end, for neither efficacy nor an exceptional circumstance would be able to justify the use of such methods."[21]

The French government attempted once more to calm opinion. The council of ministers, purposely misunderstanding the humanitarian motives of most of those who were protesting against the pacification methods, denounced on 5 April "a campaign organized by the enemies of France," which, it suggested, was trying to present the seven hundred thousand soldiers who had been in Algeria in the past year as "so many torturers." Nonetheless, since atrocities had been well documented, the council declared that "every individual failure" to carry out France's policy of safeguarding human rights had to be punished and that it was creating a Commission de Sauvegarde des Droits et Libertés Individuels to investigate all reports of abuses in Algeria.[22]

The protesting intellectuals complained of the very limited freedom of action given to the Commission de Sauvegarde and charged that its primary function was to put opinion back to sleep. This charge seemed to be confirmed when Delavignette resigned from the commission on 30 September because of its ineffectiveness and spoke out in December against the deterioration of state control in Algeria. The credibility of the commission was undermined further when the government refrained from making even its mildly condemning report public until *Le Monde* obtained a copy and printed it on 14 December 1957.

In the meantime, while defenders of the army's efforts in Algeria continued to insist that the atrocities were exceptional occurrences, more eyewitness accounts were published, and more Frenchmen spoke out in protest against the army's actions. In June, Sartre, Mauriac, Massignon, Philip, and Martinet joined with several hundred others in a silent demonstration in Paris against the war. In August, Louis Martin-Chauffier, the president of the Union des Écrivains pour la Liberté, described in *Le Figaro* the results of an investigation conducted by the International Commission against Concentration Camps. In Algeria thousands of suspects had been found in internment camps, although living under generally good conditions, and some suspects had been badly treated, even tortured, while others had "disappeared." Martin-Chauffier added that torture was "neither systematic, nor recommended, nor even authorized by the authorities," but complained later that crimes were tolerated and covered up by these authorities.[23] In the following months, scandals developed in response to the sufferings of two French Communists, Maurice Audin and Henri Alleg, both of whom had been arrested by the paratroopers in Algiers in June 1957 and allegedly had been tortured.

Audin had been a teaching assistant at the faculty of sciences in Algiers. His disappearance while in the hands of the paratroopers aroused left-wing university circles in France. In November his doctoral thesis in mathematics was sustained in absentia at a ceremony attended by Mauriac and other opponents of the war. In December the Comité Maurice Audin was formed. Headed by the mathematician Laurent Schwartz and the ancient historian Pierre Vidal-Naquet, it continued throughout the war to investigate the death of Audin and to publicize the abuses he and others had suffered.

Alleg was the editor of the banned newspaper *Alger-Républicain*. He smuggled out of prison a bloodcurdling account of the tortures he claimed to have suffered, which was published on 17 February 1958 as a pamphlet entitled *La Question. Les Temps Modernes* hailed it as paradoxically "the first optimistic book on the war in Algeria," for Alleg had triumphed over the inhumanity of torture by refusing to speak.[24] When *France-Observateur* tried to publish excerpts from it, the issue was seized by government censors, who deleted the article; when *L'Express* tried to print an essay by Sartre on Alleg, it also was seized. Finally the government banned the fast-selling pamphlet itself. In reaction, André Malraux and the Nobel laureate Roger Martin du Gard joined with Mauriac and Sartre in a petition to the president of the Fourth Republic:

The undersigned:—

—protest against the seizure of Henri Alleg's book, THE QUESTION, and against all the attacks against liberty of opinion and expression of ideas that recently preceded this seizure.

—ask that the facts reported by Henri Alleg be disclosed publicly and with complete impartiality.

—call on the Administration, in the name of the Declaration of the Rights of Man and of the Citizen, to condemn unequivocally the use of torture, which brings shame to the causes that it supposedly serves.

—and call on all Frenchmen to join us in signing this "personal petition" and in sending it to the League for the Rights of Man. . . .[25]

Meanwhile another scandal had erupted. The rebel army had been able to use Tunisia and Morocco as places of refuge. The French army was frustrated by the restrictions against pursuing its enemies across the borders. On 8 February 1958, in retaliation for antiaircraft fire, the French bombarded the Tunisian border village of Sakiet Sidi Youssef. The attack killed a large number of civilians, including many school-children. The Tunisian president, Bourguiba, was enraged and brought the question of Sakiet before the UN Security Council. In France the moralists and Communists labeled it a crime of collective reprisal.

After Sakiet and La Question, the issue of army atrocities began to lose its impact. The French were becoming accustomed to crimes in Algeria. By the end of 1957 the paratroopers had won the "battle of Algiers"; because the FLN did not start any other campaigns of urban terrorism, torture was not again used extensively. Furthermore, since French atrocities were constantly condemned by the top authorities, the French could take some comfort in the fact that, even if French soldiers might behave like the Nazis, at least France had not made the perpetration of atrocities into a principle of its warfare. In this respect, the Commission de Sauvegarde appointed by Mollet probably did serve to reassure public opinion, as did the similar commission appointed by de Gaulle. When de Gaulle came to power, the public and some intellectuals were willing to leave the problems of Algeria to him. In the Fifth Republic the far Left was the major protester against tortures and regroupment camps.

During the Fourth Republic the intellectuals had had a potentially very important role to play in opposing the war in Algeria because none of the major political parties—not even the Communists until the end of 1956—took a strong antiwar stand. The challenge faced by the intellectuals was not to rally to a political movement but to try to initiate one. Bourdet had saluted the wave of protests against the methods of pacification and declared on 4 April 1957: "We were searching for a common terrain to galvanize and unite all these citizens disoriented and discouraged by the division of the Left and the errors of its leaders: here it is!"[26]

Indeed the campaign against the methods of pacification in Algeria had been principally the work of leftist intellectuals, Catholic and non-Catholic, and their journals. It was initially publicized by *Témoignage Chrétien*, *France-Observateur*, *L'Express*, and *Le Monde*. The campaign subsequently spread to *Esprit*, *Les Temps Modernes*, and (to a much lesser extent) *Preuves*, as well as to the Communist journals. *La Nef* touched on the subject only occasionally—perhaps in part because it was closer than the others to parliamentary circles. But Bourdet's hope that the intellectuals would mobilize public opinion around this issue went unfulfilled.

The effect of the campaign on the French public had been diminished by three factors. First, the Communists were the only major political party to participate in it; thus the humanist protesters became in effect the political allies of the Communists. Accordingly, their protests lost credibility among anti-Communist opinion.[27] Second, the large-circulation newspapers kept silent about the campaign. Consequently, according to Vidal-Naquet, "although all those who really *wanted* to know were well-informed, the majority of Frenchmen knew nothing, or believed that all accusations against the army must be the work of scoundrels who invented their stories in order to distract attention from F.L.N. atrocities." Yet Vidal-Naquet probably underestimated the impact of the campaign; Sartre may have been more accurate when he charged in May 1957 that the French people actually knew the truth in spite of their efforts to hide it from themselves, but chose to accept their complicity with the torturers. As Mauriac had written in January 1955, "They get irritated, on the contrary, by the fact that they have been obliged to see what they had resolved to ignore. They admit that all civilization rests on a hidden horror: prostitution, traffic of women, policing of manners and customs, houses of correction, jails for madmen and idiots, all tortures. It is the necessary evil. Woe to him who dares to speak of it openly!"[28] Third, the implications of the campaign against the crimes of pacification were unclear. The protesting intellectuals could not agree on an answer to the question to which the issue of atrocities inevitably led—whether Algeria should be independent.

THE CASE OF TORTURE

The deficiencies of the campaign against French atrocities were revealed most clearly in the controversy over torture. Among the crimes of pacification, torture most scandalized the moralists. Bourdet, who had himself narrowly escaped torture when arrested by the Gestapo, was among the most vehement:

> If military slaughters take more lives and create a vaster suffering, they do not dishonor their authors to the same degree, they do not create the same irremediable chasm, they do not engage the same quantity of evil freely chosen, calmly accepted, savored. . . .
> There are degrees in horror, and the bloody attacks of terrorists, like the bloody violence of repression, are still crimes of men, moved by human passions. Cold-blooded torture of a defenseless prisoner, sadistic torment in order to make him talk, which destroys the body slowly and seeks to empty the soul—this is the bestial crime above all others. Bestial . . . I insult the beasts.[29]

Yet torture—in contrast to the crimes of passion—seemed to many a legitimate and necessary method of pacification in Algeria.

The major aim of the army was to destroy the FLN—to destroy the guerrilla fighters hiding in the mountains, the terrorist cells in the cities, and the clandestine political-administrative structure that the FLN had built throughout Algeria. To achieve this aim the army needed information—often quickly—and usually could obtain it only through confessions, which had to be forced. Consequently, the army officers, like the police, resorted to torture as an effective, indeed an essential, means of fulfilling their mission. In certain cases refusal to use torture actually appeared to be immoral. According to an oft-repeated tale, a member of the Commission de Sauvegarde visited the administrative head of Oran and was told: "We just captured a terrorist with a grenade in his hand. We are sure that he knows and hides from us the names of thirty other terrorists, each of whom is preparing to throw a grenade. What are we to decide? To make him spend a disagreeable quarter of an hour, or to risk three hundred innocent human lives? You are going to make the decision in my place." The visitor began to stammer but was interrupted quickly. "Set your mind at rest; the decision was made three months ago. We found the grenades and the city sleeps in peace." The moral of this tale was preached to the army by the Catholic chaplain of the tenth division of parachutists: "Between two evils—to cause a few moments of suffering to a bandit caught in the deed, who besides deserves death, and on the other hand to allow the massacre of innocent people whom you could save if, thanks to the revelations of this criminal, you could annihilate the band—it is necessary without hesitating to choose the lesser: an efficacious interrogation without sadism."[30]

In response, General Pierre Billotte, a former minister of defense, asserted that "rather than accepting a dishonoring practice," a chief should not hesitate to make his troops and even the population that he protected run a great danger. But his intransigent moral stand left him vulnerable to the sarcastic reply of General Massu that he was "ready to endure with the greatest abnegation and the greatest nobility the misfortunes of others."[31] Most opponents of torture chose not to argue on this level of pure morality. They pointed out that the cases in which torture seemed a moral duty were rare and that its use was not exceptional, as the government claimed, but widespread. They argued that the army's view of effectiveness was shortsighted.

The opponents of torture contended, in the first place, that it was counterproductive as a method of pacification. As General de Bollardière told his troops, learning about the tortures inflicted on Resistance fighters by the Gestapo had only made him fight harder. Camus affirmed: "Torture has perhaps saved some, at the expense of honor, by uncovering thirty bombs, but at the same time it arouses fifty new terrorists who, operating in some other way and in another place, will cause the death of even more innocent people." Moreover, torture was inimical to the broad aims of the pacification effort. Like other acts of violence, it hindered the reconciliation and peaceful cohabitation of the two peoples of Algeria and the acceptance by the Moslem people of unity with France. Simon thus demanded: "In a war the aim of which is to organize the cohabitation of two races on the same land, is it showing proof of political realism to multiply attacks on the rights of persons, police vexations, collective reprisals, everything that fans the flames of hatred, that sows rancor and mistrust?" General Billotte insisted that in an ideological war, in which the essential aim was to win over the civilian population, the most elevated ideology—that which most respected human values—was likely to win. Martin-Chauffier argued that the Algerian people would love and respect France if and only if France ceased to deny its own principles.[32]

This argument of the counterproductiveness of French repression was very persuasive in opposition to excesses such as collective reprisals against the civilian population, which had little justification of even short-term effectiveness. It was much less persuasive in opposition to torture. The paratroopers pointed to their dramatic successes in the "battle of Algiers," and the French of Algiers at least were convinced of the value of torture, for they no longer lived under a constant threat of terrorist attacks.[33]

The second argument offered by the opponents of torture was more eloquent and more convincing. They pointed to the effect of torture and of the other methods of pacification not on the pacification effort itself but on the soldiers and people of France. They insisted that these crimes were not only counterproductive but self-destructive—that they were undermining the moral and spiritual foundations on which the French nation had been built. Marrou, for example, proclaimed that history, theology, and common sense taught that civilizations that let the chasm widen between the ideal they claimed and the realizations they proposed died of hypocrisy.

This theme was elaborated most completely in Simon's *Contre la torture*. Simon contended that the humanist tradition in Western civilization was being threatened in the twentieth century by a double onslaught. The use of torture by the police had reappeared—and had been accepted by public opinion—as a result of a transfer of value from the individual to the group. At the same time warfare had been dehumanized because it had become scientific and total, and this in turn had resulted in "the wasting away of the chivalric traditions and of the humanitarian virtues proper to the soldier: in sum, the effacing of what made battle resemble a noble and regulated duel and the accepting of a style of massacre." The degradation of the army had then been accentuated by the new type of warfare, that of an army of occupation against a people in resistance, in which the soldiers were forced to function as policemen and thus inherited the contemporary brutalization of police methods. The aim of *Contre la torture* was to combat this threat to Western—and particularly French—humanist civilization.

Defenders of torture argued that the police, or an army functioning as a police, needed to use cruel methods in order to fight a criminal group that was the enemy of society. Simon insisted, however, that the effectiveness of these methods was not a sufficient reason "to overthrow the fundamental rules that give the social pact its value and its force," because "a society has less to fear from physical agents that try to trouble it in its visible order by infractions of the laws, than from spiritual ferments that dissolve it internally by the corruption of the law; it is less menaced by the action of its enemies than by the ruin of its principle." Torture was logical in a totalitarian regime, but not in the West. It was inimical to "the recognized principle of law and of morality" of the West, which was "the absolute value of the person as conscience and as liberty." Not only did a Western policeman act immorally when he tortured—for he attacked the "essence of humanity" in his victim—but he broke the social pact. Functioning as the very delegate of society, he violated its fundamental law and thereby worked "to overthrow the spiritual principle, to break the federating bond of the society."

Simon asserted that the injury the torturer inflicted on his society was greatest in the case of France, for he was attacking the special "historical vocation of France," the humanist mission that gave France its "true *grandeur*." Torture was thus not only an assault on the ideological bonds of French society, but "a betrayal of its soul."[34]

The moralists found the question of the effectiveness of torture as a method of pacifying Algeria of secondary importance. They were more upset at the torturer's violation of the humanist principles of the West and at his betrayal of their concept of France. As a result, they ignored the charges that their protests were demoralizing the army, encouraging the rebels, and embarrassing France. Painfully aware that French troops were behaving like the Nazis, they wanted at least to prevent the French people from being guilty, as the German people had been, of silent complicity with these crimes. Noting how much the French public acquiesced in colonial injustices, they argued that "the intransigent affirmation of man against racist brutalities" was, as Domenach wrote, "a necessary stage in the rectification of the French conscience." They contended further that public protest was the only way to save France's honor. The crucial question remained, however, of what the rejection of torture and the other abuses of pacification meant about the aim of pacifying Algeria.[35]

In *Contre la torture* Simon, like Mauriac, Camus, and Folliet, rejected the methods of pacification but not its goal. He opposed colonial injustices, but he also opposed Algerian independence—because Algeria had been fashioned by the French, because collaboration with France would give Algeria the best chance for the future, and because retreat to the European continent was not consonant with France's style and destiny. As a result, he favored the presence of the French army in order to force the enemy to negotiate. Moreover, like Servan-Schreiber, Bollardière, Barberot, and Martin-Chauffier, he believed that an army that acted in a humanitarian fashion would be able to win the hearts of the Moslem population and thus could be an instrument of reconciliation. Simon's aim, and the aim of most of the original protesters, was only to purify the pacification effort.

A crucial question, however, was whether it was possible to pacify Algeria without recourse to torture and other evils. To answer this question it was necessary first to identify the reasons for the appearance of torture in Algeria. Simon blamed torture on the degradation of Western morality and implied that the cure was to reaffirm this morality. His position was not far from that of Michel Massenet, an outspoken defender of France's efforts in Algeria, who saw "the problem of excesses" as "only a problem of discipline."[36]

Servan-Schreiber argued that the colonial system was responsible for the army's atrocities. The tangle of interests in Algeria, "the invisible, omnipresent machine" of colonialism that had "all Algeria in its grip," defeated the attempts of Bollardière and his men (including Servan-Schreiber) to make the army into an instrument to transform colonization. The army was forced to serve merely as "a police force to maintain the status quo." Unable, therefore, to rally the Moslem population, the soldiers were placed in a frustrating situation that drove them "automatically" and "inevitably" to commit atrocities. Faced with an alien people who might be hiding terrorists or at least aiding the FLN by its silence, they were forced to be suspicious of every Moslem and to live in a state of insecurity that was conducive to outbursts of cruelty. The actions of the rebels—ambushes, assassinations, mutilations—were calculated to increase the atmosphere of suspicion and hatred and to provoke reprisals by French soldiers and settlers. Desperately needing to know who were its enemies among the Moslem population, the army resorted to torture.[37]

Servan-Schreiber contended that the conditions that gave rise to torture could be remedied. If the army were freed from the grip of colonialism, it could win over the population. With the population on its side, it would not be pushed into immoral actions. Consequently, like Simon, Martin-Chauffier, and Barberot, he did not reject pacification, only its distortion.

The writers of *Esprit* and *Les Temps Modernes*, on the other hand, insisted that pacification could not be made humane. Domenach and his colleagues argued that, since nationalist sentiment was growing, the army never would be able to win the trust of the Moslem people and, therefore, never would be able to end guerrilla warfare. They agreed with the military realists, rather than with Servan-Schreiber and Bollardière, that the only way to end the atrocities was to end the war.[38]

Sartre contended that the essence of pacification was the protection of the colonial system. Accordingly, he claimed that the aim of the torturers was not just to obtain information but to force the victim to "designate himself, by his cries and by his submission, as a human beast." Sartre had argued earlier that the colonial system in Algeria was based on the dehumanization of the Moslems. When they reaffirmed their humanity by revolting, he now explained, it became necessary "to humiliate them, to burn out the pride in their hearts, to lower them again to the rank of the animal." Torture was both a manifestation of the repressive and racist basis of colonialism and an instrument created by the colonial system to protect itself. Since the Algerians no longer would submit passively to colonial rule, the only way to end torture was to abolish the colonial system.[39]

Servan-Schreiber, Domenach, and Sartre, therefore, did not blame the individual soldiers for atrocities. Even Simon was sensitive to the realistic argument in favor of torture and to the realistic excuse for reprisals. Although he insisted in *Contre la torture* that the crimes he condemned were not excusable, for the principles he upheld were absolute and could not be eclipsed by any consideration of circumstance or interest, he acknowledged that they were explicable in the situation. He even admitted that he too might have tortured in a particular situation, though he added that he would have been acting immorally. The right-wing essayist Alfred Fabre-Luce responded: "To do evil while disapproving of yourself, in order to attain the end and to save honor anyway, is that not an attitude of evasion?"[40]

Soon after the publication of *Contre la torture*, Simon was persuaded by military realists to agree that "methods more severe than those of normal inquests" should be permitted in Algeria; that is, he recognized the necessity of using moderate torture, though he refused to call it that. In his short novel *Portrait d'un officier*, which he finished in September 1957, the hero was confronted by a similar moral dilemma: "War is no longer fought between armies, but against peoples; it no longer resembles a duel but a massacre. On this basis you make a frank decision: either refuse it absolutely as absolutely inhuman; or wage it according to its necessity." No longer did Simon offer the possibility of purifying the war in Algeria; he could offer only escape. After having tried to act humanely while admitting that the military realists were more logical than he, Simon's hero left Algeria, as Bollardière had done, and left the army, as Bollardière was to do in 1961.[41]

Mauriac underwent a similar evolution. In June 1958 he was still taking a moralistic stand: he chided the intellectuals of the Left for not trying to convince the army that torture was wrong. But in November he wrote in *L'Express*:

Readers write me: "Nothing has changed, they are torturing more than ever. What you denounced yesterday, you tolerate today." No, I hate it as on the first day, but now my attention turns away from the envenomed fruits, because, thanks to de Gaulle, the axe is at the very tree that produces them: guerrilla warfare. Terrorism, torture are born from it, inevitably. No ministerial order, no official circular has ever been able to change anything about this and never will change anything. No more than the God of Malebranche, General de Gaulle does not act by specific volitions; he will end torture by ending the war.[42]

Mauriac thus resigned himself to wartime torture.

The campaigns against French atrocities no doubt had some impact on the behavior of French troops in Algeria. It resulted in official pressure to cut down on abuses and surely touched the consciences of individuals who might have engaged in them. But the atrocities did not end. The only way to end them, even the moralists came to see, was to end the war, but, since the army was unable to eradicate the rebels, the only way to end the war appeared increasingly to be to agree to the independence of an Algeria that was likely to be controlled by the rebels. Mauriac, Simon, Camus, Folliet, and (until 1958) Servan-Schreiber refused such a solution. They took the increasingly untenable position of desiring the goal of a French Algeria but despising the necessary means. When Simon's officer chose evasion and when Mauriac resigned himself to torture under de Gaulle, they were encouraging the very acceptance of "the necessary evil" that Mauriac had wanted to combat. By giving no practical solution to the problem of atrocities, their main effect may have been, as their critics charged, to demoralize the army and the French people.[43]

The other course, following the lead of the writers of *Esprit*, *France-Observateur*, and *Les Temps Modernes*, was to reject the end as well as the means. Accordingly, the positions of Jean Bloch-Michel, who was one of the editors of *Preuves*, and of the bureau of the Union Nationale des Étudiants de France were that, if atrocities were a necessary part of the war, the war must be ended. Marrou and Duverger added that the totalitarian methods needed to fight the war were creating an Algeria that they would refuse to call French. But Bloch-Michel, the student union, Marrou, and Duverger gave no positive reasons to prefer the alternative, Algerian independence.[44] By increasing the dislike of the French for the war and for Algeria and yet not offering a way to end the war, they and the other moderate protesters helped to prepare a final solution of weary abandonment—abandonment of political initiative to de Gaulle and abandonment of Algeria.

Additional factors complicated the question of Algeria's political future. The case of Merleau-Ponty is illuminating. In March 1947 he had noted in *Les Temps Modernes* that French evacuation of Indochina might "give new bases to the United States or to the USSR or to England" and mean that France would "cease to play a role in universal history." Nonetheless, France had to give independence, for the war proved that France could not stay "without exercising terror and continuing the oppression." In 1958, however, Merleau-Ponty stated that it was impossible to deduce an Algerian policy from the rejection of torture. The problem of underdevelopment was, in his opinion, an overriding factor, on the basis of which he opposed Algerian independence.[45] Two other moral issues, which served even more to complicate the Algerian problem, were the atrocities of the FLN and the rights of the French in Algeria.

THE ATROCITIES OF THE FLN

The methods of the FLN were no more humane than those of the French army—indeed less so. In its efforts to win over the Moslem population and demoralize the French, it resorted to calculated atrocities: the mutilation and assassination of Moslem political opponents and of Frenchmen and eventually bomb attacks on the European civilian population. Accustomed to nationalists imbued with French culture and to "well-behaved" movements of liberation, the humanist intellectuals were disconcerted to find themselves, in Domenach's words, "faced with people who wanted to cut our throats and who killed indiscriminately women and little children, faced with people who were rude and barbaric." They were dismayed to see the Algerian nationalists who were their friends—the moderate Amis du Manifeste led by Abbas, the more extreme Mouvement National Algérien (MNA) led by Messali Hadj—intimidated and assassinated by the FLN. Only Jeanson and his associates at Les Temps Modernes sided squarely with the FLN.[46]

Camus attempted a balanced condemnation of the excesses on both sides, an attempt consistent with his basic moral and philosophical convictions. As he explained in L'Homme révolté (1951), rebellion was the essential historical act by which humanist values, such as the life and liberty of the individual, were created and affirmed as limits to human action: it was the origin of transcendent values in a world without God. Because of the intransigent attitude that was born in the act of rebelling, however, rebellion tended to surpass the very limits that it had created and to degenerate into what Camus called "revolution." When the rebel no longer respected humanist limits, the result was nihilism. The FLN was guilty of denying these limits in Algeria, but so also were the French settlers and the army. Camus concluded that both sides were to be condemned.

The supreme fault of rebels, according to Camus, was arrogating to themselves the right to kill. In his early essays and in Le Mythe de Sisyphe (1942), Camus had revolted against a universe that condemned man to death and had rejected an escape by suicide. Although he had written in favor of the purge that followed the Liberation, he soon had admitted that Mauriac had been right in arguing for clemency for collaborators. In L'Homme révolté he countenanced murder only if the rebel agreed to give up his own life in return. Later, in Réflexions sur la guillotine (1957), he and Arthur Koestler argued against capital punishment.

One of the strongest arguments against the death penalty, Camus thought, was the danger of executing an innocent person. Indeed, as seen in his articles on the famines in Algeria and in his novel La Peste

(1947), he found the suffering and death of innocents intolerable. The aspect of the civil war in Algeria that revolted him the most was the attacks by both sides on the civilian population. In a series of articles in *L'Express* from July 1955 through February 1956, he not only condemned both French and rebel atrocities, but called for a civilian truce —an agreement by both sides to end violence against civilians. He traveled to Algiers in January 1956 to speak, alongside Abbas, in favor of this civilian truce.

Camus condemned both sides because both were using inhumane methods, thus destroying the justice of their causes. The crimes of both were responsible for creating and perpetuating an atmosphere of hatred. Moreover, in a situation in which a vicious circle of excesses had been established, both sides, he believed, had to agree simultaneously to limits before these limits could be reinstated. Only when limits were reestablished could an atmosphere be created in which reasonable discussion among the combatants and the middle groups would be possible. Only in such an atmosphere of reason could the civil war be ended.

Camus hoped that a civilian truce might be the beginning of reconciliation and that a "party of the civilian truce" might arise to mediate between the two hostile camps. But his hopes were quickly shattered. Premier Mollet expanded the military effort against the FLN. The FLN aimed its assassinations at Frenchmen who were trying to reconcile the two communities. The mass of the French of Algeria reacted to liberals like Camus with distrust and hostility, and French authorities in Algeria repressed their activities. As Camus had lamented previously in autumn 1955, "It is as if two insane people, crazed with wrath, had decided to turn into a fatal embrace the forced marriage from which they cannot free themselves. Forced to live together and incapable of uniting, they decide at least to die together. And because each of them by his excesses strengthens the motives and excesses of the other, the storm of death that has struck our country can only increase to the point of general destruction."[47]

The cycle of terror reached its most fearsome intensity when the FLN decided in 1956 to make its presence felt not only in the countryside but in Algiers itself and began the "battle of Algiers." The FLN campaign was precipitated by the execution on 19 June 1956 of two Moslems—the first time since the beginning of the rebellion that a sentence of capital punishment had been carried out. The FLN responded on the following day with some thirty attacks in Algiers, in which forty-seven Europeans were killed or wounded. At the end of July the first bomb was set off by European "counterterrorists" at the house of one of the FLN assassins who had been captured on 20 June. Fifty-three Moslems were killed and a large number wounded. On Sunday afternoon, 30 September, the first FLN bombs in Algiers exploded in the two most popular cafes, causing one death and fifty-two injuries. An atmosphere of hysteria mounted in the city as the various attacks continued. On 29 December, after the funeral of the president of the association of mayors of the department of Algiers, who had been assassinated by a Moslem, a mob of Europeans went on a bloody rampage through the Casbah.

Minister Resident Lacoste decided that drastic measures were needed to reassure the Europeans in Algiers and to combat the FLN, which was planning a general strike to show the rebel power to the United Nations. Consequently, on 7 January 1957 he gave full police powers in Algiers to the paratroopers. The terrorist attacks continued, but the paratroopers began, by means of torture, to dismantle the FLN cells. In July 1957, Germaine Tillion received a promise from Yacef Saadi, the FLN chief in Algiers, that no more civilians would be harmed. In spite of continuing exemplary executions by the French, he held to this promise, but this chance for a voluntary de-escalation of terror was ended with the arrest of Saadi on 25 September.[48] The paratroopers soon succeeded in destroying the terrorist organization, but contrary to the hope of Camus and Tillion neither side renounced the use of atrocities.

Much of the French violence against which the moralists protested occurred in response to the violence of the rebels. When the campaign against the methods of pacification began in March 1957, the defenders of the French army pointed to the barbarism of the FLN, which, they insisted, provoked and even justified the atrocities of the French. Moreover, in the eyes of much of the French public, the barbarism of the rebels discredited them and their cause—just as the Vietminh's attack on Hanoi in December 1946 had discredited it. Even Paul Rivet, the Socialist anthropologist who had been one of the most outspoken defenders of Ho Chi Minh, reacted to FLN savagery by rallying to the cause of *Algérie française*. Citing rebel atrocities, the French refused to recognize the FLN as a valid interlocutor and were all the more determined not to abandon the French of Algeria and the Moslem friends of France. In contrast, beginning in August 1956 the FLN insisted that it would not agree to a cease-fire until the French recognized the FLN as the only organization representing the Algerian people and that it would not negotiate unless it was the sole Moslem interlocutor. Consequently, the war continued even after de Gaulle admitted, on 16 September 1959, the right of Algerian self-determination.[49]

On 28 May 1957, at the peak of the campaign against the methods of pacification, a detachment of troops from the FLN army (the ALN) massacred the male inhabitants of a hamlet in the district of Melouza, probably because of their sympathies for the rival nationalist movement, the MNA. Most of the French moralists who had protested against French crimes condemned this massacre. The Comité de Résistance Spirituelle declared:

> Having raised a solemn protest of the French conscience when it saw the rights of the person and certain moral and juridical principles violated on France's side, it has the duty to address itself publicly to the leaders of the FLN and to the officers of the ALN in order to make them face their responsibilities. In systematically intensifying the terrorism, in practicing and sanctioning political assassination as a means of war, in tolerating or in organizing massacres of French and Moslem civilians, not only do they incur heavy moral responsibilities, but they discredit politically their cause and they retard and tend to render impossible the equitable solution of a cruel and unfortunate conflict, for it is evident that blackmail by terror strips the spirit of negotiation of its chances and its reasons and invites the catastrophe of war without end and without mercy.

Domenach and Bourdet charged that Melouza was a crime of collective punishment on the level of the Nazi massacres at Lidice and Oradour and insisted that blind terrorism in general was politically inept because it discredited the FLN in French and international opinion and undermined the efforts of the French Left to bring about negotiations. The intellectuals appealed to the FLN to disavow and renounce such methods.[50]

Nonetheless, Simon, Mauriac, Servan-Schreiber, Domenach, Bourdet, Sartre, and their colleagues all chose to focus their protests on French atrocities rather than to condemn both sides equally, as Camus tried to do. They gave various reasons for their choice. To begin with, they argued that they as Frenchmen were responsible for French actions. Simon explained in *Esprit* that the indignation he felt at the rebels' assassination of a fellow citizen or friend was different from the intimate suffering of his conscience at the report of tortures committed by Frenchmen; the first was "the expression of a sociological and visceral patriotism," which was aroused when France suffered, the second "the expression of a patriotism of values and responsibility," which was aroused when France sinned. Bloch-Michel asserted, as did Folliet, that the French excesses were committed by the representatives of *his* community, in *his* name, while, in contrast, the crimes of the FLN attacked neither his honor, nor his idea of what his society should be. Mauriac added that the intellectuals might have some control only over the French crimes.[51]

Several intellectuals also pointed out that the FLN's methods of combat were in large part dictated by the conditions in which it fought. Because of France's enormous military superiority, the rebels had no chance of staging a Dien Bien Phu (although they dreamed of it). Their main hope for victory was to continue the war so long and to make it so costly and painful that the French would lose their determination to stay in Algeria. Their only effective weapon against the French was terrorist attacks. Furthermore, this plan depended on the continued support of Moslem opinion. The terrorist attacks demonstrated to the Moslem population the FLN's presence and determination. Similarly, the FLN tried to eliminate the MNA because, in part, it believed that a division in the loyalty of the Moslem people would benefit the imperialists. The FLN cared little if its methods alienated French opinion as long as they enabled it to carry on the war. It did not worry about undermining the peace effort of the French Left because, with much justification, it scorned this effort. Defending the FLN's reasoning, Sartre concluded that asking the FLN to adopt morally pure means would in effect be asking it to give up its struggle.[52]

Sartre added that it was hypocritical to condemn the terrorism of the rebels because the initial and fundamental violence in the Algerian situation was colonialism. The colonial system was based on violence: first conquest, then different forms of exploitation and oppression, now "pacification." But the system contained a contradiction: its profits depended on the labor of the colonial people. In order to make sufficient profits, colonialism had to exploit these people so mercilessly that they rose in revolt; but it could not end the revolt by exterminating them, for it would thereby exterminate itself. By its own violence, colonialism had created a creature who understood only violence; by its intransigence it had forced him to resort to violence. For the colonialists to appeal to morality now that the colonial subject was turning back on colonialism its own violence was illegitimate.[53]

Sartre argued, furthermore, that the methods of the FLN actually were moral if viewed in the context of a revolutionary humanism. He applied the "engaged" morality that Merleau-Ponty and he had elaborated earlier in the debates over Communist violence. The choice in Algeria, he contended, was only between two kinds of violence. Camus's balanced moral condemnation was idealistic. Moreover, since the colonial system was the status quo, and revolution, including terrorism, the only way to change it, Camus's condemnation was reactionary: it was in effect a position in support of the Algerian colonialists. Sartre had attacked the hypocrisy of bourgeois moralism as early as his prewar novel *La Nausée*. The Algerian problem convinced him further of the Marxist claim that abstract moralism was both a luxury of the dominant class that the oppressed could not afford and a means of preserving its dominance. The violence of the FLN, he hoped, was forcing Europeans to do "the strip tease of our humanism" and to discover that it was "nothing but an ideology of lies, a perfect justification for pillage." In place of bourgeois humanism, Sartre insisted on a morality that evaluated an action as part of a concrete project in a particular situation. As he wrote later: "Since the end is defined, in effect, as the unity of the means, it is necessary that [the intellectual] examine the latter as a function of the principle that all means are good when they are effective *except* those that alter the pursued end." He chided those moralists who forgot the lessons of the French Resistance and wanted, as he put it later in comparing American and North Vietnamese massacres, to put on the same plane "the violence of a popular resistance" and "a violence of aggression." Terrorism was a moral act, Sartre concluded, because it was a necessary part of the project of destroying colonialism.[54]

In *L'Être et le néant* (1943), violence, of a largely psychological sort, had been an essential but negative element in Sartre's vision of human interaction. The other person was a constant threat to the individual; the other tried to reduce him to an object of the other's consciousness and even of his will. In the Resistance, however, Sartre had become aware of both the defensive and the constructive value of a more physical type of violence. It could be the necessary means of defending freedom, and, Sartre would conclude by the end of the Algerian war, even writers had to be willing to use it. It could also be, as Marxist revolutionaries claimed, the necessary means of building a new society. In his preface to Fanon's *Les Damnés de la terre*, written in 1961, he went one step further. Based on the lessons of Memmi in *Portrait du colonisé* as well as on his own theoretical analysis, Sartre joined Fanon in stressing the ontological value of violence.

Fanon not only insisted that the struggle against colonialism was necessarily violent but also claimed that violence invested the characters of the colonial people "with positive and creative qualities." For the individual, violence was "a cleansing force" that freed him from his inferiority complexes and restored his self-respect. Suffering from a more profound and intimate alienation than the European proletarian, the colonial subject had to strike out more forcefully and directly at his oppressor. In Sartre's words, his violence was "man recreating himself"; it alone could efface the marks on his psyche made by the colonist's violence: "We were men at his expense, he makes himself a man at ours: a different man; of higher quality." Fanon also claimed that, for the group, violence was a cement to "bind them together as a whole," a means of instilling in them "the idea of a common cause, of a national destiny, and of a collective history." This cement was important both for the current struggle and for the post-independence task of nation building. The transformation that violence produced in both the individuals and the group would prevent the betrayal of the revolution. Sartre pointed out that the Belgian Congo, which was emancipated without a struggle, immediately fell prey to neocolonialist-instigated turmoil.[55]

Sartre and Fanon employed arguments that recalled, among others, Hegel's discussion of the dialectic of master and slave, Nietzsche's revaluation of values, and Georges Sorel's appeal for proletarian violence. But they carried their advocacy of violence even further than did Sorel, for, in the name of liberation, they praised its most extreme forms: murder and even massacre. The liberation of the colonial people, therefore, was to occur at the expense of others' lives. The other intellectuals not only doubted the regenerating power of violence—and suspected it of a corrupting power instead—but wondered if the victims of FLN terrorism deserved this death sentence.[56]

These victims included French draftees, Moslems who had put their trust in France, and French settlers. The French felt a responsibility to protect all three groups. The army, in particular, which had been forced to betray its allies in Indochina, refused to do so again; it would not abandon the Moslems who, on the basis of assurances that France would remain, had taken the French side.[57] The French at home felt a stronger attachment to the settlers. Even if the intellectuals decided that French atrocities should be condemned more than Moslem ones, they could not remain indifferent to the sufferings of their compatriots.

Camus felt this dilemma acutely, for he was a native of Algeria. He remained almost completely silent during the campaign against the methods of pacification and was attacked by other intellectuals for his silence. In December 1957, Camus was awarded the Nobel Prize for literature. In his acceptance speech he talked of the role of a writer in society and stated that "the silence of an unknown prisoner abandoned to humiliations" was enough to tear the writer from his exile. But his pen and his voice did not echo the sufferings of the tortured Algerian prisoners, and when he was accosted by Algerian students in Sweden, he told them: "I have always condemned terror. I must also condemn a terrorism that operates blindly, in the streets of Algiers, for example, and that one day may strike my mother or my family. I believe in justice, but I will defend my mother before justice." In justification of his position, Camus wrote in early 1958 in the preface to his collected articles on Algeria: "When one's own family is in immediate danger of death, one may want to instill in one's family a feeling of greater generosity and fairness, as these articles clearly show; but (let there be no doubt about it!) one still feels a natural solidarity with the family in such mortal danger and hopes that it will survive at least and, by surviving, have a chance to show its fairness. If that is not honor and true justice, then I know nothing that is of any use in this world."[58]

The French of Algeria distrusted Camus for his liberalism, yet his defense of them increasingly isolated him from the Parisian intellectual community. Torn like the painter in his short story "Jonas" between a "solitary" or "solidary" way of life, Camus moved toward greater solidarity with his French Algerian compatriots. How could they be abandoned to FLN terrorism and to the political domination of the terrorists?

The presence of European settlers greatly complicated decolonization, as the British discovered in Kenya and Rhodesia. The French first encountered the problem in Morocco and Tunisia. Duverger, for example, noted in *La Nef* in 1953 that the half million Frenchmen in the two protectorates amounted to more than 4 percent of the population, making any idea of a mass evacuation impracticable, and argued that England could not have left India if the proportion of Englishmen there had been that high. He concluded that the real problem in the protectorates was the future status of the French minority.[59]

In Morocco and Tunisia, however, the juridical standing of the French always had been that of foreign residents. Consequently, they had no legal basis for objecting to independence. In contrast, Algeria was constitutionally a part of France; the numerical proportion of people of European origin in Algeria was even higher (about 12 percent) than in the protectorates; and their duration of settlement was longer. Most of their ancestors had settled in Algeria in the second half of the nineteenth century. They felt as native to Algeria as did the Moslems and took full credit for the building of modern Algeria.

The French at home had ambivalent feelings about the European community in Algeria. They believed that colonial residents in general led an easy life; the anticolonialists even portrayed them as oppressors and racists. At the same time they viewed the settlers as compatriots and knew that they had fought for France during the world wars. As Aron and *Les Temps Modernes* agreed, the French at home were willing to send a half million soldiers to Algeria mostly because they did not want to abandon the French of Algeria.[60]

The stand taken by Camus is again illuminating. He had great respect as well as sympathy for the Moslem population. In the 1930s he was a member briefly of Hadj's nationalist party and signed a manifesto in favor of the Popular Front's proposal to extend political rights to certain groups of Moslems. In his 1939 report on the misery in Kabylia he extolled the wisdom and nobility of the Kabyle people. Rejecting a policy of total cultural and administrative assimilation, even if advocating greater political assimilation, he declared that the French had the duty "to permit one of the proudest and most humane populations in the world to remain faithful to itself and to its destiny." Similarly, in 1945 he praised the Arabs as "a people of great tradition," whose virtues were "among the foremost," and in the 1950s he intervened numerous times in favor of Moslems mistreated by the police or on trial for nationalist activities.[61]

Yet the Moslem population still remained foreign to Camus. The Arabs in *L'Étranger* never assumed a personality, and the Arabs of Oran were almost totally forgotten in *La Peste*. The tragedy of the poignant short story "L'Hôte" resulted in large part from the inability of the French teacher and his Arab prisoner to engage in any sort of dialogue, in spite of good will on both sides. Written just before the outbreak of war in Algeria, this tale surely mirrored Camus's sense of helplessness, and it foretold the failure of the liberal Algerians, rejected by both sides.[62]

In 1939 and 1945, Camus had written in defense of the Moslems and had been accused of insensitivity to French victims of the uprising of 1945. In the 1950s, however, when the French of Algeria came under attack from both Parisian intellectuals and Algerian rebels, he decided that the French Algerians now needed his defense. The fullest exposition of his case was in a series of articles that appeared in *L'Express* in 1955–56.

Camus argued that the French had rights in Algeria because of their contributions and that they were "attached to the soil of Algeria" by roots that were "too old and too vigorous for us to think of tearing them up." He added that the majority of French Algerians were not responsible for the Moslems' misery and that the tendency of the anti-colonialists to put the whole blame on them was unjust. He pointed out that 80 percent of the settlers were only salaried workers or tradesmen, whose standard of living was actually lower than that of comparable workers in France. While a few of the French settlers were great exploiters of the Moslems, the mass of them benefited from the hunger of the Moslems no more than did all Frenchmen. Consequently, the vast reparation owed to the Moslems should be paid by all of France, not by the sacrifice of the French in Algeria. Camus contended further that the French Algerians, who were now scorned by many in France, deserved France's protection because they had fought to save the home country in both world wars and because, he believed, they would agree to the needed reforms if they were convinced instead of cursed. He called for justice for both communities. This excluded independence.[63]

In 1945, Camus had sympathized with Abbas's desire for a democratic Algerian state linked federally with France, but he never had supported independence. Indeed he had wanted Algeria to be an integral part of France. The aim of his series in 1945 had been to convince the French that they had to "reconquer" Algeria by means of "the infinite force of justice."[64] The constant theme of his articles on Algeria was that it contained a plurality of communities. Although he called for administrative decentralization and democratization, he always insisted that these communities had to be united from above by a French administrative structure.

Camus proposed in *L'Express* in July 1955 that the Algerian assembly created by the law of 1947 be elected fairly and given control of internal administration. This was the position of most French leftists at this time. By 1958, however, Camus had moved from support for Algerian autonomy toward the idea of "integration," espousing the plan of Marc Lauriol, a law professor in Algiers, for a "federalist integration" of Algeria into the French republic. The Moslems would be full French citizens, electing deputies to the National Assembly in Paris, not to an Algerian assembly; their sense of political identity would be with France rather than with Algeria. Since the Moslem community would have special problems and concerns, two sections would be created within the National Assembly, one representing the Moslems and deliberating separately on all questions involving them alone, the other representing the French in France and overseas. This proposal gave the Moslems equality of vote, but stripped this equality of any danger to the French Algerians by abolishing the territorial assembly and integrating the Moslem representatives into the National Assembly, where they could be outvoted by the representatives of continental France on all matters affecting the French Algerians. At the same time the mechanism of two colleges relieved some of the fear of the Frenchmen at home that in an already unstable assembly the large bloc of Moslem votes resulting from integration would have a determining influence on affairs in France.[65]

Lauriol's proposal was a final attempt to rally the Moslem population to France in a way that would be acceptable to the French in Algeria and at home—a final attempt to save both democratic principles and the privileges of the French of Algeria. The revolt of May 1958, the accession of de Gaulle, and his promise of an egalitarian society generated considerable enthusiasm for integration among French in Algeria, French at home, and even Moslems.[66] Not even de Gaulle, however, could end the rebellion.

Camus was caught in the untenable position of what Memmi labeled "the colonizer of good will." He refused to accept the authenticity and legitimacy of Algerian nationalism and, therefore, did not reject the colonial situation even though he insisted that it had to be reformed. When the civil war grew more bloody, his identification with the threatened European community grew stronger. In 1958 he collected most of his past articles on Algeria, wrote two new essays as preface and conclusion, and presented *Actuelles, III* as his final statement on the Algerian problem. Like the other defenders of *Algérie française*, he rejected even negotiations with the FLN, for he knew that negotiations would greatly increase its prestige: "Those who, in purposely vague terms, advocate negotiation with the F.L.N. cannot fail to be aware, after the precise statements of the F.L.N., that this means the independence of Algeria under the direction of the most relentless military leaders of the insurrection—in other words, the eviction of 1,200,000 Europeans from Algeria and the humiliation of millions of Frenchmen, with all the risks that such a humiliation involves."[67] How, Camus asked, could humanist principles justify a solution that might mean the sacrifice of the French of Algeria?

After Camus's death on 4 January 1960 another French Algerian writer, Jules Roy, responded to his challenge. Roy wrote that he, like Camus, had "felt torn between the justice that he demanded for the Moslems and the attachment that he kept for his racial brothers, the Europeans." Except for one article in *L'Express* in September 1955 (just after the Philippeville massacre) in which he had sympathized with the Algerian nationalists, Roy had remained silent, out of deference to his friend, but now he had to speak out.[68]

Roy traveled to Algeria in 1960, visited his family and friends, inspected the work of the army, and went to an FLN refugee camp in Tunisia near Sakiet. In November he published *La Guerre d'Algérie*. His trip had convinced him that his primary solidarity was not with his own community in Algeria but with the Moslems. He asserted that the current Frenchmen of Algeria did not deserve their privileges, nor even the compassion they demanded and that Camus had demanded for them because they were incompetent and racist; they were not worthy of keeping the inheritance of the heroic colonists who had built

Algeria. He then applied the lesson that, he said, Camus had taught him but had been unable to pursue to the end: "that justice and injustice had no frontiers and that it was necessary always to take the side of the victims." In a miserable Moslem suburb of Algiers, Roy saw a monument to the Moslems who had died fighting for France. He subsequently toured the wretched refugee camp and declared: "Between those who were hungry and those who could not eat everything offered to them, between those who bombarded and those who became crazy under the bombardments, my choice was made." He opted for independence.

Roy concluded in reply to Camus: "It is not a question of preferring your mother to justice. It is a question of loving justice as much as your own mother." Actually Roy avoided Camus's question by claiming that the two were not incompatible in the Algerian situation. He believed that the French of Algeria would be able to stay after independence and adjust to life in the Moslem-controlled state. He believed that only their illegitimate privileges would be taken from them.

This belief—or hope—was shared, or at least stated, by the majority of anticolonialists, even the Communists. They agreed with the defenders of *Algérie française* that a solution had to be found that would allow the French to continue to live in Algeria, although they added that such a situation must involve a political liberalization, perhaps even independence. As a result, the position of the opponents of the war, who insisted that the rights of the French of Algeria had to be protected, was strangely close to that of the defenders of the war, who insisted that justice had to be given to the Moslems. They differed in their assessments of the rebels.[69] Most French Algerians and many Frenchmen at home were convinced that independence—and thus even negotiations with the FLN—would be tantamount to the sacrifice of the French Algerians. The atrocities of the FLN reinforced their conviction. They, like Camus, believed that the crucial question was the one that most of the opponents of the war tried to avoid: should France sacrifice its countrymen for the sake of its principles?

Aron suggested in *La Tragédie algérienne* in 1957 that, although the preferable solution was the coexistence of the French and the Moslems, the most practical and least costly one might be the repatriation of the French of Algeria. He was widely attacked for envisaging such a cruel fate for the settlers. Soustelle, for example, contended that there was "no iniquity more atrocious, nor treatment more intolerable to inflict on a people, than to tear it from its country."[70] While Aron argued on the level of realism, his opponents replied on the level of moralism. The moral case for a sacrifice of the French of Algeria was developed by those, like Sartre, who attacked the injustices of colonialism and the incompetence, racism, and fascism of the settlers.

Sartre saw colonialism as a rigorous system, characterized by "superexploitation," which caught up the individuals within it, shaped their personalities, and directed their actions. It was a *processus*. At the same time he held the colonial residents, both the settlers and the indigenous population, responsible for the crimes of colonialism because the system had been founded and was perpetuated only by the action of individuals. It was fundamentally a *praxis*.

The aim of Sartre's discussion of Algerian colonialism in *Critique de la raison dialectique* was to refute the "economism" of Engels in general and of Tillion in particular: "Economism is false because it makes exploitation a certain *result* and that alone, whereas this result cannot maintain itself and the *processus* of capital cannot develop itself if they are not sustained by the *project of exploiting*." This project of exploiting had to be accompanied by oppression (both physical and psychological) in order to force the workers to accept their condition. The Algerian colonial situation could not continue to exist if the oppression of the system was not realized, recreated, and perpetuated, even if only passively, in the daily *praxis* of each individual in the colonial system. In Sartre's words:

We see at present that it is necessary to distinguish three levels in colonization as History in movement. The game of flat appearances that economic Reason can study has intelligibility only in relation to the antidialectical system of superexploitation. But the latter in its turn is not intelligible if we do not begin by seeing in it the product of a human labor that forged it and that does not cease to control it. . . . It is therefore perfectly clear here that superexploitation as "practico-inert" *processus* is nothing else than oppression as historical *praxis* realizing itself, determining itself, and controlling itself in the milieu of "passive activity."[71]

Sartre's analysis of Algerian colonialism demonstrated the value of the existentialist basis that he tried to give to Marxism. By this means he was able to combine and reconcile, for himself at least, the deterministic sociology and the moralistic passion that had characterized Marx. He was able to argue that the colonists were incapable of reforming the system—that it had to be destroyed, either from outside or by its own contradictions (that is, by the revolt of the colonial subjects)—

and at the same time to insist that the colonists were guilty of its injustices.

Sartre had remarked in early 1956 that he labeled as "colonists" (*colons*) "neither the small functionaries, nor the European workers at the same time victims and innocent profiteers of the regime." The Socialists and Communists also found it hard, because of the Marxist principle of proletarian solidarity, to admit that the European workers were colonialists. In July 1957, however, when Sartre reviewed Memmi's *Portrait du colonisé, précédé du portrait du colonisateur*, he stressed, like Memmi, that all European residents were privileged with respect to the Moslems and had a vital stake in the system of superexploitation. Sartre thus approached the attitude of the FLN, as expounded by Fanon in December 1957: "The Frenchmen in Algeria cannot be neutral or innocent. Every Frenchman in Algeria oppresses, despises, dominates. . . . The Álgerian experiences French colonialism as an undifferentiated whole, not out of simplemindedness or xenophobia but because in reality every Frenchman in Algeria maintains, with reference to the Algerian, relations that are based on force." According to Fanon and Sartre, no French Algerians were innocent of colonialism and, therefore, none could expect his rights or even his life to be spared by the rebels. They were complicit as long as they did not choose, as a few did, to fight on the side of the FLN. Since the defeat of the colonialists was unavoidable, the European community was, in the words of Sartre's collaborator Marcel Péju, "condemned by History."[72]

Sartre's discussion of the French Algerians revealed a basic weakness in his philosophical method. In *L'Être et le néant* he had reduced man to an idealistic abstraction by overemphasizing the dimension of the individual consciousness. After the war he remedied part of his idealism by studying man in action in his situation. Yet in his attempt to formulate a systematic anthropology he was forced to make an abstraction of this situation. By stressing the determinism of the situation, he made a new abstraction of man. In particular, by trying to reduce the French Algerians to their position as oppressors within the colonial system, he ignored some of their irreducible particularities and virtues. Although the system altered the meaning of all the parts, created its own instruments, and required certain actions, nonetheless the things and the people retained dimensions of being that transcended the system or could at least assume a different meaning in a new situation. The French of Algeria were not merely colonialists; they were human beings. Few Frenchmen could accept Sartre's judgment that the crime of participation in colonialism was sufficient to justify the death sentence.[73]

Yet the French people's compassion for their compatriots in Algeria was limited. Their feeling of solidarity with them was superficial and gradually was dispelled by the settlers' extreme behavior. Fear of abandonment caused the French of Algeria to explode into violence on several occasions in an effort to impose their will on the French government. On 6 February 1956 and on 13 May 1958 their activism seemed to pay off; they forced Mollet to back down and the Fourth Republic to abdicate to de Gaulle. Their subsequent acts of violence, however, discredited their cause and prepared French opinion for the abandonment they were desperate to avoid.

De Gaulle announced on 16 September 1959 that, after peace was restored, the Algerian people would choose their own destiny among three possibilities: complete "Frenchization," autonomy, and secession. Shortly thereafter de Gaulle removed General Massu from the command of the army in Algiers for vocalizing his opposition to self-determination. The French of Algeria felt betrayed. The extremists in Algiers revolted on 24 January 1960. The insurrection was a failure this time, for with some exceptions the army remained obedient to de Gaulle. Most Frenchmen condemned the insurrection. In the referendum of 8 January 1961 a majority of the electorate approved the principle of self-determination and de Gaulle's hope for an *Algérie algérienne* closely linked to France.[74]

De Gaulle proceeded in early 1961 to arrange for official negotiations with the FLN. In reaction to this seeming betrayal of the military's efforts, a group of army generals and colonels took control of Algiers on 22 April 1961, with the aim of preserving Algeria for France. After a few days of hesitation, however, the mass of officers failed to join the mutiny. With the collapse of the revolt, the diehard military and civilian defenders of *Algérie française* joined forces in the Organisation de l'Armée Secrète (OAS) for a terrorist campaign in Algeria and France intended to sabotage de Gaulle's peace efforts. The OAS failed on 9 September 1961 in an attempt to assassinate de Gaulle, and more generally it failed to provoke a renewal of the war. It succeeded only in producing bloodshed, turmoil, and hatred and in making it more difficult for the Europeans to remain after independence. The majority of the French people believed that the OAS was expressing the opinion of at least half of the Europeans of Algeria.[75]

Meanwhile, many of the French soldiers serving in Algeria developed little respect or affection for the settlers, who were not enthusiastic about the army officers' plans for a social revolution in Algeria. The soldiers often identified more strongly with the Moslems, whose misery they were trying to alleviate, than with the Europeans, whose privileges they were protecting.[76]

The accords of Évian, recognizing Algerian independence and ending the war, were signed on 18 March 1962. By this time the French at home, as well as de Gaulle, were ready to sacrifice the French of Algeria. As an excuse for abandonment, they wanted to think that the settlers would be able to remain in FLN-controlled Algeria. In fact, in spite of the paper guarantees of the settlers' rights and safety in the new Algeria, most of them felt unsafe and persecuted and quickly fled to France. Although the French at home were more willing to express their solidarity with the French Algerians as OAS violence subsided and the settlers were forced to evacuate, they were unwilling to recommend the expenditure of French tax dollars to aid the refugees. The public's initial ambivalence about the French of Algeria had turned into hostility.[77] Meanwhile, on 1 July the French voters were nearly unanimous in approving the independence of Algeria.

THE THREAT OF "FASCISM"

The immorality of the methods of pacification and the violence of the French of Algeria underlined an alarming potential consequence of the war to France itself. Duverger echoed the fears of most of the leftist intellectuals when he declared in Le Monde on 22 March 1957 that "for the first time in ten years" the danger of "fascism" was "becoming truly serious." The intellectuals warned that the war in Algeria was leading to fascism in France by two paths: by "gangrene"—that is, by the slow spread of fascist attitudes to the government and to the people from their breeding ground in Algeria—and possibly by coup d'état.

The charge of the extreme leftists that it takes a fascist government to fight a colonial war seemed to be confirmed first by the military rule imposed on Algeria in order to prosecute the war efficiently and subsequently by attacks on liberties in France. The intellectuals were particularly alarmed by the government's interferences with the liberty of the press. At the end of the Fourth Republic and continuing into the Fifth Republic, the practice developed of seizing the whole issue of a publication, not only overseas but in France, to delete an offensive article concerning an overseas military effort. The first case occurred at the end of the war in Indochina when, on 29 May 1954, *L'Express* tried to reveal the contents of a secret report in which the army chiefs argued that the military situation was so desperate that conscripts must be sent at once. The war in Algeria, however, provoked most of the seizures of Parisian publications. On charges of undertaking an "enterprise of demoralization of the army," or of doing "injury to the security of the State," twenty-one issues of *L'Express* were seized in France from the beginning of the war to 1961, sixteen of *France-Observateur*, and four of *Témoignage Chrétien*.[78]

On the mainland the periodicals could appear after the seizure without the deleted material, but the process caused large financial losses. Since the actual information and opinions were usually reprinted or restated in other places, such as in *Le Monde*, or even summarized in the journal that had been censored, the aim of the seizures was apparently less to suppress particular material than to intimidate the journalists. By causing them financial damage, the anticolonialist journals were punished and forced to censor themselves. The governments also harassed numerous journalists by taking them to court or arresting them. Bourdet, for example, was incarcerated for twenty-four hours on 31 March 1956 in retaliation for an article opposing the sending of more troops.

These measures may have provided further reason to refrain from talking about Algerian independence. Bourdet later claimed, however, that the anticolonialists said what they wanted, that their own uncertainties about independence explained their reluctance to speak out. The Communists alone had valid reasons to fear government persecution; they did not want to revive the atmosphere of the Cold War, which in 1953 had nearly resulted in the lifting of the parliamentary immunity of their deputies. The anticolonialist press, however, quickly learned that government persecution served to give publicity to their cause while the financial damages could be repaired by contributions. The repressive measures had more effect, therefore, in discrediting the governments and in dramatizing the danger of fascism than in limiting protest. When the first of Bourdet's articles was seized, he responded: "We are scandalized and overwhelmed to see men who, a few years ago, struggled with courage against another *vérité d'État* imitate today the enemies that they fought yesterday. We have always said: colonial fascism leads to fascism in the home country. We are approaching it."[79]

The state of mind of the French people, however, was more alarming than the behavior of the governments. Simon and Mauriac asserted that the public's acceptance of the immoral methods of pacification was more frightening than the actual crimes. When in March 1958, *L'Express, France-Observateur*, and the Communist weekly *France Nouvelle* were all seized in the same week, one of the editors of *Preuves* lamented: "French public opinion, unfortunately, does not judge. It remains perfectly indifferent, and this apathy, which permits all the abuses of power, appears to us even more dangerous to the institutions than the abuses themselves." The people who learned to tolerate a colonial war and its methods would tolerate a fascist regime.[80]

The most direct source for this degradation of French morals was, according to the opponents of the war, the conscript army in Algeria. Colonial service had been seen by rightists since the end of the nineteenth century as a school to form a new elite to regenerate France. Many French officers continued to believe this. Servan-Schreiber hoped when he left for Algeria that the youths who served there would return to form "a powerful democratic legion to reconstruct the Republic." In Algeria he discovered that instead the youths were being poisoned by their service. As Domenach complained:

> This war in Algeria is, for too many youths, the most frightful of initiations to life—an initiation by violence, without limit and without aim. . . . French youth has been placed in this untenable situation of resisting a people struggling for its dignity. People are very busy these days with preserving the morale of the nation. But do they think about the morale of the nation of tomorrow? About the brutalizing of a whole youth, which will return from this Algerian service less unruly perhaps than is thought, but habituated, disgusted, withered? Fascism is made with cynics more than with fanatics.[81]

The war in Algeria not only was corrupting individuals, but was nourishing an army that, the leftist intellectuals feared, one day might strike at the Fourth Republic that it loudly accused of incompetence and defeatism. Leftists long had suspected the professional army because, in part, of the Vichy past of many of its officers. In the early

1950s Bourdet and Rous had begun to warn that Marshal Juin was planning to use North Africa as a base to impose army rule on France in the manner of Franco in Spain.[82] The grounds for this fear may have been only the desire of the French army to be able to retreat to a North African bastion in case of a Soviet invasion of Europe. But the subsequent alliance of the army and the French Algerian extremists gave a new focus and substance to Bourdet's fears.

The main theme of Bourdet's articles beginning in May 1955 was that the French leftists must unite to oppose both the war and the rising fascism. As the war continued, as the settlers and army officers grew more unruly, and as the defenders of *Algérie française* began to stress the need to change the regime in order to create a state with more authority, fear of a coup d'état began to dominate the writings of the anticolonialists. The general public, however, did not share this fear; few people expected a coup d'état, and in January 1958 only 4 percent told poll takers that they would actively oppose a military uprising if one should occur.[83] When the Europeans of Algiers revolted on 13 May 1958, they were joined by the army leaders in Algeria. Under threat of an invasion of Paris, the National Assembly agreed to invest General de Gaulle as premier.

France had not succumbed to fascism, but the Fourth Republic had fallen and the Algerian army and settlers remained as an even greater threat to France. Yet, in contrast to the leftist intellectuals, the French public still did not repudiate the army of Algeria; no more than a fifth thought that it was endangering republican liberties. Only after the abortive generals' revolt in April 1961 did the public lose confidence in the loyalty of the army in Algeria and realize that the OAS, under the leadership of General Raoul Salan, who had been the commander in Algeria until the end of 1958, was a serious threat to the French government.[84]

The specter of fascism provided the intellectuals with perhaps their most powerful argument against the war, for it concerned the immediate fate of France rather than of an overseas land. It led to acceptance of drastic means to end the war, namely by granting independence. To be sure, the defenders of French Algeria argued—or threatened—that the attempt to abandon Algeria would provoke a coup d'état, and this possibility gave some anticolonialists an additional reason to hesitate to advocate independence.[85] The violence of the French Algerians and of the army, however, decreased public sympathy for the cause of *Algérie française*, underlined the charge of the Left that France was defending an oppressive colonial system, and helped to prepare the French public for a solution that would repudiate the army's efforts and sacrifice the French Algerians. As with the protests against the methods of pacification, the intellectuals' campaign against fascism prepared for an independence that would be viewed as an abandonment.

Servan-Schreiber had insisted in 1955 that French youths had the duty to fight to protect their compatriots in Algeria. In November 1961 he declared: "To install the FLN in Algiers is painful. Yes, it's painful. But there is no alternative. If it is not the FLN in Algiers, it will be the OAS in Paris. What is your choice?"[86]

6 ∾THE NEW RESISTANCE

In early 1960 the French public discovered that the antiwar movement had begun to conduct illegal activities. In February the police arrested members of a ring of Frenchmen, led by Francis Jeanson, who were giving aid to the FLN. Further arrests revealed that another movement, called "Jeune Résistance," was helping youths to evade the draft or to desert from the army. Faced with almost unanimous condemnation, the extremists claimed that their actions were not only moral acts of refusal to accept the war, but also political acts of resistance against fascism and, for some of them, revolutionary acts aimed at instituting socialism.[1]

THE MORALITY OF ILLEGAL ACTION

The Communist party was the first during the Fourth Republic to suggest that it was legitimate to disobey a government that was fighting a colonial war. At the end of December 1949 the Communist labor union began to call for strikes to prevent the departure of trains and ships carrying war goods; on several occasions in January and February dockers, in particular, refused to handle American war material destined for Indochina. In late 1951 the party started the campaign to free Henri Martin. Although the Communists' aims were largely practical—to harm the French war effort—the intellectuals who sympathized with these two cases of disobedience justified them on moral grounds. In the process they uncovered two basic tensions in French political morality that became critical problems during the Algerian war.

Bourdet defended the strike of the Communist dockers in *Combat*.

He argued that, since the war in Indochina was unpopular and was being fought only with career soldiers and volunteers, it did not commit the nation, and the workers were under no obligation to support it. Since volunteers fought the war, only volunteers had to transport the arms. Mauriac, replying to Bourdet in *Le Figaro*, contended that in a democracy the citizens were committed by the decisions of the majority, that is, of the majority of their duly elected deputies in parliament. Democracy could not function unless the citizens agreed to obey these decisions, among them the decision to fight in Indochina. In response, Bourdet abandoned his argument that the war was voluntary and declared instead that in a truly free democracy the right of the majority to impose its decisions was superseded by the right of individual consciences to reject morally revolting acts. Although Bourdet initially had described the strike as a political act designed to hurt the war effort arid to catalyze antiwar sentiment, ultimately he was forced to defend it as an objection of conscience to an immoral war.[2]

The dispute between Bourdet and Mauriac thus reached the impasse of the unresolved tension in Western democracy between the rights of the individual and the requirements of the collectivity, the nation. This tension was also at the root of much of the debate over the numerous acts of disobedience by those who had to fight the colonial wars.

In the campaign to vindicate Martin, the intellectuals offered two kinds of moral justification of his actions. Domenach defended the right of the individual, even when subject to military discipline, to refuse to participate in a war that revolted his conscience. He noted that the Nuremberg tribunal had not recognized military discipline as an excuse for committing crimes against humanity. He asked, moreover, if Frenchmen would refuse to a soldier the autonomy of conscience to which they appealed every day as the foundation of democracy and which ten years before had been "the origin of our resistance to Hitlerian power." In defending Martin, therefore, Domenach, like Bourdet before him, was also defending "our right to objection of conscience, that is, our liberty not to let ourselves be led to the massacre for no matter whom and for no matter what."[3]

Domenach was concerned primarily with Martin's refusal to serve in Indochina. He briefly discussed Martin's attempt to convince others not to serve and excused it by noting that silence would have meant complicity with the immoral war. But Domenach ignored the political dimension of this incident. Sartre, in contrast, acknowledged that Martin's distribution of leaflets was a political act—an act intended not just to reject his own complicity, but to harm the French war effort. Sartre admitted that no armed forces could tolerate such action, and he did not dispute the right of the military to punish Martin. Rather, he and most of the other protesters contended that, even from the perspective of military justice, the penalty was too severe for the crime of which Martin had been convicted. Furthermore, they all pointed to Martin's patriotic intentions as constituting extenuating circumstances. He was a Resistance fighter who had enlisted voluntarily in the navy in order to fight the Japanese, but who had found himself instead fighting a war in Indochina that, he was sincerely convinced, was contrary to the principles and interests of France.

Most of Martin's defenders implied that, if he was correct in condemning the war, as they believed he was, his political act of distributing antiwar tracts was not a crime. They thus referred obliquely to a second fundamental tension in French political morality—that between any current government and "eternal France." The question raised by de Gaulle in 1940 continued to be revived by those on both Left and Right who criticized colonial policy in the Fourth and Fifth Republics: was it legitimate to disobey a government that apparently was betraying France?[4]

The right of disobedience became a major issue during the Algerian war. In contrast to the war in Indochina, the conflict in Algeria clearly was supported by the nation. It was fought not by volunteers like Martin, who could claim that the French state had broken its contract with them, but by conscripts who were called to do their patriotic duty. Even if the nation was committed to the war, however, many individuals found it immoral. Some of the youths called to fight in Algeria responded by a more or less radical disobedience.

Soldiers who objected only to the means of warfare as immoral could adopt a limited disobedience by refusing to participate in crimes of pacification. This attitude was encouraged by the intellectuals who protested against the methods of pacification and who pointed out, in particular, that the judgment at Nuremberg obliged the individual soldier thenceforth to judge for himself the legality and morality of the orders he received.[5]

The conscientious soldier found it difficult to remain in the army while objecting to its methods; he was isolated and in danger of persecution, and at the same time he felt a complicity with the crimes of the army. In the words of the Catholic soldier Jean Le Meur, "Even if you are hidden, if you are in an office, in the signal corps, in supplies, you are an organ of the repressive machine, in solidarity with the whole organization—and responsible. What I believe I have discovered is precisely the permanence of individual responsibility within a system that claims wrongly to abolish it."[6] A few like General de Bollardière and the hero of Simon's *Portrait d'un officier* were able to quit the war and the army, but this option was not available to conscripts. Moreover, many of the youths called to fight the war believed that its aim was to oppress the Algerian people and that the conflict was unjust in its end as well as its means. Consequently, a more serious variety of disobedience became increasingly common: refusal to serve in Algeria.

The intellectuals first were faced with this issue when the Faure government mobilized fifty thousand reservists after the massacre of 20 August 1955. Some of the youths demonstrated against their recall. In Paris on 11 September four hundred of them refused for a day to board the troop train; similar actions occurred elsewhere in the following days. The protesters received almost no support from the anticolonialist intellectuals. Only *Les Temps Modernes* approved of their action. In an editorial entitled "Refusal of Obedience," the review asserted that the aim of the war was necessarily immoral because the rebels were "the soldiers of a Resistance" protected and aided by "an entire people." It recalled that "the Fourth Republic, after all, was born of a refusal of obedience." Yet even *Les Temps Modernes* dared to support the protesting reservists only obliquely. Bourdet and Mauriac wrote nothing. Servan-Schreiber and *Esprit* opposed disobedience. Servan-Schreiber declared that the soldiers had a valid reason to go to Algeria: to protect and reassure the French of Algeria. Moreover, he contended, as Mauriac had in 1950, that soldiers would be unpatriotic if they refused their duty. While Mauriac had stressed the sanctity of democratic procedures, Servan-Schreiber, like *Esprit*, worried about the cohesion of the nation. He claimed that refusing to serve in Algeria would be "denying the very existence of the national collectivity."[7]

In April and May 1956 the Mollet government recalled more reservists and began to send current conscripts to Algeria. Once more troop trains were held up in Paris and Grenoble by demonstrating youths, but, to their disappointment, they again received little encouragement from the Left. The only political party to give complete support was the tiny Union de la Gauche Socialiste, formed largely of non-Communist intellectuals like Bourdet. Servan-Schreiber continued to warn the youths not to shatter national cohesion—or at least not to splinter it any more than had already occurred. He had been a fighter pilot for the Free French and did not object when he himself was mobilized, seemingly in retaliation for his criticism of government policy.[8]

Unrest among the mobilized youths never became serious, but, pushed by their consciences, dozens of individuals like Le Meur refused to fight in Algeria and were sent to military prisons for their disobedience. In France conscientious objection was not permitted; every citizen was expected, if called, to do his patriotic duty, regardless of his personal beliefs, or else to go to prison.

Some youths took a more drastic step: they not only refused to serve in the army, but fled from punishment, indicating, as they meant it to, rejection of the French state that was waging the war. A group of draft evaders and deserters declared in 1960: "Our decision signifies our will not to participate in the apparatus of colonial repression. It signifies our will to weaken this apparatus by contesting its right to make use of French youth for a task to which the latter objects. It signifies also that we question a certain legality from the moment that this legality is entirely in the service of a regime and of a colonialist repression that we condemn irremediably."[9]

One draft evader, Maurice Maschino, claimed in *Les Temps Modernes* in October 1958 that his extremism was merely an extension of the values of French humanism. Maschino was a young teacher in Morocco and had written several radical criticisms of the war in Algeria for Moroccan papers when in 1957 his draft deferment was canceled. Certain that he was destined for immediate imprisonment for his attacks on the army and desirous of continuing his work against the war, he refused to report for induction and sought refuge in Tunisia. The choice of exile was painful, Maschino reported; he was greatly upset by his estrangement from France. As long as he was able to distinguish between humanist France and colonialist Algeria, to "maintain the fiction of a duality of France," he contemplated reintegrating himself into the nation by surrendering and accepting punishment for his disobedience.

The crisis was resolved for Maschino with the settler uprising of 13 May 1958. In April 1956, Marrou (like Martin) had declared when attacking French atrocities in Algeria, "France is not France if it is unfaithful to the ideal image that it proposed to incarnate." The fall of the Fourth Republic, Maschino wrote, convinced him that the France he had idealized no longer existed. Events seemed to justify his draft evasion:

The ulcer, as was bound to happen, devours the home country; colonial fascism becomes *its truth*, so true it is that acts end always by producing *their* men or *their* nations. Then all becomes simple again; history, after having robbed me, decides in my favor. I did not lose my quality of being French; France lost its. I was not unfaithful to it; it was to itself. I did not deny it; it denied everything that it could have of merit for men. It put itself outside humanity, not I outside France. It is no longer a question for me to have my act judged by the France of Soustelle and Massu. If I am to be judged one day, it will be with head held high, by those who will have defeated fascism in the home country, recognized the Algerian nation, and who will recognize me as one of theirs. My isolated combat will become theirs. My only wrong will have been to have been right too soon (at a moment when I could not yet be certain that I was right). History will have reintegrated me because France will have begun to live it correctly, to rediscover its sense and its values.[10]

More and more youths came to share the view of Maschino and of one of the arrested members of the Jeanson ring that entering into illegality was the way "to remain in the spiritual legality" of France.[11] Meanwhile, rumors spread of the sufferings and dangers faced by those who chose to go to military prison. By 1960, according to Jeanson and Maschino, three thousand youths had refused both the war and French legality. In 1959, Jeune Résistance was organized by a group of draft evaders and deserters to unite the refractory youths, to ameliorate the conditions of life in exile, and to encourage other youths to refuse military service.

Maschino and many other draft evaders and deserters—though not Jeune Résistance as a whole—went one step further in their disobedience. Convinced of the injustice of the French effort, they began to believe in the justice of the Algerian rebels' cause and decided to engage themselves on the side of the Algerian nation. With the knowledge that their criticism of the war and their refusal to serve were aiding the rebels in any case, they accepted this complicity and transformed it into direct involvement with the FLN.[12]

Others, like Jeanson, who were not faced with military service, were also actively supporting the FLN. Jeanson, a writer and teacher of philosophy, had condemned French colonialism in Algeria in *Esprit* and *Les Temps Modernes* as early as 1950, and in 1955 he and his wife wrote the first book favorable to the revolution. When asked by youths in 1955, Jeanson did not feel that he had the right to recommend desertion or draft evasion because he himself did not have to face that choice. But when Algerian friends asked him in 1956 to transport and shelter FLN militants, he accepted without hesitation. Within six months he had in his hands almost all the funds of the FLN's branch in France. At this time he decided to organize a French ring that would aid the FLN while remaining separate from it. His movement did not begin to coordinate its efforts with those of Jeune Résistance until the middle of 1960.[13] Frenchmen like Maschino and Jeanson—as well as the occasional Europeans of Algeria who crossed over to the side of the FLN—were charged by the government and the press not merely with refusal to discharge a patriotic duty, but with treason.

The moralist intellectuals reacted in various ways to these two radical acts of draft refusal and aid to the FLN. The novelists Claude Simon and Vercors argued that both were morally justified because of the immorality of French methods and aims in Algeria and because of the justice of the Algerian rebels' struggle for independence.[14] The men of *Esprit*, on the other hand, were more typical in insisting that only certain acts of disobedience were morally defensible.

Because of their belief in the moral primacy of the individual conscience, Domenach and his colleagues continued to assert that the right of the individual to refuse to serve in the army was "sacred and indispensable." They also were willing to approve of illegal acts that sprang from an "ethic of distress," as defined by the philosopher Paul Ricoeur. In March 1958, Ricoeur defended a pastor, Étienne Mathiot, who had helped an FLN leader to escape from France to Switzerland in order, according to Ricoeur, to save him from torture. Since France was allowing torture to become an integral part of its system of war, Ricoeur contended, Mathiot's act was justifiable: "The betrayal of legality by the state forces the citizen to bear witness by illegality. The gesture of Mathiot is one of the paths—the path of scandal—by which justice, exiled from the official policy, takes refuge and protests. The gesture of Mathiot is one of an ethic of distress. It is the product of the demoralization of the nation by the state and the refusal, by the citizen, of this moral corruption."[15] The ethic of distress directed an individual to resort to illegal nonviolence in order to prevent unjustifiable violence. On this basis Domenach and Ricoeur also defended both draft evasion (although Domenach excluded desertion) and aid to conscripts in fleeing France.

Esprit's ethic of distress was limited by patriotic obligations. Domenach and Ricoeur insisted that an act such as refusal of military service had to remain an act of the individual conscience, addressed at most to other consciences, in particular, to those of the heads of government. Its aim was to reassert, and to put into practice, values that transcended politics. To make it an instrument of partisan propaganda —a means of opposing the regime—was to contradict what was essential to all political life: "the obedience due to the lawful orders of the legitimate state." Unlike Jeune Résistance and Maschino, they believed that the Gaullist regime was the legal and legitimate government, even if it had been imposed by the rebellious army and settlers and was pursuing the war. Consequently, the men of *Esprit* contended that they, as intellectuals, could not try to stimulate a movement of disobedience. This argument, however, relied on a delicate distinction between publicly approving such acts, which *Esprit* did, and encouraging them, which Jeune Résistance and *Les Temps Modernes* did.

Domenach and Ricoeur also condemned the giving of aid to the FLN. They argued that even the nonviolent efforts of the Jeanson ring, such as transporting money, papers, and militants, were in fact a deliberate participation in an enterprise that was both violent and political and, therefore, contradicted the obligation of solidarity with the French nation. In *Le Monde*, Pierre-Henri Simon agreed with them, while Duverger bluntly labeled Jeanson and his colleagues as traitors.[16]

Those who defended desertion and aid to the FLN were sensitive to the charge of antipatriotic activity. Simone de Beauvoir underwent an emotional and political evolution not unlike Maschino's. As the war continued, she and Sartre grew disgusted with France: "We had begun by loathing a few men and a few factions; little by little we were made forcibly aware that all our fellow countrymen were accomplices in this crime and that we were exiles in our own country. . . . I had been labeled, along with several others, anti-French. I became so. I could no longer bear my fellow citizens." De Beauvoir continued both to love and to feel responsible for her country, and this made her anger at the crimes more intense and her alienation more dreadful: "What I find physically intolerable is being forced to be an accomplice of drumbeaters, incendiaries, torturers, and mass murderers; it's my country all this is happening to, and I used to love it; and without chauvinism or jingoism, it's pretty difficult to be against one's own country."[17]

Jeanson had been the managing editor of *Les Temps Modernes* but had left in 1956 after a dispute over Sartre's signing of a manifesto condemning the Soviet invasion of Hungary. When de Beauvoir and Sartre had heard in 1957 of Jeanson's aid to the FLN, they had not yet been ready to assist him. They had believed, like Domenach, that France was not Algeria and that it was possible to work for independence legally. According to Jeanson, Sartre had been upset at first by the violence of the Algerian rebels. De Beauvoir had been restrained by sentiments of national solidarity and had failed to understand "that Jeanson was not rejecting his status as a Frenchman by helping the FLN." By 1959, however, when finally contacted by Jeanson, they immediately agreed to aid his endeavors.[18]

Neither Jeanson nor Sartre shared de Beauvoir's deep patriotism, but Jeanson insisted that he was a Frenchman and wanted to live only in France. Like Martin earlier, he contended that he was not betraying France but acting in its true interests. He pointed out, like Maschino and others who refused to fight in Algeria, that the French community already was shattered, the order of law already overthrown. He was betraying only "the community of the bazooka, the tortures, and the camps." Although Jeanson agreed that he was participating in a movement that killed Frenchmen, he noted that, according to the law, the rebels were Frenchmen too. He claimed that so far his engagement had enabled him to exert a moderating influence on the FLN—to save French lives by convincing the FLN, except for a period right after the fall of the Fourth Republic, not to carry the terrorist war to the French-men of the mainland. Jeanson and his companions also insisted that one of their aims was "to maintain the chances of a Franco-Algerian friendship" in the interests of both countries. Jeanson warned that these chances were disappearing quickly because the original combatants, who were deeply attached to France by education, military service, and work in France, were being replaced by a new generation of youths who knew France solely as the war enemy. Only those who aided the FLN, he argued, would prevent the rebels from turning elsewhere for support and would convince the Algerian people that France was more than colonialism and repression. Finally, like those who protested against the methods of pacification, Jeanson asserted that he wanted "to save the honor of France and of its most valid traditions" in world opinion.[19]

Domenach admitted that at the base of this reputedly anti-French action was "a will of reparation, that is, a consciousness of national solidarity incomparably superior to the patriotism of those who have reproached them for lacking it." Bourdet described aid to the FLN as a courageous act of moral "witnessing," which would have a positive influence on the Algerian people, if not on the French. Both saw it primarily as the desperate act of the outraged individual conscience. Both focused on its moral dimension.[20]

Jeanson, Sartre, Maschino, and Jeune Résistance insisted, on the contrary, on the political dimension of their illegal actions, which, they claimed, were the result of rational political decisions and were the most effective means to achieve "a true democracy" in France.[21] The claim of political effectiveness was hotly debated in 1960 by the French leftists.

THE NEED FOR ACTION

The initial political reason for choosing radical action, Jeanson explained, was the impotence of the French Left. None of the large parties of the Left was actively and effectively opposed to the war in Algeria. The leader of the left wing of the Radical party, Mendès-France, was premier at the beginning of the war and affirmed that Algeria would remain French. Even when he resigned as a minister in the Mollet government in May 1956, he did not condemn the military effort, but complained that the lack of economic and political reforms would lead "from the loss of the Algerian people to that of Algeria, and then unfailingly to the loss of the whole of our Africa."[22] The Socialist chief, Mollet, was premier during the most intense period of the war, January 1956 to June 1957, and the former Socialist union leader Lacoste was resident minister in Algeria from January 1956 until May 1958. Their policy, which was not repudiated by the mass of the party militants, was to force the FLN to agree to a cease-fire, to try in effect to crush the rebellion. Even the Communist party did not vigorously oppose the war. The Communists' restraint was crucial, since their abandonment of radical activity left the political vacuum filled by Jeanson and his colleagues.[23]

The French Communists, though more sympathetic than most Frenchmen to the nationalist desires of the Algerians, were slow to espouse the cause of the FLN. One reason is that they had misgivings about the nature of the revolution. Suspicious of any adventurist actions that lacked obvious mass support and fearing imperialist maneuvers, they initially condemned the rebels. Insisting on proletarian internationalism, they continued to criticize nationalist rhetoric and terrorist methods that deprived the FLN of the solidarity of the French working class. This solidarity was deemed important for forcing the French government to end the war and for permitting a future "union with the working people of France" that would benefit the Algerians. The Communists knew that the FLN, with its nationalist and Islamic bent, did not entirely share Communist ideas on the future of Algerian society. The Algerian Communist party remained small and could play only a minimal role in the revolution.

The Communists were further deterred from support of the rebellion by political considerations in France. The party initially subordinated the Algerian question to its continuing struggle against the rearmament of Germany. In conformity with Soviet policy, it hoped to join with nationalists to prevent German remilitarization. Moreover, in 1955 the party had hopes of ending the isolation it had endured since 1947 and of obtaining a share of government power. It dreamed of the Popular Front of 1936 or even of the tripartite government at the end of World War II. The party chief, Thorez, declared during the electoral campaign of December 1955 that the Communist party was ready to cooperate after the elections with the Socialist party and other leftists to create a government that would "apply the solutions of negotiation and conciliation in Algeria and work to create a true French Union."

The elections of 2 January 1956 were a success for the Communists; the party increased its delegation in the National Assembly from 99 out of 626 deputies to 144 out of 596. The elections also were a success for the Left in general. For the first time since the elections of 1936 the Left—Communists, Socialists, and Radicals—won a majority of the seats. The "Republican Front" of the Socialists, the Mendèsists, and the small Union Démocratique et Socialiste de la Résistance headed the new government. Although spurned during and after the electoral campaign, the Communists continued to strive for an alliance with the Socialists. In March 1956, Mollet requested special civil and military powers in Algeria to end the war. As in 1947, the Communist deputies faced a crisis. They were worried by Mollet's apparent capitulation to the French Algerian extremists in February, when he rescinded his appointment of Catroux as resident minister. Nonetheless, the Communists decided to vote for the special powers in order to keep the center of gravity of the government as far to the left as possible and "to preserve the possibilities of a wide development of the single front with the Socialist workers."

In summer and fall 1956, however, the Communist deputies shifted their position. The rebellion was continuing to spread. The Communist rank and file disliked the party's support of Mollet, particularly when he continued to show little evidence of trying to end the war. On 5 June the Communists abstained on a vote of confidence. On 29 July they voted against Algerian war credits. Their return to isolation was finalized by their criticism of the Suez adventure and support of the Soviet repression of the Hungarian revolution in November 1956.

Meanwhile, at the twentieth congress of the Soviet Communist party in February 1956, Khrushchev had denounced Stalin, rejected the Manichean universe of the Cold War, and affirmed a policy of peaceful competition with American imperialism. Corresponding to this change of policy was a renewed confidence in the progressive nature even of bourgeois-led movements of national liberation. On 1 July 1956 the Algerian Communist party counseled its members to join the FLN. In February 1957, Thorez declared that the Algerian nation, defined since 1939 as a "nation in formation," had become a fact.

Nonetheless, the Communists never acted against the war in Algeria as vigorously as against that in Indochina. They continued to be suspicious of the FLN and to define the Algerian nation as the amalgam of the Moslem and European populations. They also continued to court the votes of those, including many workers, who disliked the thousands of North Africans who worked in France and who wanted Algeria to remain French. Believing in mass action, the party contended that the masses, still largely colonialist, had to be educated before they could be expected to act. It continued to subordinate colonial liberation to the apparent demands of domestic politics. In addition, the party feared that it would be penalized, even outlawed, if its opposition to the war was too vigorous. Furthermore, in the era of peaceful competition the Soviets no longer encouraged the shrill attacks on French governments that had characterized the French Communists during the Cold War period. When de Gaulle came to power, the Soviets approved of his anti-American foreign policy.

Consequently, the Communists largely restricted themselves to antiwar propaganda. They did not call disruptive strikes, nor even massive demonstrations. They opposed the refusal of military service; Thorez recalled Lenin's directive to work within the army rather than, by deserting it, to leave the mass of soldiers in the hands of rightist officers. The party also disapproved of Frenchmen giving aid to the FLN as an act "running counter to the mass politics" of the French Communist party. Yet it was not clear, at least to critics of the Communist party's moderation, that mere propaganda was the most effective way to educate the masses. Meanwhile, the de-Stalinization campaign, followed by the Soviet's brutal suppression of the Hungarian revolution, stimulated a number of Communist supporters, especially among the intellectuals, to question party dogmas. Jeanson provided an outlet for some of the people who were dissatisfied with the policies of the French Communist party.

The Left was incapable not only of stopping the Algerian war, but also of opposing the rise of "fascism." When the Algerian settlers and officers revolted in May 1958, the Left could not arouse mass resistance against the threat of coup d'état and had to accept a new regime under de Gaulle. The French people abandoned major political decisions to de Gaulle, enfeebling French political life and rendering it even more futile. Political discussion of the Algerian problem resembled an *explication de texte*: the exegesis of the purposely ambiguous statements of France's uncrowned monarch. The army and the settlers continued to threaten the freedom that remained in the Fifth Republic, and the Left continued to be disunited and inactive.

Jeanson aimed by his radical action to revitalize the democratic forces in France. He condemned the timidity of what Marcel Péju, one of the editors of *Les Temps Modernes*, labeled "the respectful Left":

They wrote articles, they put up posters, they gave speeches, they addressed themselves to Public Opinion. By misfortune, this public opinion was not spontaneously anticolonialist; it did not spontaneously demand that France negotiate with its various rebels; and the mere idea of according them independence took opinion a little unawares. It was necessary therefore to WAIT. To wait until opinion was ripe, and while waiting to say nothing to it that might risk offending it. They spoke to it very much therefore, and did not cease speaking to it, but with carefully chosen words and infinite precautions.

The Left, therefore, had "confused political action and the opinion poll." Jeanson argued that, since the masses never moved themselves spontaneously, "the art of adhering to the masses by following their inclinations" resulted only in political immobility. The role of the Left should be instead to shape public opinion and to mobilize democratic elements in France.[24]

Jeanson insisted that words alone were incapable of reviving democratic forces. He had contributed to the flood of rhetoric on the issues of the Algerian war and had concluded: "In a period in which political engagement dissolves into words, words are powerless to combat inaction; the reaffirmation of theories does not make an advance of a single step toward their application in practice. Only action can engender action, by showing here and there *the proof of its own possibility.*" Jeanson claimed that he and his colleagues were offering the French a new, morally justified form of action. He insisted that only such avant-garde action could arouse the Left. No doubt he was inspired by the FLN, which, by taking the risk of radical action, had succeeded in mobilizing the Algerian people.[25]

The other leftist intellectuals did not dispute the need for greater activism, but they questioned the value of the particular forms of action the extremists were proposing. The program practiced and advocated by Jeanson and Jeune Résistance was not solely, as some youths envisaged, the instigation of a massive refusal of French youth to fight in the colonialist war. For both it was the creation of a "new Resistance" against fascism. This task involved building an illegal, clandestine movement. For some of the *résistants*, it also involved collaborating with the FLN. The issue of debate was whether these avant-garde actions were appropriate to the French political context.

THE LOGIC OF THE UNDERGROUND

The leftist intellectuals agreed that, although de Gaulle was authoritarian, he was monarchical rather than fascist and that he would like to end the war. They concluded that the Algerian fascists would not remain satisfied with the regime they had helped to install in Paris and eventually would try to overthrow de Gaulle. They disagreed, however, on the attitude the Left should, in consequence, adopt in regard to the Gaullist regime. Out of the multitude of individual opinions, differing mostly in emphasis, three general positions emerged.

Mauriac, Duverger, *Le Monde*, and *La Nef* supported de Gaulle, although in different degrees and not without reservations. They argued that de Gaulle was trying to end the war as fast as possible, that he intended to reassert civilian control over the army, and that he was the only political personality who could achieve both of these goals. They insisted that, because of the impotence of the Left, he was the sole bulwark of French liberties against the fascist threat. Consequently, they contended that the leftists should support de Gaulle, or at least that a leftist opposition party should be formed to work within the political system he had created.

Their confidence in de Gaulle was shaken by the continuation of the war, by repeated cases of repression in France, and above all by the collaboration of part of the Gaullist administration with the OAS. Even Mauriac, who was inclined to see de Gaulle as the divine savior of France, was nearly driven to despair by events. Yet he kept his faith in de Gaulle: "I hold tightly to an end of the thread that is my admiration for de Gaulle, and the confidence in him that I retain, and the certitude that he is France's good fortune, that he is drawing near to the end, that he is going to win finally, and we with him."[26]

A second group, including Servan-Schreiber and Bourdet, were openly hostile to de Gaulle. They insisted that the real power in the Gaullist regime lay with the army of Algeria, argued that de Gaulle was a necessary tool of the army because he alone was able to rally France to the war, and suggested that he in turn might be content to let the war continue because it made his monarchical power indispensable to France. If he did try to end the war, he would be unable to dominate the army. His reign, they asserted, masked the real struggle, which was between military fascism and democracy, and aided the fascist cause by paralyzing the republican reactions of the French people. Servan-Schreiber and Bourdet declared that the Left must mobilize and organize popular forces to compel de Gaulle to end the war and to prepare for the subsequent trial of strength with Algerian fascism. The appearance of the OAS in 1961 seemed to confirm fears that such a confrontation was inevitable.[27]

The dispute over de Gaulle became so intense at *L'Express* that Mauriac left the paper in early 1961 and took his "Bloc-Notes" to the weekly *Le Figaro-Littéraire*. Both camps did agree, however, that the first step in combating fascism was to end the war, which could not be won and was spawning fascists, and that de Gaulle was the only one able to end it, since he governed France. When de Gaulle did conclude the war in 1962 and when the OAS threat eventually subsided, Mauriac was contented, and Servan-Schreiber and Bourdet (and Domenach, Duverger, and *Le Monde* as well) turned to the remaining task of reforming or combating the Gaullist regime itself.

Jeanson, the new Resistance as a whole, and to a certain extent *Les Temps Modernes*, formed still a third camp. They agreed with the more moderate leftists that the tendency of some members of the new Resistance to equate the Gaullist regime with that of the Nazis was abusive and unjustified. Nonetheless, on the basis of a more purely Marxist analysis, they disagreed with the others' separation in practice of the struggles against Algerian fascism and against Gaullism.

The proponents of resistance argued that the Gaullist regime, although not itself fascist, was "objectively placed" in a situation that made it favor the spread of fascism. Jeanson's group believed that de Gaulle was serving the interests of French high finance and big business rather than those of the army. They thought initially that he would try to end the war quickly, sacrificing the French Algerians for the benefit of French capitalism. As the war continued, however, de Gaulle appeared unable to end it. Jeanson and his colleagues began to contend that the capitalist forces behind de Gaulle were unwilling to agree to independence, in spite of the damage done by the war to France's economy, because the FLN was espousing socialism. "The Algerian struggle for independence is more and more openly linked to a revolution. To want peace is to want to support this revolution. The Gaullist regime, a circumstantial form of the capitalist regime, can *by its very nature* only oppose it."[28]

The Gaullist regime, accordingly, was seen as the "antechamber" to fascism. By perpetuating the war, it was increasing the chances that the military chiefs would take over Algeria once again and extend their rule of terror to France. Moreover, it was undergoing a rapid internal evolution toward fascism, as the administration's complicity with the OAS was to demonstrate. De Gaulle was not a bulwark against fascism; he was the instrument of French capitalism, which, to attain its objectives of defeating the FLN while also stifling the French Left, would be forced to resort, in alliance with the army, to a fascism that it had not wanted in France. The Gaullist regime would not find fascism imposed on it from outside by the extremists in Algeria, but would choose to adopt it. To support the Gaullist regime or even to respect its legality, therefore, was senseless and self-destructive, as its legality was founded on blackmail and mystification and was being used as a cover for the destruction of French liberties.

The extremists urged the Left to begin immediately, before it was too late, to oppose the Gaullist regime and to prepare for the near future when combat against fascism in France would have to be generalized. They declared after the short-lived uprising at the end of January 1960 of Europeans in Algiers: "The criminal pursuit of the colonial war in Algeria has brought FASCISM and civil war to our doors. The decisive test of force has begun; it can end only by the installation of military dictatorship or by the total victory of democracy. The hour of a new resistance has struck. All can still be saved if we know how to mobilize the people."[29] The new Resistance, therefore, was oriented toward the future: it saw an impending fascist transformation as the essence of the Gaullist regime and a future civil war as its own raison d'être.

Critics challenged both the analysis of the situation and the choice of methods of combat. They argued that the present order was neither fascist nor necessarily evolving toward fascism. Even Bourdet, a leader and hero of the Resistance against the Nazis, declared that clandestine action was not in this case an effective means of opposing fascism; it was instead a romantic and illusory adventure.

Jeanson and Sartre replied that precisely such a complacency made the French vulnerable to fascism; the dream of de Gaulle the protector was enervating the masses, reducing their ability to oppose a military coup d'état. They were not suggesting that the whole Left abandon legal efforts, but that it finally undertake them with vigor. Paralleling the reasoning of Sorel, the philosopher of the myth of the general strike, Jeanson argued that the only way the Left could regain this vigor was to prepare itself for civil war. If the Left—and the French people as a whole—subsequently could force an end to the war in Algeria, prevent the transformation of Gaullism into fascism, and even perhaps avoid a civil war, these achievements all would be due to the revitalization provoked by the illegal acts of the Resistance. If, however, the fascist forces did strike, the battle against them would be greatly facilitated by the advance preparation of a clandestine organization.[30]

Jeanson, many in the new Resistance, and eventually *Les Temps Modernes* disagreed with the other leftists for another reason: a different assessment of priorities. Simon, Servan-Schreiber, Domenach, Bourdet, and even the Communists seemed to be concerned above all with ending the war and fighting fascism; they would force de Gaulle to be an ally in this fight and afterward turn to the task of transforming the Gaullist regime. Jeanson and his colleagues asserted that the fundamental aim of the Left was still to institute socialism. The real foe, therefore, was not colonialism or fascism or the Gaullist regime; it was capitalism, or, more precisely, the "neocapitalism" of modern big business. The particular form of government utilized by the French capitalists—whether fascist or Gaullist—was of secondary importance; the crucial fact was that they had taken control of the state apparatus. The postponement of the struggle against French capitalism would only make its reign more difficult to overturn.

This was a critical moment, Jeanson and Sartre asserted, in the struggle for social democracy in France. If the army was permitted to continue to occupy Algeria, it would be increasingly tempted to strike at France. If, on the other hand, the Left allowed de Gaulle to make peace and give independence to Algeria—and Jeanson and Sartre admitted that it was possible, if not probable, that he could both do this and master the fascist reaction—this outcome too would be a disaster. With de Gaulle celebrated as the bringer of peace and defender of democracy, his regime—the rule of "neocapitalism" with de Gaulle, its instrument, as temporary monarch—would be strengthened. By allowing de Gaulle to make peace, the Left would acquiesce in its own impotence and further its disintegration, as well as help to spread the mystification of Gaullist liberalism. The Left would emerge from the war even more disunited, impotent, discouraged, and discredited than it was already. Only a peace imposed by the Left would be positive.

The current crisis, however, offered an opportunity for the socialist forces to revitalize themselves. By organizing to fight for peace and against fascism, they also would be organizing to fight for socialism. The ultimate aim of the new Resistance was to arouse "revolutionary consciousnesses"—to prepare for a socialist revolution in France. The war in Algeria offered the revolutionaries an opportunity that might not recur and must be exploited by avant-garde action.[31]

In 1947, in an editorial written by Merleau-Ponty, *Les Temps*

Modernes had defended the prudence of Ho Chi Minh against the Trotskyist sociologist Lefort, who had criticized the compromising of the revolution in the accords with France of March 1946.[32] In 1960, however, the question was not whether to curb a revolution but how to incite one. *Les Temps Modernes* now argued that the only chance of starting a revolution in France was to seize upon and exploit potentialities that would not develop by themselves. The inapplicability in France of Marxism's deterministic prophecies and the inspiration of Jeanson had turned Sartre toward an activist theory of revolution that was, in addition, compatible with the existentialist base he gave to Marxism. *Les Temps Modernes* supported Jeanson, while, paradoxically, Lefort as well as Merleau-Ponty, who had broken with Sartre and rejected the Marxist revolutionary vision in the early 1950s, did not.

ALLIANCE WITH THE FLN

Jeanson and his colleagues differed from Jeune Résistance in their conviction that the French Left should form a practical alliance with the FLN. The leftist press condemned this proposal even more vigorously than the call for a new Resistance; once again only *Les Temps Modernes* supported Jeanson. Jeanson contended that aid to the FLN, even more than refusal to serve in the army and clandestine organization against fascism, was the "shock therapy" necessary to awaken the Left. He claimed that his group was putting into practice the very solidarity with the colonial liberation movements about which the Left so often talked. In the case of the Algerian revolution, this solidarity could be seen on two levels.

Those who aided the FLN pointed out that the French Left and the FLN were already allies because they had the same enemy. The army and the settlers who were fighting the FLN were the same forces that had installed an authoritarian regime in France and were threatening to establish a fascist one. France's political future depended in part on the result of the FLN's struggle. More generally, the capitalist system that exploited the French proletariat was, in the form of colonialism, exploiting the Algerian people as well. The defeat of capitalism abroad would weaken it at home. Jeanson and his comrades criticized the other leftists for taking too nationalist a view of political action and reminded the Communists that Lenin too had stressed the solidarity of the colonial peoples and the European workers in the struggle against capitalist imperialism.[33]

Jeanson and his supporters argued further that the FLN had not only the same enemy, but also the same aims as the French Left. Both were struggling for liberty and for social justice. The French Left, with its inveterate paternalism, doubted for a long time that the Algerian revolt was socially progressive. Jeanson, however, had written in L'Algérie hors la loi (1955) that the logic of the rebellion would carry it to socialist as well as nationalist objectives. He had explained that the movement was not controlled by traditional authorities, who had been compromised by cooperation with the French, nor by a strong indigenous bourgeoisie; it was a popular movement, and as such necessarily would express the social as well as political aspirations of the Algerian people. He added in Notre Guerre in 1960 that the gravity of its economic problems would force independent Algeria to adopt socialism. Sartre and Maschino contended that some of the leaders of the FLN already were aiming beyond nationalism to socialism. Péju suggested that, by an alliance with the rebels, French socialists would facilitate this shift to a socialist orientation.[34]

The less extreme leftist intellectuals were willing to agree that the French democrats and the FLN were partial allies, but argued that active collaboration with the FLN would be politically very unwise for the Left. Bourdet pointed out that an analogy with the Resistance against the Nazis was invalid. In its support of the Allies the Resistance had expressed the profound will of the French people, while precisely the opposite was true in the case of the groups that aided the FLN; the nationalist sentiment that had motivated the Resistance against the Nazis was aroused in opposition to collaboration with the FLN. Bourdet had distinguished in 1950 between the political strikes of the Communists, which he supported because he believed they would rally antiwar opinion, and acts of sabotage, which would only offend the French public. He made the same type of distinction in 1960. Like Domenach, Servan-Schreiber, Simon, and the Communists, he argued that the French people disapproved so strongly of desertion and aid to the enemy that the association of these extreme acts with the antiwar and antifascist movement would discredit the movement and isolate it from the mass of the French nation. Domenach and Simon warned that the spread of radicalism actually would increase the chances of success of a military coup d'état since the nation would choose the army activists rather than the disciples of Sartre. Most of the intellectuals, therefore, insisted that the alliance with the FLN should remain merely an "objective" one.[35]

Jeanson replied that support of the FLN would be legitimized a posteriori. The French people eventually would seek to make peace with the Algerian people. If battle with the fascists in France became necessary, the solidarity of the FLN and the French Left would become very real and practical. The bonds formed by those who were aiding the FLN would enable the French Left to rely on the strength of the FLN in the struggle against fascism and for socialism in France. Furthermore, the will of the French people might evolve; Jeanson reminded Bourdet that few Frenchmen had decided to fight against the Nazis when he had begun his Resistance career.[36]

Jeanson was aware that the spread of his movement would incite the fascists. Indeed, the new Resistance must have been tempted to do so deliberately. The movement was meaningful only in terms of a future battle against fascism, and such a battle may have appeared to be the quickest way to a socialist revolution. Nonetheless, Jeanson later insisted that he did not want to provoke the fascists to action because he was hostile on principle to a *politique du pire* and because the French people were insufficiently prepared to resist them. At the same time he believed that, as the Munich pact had shown, nothing was to be gained from avoiding a confrontation with the adversary. The risk of inciting the army and the settlers had to be taken in order to revitalize the Left.[37]

Jeanson and his supporters suggested that the Left would gain from an alliance with the FLN not only material support but also inspiration. By joining with a people fighting for its liberation, the French Left would recover more fully its sense of action.[38] Behind this suggestion was a new vision, expounded in *Les Temps Modernes*, of the important historical role of the revolutionaries of the Third World.

In 1948, Sartre had described the poetry of France's black writers as "the sole great revolutionary poetry" in the contemporary world. He had predicted that the blacks eventually would shed their subjective racial identities and take up their objective identities as a revolutionary proletariat. But this view of the oppressed people of the Third World as the vanguard of world revolution remained germinal until the late 1950s. The Algerian revolution demonstrated both the dynamism of the overseas peoples and the immobility of the French proletariat. In spring 1960, Sartre and de Beauvoir traveled to Castro's Cuba, and at the same time the Chinese began their attack on Soviet moderation. Sartre and his colleagues were ready to abandon the traditional Marxist view that the important acts of revolution would be done by the proletariat and in the developed countries.

In October 1960, Péju charged in *Les Temps Modernes* that Western socialists had neglected the Third World and egotistically had wanted "to construct a luxury socialism on the fruits of imperial rapine"; as a result, they had lost their way, and the revolutionary actors in history were no longer the Western proletarians, but the combatants of the Third World. Traditional Marxists, however, such as the French Communists, continued to believe that the political and social consciousness of the peasantry could not be trusted. In response, Fanon argued in *Les Damnés de la terre* (1961) that in the Third World the revolutionary will of the rural masses was more fervent and less corruptible than that of the indigenous proletariat, for they experienced more acutely the exploitation and oppression that resulted from capitalism. Sartre, in his preface to Fanon's book, echoed Fanon's glorification of Third World peasant revolution. Like Hegel's slave and Marx's proletarian, the colonial rebel, as envisaged by Fanon and Sartre, emerged from his enslavement as a superior being. With masochistic relish, Sartre declared that Europe was in its death throes and that the peasantry of the Third World had become the subjects of history. Yet the Algerian war offered to the French Left the opportunity to join with Third World rebels and thereby, in Péju's words, "to make contact again with the evolution of the world."[39]

Sartre, Jeanson, and their comrades were severely attacked for their vision of the Third World. Their critics charged that, by transferring the nineteenth-century Marxist scheme of proletarian revolution from Europe (where it had not applied) to the world situation in general, they were distorting and romanticizing reality: "In the ascetic universe of the intellectual of the far Left, a mythical Third World replaced the myth of the proletariat." In suggesting that "socialism" was the common destiny of France and Algeria, they were attaching too little importance to the current realities of the Algerian revolution —the importance of Islam, for example—and were inclined to believe that only the faction of the FLN that wanted to construct a Marxist socialism was the valid expression of the Algerian people. The critics charged, in summary, that the neo-Leninist intellectuals had missed the opportunity provided by decolonization to revise a vision of the world based exclusively on Western and outdated models.[40]

The critics were correct that the French ideologues of Third World revolution undervalued the diversity of the world, that their revolutionary vision was ethnocentric and tended toward monism. Sartre, for example, declared, in the spirit of Hegel and Marx: "Our historical task, at the heart of this polyvalent world, is to bring closer the moment when History will have *only one meaning*, when it will tend to be dissolved in the concrete men who will make it in common." Because of the exportation of Marxist ideology and the general Westernization of the world, Sartre and the others could reply to their critics that their vision of the Third World was becoming increasingly widespread and applicable and ultimately would be validated. It was difficult to disprove Sartre's conception of history as a "totalization in process." But even if the world were tending toward unity, it still could be doubted that Marxist categories provided the key to understanding this process.[41]

THE IMPACT OF THE NEW RESISTANCE

Jeanson had hoped to awaken the Left and the French people, but he was hampered by the difficulty of reaching a wide audience while remaining underground. Beginning in September 1958 he put out a small newspaper, *Vérités Pour*, with a limited circulation of about five thousand copies. Its main function was to unify the various clandestine groups that were helping draft resisters and aiding the FLN.

The French government solved Jeanson's publicity problem when it arrested members of his ring in February 1960. The score of arrests, which did not include Jeanson himself, did not disrupt the movement's activities and aided greatly in recruitment of new members. The question of radical action was thenceforth a much-debated topic in the antiwar press, even if only *Les Temps Modernes* supported Jeanson. In April the government was unable to prevent Jeanson from holding a clandestine press conference in Paris, which was reported in the popular daily newspaper *Paris-Presse*, and it gave further publicity to the "new Resistance" by seizing articles in *L'Express* and *France-Observateur* on the inaccurate charge of inciting to desertion.[42]

In early September the trial of the Jeanson ring opened. The day before the trial started the literary critics Maurice Blanchot and Maurice Nadeau began to circulate a "Declaration of the Right of Draft Evasion in the Algerian War." Signed originally by 121 intellectuals, it was more commonly known as the "Manifesto of the 121." They asserted:

—We respect and deem justified the refusal to take arms against the Algerian people.

—We respect and deem justified the conduct of the French who consider it their duty to bring aid and protection to the Algerians oppressed in the name of the French people.

—The cause of the Algerian people, which contributes in a decisive fashion to ruin the colonial system, is the cause of all free men.[43]

Among the original signers of the declaration were the staff of *Les Temps Modernes*, led by Sartre, Péju, and de Beauvoir; the anticolonialist militant Guérin; the surrealist poets Leiris and André Breton; the novelists Marguerite Duras, Alain Robbe-Grillet, Florence Malraux (the daughter of André Malraux), Christiane Rochefort, Claude Roy, Nathalie Sarraute, Claude Simon, and Vercors; the composer Pierre Boulez; the film director Alain Resnais and the actress Simone Signoret; the Marxist philosopher Henri Lefebvre; the psychologist Maud Mannoni; the publishers Jérôme Lindon (of Éditions de Minuit) and François Maspero; and the political cartoonist Siné.

One hundred twenty-four other intellectuals added their signatures later. These included the novelists Michel Butor, Clara Malraux (the former wife of André Malraux), and Françoise Sagan; the poet Tristan Tzara; the film director François Truffaut; the agronomist René Dumont; the sociologist Maxime Rodinson; and the political cartoonist Tim.

The French government prevented widespread public diffusion of the text of the manifesto. One of the original signers, the Catholic journalist Barrat, was imprisoned for two weeks because the police found 170 copies in his office. But the government could not repress the news that a large number of intellectuals had supported refusal to serve in Algeria. Indeed, punishing or threatening to punish the signers gave notoriety to the manifesto. The professors Schwartz and Vidal-Naquet, for example, were suspended along with several other government employees who had signed. Signers were prohibited from appearing on radio and television and in state-subsidized theaters. The French Left was unified in its condemnation of these repressive measures.[44]

Most of the intellectuals who opposed the war in Algeria did not sign the Manifesto of the 121. Many signed instead a more moderate "Call to Opinion for a Negotiated Peace in Algeria." This latter manifesto insisted on a "real self-determination," but it avoided the crucial issues: it did not call specifically for independence and did not suggest how important a role the FLN should play in the negotiations and in postwar Algeria. It did not support refusal to serve in the war, but argued instead that the crisis of conscience and spirit of revolt of the French youth was a new and urgent reason to end the war. The signers included Domenach; Pierre Gaudez, the president of the Union Nationale des Étudiants de France (UNEF); the literary critics Roland Barthes and René Etiemble; the philosophers Merleau-Ponty and Ricoeur; the sociologists Lefort, Edgar Morin, and Georges Gurvitch; the geographer Jean Dresch and the historian Ernest Labrousse; the poet Prévert and the writer Colette Audry; and Mayer, the president of the Ligue des Droits de l'Homme.[45]

If Jeanson's actions did not provoke a rallying of leftist intellectuals around his ideas concerning the future of Algeria and the tactics of the French Left, they did at least force the more moderate intellectuals to evaluate their own previous efforts, which Bourdet, Domenach, and Servan-Schreiber admitted had been ineffective. They concluded that their refusal to follow Jeanson compelled them to find alternative modes of engagement for the antiwar movement that would be more effective than either the past protests or the new Resistance.[46] Jeanson, of course, had not rejected legal efforts, but only insisted that clandestine action was necessary to stimulate and accompany them.

Servan-Schreiber and Duverger offered the most moderate suggestion. Like the Communists and the Parti Socialiste Unifié (PSU, the small non-Communist party of the far Left, which Bourdet had helped to form), they argued that draftees should fight fascism from within the army. Servan-Schreiber proposed that the Left undertake a campaign to encourage soldiers to disobey illegal orders. This belief in the democratic conscripts was partly justified in April 1961, as Servan-Schreiber and the Communists declared, when many of them refused to participate in the attempted coup d'état by the four generals.[47]

Bourdet and Domenach called for radical, but nonviolent, acts of civil disobedience in protest against the war and its crimes. Bourdet reminded his readers of the victories of nonviolent "direct action" in India and the Gold Coast (Ghana). Such acts of civil disobedience spread during the late spring. For example, to protest against internment camps for Algerians in France, a group of demonstrators, including Bourdet, Ricoeur, Massignon, and Stibbe, sat down in front of the Ministry of Interior in Paris, refused to move, and had to be taken away by the police. But these acts never became numerous enough to have much impact.[48]

In October 1960, however, Bourdet was encouraged when several thousand people demonstrated in the Paris streets after a meeting against the war. In spite of government obstruction of the meeting and police repression of the demonstration, in spite of the refusal of the Communists to participate, the Left had successfully taken to the streets to oppose the war. Bourdet believed that a turning point had been reached and called for more street demonstrations. Yet not until autumn 1961 did the far Left, aroused by the OAS bombings and led by the PSU, demonstrate frequently in the streets of Paris.[49]

Meanwhile, a more dramatic awakening had occurred among the university students. The major student union, the UNEF, had been torn apart by the war. The branch of Moslem Algerian students, supported by other groups of overseas students, withdrew in January 1957 because the UNEF would not condemn the repression of the rebellion. A few months later, the most conservative student groups left the union for a year because the left-wing majority in the UNEF was considering a call for negotiations. The issue of Algeria was so divisive that the UNEF chose not to take a stand.

Gradually the student mood changed. At its annual congress in April 1959 the UNEF authorized its administrative board to prepare a study of the war and its effects on the students. In August the minister of the army issued a decree restricting the granting and renewal of draft deferments for students, but after UNEF protests culminating in student strikes on 15 and 16 March 1960, the decree was revised. At its congress in April 1960 the union broke its silence, denounced the war, and called for negotiations with the FLN, which at the time de Gaulle still was trying to avoid. The directors of the UNEF daringly joined with the outlawed Algerian student union in June in a common appeal for negotiations, though they also spoke out against direct aid to the FLN. The government responded immediately by suspending its subsidy to the UNEF and later by trying to end the draft deferment of the UNEF vice-president, who had met with the Algerian student leaders. But Gaudez, the president of the UNEF, took the initiative in organizing the October demonstration. The leftist intellectuals were greatly excited by the new activism of the youth.[50]

The radicalization of antiwar protest in 1960 was in part the consequence of the continuation of the war even after de Gaulle's promise of Algerian self-determination. The youths who were liable for military service knew that their sacrifice on the battlefield would have little meaning. They and the intellectuals were dismayed by the failure in June of the first official talks with the FLN. In addition, the revolt of the extremist settlers in Algiers in January had underlined the threat of Algerian fascism.

Nonetheless, Jeanson, Jeune Résistance, and the Manifesto of the 121 contributed to this radicalization. In 1960 the number of youths who refused to serve increased markedly, even if not on a scale to hurt the military effort, and Jeune Résistance was responsible for showing them the way. The number who aided the FLN was never large—a few hundred activists drawn from all segments of the Left—but the arrest of Jeanson's colleagues pushed Sartre and *Les Temps Modernes* to declare publicly their support of his action and helped to awaken the rest of the Left. Jeanson, Sartre, and Péju provided an outlet for action to many Frenchmen on the far Left who were discouraged by the immobility of the Communists and the ineffectiveness of legal protest. They provided reasons not only to support but to work for Algerian independence and the victory of the FLN.

Yet the extremists probably did little to end the war. The general public was not likely to be swayed by them. The unrest among the youth did not become dangerous to the war effort; indeed, in contrast to the French student riots of 1968 or the protests of American students against the American war in Vietnam, the lack of student activity against the Algerian war is striking. Nor did the Left become a powerful force. De Gaulle, who was solely responsible for French policy on Algeria, doubtless was much less impressed by protest at home than by the perseverance of the FLN and by the dramatic Moslem demonstrations in December 1960 in favor of the FLN.[51] The opening in May 1961 of serious negotiations with the FLN defused the militant antiwar movement.

In the following months, however, the OAS bombed the offices and homes of left-wing opponents of the war and threatened to overthrow the Fifth Republic by internal subversion and violence. The leftist intellectuals founded a Ligue pour le Rassemblement Antifasciste and participated in numerous demonstrations against the OAS. The culmination was a march through Paris of a half million people on 13 February 1962 for the funeral of eight Communist demonstrators allegedly killed by the police. It was the largest leftist demonstration in a generation. But the momentum could not be maintained. The Communists refused to make the fight against the OAS the basis for a united and active Left. The peace treaty was signed on 19 March 1962. France's minor civil war soon subsided. Before the Left had been revitalized, de Gaulle, as Sartre had feared, had been able to agree to Algerian independence under FLN control and to quell the army and the OAS terrorists. France emerged from the war not at all ripe for a socialist revolution.[52]

The group of Frenchmen whose reasoning was closest to that of Jeanson, Sartre, and their supporters was, paradoxically, not the other leftists but their most bitter enemies, the diehard advocates of *Algérie française*. These extremists, who revolted against the Parisian governments and ultimately, in many cases, joined the OAS, included numerous military officers and politicians like Soustelle and Bidault. They declared, like their French and FLN opponents, that the colonial regime in Algeria had to be abolished and Algerian society revolutionized, but under the direction of the French army, not of the FLN. They believed that in Algeria the French army was fighting a Marxist revolution that, unless stopped, might engulf France and the rest of Europe, but they were intent on defeating, not promoting, it. They agreed that the decadent bourgeois order in France had to be replaced, but by a regime of nationalist revival. They agreed that the future of France was at stake in the war in Algeria and that the war offered them a revolutionary opportunity that ought to be exploited. They carried their revolutionary efforts much further than did the leftist extremists, but, beyond the establishment of the Fifth Republic, they had no more success.[53]

Between these two revolutionary minorities was the vast majority of the French people, who were happy to see the return of peace after fifteen years of futile colonial warfare.

7 &THE TRIUMPH OF REALISM

The moralists were unable to offer France's leaders and public a clear and convincing set of arguments in support of any particular policy. Many anticolonialist intellectuals approached the problems of decolonization from a "realist" perspective in addition to or instead of a moralist one. Realizing that the French were more concerned with their own interests than with those of the colonial peoples, they examined not only the justice of France's overseas policy but also its effectiveness in furthering French interests. They argued that a more liberal overseas policy would be beneficial to France.

THE INEFFECTIVENESS OF FRENCH POLICY

France's military efforts in Indochina, however debatable their moral foundation, clearly were unsuccessful in ending the war. It is not surprising, therefore, that the intellectuals who opposed the war chose to stress realist rather than moralist objections. They argued that the means used by the French authorities were not the ones that would lead to the declared goals of restoring peace and keeping the Indochinese states in the French Union. This was the message of, for example, a manifesto of intellectuals that was published in January 1949 in *Les Temps Modernes* and *Esprit*. Its signers included a number of the more active anticolonialists—Bourdet, Sartre, de Beauvoir, Merleau-Ponty, Rous, Bernard, Rivet, Philip, Julien, Domenach, Mounier, Massignon, Martin-Chauffier—as well as such other luminaries as Breton, Jean Cocteau, Vercors, Jean-Louis Barrault, and Henri Matisse.

The loudest and most persistent critic of the stupidity of French policy in Indochina was Bourdet. Although he has been described as initially a left-wing Catholic and a disciple of Maritain and Mounier, he tried to avoid moralistic arguments. Educated as an engineer before the war, he demanded that France be "scientific" in its overseas policy —that it set realistic goals and use effective means. The antifascist oratory of the thirties that had been followed by France's abdication to Hitler and the Resistance dreams that had been betrayed after the Liberation had convinced Bourdet that idealistic talk was ineffective because people acted for selfish reasons: "We know now that people do not react that way, that it is useless appealing to their better feelings, because they have no better feelings, because all that is loose and empty words. We know that maybe you can have some action by appealing to their worst feelings, to their selfishness, to their hope of a better life, to their feelings that they are being gypped by their leaders, and so on. Then maybe you can get something."[1]

Bourdet insisted, as soon as hostilities began and throughout the war, that France had no chance of defeating the Vietminh either militarily or politically. He argued in his editorials in *Octobre*, *Combat*, and *L'Observateur* that the facts of the war showed that the French army was incapable of crushing a nationalist movement supported by the mass of the people. The war was even more hopeless, he maintained, after the victory of the Communists in China in 1949, for the Vietminh could receive unlimited aid from their Chinese neighbors. He contended subsequently that even American aid did not increase France's chances and warned that the actual intervention of American forces would turn the conflict into a world war. This somber appraisal of France's military chances was echoed by other intellectuals. Duverger added that French plans for "vietnamization" of the war were futile since the recent history of China and Korea had shown what became of "these national armies under the orders of feeble and corrupt regimes, supported by the West."[2]

Meanwhile, France was attempting to create a moderate government around Bao Dai. As late as July 1950, the majority of Frenchmen of all political tendencies except the Communists thought that Bao Dai would triumph over Ho Chi Minh. The antiwar intellectuals, however, argued that, since the Vietnamese people wanted independence, this maneuver had no chance of succeeding until the French conceded to Bao Dai the independence they had refused to grant to Ho Chi Minh. Bourdet added that, even if France conceded independence to Bao Dai, and even after it finally did in 1953, Bao Dai had no chance of rallying popular support. As long as the Vietminh were fighting, he would be unable to forego the protection of foreign troops. He also would be unable to make popular agrarian reforms because this action would contradict his base of power among the landowners. Moreover, the prestige and popularity of Ho Chi Minh were immense. Bourdet doubted that the Vietnamese people would betray the leader whose armed struggle alone made possible the concessions that Bao Dai was winning from the French.[3]

France thus appeared to be fighting a war it could not win in order to install a leader who could not rally popular support. Such a policy, the critics asserted, was completely wrong from the point of view of French interests. The declaration of intellectuals charged that the war was "an apple of discord among Frenchmen" and "a veritable ferment of hate and dissociation for the French Union." Duverger noted that the war was taking away troops needed to defend France and Europe against the Soviets and thereby was reducing French weight within the Atlantic alliance. Beuve-Méry pointed out, as did the declaration and Bourdet, that the war was destroying France's army, ruining its finances, and increasing its dependence on American financial and diplomatic support. By August 1953 four-fifths of the French people agreed that stopping the war in Indochina would help solve France's most important problem, its living standard.[4]

At the same time, Bourdet and others argued, the French were undermining the respect, trust, and friendship on which their future presence in Indochina must be based. Their pursuit of the war was pushing Ho Chi Minh into the arms of China; their hesitation on independence was turning their Indochinese allies toward the Americans, whose increasing involvement in the war was solicited by the French governments. The only way for France to save any of its influence in Vietnam, the critics concluded, was to negotiate with Ho Chi Minh and, Bourdet added, to accept a Vietnam controlled by the Vietminh.[5]

By the early 1950s the French governments were trying to justify the war in the context not only of the French Union but also of the struggle of the Free World against communism. In support of this position, Aron asserted in *Le Figaro* that, although France was incapable of winning the war alone, a common effort of the Western powers was preferable, in spite of the danger of Chinese intervention, to a victory by Ho Chi Minh. Regardless of France's past errors, he wrote,

France currently was defending "a position of vital importance." The victory of Ho Chi Minh would mean the subsequent "Sovietization" of all Indochina, Siam, and Burma.[6]

Duverger, in contrast, argued that the war in Indochina was unrealistic even in terms of a common effort of the West against communism. The greatest danger to the Free World, he asserted, was still in Europe, not in the Far East. The Far East should be defended by those with important interests there and with an aptitude for it, presumably by the Asians themselves. The French should instead man the European lines of defense of the Free World. Furthermore, Indochina was not a key region in the anti-Communist struggle in Asia. The victory of the Soviets in Hanoi and Saigon hardly would affect the world balance of forces, either materially or morally. Rather than dispersing democratic forces in Asia and fixing them on "a theater of operations of local and limited interest," the Free World should concentrate on reinforcing India and Japan.

Duverger contended, finally, that even within the context of Indochina alone France was trying to combat communism in an unrealistic fashion. France was committing the general error made by the West in Asia in thinking that military intervention was capable of stopping the expansion of communism. The Communists promised social reforms, but all that the West offered to the peoples of the Far East was "the maintenance of the ancient feudal powers under the appearance of a parliamentary regime in the European mode." The creation of such a parliament could not possibly compensate for the lack of social reforms because it did not correspond to the economic and social structure of Asia, nor to its mentality: "Our Western political system rests on the middle classes, on a bourgeois and liberal tradition, and on a people possessing on the whole a quite elevated material and intellectual level. Nothing like that exists over there." The only way to combat Communist nationalism in Asia was to oppose to it "another nationalism, more authentic than it and just as progressive." But in Vietnam, Duverger concluded, such a nationalism did not exist and could never be elicited by white troops. By early 1954, Aron, too, had decided that, if communism was to be contained in Asia, it would be contained "not by the armies of the West, but by the peoples of Asia."[7]

The ineffectiveness of a policy of force was demonstrated further by the events in Tunisia and Morocco in the early 1950s. French repression caused widespread bloodshed and bitterness but did not prevent both countries from gaining total independence in 1956. India, Pakistan, Ceylon, Burma, Indonesia, Libya, and Sudan had become independent; Ghana and Malaysia were approaching independence; and the Bandung conference of Asian and African nations in April 1955 had denounced the remaining colonial dominations. By the mid-fifties it was clear that the French were trying to oppose a major historical force. French policy was unrealistic in relation not only to the particular situations overseas, but to the general evolution of the world. The ideology of national liberation was sweeping Asia and Africa.

Some of the intellectuals had understood this evolution early, but their warnings had been in vain.[8] In the mid-fifties a number of realists argued that experience had proved that to try to prevent decolonization was futile and self-defeating. By accepting the inevitable, Aron claimed, France might have mastered the events and lessened the perils. When all could not be saved, the only way to save something was "to give in time, with generosity." Duverger argued that, since the movement that pushed Africa and Asia toward nationalism was "too powerful for us to dam it up," the "only realistic policy" was "to channel it."[9]

The realists also cited the experiences of other times and countries. Bourdet pointed to Napoleon in Haiti and the Dutch recently in Indonesia; in both cases attempts at reconquest had led to complete eviction. Others pointed to Spain in South America; when Spain had refused political liberalization, the colonies had broken all ties and Spain had sunk into "an irremediable decadence."[10] In contrast, they looked with envy at the British, who had known how to give independence to India and Pakistan in 1947 in time to avoid a colonial war and to save their economic and cultural interests and who had taken Nkrumah out of prison in 1951 to make him the head of the government of the Gold Coast. Idealizing the behavior of the British, the French anticolonialists held up British realism as a model to the French to demonstrate that cooperation with the nationalists was in the interests of the home country.[11]

Nonetheless, the policy of force was applied to Algeria. Neither situational nor historical realism became a dominating force in French overseas policy until the Fifth Republic.

The French policymakers refused to follow the teachings of the realists. They continued to be willing to resort to force, in spite of its great cost to France and its apparent counterproductiveness, in an attempt to preserve France's sovereignty in the overseas lands. Factors such as the paralysis of the political system, the influence of special interests, ignorance of the facts, the inability of the humanist intellectuals to justify independence, and even the widespread belief in empire cannot account for this intransigence. Why was it so difficult to revise the policy of imperial preservation?

France's colonial traditions were one barrier to decolonization. The emphases on territorial aggrandizement, administrative centralization, and assimilation characterized French much more than British colonization and were obstacles to the liberal reforms that the colonial peoples demanded, the realists advocated, and the British were able to make.

These traditions help to account for the inability of the French to decolonize. It was easy to continue in the pattern set by predecessors; the French were very conscious of and had great respect for their past; policymakers used the past—or a particular interpretation of it—to validate current programs and acts. But the persisting strength and appeal of traditions cannot be fully explained by the mere fact that things were done this way in the past—not at least in a modern society that claimed to base the legitimacy of its social norms and political policies on rational as well as traditional grounds. In order to persist, traditions must be renewed by each generation. Since the colonial traditions never went uncontested by Frenchmen, by colonial subjects, or by foreigners, the French had to make a choice, even if unconsciously, to renew them. The French of the Fourth Republic had to reaffirm them in opposition to the general awakening of the colonial peoples, to the ill will of the Americans and Soviets, and even to their own admission, as seen in the vision of a "French Union," that the empire had to be liberalized.

The continuation, in spite of all, of the tendencies toward territorial possession, centralization, and assimilation can be understood better if placed in a broader context. They were expressions of general characteristics of French history.

The stress on territorial aggrandizement was inherited from two sources. The peasants, who formed the largest segment of the population well into the twentieth century, cultivated their land intensively and desired to acquire more land. In England, in contrast, a far greater proportion of the people worked in trade and industry. The wars of the Old Regime and the conquests of Napoleon had established the tradition that French national glory was a function of territorial sovereignty. The expedition to Algiers in 1830, the Mexican fiasco under Napoleon III, and the imperial conquests of the early Third Republic all were attempts to increase the glory of the regime and of France. In contrast, the primary aims of British colonization in the nineteenth century were material advantage and, in some cases, the suppression of the slave trade. The British idea that abandonment of sovereignty could be profitable was, in Aron's words, "foreign to the traditional way of thinking of the French." Instead, "the spirit of the jurist, of the peasant, of the Roman" survived: "You keep or else you lose."[12]

The efforts to unify the conquered territories and to rule them from Paris were part of a centralizing tendency that has characterized France since the Middle Ages. In all realms—political, administrative, economic, cultural—France became increasingly unified and hierarchically organized around Paris (or, before the Revolution, around Versailles-Paris). Postwar attempts at decentralization, including those within the empire, were not very successful.

The revival of Jacobism during the Resistance and the dominance of the political heirs of the Jacobins at the end of the war helped to limit decentralization in the structures of the French Union. Domenach admitted in 1949 that the leftists had not been sufficiently aware of the flaws in these structures: "It is difficult to change your categories: like the others, even if we were against the others, we have perhaps continued too much to 'think French'; that is, our Jacobin, Napoleonic, Hugoist, Resistance pride led us unconsciously back to the image of a centralizing, administrating France, dispenser of enlightenment and well-being." When, in response to the demands of the colonial elites, the empire did become increasingly decentralized by law during the Fourth and Fifth Republics, this change was resisted by French officials. As the French political scientist Alfred Grosser has explained, they as Frenchmen were "psychologically incapable of imagining and thus of respecting a decentralized system of decision-making."[13]

The insistence on centralization led logically to a colonial policy of assimilation as the only way to combine liberalism and centralism. The conquest of territory, the resistance to decentralization, and the efforts at assimilation were further legitimized by the widespread belief in France's humanist vocation in the world.

The French thus exhibited certain characteristics in their history that ran counter to the requirements of a smooth decolonization. To account for French peculiarities, most commentators have, like Aron and Grosser, referred in some way to a historically developed French "national character." Jean-Baptiste Duroselle, a specialist on French foreign policy, asserted, for example, that "the French national personality" was "more conservative, or in any case less adaptable to the bitter necessity" of decolonization than was the British. The colonial historian Hubert Deschamps contended that the French were Platonists and geometricians "by instinct": "We do not possess the commercial realism of the Englishman, his sense of adaptations, of partial progresses, of the balance of profits and losses. We are a nation of landowners and of jurists, avid for stable constructions, not always comfortable, but of a beautiful logical order. The idea of modifying them is considered for a long time to be sacrilegious; then suddenly the taste for sacrilege triumphs; they then are torn down to be replaced by others."[14] But the recourse to national character only transfers the question. Why were the French so legalistic and so "avid for stable constructions"? Why were they less "adaptable" than the British? Why were they "psychologically incapable" of decentralizing the system of making decisions in the empire? Why did the "way of thinking" of the territorially possessive peasant endure?

These questions point to answers in the realm of social psychology. French colonial history reveals a strong desire for order and stability that, although seemingly contradicted by much surface chaos (strikes and government instability, for example), has been reflected in and reinforced by various substructures of French life. The language has been carefully, even if unsuccessfully, protected from corruption, unregulated growth, and misuse. The child-rearing patterns and educational system have taught rigorous self-discipline. The public and private bureaucracies have operated according to sets of rigid and impersonal rules. Both economic policy makers and private citizens have insisted that a sound monetary system must have a tangible basis, gold.

This desire for order and stability has been, in part, a response to feelings of insecurity and inferiority. The French individual tends to learn, as he is growing up, to be suspicious of other people and to react by turning in on himself, by forming strong family ties, and by hiding behind bureaucratic regulations. Faced with the prospect of economic and social change, large groups of the population, especially before World War II, formed defensive groups and adopted "Malthusian" social strategies in order to protect their own positions and, more generally, to preserve what the political scientist Stanley Hoffmann has labeled "the stalemate society." Aware of their inferiority to foreigners, prewar French businessmen sought the protection of tariff barriers while the French military withdrew behind the Maginot line. The anxiety that Frenchmen experienced must have remained high during the postwar period of economic scarcity, political turmoil, social strife, and international tension. [15]

The French were sensitive also to France's status in the world. Its sinking fortunes—culminating in the catastrophe of humiliating defeat and debilitating occupation during World War II—increased their personal insecurity and denied them the compensation of national *grandeur*. They wanted to believe at the end of the war that France was still a great power, but were faced with the reality of impotence, in relation first to Nazi Germany and subsequently to the United States and the Soviet Union. As a result, France's postwar history was to a large extent "a battle against humiliation." Britain's decline, in contrast, was more recent and less evident; its record during the war was glorious. [16]

The empire had come to play an important, though largely symbolic, role in compensating the French for their multiple feelings of insecurity and inferiority. The colonies had been conquered in large part to offset France's crushing defeat by Prussia in 1870. The resulting empire had been presented for a half century as the nation's military, demographic, and economic hope. By the time a worn-out and internally divided France found itself reduced to a minor role in world affairs, the empire was widely seen as a vital source of power and prestige, a clear sign of national *grandeur*. The leaders of the Liberation agreed that greatness could not be restored without the empire. De Gaulle even declared: "For us, in a world such as it is and is going to be, to lose the French Union would be a decline that could cost us our independence. To keep it and to make it live is to stay great and, in consequence, to stay free." [17]

The empire was guarded all the more jealously because its value was not real and material, but symbolic and compensatory. Attitudes that externalize inner problems become, in general, increasingly rigid as the level of anxiety and the sense of threat increase.[18] Accordingly, the French reacted to threats of the dissolution of their empire by a more stubborn defense of it. They had been taught in school that, as in the case of Rome, loss of empire was a sign of historical decadence. Suspecting that this decadence was progressing rapidly, many Frenchmen passionately opposed any loss of territory. In a sense, they opposed the loss of the symbol so as not to acknowledge the loss of the reality of national power. The demands of the colonial peoples for independence, therefore, instead of provoking a more liberal attitude, added to the anxiety about national status. Without the confidence to base the French Union on the same sort of tenuous bonds that linked the members of the British Commonwealth, the French insisted on preserving actual sovereignty. They recalled that France had yielded at Munich rather than fight and had surrendered at Compiègne rather than exhaust all means of resistance. The loss of Indochina, Morocco, and Tunisia pushed them to greater efforts in defense of Algeria. In response to the series of humiliations suffered by France since 1940, many Frenchmen chose Algeria to be "the last line of resistance," a new Verdun.

Other Europeans reacted similarly when the disintegration of their empires threatened their senses of national greatness. The Dutch, after being forced out of Indonesia in 1949, struggled until 1962 to retain a land of little real value to them, West New Guinea. Even the British, declining in power and facing humiliation by Nasser, made a futile attempt in 1956 to regain control over the Suez. Yet only the Portuguese, whose self-image was much more completely bound up with their imperial tradition than was the French, devoted more energy than the French in trying to preserve their imperial outposts.[19]

A REALISM OF PRESERVATION

Most of the anticolonialist intellectuals both sympathized with and manifested the widespread desire to preserve the empire. Denying the frequent charge that they were proponents of "abandonment," they contended that reforms were the true means of safeguarding French presence, while attempts to conserve the status quo were losing everything. Even the most moralistic of the French intellectuals—Camus,

Mauriac, and Domenach, for example—tried to increase the appeal of the humanist policies they advocated by linking them with realism and French national interest. They argued that durable and useful bonds with the overseas peoples could be created only by a policy of justice.[20]

More specifically, it became increasingly clear to the anticolonialists that political as well as economic and social reforms were necessary to reestablish the confidence in France on which the French Union, or a looser association of states, must be built. The prominent left-centrist politician Mitterrand, for example, used this argument in his widely read book *Présence française et abandon* (1957) to defend the assembly's decision in 1956 to split French West Africa and French Equatorial Africa into twelve states, each of which would elect an assembly with considerable power over local matters: "The only effective means of opposing separatism was to cede the reins of local power to the African leaders who aspire to the emancipation of their people but who are equally desirous of inserting it in a vaster and more powerful community." The declared aim of such reforms remained the preservation of France's presence overseas. Arguing that the loss of Indochina, Morocco, and Tunisia demonstrated the bankruptcy of efforts to resist political liberalization, Mitterrand offered the vision of a new empire: "A strongly structured central power in Paris, autonomous States and territories federated in the bosom of an egalitarian and fraternal community, the frontiers of which will go from the plains of Flanders to the forests of the equator, such is the perspective that it is up to us to define and propose, for without Africa there will be no History of France in the XXIst century." Like Mitterrand, most of the anticolonialist intellectuals based their criticisms of the ineffectiveness of French policy on a "realism of preservation." They disagreed with their imperialist opponents on the means, on the form the goal should take, but not on the goal itself.[21]

L'Express provides a good example of this realism of preservation. The weekly was notorious for its opposition to French policy in the overseas lands and, in particular, to the war in Algeria. While Mauriac questioned in his articles the morality of French actions, Servan-Schreiber, the editor, challenged their effectiveness. Like Bourdet, Servan-Schreiber was an engineer by education, a journalist by profession, and aspired to a political career. He was, however, more moderate politically than Bourdet: he was a Radical party supporter rather than a socialist. Unlike Bourdet, Servan-Schreiber did not attack the goal of a French Union.

Servan-Schreiber's aim was to stimulate a renaissance of France's "imperial destiny" on a more realistic basis. He and Mendès-France urged France in 1956 "to reconstitute for itself a vast empire in loyal, equitable collaboration with the Moslem peoples and the black peoples." Unwilling to "abandon" all of North Africa, he opposed Algerian independence until forced during the Fifth Republic to admit that it was inevitable. Instead he wanted a strong government—though not de Gaulle backed by the army—to carry on negotiations that would not be a "capitulation," but rather "the instrument of a new community, safeguarding the interests of the French future." As late as February 1961, Servan-Schreiber continued to hope that France's imperial genius would permit it to be the link between Europe and the young states of Africa so that a Eurafrican community would arise from the foundation of Franco-African cooperation. The war in Algeria had to be ended, he argued, because it was driving the African nationalists into the arms of the Soviets and the Chinese.[22]

Others more favorable to total liberation, like the Communists, also stressed their desire to maintain French presence, partly because they feared the political consequences of the charge of advocating abandonment. Even those who were willing to propose independence, such as Rous, the men of *Les Temps Modernes*, and Bourdet, argued in terms of a realism of preservation. Rous, for example, insisted in *Tunisie . . . Attention!* that decolonization did not have to mean the end of "a legitimate cultural radiance," nor of fruitful economic relations, nor even of a military and strategic presence in the former colonies. But to preserve these bonds—the only ones still possible, according to Rous —it was necessary to decolonize in time; the way to maintain French presence was to grant independence. Jeanson defended even aid to the FLN by arguing that it was the best means to retain ties with Algeria. Echoing the words not only of Mitterrand but of mortal enemies like Soustelle, he warned: "An Algeria hostile to France means a Maghreb hostile to France; it means the radical cleavage between our old continent and the African New World; it means asphyxiation finally for a Europe pulled back on itself and condemned to stagnation, that is, to decadence."[23]

Both the leaders and the people of France demanded more than assurances from the reformers that they too wanted to preserve French sovereignty or at least French "presence." They demanded more than arguments that a policy of force was the way to lose everything. They had to be convinced that a reformed political structure could be erected that would be stable and would ensure the preservation of which the anticolonialists talked. The reformers responded with a variety of projects based on the idea of federalism.

Federalism was in vogue at the end of the war and throughout the Fourth Republic as a solution to France's overseas problems. It was popular because it was ambiguous, because it appeared to satisfy a number of different aims. Federalism was a means for the French to avoid the undesirable consequences of centralization and assimilation while still retaining control of the overseas lands. Critics of France's imperial tradition pointed to several major flaws in the policy of assimilation. To begin with, unity of legislation was harmful because of the irreducible particularities of the various territories in the French Union. On this level the drive for federalism, or at least for greater decentralization, in the French empire joined with the minority tradition of opposition to the centralized French state. Furthermore, it was clear that the French people would never tolerate the complete integration of the overseas peoples into the French political system because they would have fewer representatives in parliament than the overseas peoples. They feared, in the words of Édouard Herriot, that "France would thus become the colony of its former colonies." The deputies of the Algerian Moslems alone threatened to be a large enough bloc to be able to control the destiny of the home country. Finally, as became apparent by the mid-fifties, the French people would be unwilling to accept the economic sacrifices required to bring the living standards of the overseas peoples up to their level.[24]

Because federalism was also seen as a means to satisfy colonial political demands short of independence, it became increasingly popular in the mid-fifties. For example, in *La Nef*'s issue on the French Union in June 1955, most commentators wanted to revise the constitution to make the union more federalist. Mitterrand asserted that this was the only way to protect French interests. Domenach and Senghor hoped to create a great common civilization of France and the overseas peoples.[25] The growing movement for revision of the French Union culminated in de Gaulle's attempt in the constitution of the Fifth Republic to create a voluntary federation labeled the "Community." It was, to a large extent, a revival of the second Constituent Assembly's initial plan that de Gaulle had vehemently attacked and Bidault had scuttled.

Federalism was advocated as the solution to the particular problem of Algeria. In May 1955, *Esprit* began to call for internal autonomy for Algeria as a step toward creating an Algerian state within a French federal system. A year and a half later *La Nef* also espoused federalism for Algeria; Duverger wrote in the December 1956 issue that, since an Algerian republic necessarily would exist one day, the task was, by transforming Algeria into a federal state within a "French Commonwealth," to prevent it from becoming independent. In May 1957, *La Nef* conjectured in an editorial that an Algerian state might become part both of a federation of the Maghreb and of a federal French Union; it suggested that in this way both the Europeans and the Moslems of Algeria could feel secure. In January 1958, *La Nef* proposed that France recognize Algeria's independence if the Algerians would agree to be part of a "confederation" of states led by France. It declared in support of its scheme: "In order to conserve the empire, France must henceforth create States." When de Gaulle came to power, *La Nef* hoped that he would fit an Algerian state into the federal Franco-African structure he was erecting. In his speech of 16 September 1959, de Gaulle did offer the terms of the Community to Algeria.[26]

Federalism was a particularly attractive slogan because it concealed the crucial issue in the disputes among colonial nationalists, French reformers, and French conservatives—the question of sovereignty. Like the self-contradictory formula of "independence within the framework of the French Union" applied to Vietnam at the end of World War II, federalism was a term that could be used to signify very different arrangements. A means both of loosening the bonds of political subordination and of preserving them, it might be seen as a form of political autonomy, perhaps as a step toward independence, or merely as a form of administrative decentralization. It could be used to disguise independence or to disguise continued domination by France. The apparent consensus for federalism, therefore, was to a large extent only a verbal illusion.[27] The disintegration of de Gaulle's Community in 1960 showed that the question of sovereignty could not be avoided.

If federalism was unsuccessful, looser ties between France and its former colonies still might be possible. The anticolonialists who gradually began to advocate independence because it seemed desirable or inevitable contended that it could and should be followed by "special relations," "association," "community," "cooperation," or "interdependence." They pointed to the British Commonwealth as an inspiration for France, but they differed among themselves in their conception of the goal. Rous and Bourdet envisioned a cooperation of independent states based on bonds of mutual interest, culture, and friendship. Both *Esprit* and *La Nef* hoped for an association that would limit independence. *Esprit* wanted to protect the young nations and to temper nationalist passions, while *La Nef* was concerned more with preserving French interests.

The anticolonialists argued on the grounds of a "realism of preservation" in order to appeal to the French leaders and public. But this argument had a major weakness. The policy of force obviously was not working—at least not the amount of force the French were willing to commit to the defense of the empire. Yet there was little reason to believe that political reforms would be more successful.

The anticolonialists constantly pointed to the many reasons the colonial peoples had for staying with France. First, the overseas peoples were tied to France by bonds of friendship, a shared past, and a common culture. The intellectuals argued that such bonds were more durable than those of political subordination. Second, association with France was required by the vital interests of the colonies, which could not afford complete independence because they needed France's protection from other imperialists and France's aid to develop their economies. The evolution of the world, even if it tended provisionally to develop nationalisms, was tending to regroup states into constellations. Third, France would attract the colonial peoples because of its traditional humanist mission and its culture. Instead of turning to the United States or to the Soviet Union, they would want to stay with France, which could offer them a humanist path to modernity.[28]

Proposals based on a realism of preservation were unconvincing, however, because they were impracticable. It is doubtful that a true, egalitarian federation could have worked when the peoples were so different and that the people of France would have agreed to enter such an egalitarian federation with their former colonies. Even if the French actually had offered equality, the proposal probably would not have had sufficient appeal to suppress the rising desire for independence.

Imperialists were quick to stress the impracticability of the federalist schemes. For example, the Independents warned during the electoral campaign of December 1955: "In Algeria, the federalist solution would lead to the Algerian Republic, and this would lead to autonomy, then to independence, thus to the eviction of France." Such assessments were confirmed by events. France granted internal autonomy to Tunisia in 1955, but had to agree to the independence of Morocco and Tunisia in 1956. France granted partial local autonomy to sub-Saharan Africa in 1956 and the Community to it in 1958, but by the end of 1960 all the states had seceded. De Gaulle offered autonomy to Algeria, but was forced to acquiesce in its independence in 1962. The French people not only had followed de Gaulle in favoring an intermediate solution in Algeria but also had told pollsters that it could work. Yet they surely must have sensed the fragility of efforts at federalist reform.[29]

The argument that independence would lead to association was also unconvincing. France's Vietnamese allies rejected the French Union and turned to the Americans. The Moroccans and Tunisians agreed to "interdependence," but this did not prevent them from aiding their Moslem brothers of the FLN and did not prevent President Bourguiba from forcing the French to abandon their military bases in Tunisia. Accordingly, the French public was not optimistic about the continuation of close and useful ties after independence. Ironically, the widespread use of arguments of preservation may have helped to decrease the possibility of this preservation by increasing the nationalists' distrust of French intentions. As Aron warned in 1959, the project of associating with France the weak new states of Africa was "condemned in advance" if France appeared "desirous of maintaining or of restoring the empire."[30]

The anticolonialists stressed a realism of preservation in order to reach an audience that desired to retain the security and prestige of imperial sovereignty. But the widespread use of this kind of argument may have had harmful effects on the French public. To the extent that the French let themselves believe this reasoning, it created unrealistic expectations, and the denial of these expectations by subsequent events must have produced bitterness and resentment. Furthermore, the anticolonialists who used this argument did not accustom the French to the idea of independence; indeed, by catering to rather than combating the desire to preserve France's presence, they may have helped to perpetuate the imperialist state of mind of the public and thus to make the mental adjustment to the end of empire more brutal. In both ways these intellectuals may have increased the danger that the colonial peoples who insisted on their national liberty would be abandoned suddenly and completely by the disillusioned French people.

THE LOGIC OF ABANDONMENT

The most persuasive realist cases for decolonization were formulated not by the leftists, but by two writers associated with the moderate Right, Aron and Raymond Cartier. Aron was postwar France's most renowned social scientist and defender of liberal doctrines. Like Sartre, his fellow student at the École Normale Supérieure, he studied in Germany in the early 1930s. Sartre returned with the philosophy of Heidegger; Aron brought back as well the political sociology of Max Weber. When the Germans invaded France, Sartre's outfit was captured; Aron's was evacuated to England. In England, Aron became one of the editors of the monthly *La France Libre*. At the Liberation he collaborated very briefly with Sartre in *Les Temps Modernes*, but soon quit and became Sartre's main liberal opponent on the ideological questions of the Cold War. He directed the cabinet of André Malraux, de Gaulle's minister of information in 1945–46; wrote for Camus's *Combat*; and subsequently contributed regular editorials on current political and economic issues to *Le Figaro* as well as occasional articles to *Preuves* and other periodicals. He also taught at the Institut d'Études Politiques and, beginning in 1955, at the Sorbonne and published numerous books on sociological theory, philosophy of history, French politics, and international relations.[31]

Aron was an advocate of empire at the time of the Liberation. He offered both nationalist and humanist reasons for its preservation. He believed that the empire, particularly North Africa, could be an important source of strength and wrote, accordingly, that the first essential task of French external policy was to maintain the integrity of the empire. He also believed that France had a world mission—to refuse the mystique of the machines and to keep human proportions in a world in which everything was conspiring to deliver societies to "the inhumanity of enslaved crowds and steel pyramids."[32] He implied that humanist France was for this reason the best agent in the inevitable Westernization of the world.

Aron insisted from the beginning, however, that the possibility of preserving the empire had to be assessed realistically. He argued on several occasions that France would be able to retain its colonies only by an audacious and generous policy of liberalization. As early as 1943 he tried to convince the Gaullists in London that France should abandon Indochina because it would be unable to preserve it and should instead concentrate on saving Africa, which was "essential" to France. Since France no longer had the means to be a world power, it should resign itself to a new role as a Mediterranean power. Although he defended Blum's decision to react with force to the Vietnamese attack on Hanoi, Aron nonetheless continued to assert that France had to give up its sovereignty in Indochina.[33]

Aron did not believe that empire was an end in itself; rather it was principally a means to national greatness, and its value had to be judged soberly in terms of its contribution to the overall interests of France. Representing the expanding technocratic segment of the intelligentsia, Aron constantly preached that the crucial, essential task for France was the reconstruction and modernization of its economy. He argued in 1945 and into the Fifth Republic that the increase of production through mechanization was the indispensable means to social peace in France, to influence in international affairs, and to the protection of the empire—in short, to "the *grandeur* of the reconciled fatherland." He insisted that economic modernization was a prerequisite for France's mission, for others would listen to its humanist message only if France became one of "the lords of the mechanical civilization." Only then would the rest of the world admire France's refusal to worship machines, to give "these gigantic playthings the naive admiration of the barbarian."[34]

If the attempt to preserve the empire harmed the interests of France—in particular, if it prevented economic modernization—Aron was ready to advocate the abandonment of empire. This situation clearly had arrived in the mid-1950s. In Africa, furthermore, the issue of decolonization was not overshadowed by the Cold War. Even though he feared the spread of Nasserism and communism to North Africa, this fear was secondary. More important to him was the fact that the war to protect France's most prized overseas possession, Algeria, was threatening to ruin France. Regretting the infrequency of his criticisms of French actions in Indochina, Aron intervened vigorously and repeatedly in opposition to French policy in Algeria.[35]

Early in 1957, Aron published a collection of essays, *Espoir et peur du siècle*, in which he recommended the progressive creation of an

Algerian state.[36] Partly to clarify his position, he published in June the short book *La Tragédie algérienne*, which, in terms of its impact both on government circles and on public opinion, was probably the single most influential writing on the Algerian problem. The first half had been written in May 1956, sent to Premier Mollet, and circulated among a few friends, including the editor of *Le Figaro*. In both parts of the book—and the following year in the more detailed *L'Algérie et la république*—Aron developed the arguments of a realism of national interest in favor not merely of Algerian statehood but of independence.

Aron insisted that it was useless to deny the existence of an Algerian nation. The proposition that Algeria was a part of France was refuted by economic and social realities. Algeria was an underdeveloped country with a high birth rate, and to try to apply to it laws designed for France was absurd. Moreover, the Algerians were becoming conscious of their national particularity, an unavoidable development after Morocco and Tunisia had achieved independence. Since this consciousness was arising in opposition to France, no reform would be satisfactory, no reform could end the war, if it excluded "the magic word, independence." The minority would continue to fight, and the majority would feel solidarity with them. Since the educated tended to be the most nationalist, the progress of France's *oeuvre* was likely to facilitate, rather than to impede, the spread of a nationalist consciousness.[37]

Aron added that the French could not end the war by military means. He had been awed by the military power of the Soviets and Americans at the end of World War II and continued to be interested in the world struggle of the two nuclear giants. But the successes of guerrilla warfare in Asia convinced him that it was "one of the century's demiurges on a par with the atom bomb." Guerrillas were unable to defeat a regular army by themselves—the Communist victories in China and Vietnam would have been impossible without external aid. But the insurgents did not need a military victory; all they had to do was to prevent the colonial power from establishing order and security. The latter, on the other hand, needed a total victory. As long as the guerrillas enjoyed the complicity of the population—and especially if they also had a place of refuge in a neighboring country—total victory was impossible unless the colonial power was willing to resort to total repression. Consequently, even when military campaigns during the

Fifth Republic appeared to reduce the rebel army to scattered bands, Aron continued to assert that the French army could not succeed in the pacification of Algeria.[38]

Furthermore, Aron contended, the project of integration surpassed France's financial resources. He calculated that the investments necessary to raise the Algerian standard of living only 4 percent a year would prevent the standard of living in France from rising at all. Aron doubted that the French people would tolerate such a sacrifice. Meanwhile, the war itself was extremely expensive and made the work of economic reconstruction more precarious. In sum, contrary to popular belief, France would ruin itself while trying in vain to cope with the problems of Algerian underdevelopment and would be blamed in world opinion for its inability to solve them.[39]

Aron argued, finally, that the loss of Algeria would not harm France's economy. The defenders of French sovereignty contended that Algeria played a vital economic role. Aron replied that economic ties were not likely to be cut by independence; an independent Algeria would have difficulty finding new markets to replace those already established with France. By continuing the war, however, France would reduce its future clientele in Algeria and would endanger its investments in, and relations with, Tunisia and Morocco, as well as its cultural and economic positions in the Arab Near East. Aron added that the exports to the colonies were a minority of French exports and were in fact a long-term hindrance to French trade because the protected markets encouraged laziness. Some readjustment would be necessary, but both Great Britain and the Netherlands had done it successfully, he claimed, even though Indonesia had been more important economically to the Netherlands than Algeria was to France. Aron noted that the money spent on the war and invested in Algeria could be used more profitably to modernize the French economy, which was a necessity since France was going to enter a competitive European common market.

Critics replied that Aron's analysis was shortsighted. Investments at home would be fruitless when, because of the loss of Algeria and hence of all Africa, Western Europe found that, in its contracted condition, it was no longer economically viable and was being absorbed into a larger, possibly Communist, economic bloc. Such apocalyptic visions did not disturb the reasoning of realists like Aron.[40]

The discovery of oil and gas in the Sahara in April 1956, however, appeared to give France a new, concrete economic reason to stay in Algeria. The advocates of *Algérie française* claimed that the mineral potential of the Sahara ultimately would redeem the present financial sacrifices and, in particular, would provide France with an independent source of vital raw materials. Old dreams of autarky and of engineering feats that would transform the African wastelands into France's California were revived. Few people believed in 1957 that France would be able to continue to exploit the oil of the Sahara if Algeria became independent.[41]

Aron admitted that control of the oil would give France more security, but not enough to be worth a war. Independent energy sources would do little to alter the fundamental dependence of France's economy on overseas imports. In peacetime, he believed, France easily could buy all the oil it needed, while in wartime, control of the seas would matter more than sovereignty over the Sahara. He added that, since the Saharan oil and gas would be difficult and expensive to exploit, profits would be slow in arriving and would not be great; France would get little financial relief in the near future and would invest in French Algeria at least as much of the profits as an independent Algerian state would take in royalties. Aron concluded that the greatest benefit of the Saharan oil would be to France's balance of payments. The crucial point was not French sovereignty, but only the continued membership of North Africa in the franc zone, which would enable France to pay for the oil in francs. Meanwhile, the pursuit of war made the development of the Sahara impossible.[42]

The French taxpayer apparently was calmed by what *La Nef* called in 1959 the "mirage" of the Sahara, and *La Nef* itself helped to sustain this vision in its special issue on the Sahara in January 1960.[43] Yet the French, unaware of how valuable the Saharan oil would become in a decade, did not consider it important enough to fight for. De Gaulle initially attempted to separate the Sahara from Algeria when dealing with the FLN, but ultimately had to agree to include it in the independent Algeria. The FLN promised in return to respect French investments in the Sahara, to give preference to French companies in future projects to exploit hydrocarbons, and to allow France to pay for oil and gas in francs.

Aron thus explained that the independence of Algeria would not be a severe blow to France. Like Tillion, however, he believed that an independence that meant the breaking of all ties would be a misfortune for the French of Algeria and a disaster for the Moslems. At the same time he insisted that, if there was an intermediate solution between "indefinite violence" (the policy of integration) and "sudden capitulation," it could be reached only if the French agreed without reservations to "the national vocation of Algeria." Like Berque in December 1956 and both Tillion and *La Nef* in 1958, he argued that the aim should not be to prevent the Algerian people from exercising "the right of self-determination," but "to create the conditions in which it would do it without breaking with France." The French should seek interlocutors for whom nationalism was not xenophobia—in other words, more moderate ones than the FLN. But, Aron insisted, this search would be fruitless, as it had been in Indochina, unless the French were clearly willing to let the Algerians choose independence.[44]

Aron understood the difficulty of his plan: the French army would have to continue to fight against the extremists with the sole aim of giving independence to a more moderate group. As inspiration, he offered again the example of the British, who had been willing to fight in Malaysia in order to create a non-Communist nation. Yet even if the French government and army had followed Aron's advice, it is questionable that they could have found enough moderate nationalists with the courage to risk dealing with the French and with the prestige to rally the Moslem population.

Even de Gaulle, the sole French leader whom the Moslems trusted and respected, did not take the first step of acknowledging the Algerians' right of self-determination until September 1959. He denuded the right of real meaning, Aron charged, by insisting that the referendum could occur only several years after the success of pacification and by implying that the choice of "secession" would lead to a partition of Algeria. Aron lamented that de Gaulle's style was royal: he wanted to act by granting favors to beneficiaries of his own choice. Noting that in Algeria there was not even a Bao Dai to receive these favors, Aron argued in *Preuves* in November 1960 that it was no longer possible to bypass the FLN. Echoing the statements of Bourdet during the war in Indochina, he explained: "Once the nationalist movement is incarnated in one or a few men, once this incarnation has been confirmed by events, that is, by spilled blood, it is vain for the ex-colonial state to search for a substitute incarnation: it will not find any. It has more chances to convert the leaders of the revolutionary movement to moderation than to discover moderate leaders who are at the same time acceptable to the nationalists."[45] De Gaulle eventually agreed to negotiations with the FLN alone; they began in May 1961.

Aron's influence was great because he was free from the suspicion the leftists aroused among the French public. He stated the case for emancipation of Algeria with dispassionate logic. He could command the attention of the upper levels of French society, the "directing classes," where partisans of integration tended to be more numerous. Although he was not permitted to write on Algeria in *Le Figaro*, his attitudes were well known to the conservative readers of that paper. Because of his "bourgeois respectability," the defenders of *Algérie française* saw him as their most dangerous enemy. Soustelle complained: "If *L'Express* is the *L'Humanité* of the left bank, M. Aron is the Servan-Schreiber of the rich, the Mauriac of iron metallurgy, and the Bourdet of finance." Soustelle charged him with spreading defeatism and preaching the abandonment of Algeria. Aron replied that the real defeatists were those who denied the realities and who despaired of "reconciliation with the nationalists," that real abandonment would be the rejection of "cooperation with the countries promoted to independence."[46]

Soustelle charged, in addition, that Aron callously and selfishly wanted to abandon the Algerian Moslems to their misery. In fact Aron argued that France had a "mission" to continue to aid Algeria as much as possible. He insisted only that neither this mission nor the mistaken belief in the profitableness of Algeria to France was reason to refuse independence to Algeria.[47] Nonetheless, his main impact on the French public, and especially on business circles, no doubt was to promote a selfish "realism of abandonment," for which he provided the logic even if he criticized and wanted to transcend such an attitude. A mood of abandonment was already spreading before *La Tragédie algérienne* appeared, as was proved by the reaction to the sensational articles on sub-Saharan Africa by Cartier, the editor of *Paris-Match*, in late summer 1956.

The very popular weekly magazine *Paris-Match* had been a militant and intransigent defender of the West against communism and against Moslem "fanaticism." It had passionately defended French empire in Indochina and North Africa. Yet its fundamental attitude toward sub-Saharan Africa, which was largely outside the Cold War, had stressed the argument of material interests. In 1953, Cartier had asserted in regard to troubles in Kenya and the Gold Coast: "Europe does not have a colonial empire at home like the United States and the USSR. Having lost Asia, which it besides never completely dominated, it needs more than ever the African continent as a prolongation and a complement, as a source of raw materials and a market. Without Africa, Europe is only a small, overpopulated, and dependent peninsula. This is a precise and sufficient reason not to give it up, even if it is necessary to fight to keep it."[48] In 1956, Cartier visited sub-Saharan Africa and changed his mind. He was shocked by the waste of French money and efforts; the attempts to develop France's "immense portion of the poorest part of a thankless continent" had been fruitless. He was offended by the lack of gratitude shown by the Africans. He noted that French investments would be put to much better use in France, where they were needed to modernize the economy, and pointed to the wealth of Switzerland and Sweden and of Holland after the loss of Indonesia. Since the march toward self-government was inevitable, overseas investments, where not wasted, ultimately would be lost to France. Cartier concluded that France should voluntarily give up a political sovereignty that imposed impossible financial burdens but was unnecessary for continued economic exploitation:

Today's wisdom consists in doing the opposite of what yesterday's prudence counseled: accelerate instead of braking. It is necessary to transfer as quickly as possible as many responsibilities as possible to the Africans. At their risk and peril. It will be no trouble besides to safeguard, for a reasonably long time, the respectable economic interests of the home country. Africa is not in any state to pose conditions. . . .

La politique is the art of adapting to the events that can no longer be directed. In Black Africa, France will easily conserve everything useful that it possesses. On the condition of not wanting to keep at any price forms and façades that no longer correspond to our epoch. On the condition of putting a realist mind in place of the sentimental and historical mind with which it has pondered up until now its overseas territories.[49]

The enormous circulation of *Paris-Match*—it printed over a million copies and claimed some six million readers—meant that the influence of these articles on public opinion was potentially very great. The immediate adoption by the press and politicians of the term "Cartierism" suggests that Cartier articulated a widely shared feeling. The lack of public uproar over the rapid evolution of sub-Saharan Africa and Madagascar from the local autonomy granted in 1956 to independence by 1960 suggests that the mood of abandonment spread quickly. Indeed, 51 percent of the people polled in September 1958 agreed with the opinion that France should "no longer have with its former African colonies any military and political bonds, bonds which bring heavy financial obligations," and half of these people cited the costs as the reason for their agreement.[50] The unending wars of decolonization had produced weariness; the new awareness of the gigantic problems of underdevelopment made the burdens of empire loom large. Sub-Saharan Africa and Madagascar seemed less and less to contain vital French interests.

More particularly, Cartier and Aron were expressing and provoking a general shift in opinion among French businessmen. The French prewar economy had lacked markets; the postwar economy lacked capital. Consequently, the markets of the French Union no longer seemed as important to business circles as they had in the 1930s, while at the same time these territories, in contrast to the plantation islands of the Old Regime, required huge investments of capital not only to combat misery but also to make them valuable producers. Meanwhile, by the mid-fifties the French economy had recovered from the devastation of the war, was booming, and no longer seemed to need as much protection. The old tradition of opposition to empire by the liberal economists and businessmen of the eighteenth and nineteenth centuries reemerged. Those businessmen with economic interests overseas were ready to seek their profits without the guarantee or expense of sovereignty.[51]

"Cartierism" was the variety of "realism of preservation" that many Frenchmen finally adopted. In contrast to the technocratic realism of Aron, it was a combination of weary disillusionment and selfishness. It was the policy that the French presumed the British had followed in India, but it was adopted by the French more out of bitter resignation than out of economic self-confidence. Paradoxically, as the Cartierists became aware of the burden of empire, the demands for independence of the colonial peoples were opportune for them.

The humanist intellectuals, on the other hand, were sensitive to the rising threats to the colonial peoples of abandonment and "neocolonialism." In a poll in January 1960 only 29 percent of the French people approved of the principle of financial aid to overseas countries that became independent but remained in the Community, while 36 percent disapproved, and 35 percent gave no opinion. The neocolonialist menace appeared to be dramatized by the foreign involvement in the civil war that broke out in the Congo soon after it became independent from Belgium. The spread of Cartierism thus increased the humanists' anxiety about independence.[52]

Cartierist reasoning was more difficult to apply to the Algerian problem. De Gaulle criticized it in November 1959. In April 1961, however, he joined Aron in stressing that France did not need Algeria at all and could use its men and resources to much greater advantage at home. Yet such a realism of withdrawal still ran up against the problem of the French of Algeria. Cartier himself continued to defend French sovereignty in Algeria because he refused to abandon the Frenchmen there. Aron also hoped that they could continue to live in Algeria. When de Gaulle began negotiations with representatives of the provisional government formed by the FLN (the GPRA) in May 1961, Aron wrote in *Preuves* that de Gaulle could not "abandon the Europeans of Algeria to the arbitrary control of the GPRA and to the eventual vengeance of the masses."[53]

In *La Tragédie algérienne*, however, Aron had suggested that it might be necessary to repatriate the French of Algeria. If a middle solution could not be found, the rights of the French Algerians would have to bow before the equally just claims of the Algerian nationalists. To reduce the suffering of the French Algerians, Aron later introduced the idea of a temporary partition to ease the transition.[54] De Gaulle meanwhile was threatening the FLN with the prospect of a permanent partition. Ultimately, however, he too opted for repatriation.

DECOLONIZATION AND *GRANDEUR*

The underlying theme of the agony of decolonization was *grandeur*. The French sought to retain their empire because they felt it was an essential aspect of the otherwise waning power and prestige of their nation. The Cartierists represented a shift of many Frenchmen to a narrower, more materialistic view of France's concerns. Nonetheless, the popularity of de Gaulle suggests that the theme of *grandeur* continued to be important.[55] A crucial task of the advocates of decolonization, therefore, was to convince the French that decolonization was not a sign of and contribution to the decadence of France, but rather a means to a renewed greatness.

The question of possession of colonies had been subsumed into the larger question of the nature of France's greatness at the time of their conquest. The famous debate in the Chamber of Deputies in 1885 over the vote of credits for an expedition to Madagascar had seen the confrontation of two visions of France: a choice between a continental or an imperial orientation. The proponents of a continental nationalism argued that colonial expansion was a waste of France's scarce resources. The president of the Ligue des Patriotes, Paul Déroulède, insisted that France should prepare for war against Germany to avenge its humiliation in 1870–71 and to recover Alsace-Lorraine. The radical republican Georges Clemenceau stressed the need to concentrate on internal development and on increasing the well-being of the French people. The liberal economist Frédéric Passy declared:

I believe that France has the duty to concentrate itself, to collect itself, and that if it wants to radiate and spread out, it must be like those waters that flow out while rising, not like those that lose themselves in a thousand fissures and a thousand leaks that dissipate them. It is by the natural progress of riches, of population overflowing onto foreign territories, by voluntary emigration, by fruitful and free commerce, and not by these adventurous, costly, and sterile expeditions launched haphazardly in all directions, that one can arrive at spreading the name, language, spirit, and interests of France. It is in making it stronger that one will make it radiate outside with more energy and more brilliance.

The major advocate of an imperial nationalism, the moderate republican Jules Ferry, argued that at a time when the other European powers were expanding overseas, France had to join them or else renounce definitively the status of a great nation. Charging that the policy of "abstention" was "very simply the grand path of decadence," he insisted that it was not enough for France to be a free country like Belgium or Switzerland; "it must also be a great country, exercising on the destinies of Europe all the influence that belongs to it" and "must spread this influence over the world, and carry everywhere it can its language, its customs, its flag, its arms, its genius."[56]

Ferry's conception of France won the day, and in succeeding decades it was taught to the mass of Frenchmen. This conception obviously was challenged by decolonization. Consequently, a new debate took place over the nature of France's *grandeur*. Rejecting Cartierism, most intellectuals did not dispute that France ought to play a world role. They disagreed on the nature of this role, that is, on the type of world presence that in the future would constitute French greatness.

Soustelle upheld the traditional view that empire was necessary for greatness. Echoing not only Ferry but Déroulède, he objected to the potential loss of Algeria as passionately as Déroulède had objected to the loss of Alsace-Lorraine. He argued that abandonments were a cumulative poison and that renunciation of empire, in particular of Algeria, would result in "the irremediable decadence," perhaps even the death, of France. If, however, the French responded to the challenge not with the defeatism of Aron, but with the courage of Charles Martel at Poitiers, they might be able once again to turn back the tide of history. "To abandon Algeria," Soustelle proclaimed, "is to condemn France to decadence; to save Algeria is to put a stop to the frightful process of degradation; it is to return to our country, to its people, to its youth, their chances and their future."[57]

The humanist intellectuals had a related vision of French national *grandeur*. The concept of a civilizing mission in the world was a part of the traditional ideology of French imperialism. Consequently, it is not surprising that some intellectuals continued to find in it reason for the perpetuation of France's political presence overseas. Simon, for example, declared:

Each nation has its destiny and its style, and those of France are not seclusion and withdrawal. There are flags that are made to billow in all the winds of the world, and that would droop if they remained planted in a plot of land ruled by a policy of cautious dignity. It is still necessary that the French flag raise in the temporal melee the sign of a civilizing value attached to the very idea of France; if not, we ought to blush at our passing victories, and dread in addition a definitive and total defeat in the hour in which the forces of history will act invincibly against us.

Even the writers of *Esprit*, while insisting that France had to decolonize, continued to assert that France's greatness came essentially from its outer-directed humanist vocation. Unlike Soustelle, however, they were confident that, after decolonization, France's civilization would have a continued, indeed greater, power of attraction and ability to radiate. Domenach wrote in April 1962 that "the great future task of France" was to organize a community of French-speaking countries. In November 1962, *Esprit* devoted its issue to the theme "French, Living Language," and in the introduction Domenach argued that the loss of Algeria was not the end of all France's past *grandeur* because, thanks to its language, it still had "the opportunity of participating under the best conditions in the worldwide confrontation."[58]

Aron, in contrast, proposed that France turn its energies inward. In reply to Soustelle, he argued that decadent nations refused to "adapt themselves to a changing world," that the "grave diggers of the fatherland . . . under the pretext of preventing decadence" directed patriotism into a dead end. Great Britain, the Netherlands, and Japan had proved that internal decadence need not be the consequence of the loss of empire. Since France no longer had the means to reign over other peoples, Aron asserted, it too had to renounce this outdated kind of *grandeur* in order to seek another. French greatness in the modern world had to come from its internal accomplishments: the modernization of its economy without the abandonment of its humanist culture. Echoing Passy, he concluded that on the basis of this double success, and on this basis alone, France and French thought would continue to influence the world.[59]

Aron and Domenach offered two different versions of a decolonization that would entail a revival, rather than a decline, of national *grandeur*. But de Gaulle was more effective in convincing Frenchmen that decolonization was not an intolerable blow. He seemed to believe —and many Frenchmen along with him—that he was the incarnation of eternal France and the most trustworthy defender of French greatness. When de Gaulle liberated the colonies, therefore, the imperialist segment of the French public was more willing than they were during the Fourth Republic to think that empire was no longer necessary for *grandeur*. Under his leadership France was able to give up Algeria, in particular, without an intolerable sense of defeat and humiliation.[60]

De Gaulle had insisted that, as he wrote in the celebrated opening of the first volume of his war memoirs (1954), France was "not really itself except in the first rank," that France could "not be France without *grandeur*," and, as a result, France needed to retain its empire. He had declared in 1946, for example: "United to the overseas territories, which it has opened to civilization, France is a great power. Without these territories, it risks being one no longer."[61]

De Gaulle was not only a nationalist but also a pragmatist and an empiricist. When he returned to power in 1958, he betrayed doctrinaire Gaullists like Soustelle and proceeded to decolonize. In his speeches he popularized the arguments already proposed by the realist critics of French colonial policy. Reassured by his person and impressed by his style, the French were more receptive to these arguments. He told them that the world was evolving and that France had to adapt. The peoples to whom Europe had brought "civilization" now wanted to assume responsibility for themselves. This desire was not only "natural and legitimate," but, more important, it was "irresistible." The only way to keep the former colonies close to France was not to resist the desire for self-determination but to channel it. Moreover, as he declared on 11 April 1961, all the great powers realized now that "their future, their salvation, and the possibilities of their world action" depended no longer on the domination of others but on their own internal development, above all, and on "cooperation" with the former colonial peoples.[62]

De Gaulle seemed, therefore, to rally to Aron's conception of *grandeur*. Yet in fact he placed his realism at the service of a conception more like Domenach's and Simon's, indeed one that remained largely traditional. He continued to be preoccupied with France's role in the world. "France," he proclaimed on 31 December 1963, "because it can do so, because everything invites it to do so, because it is France, must conduct in the world a policy that is worldwide." He now conceived of this global role in terms of diplomatic action and leadership of a French-speaking bloc of nations. As a result, he, like the humanist intellectuals, opposed the Cartierist spirit and convinced the French public that France should continue to aid and guide its former colonies. Like the humanist intellectuals, he was confident that France's former subjects would need the assistance of a developed country and would choose to associate with France, to which they had deep ties, rather than with the United States or the Soviet Union. Like the nationalists, he insisted that France should continue to play the role of a great power by means of an independent military policy and diplomacy.[63]

De Gaulle's withdrawal from NATO, his nuclear *force de frappe*, and his haughty anti-American diplomacy were a financial drain on France, but they gave an illusion of continued old-style *grandeur* that was agreeable even if only partly believed. In this way Gaullist foreign policy was functional, perhaps necessary, to French decolonization. It provided a psychological cushion for the modernization of France's conception of its *grandeur*.[64] De Gaulle's quasi-monarchical and prestige-conscious regime was the necessary transition from imperial France to the France of Aron and Giscard d'Estaing.

8 ❧THE ATTACK ON ETHNOCENTRISM

The belief of the French in their special colonial vocation was one of the foundations of the persisting imperial idea. The moralists were reluctant to admit that the colonial peoples might be better off without continued French tutelage. The realists tended to assume that the colonial peoples, whatever their future political status, would want to stay attached to France. A few intellectuals, however, denounced the ethnocentrism underlying these notions.

RACISM AND ETHNOCENTRISM

The French were convinced that they were able to interact more effectively with colonial peoples than were other colonial rulers. They were able to do this, they were told in school and by politicians and intellectuals, because they were less racist. As the geographer André Siegfried explained to a group of Americans, the Frenchman "oversteps the narrow limits of racial or nationalistic prejudices, and attains effortlessly a humanist, international, conception of man."[1]

The Frenchmen of the Liberation proclaimed that their victory was the defeat of a racist conception of humanity that had culminated in the Nazi atrocities. The politicians granted citizenship to the colonial peoples; admitted their representatives to French assemblies; chose a Senegalese, Senghor, to draft the Declaration of Rights included in the constitutional proposals of the first Constituent Assembly; and elected a Guianan, Gaston Monnerville, as president of the Council of the Republic. During the Fourth Republic the intellectuals wrote tracts against racism and condemned the well-publicized sufferings of black people in the American South and in South Africa. Although troubles in the French Union forced an awareness of the blatant racism of many French colonial residents, even the most severe critics of colonial racism offered explanations of it that served to reassure the people at home.

The foremost of those explanations of colonial racism were the psychoanalytic theory of Mannoni and the various existentialist-Marxist blends offered by Memmi, Sartre, and Jeanson. According to both types of explanations, colonial racism was a product of the colonial situation. It had the primary function of justifying the privileges enjoyed by the colonial masters and was activated by threats to the colonial situation and its privileges from reform projects conceived in France, from the demands of the indigenous people, or from the colonists' own consciences. The only basic disagreement among the theorists was over the nature of these privileges. Mannoni stressed the psychological value of the master-servant relationship, which gave the master easy compensation for the "inferiority complex" that plagued men raised in Western individualistic society. Memmi and the writers of *Les Temps Modernes* pointed instead to the economic exploitation of the indigenous population by the colonists. Both Mannoni and the existentialist-Marxists suggested that Frenchmen, like other people, became racist if placed in a colonial situation in which the dominated peoples were of a different race and that decolonization was a means of reducing racism. At the same time they did not deny the contention that Frenchmen normally were not racist.[2]

What can be concluded about the claims of the French? Clearly, they were exaggerated. Many individuals even in France were in fact racist. Although the French as a whole probably were less racist than their Anglo-American rivals, they were not less prejudiced.[3] The basis of prejudice is the association of value judgments with the differences that are observed in (or attributed to) another group of people. If these differences are physical, the result is racism. If they are cultural, the result is cultural prejudice. The Frenchmen who congratulated themselves on their lack of racism tended to be guilty instead of a sense of cultural superiority.

One reason for the relative absence of racism in France was precisely the particular type of ethnocentrism that was inherited from seventeenth-century neoclassicism and revolutionary political theory and that was developed into official ideology by the anticlerical Third Republic. The French were taught in school that the essence of a civilization was its culture, especially the values inherent in the culture; that this culture was acquired by the individual through his upbringing and education; and that French culture was distinguished from other Western (as well as non-Western) cultures by its "universalism," that is, by its special accessibility and applicability to all people. The historian Charles Morazé, for example, asserted: "What attracts to France and is found nowhere else is not a *specific* trait of French culture, but the coexistence of traits belonging to every culture. Coexistence? Certainly; yet even better the organic synthesis of every culture." France's "humanist" culture seemed to express the essential and supreme values of humanity. Furthermore, the key to and the instrument of this culture, the French language, was itself characterized by universalism. In Siegfried's words: "The French language, famous for its clarity, is a precision instrument. . . . Any thought whatsoever, filtered through the French spirit, thereby receives clarity and order. Even more, it acquires universality; it becomes transmissible, like a medium of exchange acceptable everywhere and usable by everyone."[4]

The French believed that the colonial peoples were capable of learning French culture and that, when they did so, they would be true Frenchmen. The French also believed that such a cultural assimilation would elevate the colonial peoples morally and intellectually. They ignored or scorned the indigenous cultures. They described a colonial subject who had learned French, passed through a French education, and adopted French customs as an *évolué*—presumably he had "evolved" from a lower to a higher stage of civilization. The French were convinced of their superiority as colonial tutors because they believed that they were not only less racist than other colonial rulers but also that they brought with them a more elevating culture. If racism was needed overseas to justify colonial privileges, ethnocentrism was sufficient in France to justify the empire.[5]

The movement of colonial liberation, therefore, was difficult for Frenchmen to understand. It was seen as the rejection of the gift of a superior culture. Duverger remarked in 1955, not without pride: "The English would be shocked that a foreigner could have the idea of becoming British; the French are shocked when a foreigner does not have the idea of becoming French." Decolonization was a challenge to the belief of the French in the universality and superiority of their culture. It came at a time when the fall of France from its old position of military and economic preeminence made many Frenchmen insist all the more on the greatness of their culture. Consequently, decolonization provoked a crisis in the French conception of their own civilization. As a Swiss observer, Herbert Luethy, declared in 1955: "The hardest question which confronts France, alike in her colonial empire and in her relations with Europe and the world, is whether her idea of civilization is capable of renewal—renewal by receptivity to the alien and the novel without which it can itself have no radiative or assimilative power—or whether it will degenerate into that crabbed and narrow cultural chauvinism which nowadays characterizes so many manifestations of the French spirit."[6]

The French had to respect other cultures before they could welcome the assertion by the colonial peoples of their own separate national and cultural identities. They needed to open themselves to the diverse cultural influences of the world to avoid a reliance on their past glories. The intellectuals who stressed the value of non-Western cultures, therefore, helped not only to facilitate decolonization but also to revitalize French civilization.

THE CHALLENGE OF NEGRITUDE

The first intellectual challenge the French of the Liberation had to face came from the colonial peoples themselves. The colonial elites had experienced the attraction of French culture. As Senghor put it, "I do not know a people more tyrannical in its love of Man [than the French people]. It wants bread for all, liberty for all; but this liberty, this culture, this bread will be *French*. The very universalism of this people is French. So much so that the barbarians of 'the French Empire' . . . ended up by persuading themselves that they could have no other destiny." But the policy of assimilation was a trap. The French could give a French education to many colonial subjects, but they could not remold the entire society. The *évolués* suffered a cultural uprooting that made them unable to return to the traditional ways of life that endured at home. At the same time they were likely to discover, both in the overseas territories and in France, that the society whose culture they had imbibed was less open to them than they had expected. The scorn they encountered reinforced their suspicion that assimilation involved a loss of authenticity and could produce only mimics. They found themselves estranged from both worlds and torn within themselves.[7]

The *évolués* thus discovered personally that "cultural imperialism" was, in Senghor's words, "the most dangerous form of Colonialism." Many of them reacted by trying both to regain their own cultural authenticity and to combat the denigration of their native cultures by the French proponents of assimilation. One result of assimilation, therefore, was an intellectual ferment and literary flowering both among the blacks of the Caribbean and Africa and among the Arabs and Berbers of the Maghreb. In contrast, the young elites of Britain's African colonies, not subjected to an assimilation policy, did not feel the same need for cultural affirmation and turned directly to political concerns.[8]

The colonial cultural movements were accessible to the French public because they were expressed in French even though their primary aim was to assert the cultural identity of the colonial peoples. The paradox of attempting to overcome cultural alienation by utilizing the very instrument of that alienation can be explained by three factors. First, the authors were *évolués*. They had learned to admire the French language, which they had at their command, and, in some cases, had lost touch with their original languages. Second, the audience for literature in the indigenous languages was limited. The educated among their own people had learned to read French in the colonial schools, and French gave them access to a wider public not only in France but also around the world. Third, the homelands of the authors were dominated by France. They had a strong interest, therefore, in convincing both themselves and their rulers of their dignity.[9]

The cultural self-affirmation of the blacks had a much greater impact in France than did the North African literary revival. It occurred earlier and reached the French public, appropriately, in the first years after their experience with the Nazis.[10] The claims of the black writers were more shocking to the French public than those of the Arabs and Berbers because African culture was generally considered to be far inferior to Islamic culture. Furthermore, in compensation for the prejudice suffered by the blacks, French intellectuals welcomed the new movement with enthusiasm and gave it publicity.

The ideology of black particularity and dignity had been forged in Paris in the early 1930s by a group of French-speaking black students who had joined in a search for the legitimate values of the Negro-African world. The most important figures were Léon Damas of

Guiana, Senghor of Senegal, and Césaire of Martinique. Damas studied law; Senghor graduated from the Sorbonne; Césaire from the elite École Normale Supérieure. Both Senghor, the first African to pass the *agrégation* exam, and Césaire taught for several years in French high schools. All three wrote superb poetry and essays in French. After the war all were elected to represent their homelands in the National Assembly. The leaders of the revolt against French culture were thus some of the most successful of the *évolués*.[11]

The fruits of the years of discussions had been made public just before the war. In particular, in 1939, Césaire launched the movement's battle cry—"negritude"—in his passionate and lengthy poem *Cahier d'un retour au pays natal*. But Césaire's poem and the new movement did not yet attract much attention. During the war the movement broadened its base. Césaire and his wife, both teaching in a high school in Martinique, spread the message of negritude to the people of the West Indies in the small surrealist review that they edited, *Tropiques*. Senghor spent two years in German prison camps before his release because of illness, but when he returned to continue teaching in France he not only participated in the Resistance but also met with a new generation of black students in Paris. After the war the themes of negritude were elaborated and achieved fame in the poetry, essays, and speeches of Senghor and Césaire; in the militant *Anthologie de la nouvelle poésie nègre et malgache de langue française*, edited by Senghor in 1948; in the first French black African review, *Présence Africaine*, founded in 1947 by a leader of the younger generation, the Senegalese Alioune Diop; and ultimately in the international congresses of black writers and artists, sponsored by the *Présence Africaine* group, held in Paris in 1956 and in Rome in 1959.

The early explorers of negritude had received inspiration from a number of sources. Their path was marked out by the Afro-American literary movement of the 1920s, the "Harlem Renaissance," and in Paris they met many of its major figures. Meanwhile the reigning picture of African barbarism began to be challenged by Western scholars —especially the German archeologist Leo Frobenius and the French anthropologist Maurice Delafosse—whose studies of African history, society, and culture provided the young blacks with a scientific foundation for their claim of dignity. The European surrealist movement also aided them by attacking Western civilization, by praising the "exotic" cultures of Africa and Asia, by proclaiming the revolutionary role of the artist, by legitimizing the descent into the torrents of the artist's unconscious, and by liberating the French language from its Cartesian and neo-classical bonds and thereby turning it into an instrument suitable for singing the black soul. Finally, the pretensions of Europe were being undermined by its own increasing self-doubt—in particular, the widespread criticism of capitalism—as it seemed headed in the 1930s toward self-destruction.

Nonetheless, the black writers did not, like the Maghrebins, have the support and inspiration of the all-pervasive Islamic religion, of the Arabic language with its roots in the Koran, or of the vast cultural and political renaissance of the Islamic and Arabic world.[12] The blacks' self-affirmation had to be based mainly on their own acts of will. The difficulty of the path of negritude—especially for the completely uprooted West Indians—was dramatized in Césaire's poem *Cahier d'un retour au pays natal*.[13]

Césaire aimed at a black audience, and his message was harsh. He described vividly the squalor that greeted his return to his native Martinique. He lamented the suffering and degradation of black people around the world. He ridiculed blacks who sought to avoid these ugly realities by denying their own negritude. He related his own futile attempts to avoid these realities by, in contrast, plunging into the black stereotype—by exalting, in defiance of Europe, "dementia praecox, flaming madness, tenacious cannibalism," by identifying with black rebels like Toussaint L'Ouverture, the liberator of Haiti, and by glorifying the African past. Césaire's attempts collapsed before the very real degradation of the blacks of Martinique and before his own cowardice. The black men of his time, he admitted, never had been princes of Ghana, wise men of Timbuktu, or warriors, but were only "quite worthless dishwashers, small-time shoeshine boys, and, at best, quite conscientious sorcerers." The race that had to be accepted and affirmed, therefore, was "my race that no ablution of hyssop mixed with lilies could purify/my race gnawed by blotches/my race a grape ripe for drunken feet."

But by daring to admit the ugliness of his race, Césaire was able to discern its authentic beauty. Descending into himself—returning in a more radical fashion to his "native land"—he discovered underneath his shame the real virtues of the blacks. Those who were scorned for erecting no buildings of stone and steel, for exploring neither the sea nor the sky, for dominating neither steam nor electricity, were at the same time those who lived in intimate communion with nature, "those without whom the earth would not be the earth." In the most famous lines of the negritude movement, Césaire proudly sang:

> my negritude is not a stone, its deafness kicked against
> the clamor of the day
> my negritude is not a film of stagnant water on the dead
> eye of the earth
> my negritude is neither a tower nor a cathedral
>
> it plunges into the red flesh of the soil
> it plunges into the burning flesh of the sky
> it digs into the dense prostration with its upright
> patience.
>
> Eia for the royal Cailcedra tree!
> Eia for those who have never invented anything
> for those who have never explored anything
> for those who have never dominated anything
> but, possessed, they abandon themselves to
> the essence of things
> ignorant of the surfaces but possessed by
> the movement of things
> not caring to dominate, but playing the game of the world.
>
> truly the elder sons of the world
> porous to all the breaths of the world
> fraternal eyrie of all the breaths of the world
> undrained bed of all the waters of the world
> spark of the sacred fire of the world
> flesh of the flesh of the world throbbing with the very
> movement of the world!

After this liberating self-discovery, Césaire could legitimately defy the white civilization that had oppressed his race. He charged that Europe had pushed the black people down their road of degradation, had "gorged them with lies and bloated them with pestilence." But now the white world, "horribly weary from its immense effort," was crumbling. It was time for the black people to free themselves, to cast off their shame, to dance their negritude, and to join with the other races to continue the work of mankind that Europe no longer was qualified to lead.

The Antilleans, uprooted from their ancestral home, could only discover their authentic negritude by "Orphic" means: a desperate "descent to the chasms of the black soul." The Africans, however, were able to study the outward manifestation of this soul in the African civilization around them. Using the term "culture" to mean "the spirit of a civilization," Senghor defined negritude as "the ensemble of the cultural values of the black world, as they are expressed in the life, institutions, and works of the blacks." In his essays he sought to describe both to his fellow blacks and to the French public the specific aspects of negritude.[14]

The essential characteristic of the black, according to Senghor as well as Césaire, is the way in which he encounters the world outside. As a man who traditionally has worked the land, the black is sensitive to the world, "docile to the rhythm of the cosmic forces," open even "to the apparently imperceptible rhythms, to all the solicitations of the world." He is not merely sensitive to the exterior of the object, but above all to its inner essence. This essence is the Life Force that penetrates the universe as rhythm. Rhythm, Senghor explained, is "the architecture of being, the internal dynamism that gives it form, the system of waves that it emits for the *Others*, the pure expression of the Life Force." Since the black penetrates the object in "an active attitude of communion, indeed of identification," he participates in the being of the object, in its rhythm, and expresses this rhythm in his art. He responds to the object and the rhythm emotionally, that is, by moving out to it with his whole being; therefore, emotion is "the royal domain of the Negro." Senghor contrasted the Negro-African with the European while commenting on the lines of Césaire quoted above:

It is known that the attitude of Man before Nature is the Problem par excellence, the solution of which determines the destiny of men. Man before Nature is the *subject* opposite the *object*. It is a question, for the European, *homo faber*, to know Nature in order to make it the instrument of his will to power: to utilize it. He will pin it down by analysis, will make it a *dead* thing in order to dissect it. But how to make Life out of a dead thing? It is, on the contrary, in his subjectivity that the Negro, "porous to all the breaths of the world," discovers the object in its reality: *rhythm*. And there he is, abandoning himself, docile to this living movement, going from subject to object, "playing the game of the world." What is there to say except that, for the Negro, to know is to live—in the life of the Other—by identifying himself with the object? To know (*Con-*

naître) is to be born (*naître*) to the Other while dying to oneself: it is to make love with the Other; it is to dance the Other. *"I feel, therefore I am."*[15]

Senghor claimed, therefore, that the mind of the black acts in a different manner from that of the white European: his reason is not "discursive" and "antagonistic," like the European's, but rather "synthetic" and "sympathetic." It is "another mode of knowledge" which is, in one sense, superior, since it does not impoverish things by fitting them into rigid schemas; instead "it slides into the arteries of things, it experiences all their contours in order to lodge itself in the living heart of reality." Senghor liked to summarize his position with the statement: "European reason is analytical by utilization; Negro reason, intuitive by participation."[16]

Senghor concluded that Negro-African culture should be recognized by both blacks and whites as worthy of confronting European culture in a dialogue of equals. He did not deny that African civilization was deficient in the area of science and technology and that Africa could not survive unless it assimilated these. But he insisted that European civilization too was deficient. Just as its art had been revitalized by an infusion of black rhythm, its society needed to regain the sense of community that still permeated African societies, its culture needed to learn the black peoples' respect for and intimacy with nature, and its war-weary population needed to rediscover the black peoples' joy of living:

> For who would teach rhythms to a world blasted by machines
> and guns?
> Who would carry the joy-cry to waken the dead and the
> orphaned at dawn?
> Say, who would bring life's memory back to the men of
> gutted hopes?
> They call us the men of cotton, of coffee, of oil,
> They call us the waking dead.
> But we are the men of the dance whose feet draw power in
> beating the solid ground.[17]

Furthermore, Senghor pointed out that many scientists and philosophers of twentieth-century Europe were abandoning the ideal of objective knowledge. The physicists had revealed, in the principles of relativity and indeterminacy, that the observer could not stand outside, detached from the things that he was observing. Philosophers such as the phenomenologists had stressed the observer's essential participation in the act of perception and had adopted a method of seeking knowledge that, Senghor claimed triumphantly, was precisely the intuitive method of the blacks. Some thinkers, such as the Catholic philosopher Pierre Teilhard de Chardin, were even proposing, like the Negro-Africans, that reality was an interaction of vital forces.[18]

The philosophy of negritude was not an ideology of revolution. It stressed the need for cultural, rather than political, liberation. It was not designed to stir up the masses, but to give new confidence and direction to the African elites and to gain the respect of European intellectuals. But this reevaluation of the role of Negro-African culture had obvious political implications. Cultural identity both presupposed and justified political autonomy. Accordingly, the concept of negritude was used by the French African elites as a basis for demands first for federation, ultimately for independence. It was also a basis for the confidence of the African nationalists—for their conviction that, because of the communitarian traditions and instincts of their peoples, their states, once liberated, could develop a new and more vital type of socialism than that attempted in Europe.[19]

Meanwhile, the impact of the negritude movement on the French public was magnified in the early postwar years by the patronage of a number of France's most celebrated intellectuals. The republication in 1947 of Césaire's *Cahier d'un retour au pays natal* carried an enthusiastic preface by the dean of the surrealists, Breton, who described Césaire's poetry as "beautiful like nascent oxygen." When Diop's journal *Présence Africain* was launched in autumn 1947, with the aim of presenting its African and French readers with both scholarly studies about Africa and literary texts by African writers, it was supported by a galaxy of great names. The "committee of patronage" included André Gide, Sartre, Camus, Mounier, Leiris, Rivet, the director of the Musée de l'Homme, and Théodore Monod, the director of the Institut Français d'Afrique Noire at Dakar, as well as Césaire, Senghor, and the black American novelist Richard Wright. The anthropologists Georges Balandier and Paul Mercier worked on the editorial board. In the first issue, the African modernist Diop stressed Africa's need for enlightenment by Europe, while the French contributors—Gide, Sartre, Mounier, Monod, and Balandier, among others—asserted that Europe had to appreciate and learn from Africa. The greatest contribution to the fame of negritude, however, was Sartre's brilliant introduction to

Senghor's *Anthologie de la nouvelle poésie nègre et malgache de langue française* (1948). Sartre's essay, entitled "Orphée noir," was highly praised by the black writers for its depth and sensitivity. It became the most influential popularizer of the concept of negritude in France and around the world.[20]

The French supporters of the black cultural revival were unwilling to grant negritude the concrete reality claimed by the black writers. The black intellectuals seemed to be glorifying their race—or a Negro-African culture that was presented as hereditary—at the very time that the French intellectuals, in reaction to the Nazis, were trying to combat racism. French support of the blacks was a part of an antiracist campaign and was not intended to promote a new racism, even if it was, in Sartre's phrase, an "antiracist racism." To make the antiracists even more uncomfortable, Césaire and Senghor deliberately chose to meet the racists on their own grounds. They agreed that all Negroes could be lumped together, and they glorified a number of traits—emotion, rhythm, intuition—that were aspects of the racist stereotype of the black. For both reasons, the ideologists of negritude were questionable allies in the fight of the European antiracists to prove a fundamental human equality.[21] Furthermore, negritude involved a glorification of the traditional values and practices of Africa at a time when Africa needed to modernize in order to survive. To be sure, Senghor, Césaire, and, above all, Diop insisted that the blacks had to assimilate European science and technology into Negro-African civilization, but it was easy for the Europeans to see negritude as an impediment in this process. In the interests of modernization, as well as in opposition to racism, the French intellectuals admitted the particularities of the black people only to dissolve them in a vision of a more universal civilization that was still essentially European.[22] The attack of the negritude movement on French ethnocentrism was, therefore, both promoted and blunted by its French patrons.

Even Sartre exhibited this ambivalence toward negritude. He tried to demonstrate in "Orphée noir" that the "antiracist racism" of negritude was in fact aiming at "the abolition of differences of race." Since the blacks were oppressed as a race, they had first to become conscious of and to take pride in their racial subjectivity. This racial consciousness, however, would lead to a realization that it was actually the capitalist system that was oppressing them and from which they had to free themselves. When they worked for their own liberation, Sartre contended, they, as the most oppressed of all men, were working objectively for the liberation of oppressed men of all colors. Some, like Césaire, who belonged to the Communist party, were conscious of their solidarity with the proletariat in the struggle against capitalism. In the minds of these black Marxists, "the subjective, existential, ethnic notion of negritude" was making its logical transformation into "the objective, positive, exact" notion of the proletariat. Sartre concluded:

In fact, negritude appears as the weak stage of a dialectical progression: the theoretical and practical affirmation of white supremacy is the thesis; the position of negritude as antithetical value is the moment of negativity. But this negative moment is not sufficient in itself and the blacks who employ it know this well; they know that it serves to prepare the synthesis or the realization of the human in a society without races. Thus negritude exists in order to destroy itself; it is the passage and not the result, the means and not the ultimate end. At the moment that the black Orpheus embraces most tightly this Eurydice, he feels her vanish between his arms.[23]

Sartre, like most other French intellectuals, was unwilling to admit that negritude had a concrete reality. His particular attitude resulted from two factors. On the one hand, Sartre continued to believe in the existential ontology expounded in *L'Être et le néant*. He believed that all humans are alike in that their fundamental condition is freedom. He viewed interpersonal relations as primarily a conflict in which each person, seeing the freedom of the other person as a threat to his own, seeks to protect his freedom by gaining possession of the other's freedom. The loser in the struggle is forced, at least temporarily, to adopt the unauthentic identity created for him by his oppressor. This identity is the reflection of the oppressor's prejudice. Accordingly, in his *Réflexions sur la question juive* (1946), as well as in "Orphée noir," Sartre neglected the ethnic or racial particularities that gave partial truth to the stereotype and that the oppressed persons themselves valued.

On the other hand, Sartre was increasingly adopting a Marxist vision of history. From the Marxist point of view, the authentic man is not, as the Romantics and the black writers suggested, the man who stays intimately linked with nature, but rather, as the Marxist philosopher Edgar Morin asserted, *"the man condemned to becoming, the man who throws himself into inquiry and evolution, the man who is practically, technically, morally, a revolutionary."*[24] The Marxist scheme of history presumably was applicable to the whole world, and in it race played almost no part. By analyzing negritude from the point of view of Marxist revolutionary internationalism, Sartre substituted a Marxist ethnocentrism for the Cartesian ethnocentrism he had rejected. He did not hope to assimilate the blacks into a universalist French civilization, but rather into the universalist proletarian civilization that would result from the future revolution defined by Marx.

Sartre's reduction of negritude to the antithetical moment of a Hegelian dialectic was facilitated by the exponents of negritude. They tended to portray Negro-African values as the exact opposite of European values, were socialists even if not orthodox Marxists, and envisioned a future civilization to which all races would contribute. They aimed, however, at a symbiosis of races, not at "the abolition of differences of races." Sartre was an inconsistent Hegelian in suggesting that negritude would "disappear completely" rather than be conserved and reconciled with the distinctive qualities of other races in a greater totality.[25]

For all the enthusiasm of the black writers over Sartre's essay, they held fast to a black identity that for them was concrete and valuable in itself. Negritude led the Africans not to Marxism, but to African nationalism, combined with dreams of African unity, and to "the African way of socialism." Even Césaire appeared to betray Sartre's expectations when in 1956 he resigned from the Communist party. In a scorching open letter Césaire denounced not only the ethnocentric and paternalistic attitude of the French Communist party, but the very doctrine of international proletarian solidarity: "It is an established fact that our struggle, the struggle of the colonial peoples against colonialism, the struggle of the colored peoples against racism, is much more complex, indeed of an entirely different nature than the struggle of the French worker against French capitalism and cannot in any way be considered a part, a fragment of that struggle."[26]

Sartre's essay had a different effect on Fanon, a member of a younger generation of blacks. It hurled him into despair. Sartre's demonstration that negritude was only an incomplete and transitional concept dried up the "black zeal" that Fanon, as a medical student in Paris, needed psychologically in order to reply to white racism.

When I read that page, I felt that I had been robbed of my last chance. I declared to my friends: "The generation of young black poets just received an unpardonable blow." An appeal had been made to a friend of the colored peoples, and this friend had found nothing better to do than to demonstrate the relativity of their action. For once, this born Hegelian had forgotten that consciousness needs to lose itself in the night of the absolute, the only condition for it to attain to consciousness of self. . . . Without a Negro past, without a Negro future, it was impossible for me to live my Negrohood. Not yet white, no longer completely black, I was damned.[27]

Yet Fanon soon developed a position not far from Sartre's. In his passionate analysis of the neurosis of the black man, *Peau noire, masques blancs* (1952), he argued, like Sartre, that the negritude movement was basically a reaction to and a reflection of the racism of the white oppressor. In spite of its value in restoring black self-esteem, it led to an unauthentic plunge into what Fanon called, recalling the last lines of Césaire's *Cahier d'un retour au pays natal*, "the great black hole." Fanon believed, like Sartre, that the individual is not only free to go beyond his given situation—in the case of the black, a racist situation—but that he has the duty to do so. Fanon insisted that the black man does not have the right to become mired in his blackness. Rather, he has the duty to assert his essential humanity, that is, to live in the "permanent tension" of human freedom. The black man must make himself a man.[28]

The authentic response to white racism, Fanon concluded, was not black cultural protest, but revolt. In *Peau noire, masques blancs* Fanon focused on psychological rebellion against the alienation suffered by the black man. The next step was already implied: the black must shatter the alienating situation through political and social revolution. In 1956, after three years as a psychiatrist in an Algerian hospital, Fanon quit to join the FLN. The revolutionary schema of orthodox Marxism utilized by Sartre in 1947, however, continued to make as little sense to Fanon as it did by this time to Césaire. Instead of either proletarian or black solidarity Fanon preached the solidarity of the revolutionary peasants of the Third World. Like Sartre, he moved from an existentialist to a Marxist type of universalism, but he adapted Marxism to the perspective of the Third World.[29]

THE WISDOM OF THE SAVAGES

The negritude movement challenged French cultural prejudice and was given substance by the liberation of the African territories. But the French conviction that the goal of even an independent Africa ought to be Westernization, preferably in the French manner, nourished a persisting ethnocentrism. Meanwhile, a more radical attack on this ethnocentrism was coming from a Western source, the anthropologists. The most celebrated of these anthropologists was Claude Lévi-Strauss.

Lévi-Strauss had turned to anthropology in the 1930s in revolt not only against the sterile narcissism of the Western philosophy that he was studying but also against Western society in general. His esteem for exotic societies was "a function of the disdain, not to say the hostility," that he felt for the customs of his own society.[30] Like other anthropologists of the era of decolonization, Lévi-Strauss became aware that his discipline had been a product of colonization. Anthropologists had been able to study non-Western peoples as objects, he charged, only because the West had treated them as objects since the Renaissance. Anthropology had served as an outright apologist for colonization in the era of conquest before World War I. Lévi-Strauss suggested, therefore, that anthropology now had a mission to be "an enterprise reviewing and atoning for the Renaissance, in order to spread humanism to all humanity."[31] Accordingly, he tried to rehabilitate the so-called primitive peoples in Western eyes.

Lévi-Strauss began his attack on Western ethnocentrism by criticizing the theory of "evolutionism." The major philosophers and anthropologists of the nineteenth century—Comte, Spencer, Marx, Tylor, Morgan—had viewed different societies, both in distant lands and in the past, as representing stages in a single line of development that culminated in Western civilization. They recognized the diversity of cultures in the world only to abolish it in their typology and in their theory of change. This vision had been, and continued to be, a basis of the idea of the civilizing mission of Western colonization. After World War I, however, anthropologists had begun to study the primitive societies closely and to see them as unique and complex wholes that could not be reduced to the evolutionist schemas and that had intrinsic value. As a result, a movement of cultural relativism had emerged, expressed in France in two pamphlets written for a UNESCO series against racism: Leiris's *Race et civilisation* (1951) and Lévi-Strauss's *Race et histoire* (1952).

In *Race et histoire*, Lévi-Strauss challenged the scientific foundation of the evolutionist vision as based on a false analogy of social change with biological processes. Prehistoric societies were ordered by the evolutionists according to the material remains they left, and present societies were compared to them on the basis of such products. Lévi-Strauss pointed out, however, that while an animal gave birth to another animal, an axe did not give birth to an axe. Basing a schema on changes in technology ignored the social reality of which the technology was only one expression. Within two different societies, axes might have radically different meanings, which would make their comparison very misleading. Furthermore, Lévi-Strauss argued that the evolutionists' attempt to equate some contemporary societies with the prehistoric ancestors of Western societies was absurd because all existing societies were the products of long periods of development.[32]

Lévi-Strauss charged that evolutionism was founded on the very ethnocentrism that it tried to rationalize. Other cultures seemed primitive or stationary or underdeveloped only because their lines of development had no meaning for Westerners and could not be measured by the criteria Westerners employed. Westerners judged others in terms of the particular pursuit in which the West had excelled—the enterprise of equipping man with "increasingly powerful mechanical resources" in order to augment "the quantity of energy available for each member of the population." But, as Leiris, too, pointed out, the very diverse societies that the West lumped into the single category of "underdeveloped" had in fact followed other lines of development in areas in which the West itself was relatively underdeveloped.

As examples, Lévi-Strauss praised the Polynesians for their remarkably free and generous social and ethical organization and the Eskimos and Bedouins for their "ability to overcome even the most inhospitable geographic conditions." He asserted that Indian Yoga, Chinese breathing techniques, and the ancient Maoris' visceral control were evidence of a profound mastery of "that supermachine, the human body." He claimed that the Australian aborigines, who made elaborate theories about their family connections, were not merely "the founders of general sociology as a whole," but "the real innovators of measurement in the social sciences." He concluded that progress occurred in a multitude of different directions and on a multitude of different levels, but that men were in general too culture-bound to appreciate this variety.[33]

Furthermore, Lévi-Strauss insisted that the West should not be too proud even of its extraordinary progress in the single direction of technology. He claimed that a more accurate biological analogy for social change than evolution was mutation—change by "a series of leaps and bounds" not always in the same direction. Comparing social change to a game of dice or roulette, he contended that exceptional progress in a single direction was largely a result of the good fortune of achieving the combination of dice throws (or cultural traits) needed to win (to progress). The chances of achieving a long enough series to set off, for example, a scientific revolution were very small unless a coalition of gamblers, or cultures, formed to pool their individual successes.

Lévi-Strauss and Leiris pointed that Renaissance Europe had had the good fortune to be a meeting place and melting pot of very diverse cultures—Greek, Roman, Germanic, Anglo-Saxon, Arabian, Chinese. At the same time pre-Colombian America and sub-Saharan Africa had been relatively isolated and homogeneous. Lévi-Strauss and Leiris believed that such isolation was one of the greatest calamities that could afflict a group of men. Consequently, in 1955, Lévi-Strauss recommended in his popular work *Tristes Tropiques* that France overcome the insularity that menaced both it and Islam by opening its doors to the twenty-five million Moslems in its empire. Making a dubious analogy, he argued that the United States had made a similar wager in the nineteenth century in accepting masses of immigrants and had won.[34]

Lévi-Strauss's defense of non-Western civilizations did not go unchallenged by the high priests of French culture. The lyrical essayist Roger Caillois undertook to refute *Race et histoire* in the columns of the prestigious literary review *La Nouvelle Nouvelle Revue Française*. Caillois saw in Lévi-Strauss's pamphlet the climax of an attack on all the ideals and values of the Christian West by a pack of spiteful intellectuals—surrealists and anthropologists, in particular—who celebrated Europe's decline by exalting "barbarism" and "fanaticism."

Caillois argued that Lévi-Strauss's cultural relativism—his contention that a man of one culture could not fully appreciate the lines of development followed by another culture—prohibited him from making any cross-cultural judgments. Hence Lévi-Strauss's persistence in showing where other societies were superior to the West was inconsistent with his premises. Paradoxically, his judgments were also irrefutable evidence of the superiority of Western civilization. Caillois concluded triumphantly:

The West has not only unified history and the planet; it has not only produced a solidarity of all civilizations by the progress of its techniques, by its commerce, its conquests, and its wars. It has invented archaeology, anthropology,

and museums; this is an originality that the visitors to museums, the archae-
ologists, and the anthropologists would be ungracious to contest. . . . But
their injustice toward their civilization is such that they forget that it is up to the
present the only one that has produced the material and spiritual conditions
for their own researches, the only one that permits and creates those for their
ingratitude.[35]

In his rebuttal in *Les Temps Modernes*, Lévi-Strauss explained that it
was entirely consistent to contend, on the one hand, that an observer
could rank cultures according to their apparent ability to satisfy a single, isolated criterion and, on the other hand, that he would be unable
to rank them when they were considered as living wholes, satisfying a
variety of different and perhaps unsuspected criteria. He charged that
Caillois's doctrine that the anthropologist should not criticize the civilization that produced him was repressive. He could not forget that the
expanding West had created anthropologists at the very moment that it
was undertaking to destroy the object of their studies. The subsequent
haughty response of the editors of *La Nouvelle Nouvelle Revue Française*,
who dismissed Lévi-Strauss by ignoring the entire substance of the
debate, only demonstrated the depth of the roots of French ethnocentrism.[36]

In Lévi-Strauss's later writings he attacked Western civilization
with much greater vehemence, but he also moved a step in Caillois's
direction. He now stressed that continued progress in a single direction was a result not only of a fortuitous meeting of cultures, but of
a deliberate fostering of historical change. All societies had accomplished the "neolithic revolution"—the fundamental advances in agri-
culture, domestication of animals, weaving, and pottery making that
were the basis of all civilizations. Societies could be divided roughly
into two groups according to their subsequent attitude toward historical factors that threatened to upset the social equilibrium based on the
neolithic revolution. "Cold" societies sought to give themselves institutions that would annul, in a quasi-automatic fashion, the effects of
history. "Hot" societies, such as those in the West, internalized historical change and made it "the moving power of their development."[37]

The problem faced by "hot" societies was to overcome the contradiction of progress. The cultural diversity on which progress was
based tended to be eliminated by this very collaboration. Continued
progress was possible only if this diversity were constantly renewed
either internally by provoking social cleavages or externally by widen-

ing the circle of partners. Like the Marxists, Lévi-Strauss charged that the West had progressed only by means of exploiting slaves, serfs, and finally proletarians and ultimately by subjugating most of the peoples of the world. In the manner of a thermodynamic versus a mechanical machine, "hot" societies did more work than "cold" ones, but consumed more fuel; like a steam engine, they created more order in the area of mastery over nature, but created more disorder in the area of relations among men.

Lévi-Strauss believed that the technological advances of the West were not worth the human price. He preferred the "cold" societies, which chose to try to "perpetuate themselves like a clock in which all the cogwheels participate harmoniously in the same activity." In these societies, authentic human relations were still possible; politics was still based on consent, as Rousseau had seen, rather than on coercion; and men lived in close and harmonious accord with their natural environment. Lévi-Strauss not only attacked the concept of evolutionism; he also sided with the societies that tried not to evolve.[38]

Westerners prided themselves not only on their scientific and technological advances but also on the type of thinking that had produced these inventions. The philosopher Lucien Lévy-Bruhl had claimed in the early twentieth century that "primitive" peoples had a "prelogical" mentality different from the scientific way of thinking of the European colonizers; their thinking was mystical, was hardly differentiated from their emotions, and was indifferent to the logical principle of noncontradiction. Although Lévy-Bruhl himself attributed the difference to the social group's view of reality rather than to biology, his theory harmonized poorly with France's egalitarian ideology and could even be utilized by racists. Nonetheless, it was widely diffused and was espoused by Frenchmen from Gide to Caillois. Even Senghor, although he naturally rejected the denigration of the "primitive" mind, stressed the emotion and intuition of the Negro-African people. The anthropologists reaffirmed the essential similarity of the mental processes of all humanity.[39]

Near the end of his life Lévy-Bruhl himself sought to explain the apparent difference in thinking as a result of a difference in experience rather than in mental structure. He argued that primitive peoples had mystical experiences that civilized men did not have. Mannoni, a spokesman for postwar antiracism, replied that these so-called primitives and Westerners had similar psychic experiences; they differed only in their interpretation of these experiences: "Modern science was the result, not of a change in the nature of experience but of a change in the attitude of the observer. Before this change came about—and it was a change affecting the whole structure of the personality—man had learned not to heed, or to heed as little as possible, the daily lessons of the world of sense-perception."[40]

Lévi-Strauss agreed that there were two different types of thinking, for in no other way could he account for man's long scientific stagnation between the neolithic revolution and the modern scientific revolution. Like Mannoni, he insisted that the difference was not a result of biology, but of a choice in objects of thought—"that the kind of logic in mythical thought is as rigorous as that of modern science, and that the difference lies, not in the quality of the intellectual process, but in the nature of the things to which it is applied."[41] Unlike Mannoni and other humanist colonial reformers, however, he questioned whether Western logic was always superior to that of the "primitives."

The "primitive" societies as well as the Western ones had accomplished the neolithic revolution. Lévi-Strauss asserted that these complex technical advances could not have been made by chance, but must have been a product of "centuries of active and methodical observation, of bold hypotheses tested by means of endlessly repeated experiments." They "required a genuinely scientific attitude, sustained and watchful interest, and a desire for knowledge for its own sake." Further proof of the intellectual prowess of the so-called primitives was provided by the sophisticated systems of classification that Lévi-Strauss studied in his renowned book *La Pensée sauvage* (1962). Motivated by a "thirst for objective knowledge," these people carefully studied and cataloged their natural environment. Impelled by a "demand for order" in the world, they subsequently constructed complex systems in which they classified the whole universe and put all levels of being into analogical relation.[42]

Lévi-Strauss argued that "savage thought" was as scientific as modern Western thought. He labeled it "the science of the concrete," for, in contrast to Mannoni, Lévi-Strauss contended that "primitives" paid more rather than less attention to the world of sense perception. In its search for necessary connections, the savage mind applied itself to the level of concrete reality, while modern science withdrew to the more abstract.

The difference between the methods of the two sciences, Lévi-Strauss explained, was analogous to the difference between the methods of the home handyman and of the engineer. Mythical thought, like the handyman, used the concrete debris of old intellectual systems to build new ones. It organized and reorganized a given set in the manner of a kaleidoscope in its search to make a meaningful order of all elements of the set. The units of concrete science, such as natural species, therefore, were preconstrained, limited in number, and already possessed of meaning owing to their previously determined qualities. Yet they pointed beyond themselves. By their position in the structure of the whole system, they helped, like parts of a coded message, to give meaning to the system. In contrast, modern scientific thought, like the engineer, sought to open up the given set and go beyond it by creating new elements through abstraction from the observed. It manipulated not "signs," but "concepts." Lévi-Strauss paid no attention to Senghor's distinction between intuition and analysis since he was concerned only with logical processes; but this distinction was in accord with the different attitudes toward concrete things taken by the savage and the modern scientists.[43]

Lévi-Strauss pointed out many examples of savage thinking in modern Europe, and near the end of the book he revealed that the term "savage mind" actually signified "neither the mind of savages nor that of primitive or archaic humanity, but rather mind in its untamed state as distinct from mind cultivated or domesticated for the purpose of yielding a return." He admitted that modern science, by overcoming the limitation of the logic of the concrete to a closed set, had been able to surpass by far the achievements of the neolithic revolution. But he insisted that neither the strengths of savage thought nor the deficiencies of modern science should be underestimated. The West's increased conceptual and practical mastery over nature had been achieved at the cost not only of social evils but of a certain intellectual impoverishment.[44]

A keystone of the scientific revolution had been the distinction between "primary qualities" such as mass, extension, and velocity, which could be formulated quantitatively, and "secondary qualities" such as color and taste, which were neglected as merely sense perceptions. The qualities modern science labeled as peculiarly scientific, Lévi-Strauss noted, were "precisely those which formed no part of living experience and remained outside and, as it were, unrelated to events."[45] Lévi-Strauss was, according to his own definition, among the most modern of social scientists. His primary aim was to discover constraints of the human mind that were necessary and universal. He believed that these invariable laws of logic were objectified in all of man's products. By finding the immanent structures of social customs and institutions and of myths, he hoped "to understand how the human mind functions."[46] At the same time Lévi-Strauss believed that his work was part of a trend in modern science that was demonstrating, in a very different way than that suggested by Senghor, the scientific validity of savage thinking.

Lévi-Strauss declared at the end of La Pensée sauvage that the current attempt of modern science to integrate the hitherto neglected "secondary qualities" into its theories had resulted in a shift of concern from concepts back to signs. Modern science, in turning to problems similar to those undertaken by savage thought, had vindicated the methodology of the science of the concrete. For example, structural linguistics, which had inspired Lévi-Strauss's structural approach to anthropology, had been successful because the linguists had treated the semantic universe in the same way the savage thinkers treated the physical universe. Language, like the "primitives'" universe, appeared to consist of messages that were meaningful only in terms of a linguistic system that had been constructed by means of contrasting pairs of signs (the phonemes). While savage thought treated the physical world as a universe of information, modern information theory treated the world of communication as a universe of physical objects. The two "distinct though equally positive sciences" had crossed paths, although one was "supremely concrete" and the other "supremely abstract." As a result, Lévi-Strauss concluded, the entire process of humanity's search for knowledge had assumed "the character of a closed system."[47]

Lévi-Strauss was a type of naturalist—he was preserving the memory of the exotic societies in which la pensée sauvage still flourished. In his inaugural lecture at the Collège de France on 5 January 1960, he suggested that, if the triumphs of modern science succeeded in freeing society from "the millennial curse" that compelled it to enslave men in order to progress, then society could return to the "crystalline structure" that characterized primitive societies. But the note of optimism in this lecture was not genuine. Lévi-Strauss was resigned to the disappearance of the societies he studied and to the degradation of humanity by the spread of a uniform Western civilization. He attacked Western ethnocentrism but had no expectation of curing it. His primary aim was merely to study the human mind, not to improve it.[48]

Lévi-Strauss turned his back on a contemporary history of which he disapproved. But such an attitude, if understandable, was no longer practicable. The population explosion made the achievements of the neolithic revolution insufficient for the continued physical survival of the "underdeveloped" societies. In this light, the tenets of cultural relativism seemed outmoded. A new evolutionism emerged, based not on the alleged similar histories of societies but on their similar needs, that is, on the need for economic "modernization." It seemed obvious that only those non-Western societies that adopted modern science and industry would escape stagnation and eventual annihilation. With decolonization taking place, even anthropologists shifted their concern from indigenous traditions to social change. As early as 1950, Leiris and Balandier charged that the anthropologists' praise of traditional cultures was both an anachronism and a hindrance to the political and economic emancipation of the colonial peoples. The need for development, therefore, seemed to confirm the West's role as the leader and guide of the peoples of the world. The cultural criticism of Lévi-Strauss could not refute such a mission, even if it made clear the mission's apparent cost, a great cultural impoverishment.[49]

RETURN TO THE EAST

In the late 1950s and early 1960s Lévi-Strauss was an extremely popular intellectual figure in France. He was able to teach his readers a new respect for the "savages," but his message was rejected by many as antimodern, and the peoples whom he praised could be dismissed as having a negligible importance in the contemporary world. French ethnocentrism needed to be confronted by non-Western peoples who appeared to present a more viable alternative to Westernization than the peoples praised by Lévi-Strauss. This challenge came not only from Maoist China, but also from a source with which the French were more intimately acquainted, the Arab peoples. The principal interpreter of the Arabs to the French was Jacques Berque, who offered the most inspiring vision of the world that was emerging from decolonization.

Berque was born in Algeria, served in the Moroccan rural administration, represented Morocco at the Brazzaville conference of 1944,
and founded a short-lived project of rural modernization in Morocco in
1945. He wrote specialized works on the sociology of Moroccan peasant communities and in 1956 was appointed professor of the social
history of contemporary Islam at the Collège de France. In response to
the Algerian war, Berque wrote in favor of Algerian independence and
participated in the efforts of the university community to convince the
French to end the war. In this activity he followed in the tradition of
France's greatest scholars of overseas societies, like his own teacher
Massignon and like the Asian expert Mus, who also responded to
colonial uprisings by speaking out in sympathy with the rebellious
peoples they knew so well. At the end of the period of decolonization,
Berque wrote a series of important books, notably *Dépossession du
monde* (1964), in which he contemplated the fundamental meaning of
decolonization.

Berque contended that society was articulated in a series of stages,
the basic level of which was man's relation to his natural environment.
At this base of immediacy and ecological authenticity, all modes of
subsequent development of man and society—erotic, sportive, aes-
thetic, spiritual, economic, and so forth—originally were possible and
remained potential. This was the level of unexpressed meanings, the
level at which the sign, "like the Delphic oracle," meant nothing yet,
but was "content to vibrate." All semantic activity and all elaboration
of more complex levels of society necessarily involved the arbitrary
selection and reduction of "these unfathomable riches."[50] The extreme
of impoverishment had been achieved, according to Berque, by Western industrial society. It had reduced man to a single dimension, the
economic, and had severed him from his roots in nature.

The critical moment of Western history, Berque believed, had been
the middle of the eighteenth century. At that time the West had had the
opportunity to make a creative synthesis of three elements: its growing
awareness of the rest of the world, the new power of its machines, and
its close relation to nature. But the West had retained only the first two
elements and had abandoned nature to artists and adversaries of progress. The cause of this failure, Berque charged, was capitalism. In its
search for surplus economic value, capitalist production, more than
any other social expression, consumed "the surpluses of man and
nature." It conducted "a plundering raid" on the unexpressed mean-

ings and annihilated the anthropological values arising from man's essential multidimensionality and from his rootedness in nature.

Still searching for economic profit and not content with impoverishing themselves, the European bourgeois imposed, or tried to impose, this impoverishment on the rest of the world. Colonial imperialism was, according to Berque, a gigantic "consumption of signs." It was "the quest and liquidation of the diverse in the world," the destruction of all but one type of social expression, the narrow "economism" of the West. Moreover, this Western mode of being was especially alienating when imposed on subjugated peoples from the outside.

The radical unauthenticity of this imported Western social expression, however, was the very reason for the failure of imperialism. Berque supported and went beyond the arguments of various economists that colonialism was incapable of developing the colonial territories. He explained that colonialism, confronted by societies still partly rooted in authentic relations with their natural surroundings, could do no more than create horizontal integrations on the surfaces of these societies. It was unable to touch the profound forces of the indigenous society, which alone could have achieved the necessary vertical integrations. These forces instead had reacted to the shock of colonization by withdrawing into "continental" strongholds: religion, the veiled women, the peasant communities of the mountains. In these retreats the subsequent revolts were nourished. Unlike most French colonial historians, who treated colonial nationalism as a reflection of Western ideas, Berque saw the forces of liberation developing from within the indigenous society.[51]

Decolonization was the exorcism of a world that had been possessed by the demons of the West. Elaborating on Memmi's ideas, Berque argued that decolonization was the moment not only in which the subjugated peoples reentered history, but in which they became the active and creative forces of a new era of history. Unlike Sartre and Fanon, however, Berque did not structure his vision in accordance with a revised Leninist doctrine. He saw a more intimate dialectic at work. He believed that, while the capitalist West had exhausted its creative energy and had become decadent and passive, as evidenced by the popularity of ahistorical structuralist theories like Lévi-Strauss's, the colonial peoples had retained contact, in their continental retreats, with their fundamental level of immediacy and authenticity. He declared that decolonization was a return to the spring of a rediscovered and released nature. It was a bubbling up and gushing forth of hidden energies and new meanings from the creative anthropological base of humanity. It was a new beginning, not only for the liberated colonies, but for the whole world.

With the world threatened by the spread of the West's "pseudo-civilization of consumption," Berque believed that these rejuvenated, former colonial peoples could be "the saviors of history." With them, the world had been given a second chance to integrate ecological authenticity into an industrial civilization. Berque contended that the potential for success was greater now than in the eighteenth century because the new anthropological creativity was occurring when both technology and critical reflection on technology were mature. The newly liberated peoples would show that technological development could occur without the drastic anthropological impoverishment of Westernization. Because of the vastness of the enterprise, he was not surprised by the temporary failures of these peoples, but he did not lose confidence in them. He called on Westerners to follow the inspiration of the Third World and to rediscover their own East—to return to "the place of the immediacy of relations between nature and culture."[52]

Berque criticized the effects of industrialization, but did not reject modernity, as did Lévi-Strauss. The task was to transcend the present sterile antithesis between cultural authenticity and technology by creating a true industrial civilization. The nature Berque wanted the peoples of the world to rediscover was not the virgin nature of the reactionary Romantics, but a "second nature," a socialized nature, the nature worked on and reconstituted by man. The initial objective of the new era of history was to forge new bonds between industrial society and its ecological base. The second objective, and an outcome of the first, was to revive the multiplicity of human dimensions that the capitalist West had eliminated and to assure within industrial society a continual conversion between these modes of being. The third objective was to protect and stimulate cultural multiplicity within the worldwide industrial civilization. This third objective was closely linked to the preceding two: "The plurality of man's dimensions is itself the foundation for and injunction to the plurality of the world's cultures."[53]

Berque tried to convince Frenchmen that decolonization was not the defeat of France, but the end of a sterile period of history and the rebirth of the world. It was difficult not to greet his hopes with some skepticism, for it was difficult to believe that a modern industrial civilization could renew or retain ties with nature and preserve human and cultural multiplicity. Lévi-Strauss, for example, retorted that several variations on the single theme of industrial civilization would in no way compensate for the destruction of genuine cultural diversity by the spread of Western influence. Berque was aware of the danger that modernization would result merely in Westernization, but had faith in the creative power of peoples like the Arabs. Yet it was easy to believe that Berque, like Sartre and Fanon, was only expressing a new type of romanticism. Not surprisingly, his message was appreciated more in the Arab countries than in France.[54]

THE PLURALITY OF THE WORLD

Decolonization forced the French to question the universal applicability of their civilization. The cultural self-affirmation of the colonial peoples, the cultural criticism of anthropologists like Lévi-Strauss, and the vision of Berque were parts of a process in which French intellectuals learned to prize the cultural plurality of the world. The intellectuals who attacked French ethnocentrism invited the French people to participate in a worldwide dialogue of cultures from which they had as much to learn as to teach. They did not want France to withdraw into isolation, but rather to continue its humanist vocation with a new modesty.

The review *Esprit* was foremost in transmitting this vision of a collaboration of peoples. Though not free of ethnocentrism themselves, its editors welcomed the articles of intellectuals like Senghor and Berque who tried to widen the perspective of the French. In the special issue of October 1961 entitled "From Assistance to Solidarity," Domenach declared that the French, in dealing with the plight of the underdeveloped countries, must ask "not what can *we* bring *them*? but first, in the midst of a common 'we,' what services can we mutually do for each other?"[55] The time had come to build a unified yet pluralistic world civilization in which each culture preserved its specificity within a general dialogue and solidarity.

The expansion of cultural perspective illustrated and promoted by *Esprit* was not a refutation of French universalism. The admission that French values and practices might not be superior to those of other peoples—the willingness to praise and learn from different cultures

—was a further sign of the basic universality of the French spirit. The call for a symbiosis of cultures represented a healthy and realistic revision rather than a denial of France's particular form of ethnocentrism. By this means the crisis of French civilization diagnosed by Luethy could be overcome: the French could demonstrate the vitality of their civilization by their ability to engage in a creative interchange with other cultures. From decolonization would emerge a "new French universalism."[56]

Yet it was hard for the French to see their culture as merely one among equals. In *Esprit*'s special issue of November 1962 on "French, Living Language," Domenach suggested that France's participation in the future interaction of world cultures could be based on a linguistic community that would, in effect, replace the ruptured political community. Realizing that the French language carried French culture along with it, the contributors to the issue nevertheless denied that the teaching of French abroad would undermine the local cultures. Instead, they claimed, it would provide the overseas peoples with access to the "universal" and with their "only means of opening on and grasping the modern world." The spread of the French language, it was maintained, would not be "intellectual imperialism," but an effort "to maintain certain of the highest spiritual values of humanity."[57]

This vision of a French-speaking community illustrated a basic hindrance to the acceptance of a real cultural pluralism. The French intellectuals found it difficult not to be concerned with universal values; without them, as Domenach objected, the humanity of Berque would be "a sort of gigantic volcanic disorder."[58] But they continued to look to Western values—of Christianity, of the Enlightenment, of Marxism.

∾ Conclusion

DECOLONIZATION AND THE INTELLECTUALS

The French fought long and hard to prevent the loss of their colonies. Their actions were to a great extent the consequence of the imperialist ideas that persisted among the political elite and the public. They believed that France had a humanist colonial vocation and that empire was part of the nation's greatness. The critics of France's actions were not able to transform this imperialist state of mind. Their failure was the result both of the French people's lack of receptivity to anti-imperialist messages and of the shortcomings of the critics' arguments.

The ideas possessed by an individual or a social group are difficult to change. Ideas are not likely to be discarded without good reason. They may be the product of a child's basic education and usually are part of a reinforcing set of concepts, closely related to other characteristics of the individual or group. The resistance of ideas to change is particularly great when these ideas are involved in individual or collective self-esteem.[1]

As a result, intellectuals who try to effect fundamental changes in ideas are unlikely to have a great impact unless other forces have made people receptive to the new ideas. The eighteenth-century *philosophes*, for example, appeared in the midst of a vast internal transformation of French society that had created for them an audience whose emerging consciousness the *philosophes* were able to articulate and shape. In contrast, the advocates of decolonization confronted a public whose hostility to anti-imperialist ideas was increased by their recent experiences. The decline in France's status in the world, culminating in its collapse in World War II and its impotence in the immediate postwar period, added a nonrational force to the belief in the legitimacy and value of France's empire. The movement for colonial liberation was seen as another external threat to France. The audience that was receptive to anti-imperialist ideas was in the colonies, not in France. In Britain, in contrast, the political leaders and the public were prepared by their imperial traditions and by the wartime reassertion of Britain's prestige to agree to a transformation of their empire into a loose Commonwealth.

The French intellectuals felt pressure from both the public and the governments to conform to the general desire to preserve the empire. No doubt they were sensitive both to patriotic appeals and to the financial threats of the loss of readers and, during the Algerian war, of government confiscation. Yet, as intellectuals, they were committed to an effort to analyze the situation honestly and objectively and to make their conclusions public. They had the duty to try to educate their compatriots.

The intellectuals did not at the end of World War II call for the complete independence of the colonies. Few advocated this even as late as the mid-fifties. Most of those who did were far leftists who already had lost a great deal of credibility among the political elite and the general public either, like the writers of *Les Temps Modernes*, because of their support of the Soviet Union and the French Communist party or, like Rous and Lefort, because of their Trotskyist leanings.[2] In addition, a handful of writers of the liberal Right—in particular, Aron on Algeria and Cartier on sub-Saharan Africa—came out for independence in the mid-fifties on grounds of economic liberalism and political realism. Both far leftists and liberals were out of tune with the still-dominant rhetoric of missionary idealism and *grandeur*. The other intellectuals, from the writers of *Esprit* to Soustelle, called for extensive reforms but stopped short of independence. They defended their proposals for reform with arguments that were in accord with the traditional ideology of French imperialism.

Among these advocates of reform, the moralist critics of French colonial policies wanted the French to act justly in the colonies. But they feared that because of the immaturity of the colonial peoples, the external threat of other imperialisms, and the internal threat of underdevelopment, separation from France would be a misfortune for the colonial peoples. They also worried, especially in the case of Algeria, about the fate of the French settlers and the indigenous supporters of

France if control was turned over to the colonial nationalists. The "humanist" principles that inspired their anticolonialism, therefore, prevented them from moving to an anti-imperialist position.

The realist reformers continued for the most part to assert, like their imperialist opponents, that some kind of overseas presence served France's interests and increased its *grandeur*. Consequently, when they charged that the methods the French were employing to maintain the empire were ineffective and that the aim of continued imperial domination was unrealistic, they argued in the name of preserving rather than ending France's ties with overseas lands. Like the moralists, they proposed more liberal forms of association, not separation.

Ironically, the reform-minded intellectuals had a more radical impact both on events and on French ideas than they apparently intended. Both the overseas elites and the French leaders and people were encouraged by their arguments to engage in the process of colonial demands and French concessions that led inexorably to independence. Furthermore, the imperialists themselves helped to make the anticolonialists' messages appear more radical than they were. Hoping to discredit even moderate reforms, the imperialists claimed that the reformers foresaw and wanted the "abandonment" that was implied by their proposals.

It is easy, from a retrospective and non-French viewpoint, to criticize the French intellectuals who were unwilling to call for independence. Their arguments seem morally questionable: they furnished justifications for the continued dominance of one group of people over another. Their arguments also seem unrealistic: they paid insufficient heed to certain aspects of the postwar world—the rise of colonial nationalism, the hostility of the Americans and the Soviets to European empires, the weakness of France—that already could be seen as condemning any sort of political ties between France and its colonies. Yet such an appraisal is incomplete.

The intellectuals' embarrassment before the question of independence was a result of the shaping of their visions by their culture and profession. They judged overseas issues in terms of the values they shared, for the most part, with other Frenchmen and intellectuals. In particular, in accordance both with the Declaration of the Rights of Man and the Citizen and with the calling of the intellectual, they believed that individual rights, especially the freedom of thought and expression, were more important than, and should not be sacrificed to, the interests of the collectivity. Consequently, they were very concerned about the threats to individual liberty and well-being that might accompany the achievement of national sovereignty.

Indeed, their hesitations were in large part a product of their honesty in applying these values. Intellectuals often are accused of abstract and idealistic thinking, but in the case of decolonization most of them, except for some on either extreme, sought to deal with the concrete situations. They saw that the issues were complex and contradictory and that the problems confronting newly independent states were real and tragic. The economic and political difficulties of France's former colonies have confirmed that some of the intellectuals' fears were valid, even if these difficulties do not demonstrate that the states would have been better off under a continuing French rule.

Forseeing these difficulties and sharing with other Frenchmen the conviction that France had a special vocation to aid the peoples who were struggling to reach modernity, the intellectuals tended to see independence as the abandonment of their tutorship to hands, whether foreign or indigenous, that were less worthy. The more "humanist" policy seemed to be to create a just French Union. Believing that the overseas peoples shared their idealization of France and its culture, they expected that these peoples would want to remain associated in some way with France. The ethnocentrism on which French colonization had been based continued, in spite of diverse attacks on it, to pervade the thinking of most of the intellectuals throughout the period of decolonization. It was the intellectuals, after all, whose self-esteem was most closely bound up with the idea that France's culture and language had a universal appeal. In sum, to ask the intellectuals to support colonial independence was to ask them to change their most fundamental values and beliefs.

The intellectuals' contributions to decolonization must not be underestimated. They insisted that French policies had to be guided by certain humanist values and realist criteria which, at the least, limited the means the governments could employ. The campaign against French atrocities in Algeria, for example, showed that the French governments could not afford to violate moral principles too blatantly without provoking a storm of protest from the intellectuals. The campaign also suggested that such protest is necessary to impose some limits on government actions. It demonstrated the importance of the intellectual's role as the conscience of his society. Furthermore, even if the intellectuals wrote neither boldly nor unambiguously about the ends of overseas policy, they did at least raise and discuss the important questions.

The impact of "engaged" intellectuals is in any case probably greater after the fact than before. Even if they have little influence on immediate policies, they still can prepare the ways in which people will eventually conceptualize their experiences. When the external situation has changed, people must find a means of integrating the new situation into their world view and, therefore, may have to accept ideas they formerly rejected. Furthermore, the intellectuals' immediate audience will have included many of the school teachers and textbook authors who will shape the views of the youths.[3]

After the French had failed to prevent the loss of their empire, they needed to adjust their vision of France and the world to the fact of decolonization. Aside from Sartre and Berque, who glorified the peoples of the Third World, the intellectuals could offer the French little reason other than "Cartierist" selfishness to welcome, even in retrospect, the independence of their former colonies. The French viewed decolonization as a defeat. Yet the intellectuals helped to minimize some of the potentially unpleasant consequences of this view. The humanist intellectuals' stress on France's continuing overseas mission hindered the spread of the Cartierist vision of the former subjects as ungrateful people who deserved no further aid from France. It prepared the public to accept de Gaulle's linking of aid to the former colonies with the reassertion of France's *grandeur*. Even if the percentage of France's GNP devoted to foreign aid (mostly to its former colonies) declined during the decade after the Algerian war, it remained higher than that of any other Western country.[4]

The most traumatic part of decolonization was the Algerian war. The French tried to forget about it as quickly as possible. The leftists were embarrassed about the Left's behavior during the war and critical of conditions in independent Algeria.[5] The mass of the people returned to the private concerns from which the war had dragged them. In time, however, the memories of the war became less immediate and painful. The spectacles of the American war in Vietnam and the struggles for national liberation in the Portuguese empire permitted the French to look at their own experiences in Indochina and Algeria from a more favorable perspective. With the sole apparent motive of preventing Communists from coming to power in South Vietnam, the Americans fought as unsuccessfully as had the French and far more destructively. The Portuguese leaders, who talked even more than the French about their country's civilizing mission, devoted Portugal's scarce resources to long wars in Africa that the army itself finally decided could not be won. The French also were able to see a judgment on British colonization in the troubles that erupted in, for example, Nigeria, Rhodesia, Bangladesh, the Near East, and Northern Ireland.

In the early 1970s, a decade after Algerian independence, the French were willing again to think seriously about the war and its meaning. The French Algerians who had fled to France brought to public attention the injustices done to them at the end of the war by the FLN, the Gaullists, and the French people. The military leaders of the war and of the OAS presented chronicles of their activities. The anticolonialist intellectuals responded to the challenge. In a flood of memoirs and histories, in films and on television, the issues of decolonization were debated once again, but in a calmer atmosphere. The intellectuals' ideas about decolonization were given another opportunity to influence the French people.[6]

Yet the time when intellectuals could exert considerable influence in France may be gone. The contention of many Liberation intellectuals that the intellectual should be actively involved in the issues of his time has received multiple challenges. Some critics have charged that political commitment distracts the intellectual from his true role, which is "the exercise of creative imagination." The novels of Sartre and Camus gave way in the late 1950s to the "new novel," concentrating on descriptions of physical objects and rejecting all moralizing. Other critics were dismayed by the seeming irresponsibility of the public posturing of those intellectuals who issued statements and signed manifestos on a multitude of subjects. Lévi-Strauss pointed out that the intellectual's opinion is sought only because of "the concern imputed to him for never saying anything in public that hasn't been solidly thought out." If the intellectual "lets himself be cajoled into hasty statements about a subject in which he is without any particular competence or deeply grounded knowledge, he would betray the confidence of those who take him seriously on the basis of more considered judgements."[7]

Jeanson and Sartre, on the other hand, decided that the type of involvement practiced by the Liberation intellectuals was insufficient. During the Algerian war they came to the conclusion that the intellectual not only must think and write, but must take concrete action as well: the intellectual himself must unite theory and practice. The failure of Jeanson's avant-garde effort to revitalize the Left and to arouse the masses, however, convinced them that the intellectual must abandon his traditional posture even further. Radical politics could not succeed, it seemed, until the masses developed the ability of self-expression and communication necessary to forge a "proletarian" consciousness. The intellectual must cease speaking at the masses and instead help them to express themselves. In 1967, Jeanson formed a "team of cultural action" from the Théâtre de Bourgogne to bring theater into the countryside, and in 1969, to the dismay of both far leftists and rightists, he accepted a government appointment to set up a multipurpose arts center (*maison de la culture*) in Chalon-sur-Saône. Sartre, after the shock of the student revolt of May 1968, actively supported the young radicals, becoming in 1970 the nominal editor of *La Cause du Peuple* and numerous other banned publications. While not entirely discontinuing his own writing, Sartre argued that the role of the intellectual in a capitalist society was to blend with and to become the mouthpiece of the masses.[8]

Meanwhile, the composition of the intellectual stratum was changing. As the French economy began to boom in the early 1950s, industrial technology became more widely used and more complex; the creed of scientific research and technical proficiency spread through private industry and public administration; and the universities expanded. In France as in other advanced industrial states, increasingly large numbers of highly educated people were employed by private and public concerns to work in specialized areas. In addition, the change of regimes in 1958 meant a shift in power from the old-style politicians, with their respect for general culture and verbal skill, to the technocrats. Observers wondered if the classical intellectual was being superseded by the specialist.[9]

There will always be issues of general interest that need to be analyzed and solved. There will always be injustices that need to be denounced. There will always be authors, journalists, and academics in France who will choose to fill this role. The importance of the role itself, however, has declined in contemporary France. The involvement of the French intellectuals in decolonization, especially their activities during the war in Algeria, may prove to have been the final great battle in the long tradition of France's "engaged" intellectuals.[10]

᭳ Notes

NOTES TO CHAPTER ONE

1. The following analysis of the political system is based primarily on Duncan Mac-Rae, Jr., *Parliament, Parties, and Society in France, 1946–1958*; Robert Schuman, "Nécessité d'une politique"; Pierre Gerbet, "L'Influence de l'opinion publique et des partis sur la politique étrangère de la France," pp. 91–103; Alfred Grosser, *La IVe République et sa politique extérieure*, pp. 48–55, 79–101; Harvey G. Simmons, *French Socialists in Search of a Role, 1956–1967*, pp. 26, 28–29, 32, 78–79, 227–29.

2. See Tony Smith, "The French Colonial Consensus and People's War, 1946–58," pp. 217–22.

3. Philippe Devillers, *Histoire du Viêt-Nam de 1940 à 1952*. Public opinion polls were taken regularly by the Institut Français d'Opinion Publique and published in a periodical entitled for a short time *Bulletin d'Informations* and subsequently *Sondages*. See, in particular, the polls reported in *Sondages* 7 (1 Oct. 1945): 182; 9 (1 March 1947): 59–60; 9 (1 June 1947): 119; 16, no. 4 (1954): 10–14; 18, no. 3 (1956): 32. The Ministry of Overseas France conducted polls in 1949–50 to discover to what degree the public was aware of the overseas lands: "Connaissez-vous la France d'outre-mer?" pp. 19, 35. The results of opinion polls obviously are not completely trustworthy. Distortions might be introduced by the sample, by the choice and phrasing of the questions, and by the interpretation of the answers both by poll takers and by analysts. Nonetheless, polls seem to provide the most reliable indication of public opinion. In making generalizations about French opinion, I will assume that the IFOP polls are accurate.

4. See also *Sondages* 8 (1 April 1946): 146; 8 (16 June 1946): 146; 9 (1 March 1947): 60; 13, no. 1 (1951): 17–19; 15, no. 3 (1953): 6; 20, no. 3 (1958): 45; 20, no. 4 (1958): 56–59; and table 5.

5. *Sondages* 9 (1 April 1947): 64; 10 (15 Sept. 1948): 168; 13, no. 3 (1951): 4–5; 16, no. 4 (1954): 5–8; "Connaissez-vous la France d'outre-mer?" pp. 7–18. The British public was just as ignorant about the British empire, according to "Connaissez-vous la France d'outre-mer?" pp. 54–57.

6. Gerbet, "Influence de l'opinion publique," p. 88. Also *Sondages* 16, no. 1 (1954): 8, 10. Compare Pierre Fougeyrollas, *La Conscience politique dans la France contemporaine*, p. 271.

7. MacRae, *Parliament, Parties, and Society*, pp. 230–31. Also Jacques Chapsal, "Le Suffrage politique et l'expression de l'opinion publique française depuis 1945," pp. 263, 289; Henry W. Ehrmann, *Politics in France*, pp. 92–95.

8. Philip E. Converse and Georges Dupeux, "Politicization of the Electorate in France and the United States," pp. 41–63; MacRae, *Parliament, Parties, and Society*, p. 260; Gerbet, "Influence de l'opinion publique," p. 89. Compare the similar conclusions about American opinion in Bernard C. Hennessy, *Public Opinion*, pp. 46–47, 50–51; Herbert McClosky, "Consensus and Ideology in American Politics," pp. 378–83.

9. Income, education, and social status are correlated with opinion in *Sondages* 8 (1 April 1946): 85; 13, no. 1 (1951): 56–59; 19, no. 2 (1957): 50; 20, no. 3 (1958): 45; 20, no. 4 (1958): 23–24, 50–59; 22, no. 3 (1960): 46–48, 58. Similarly, for the United States, see John E. Mueller, *War, Presidents and Public Opinion*, pp. 122–23. On the war in Indochina see table 2; breakdowns by party preference are given in *Sondages* 13, no. 1 (1951): 19; 15, no. 3 (1953): 6. The exception to the statement in the text is 1950, when the outbreak of the Korean war seems to have provoked a temporary burst of determination in France to defeat the Vietminh. See also D. Bruce Marshall, *The French Colonial Myth and Constitution-Making in the Fourth Republic*, especially p. 2; William G. Andrews, *French Politics and Algeria*, pp. 35–64; Gerbet, "Influence de l'opinion publique," pp. 104–5.

10. Various definitions have been proposed in the vast literature by and about intellectuals. See, for example, Philip Rieff, ed., *On Intellectuals*; Lewis A. Coser, *Men of Ideas*; "Intellectuals and Tradition"; "Intellectuals and Change"; Louis Bodin, *Les Intellectuels*; "Les Intellectuels dans la société française contemporaine"; Jean-Paul Sartre, *What Is Literature?*; Jean-Paul Sartre, *Plaidoyer pour les intellectuels*; Raymond Aron, *The Opium of the Intellectuals*, especially chap. 7; Albert Camus, *Resistance, Rebellion, and Death*, pp. 181–209; "Les Intellectuels"; "French Intellectuals: Do They Serve a Purpose?" p. 14. The term "the sacred" comes from Edward Shils, "The Intellectuals and the Powers," in Rieff, *On Intellectuals*, pp. 27–35. Otherwise the definition proposed here is not quite like any of the above, but is derived largely from the definition that the protagonists of this book gave in their actual practice.

11. The importance of "world images" is stressed in Max Weber, *From Max Weber*, pp. 280, 286–87. Recent studies have suggested, however, that, in the United States at least, only a minimal consensus on fundamental values exists among the mass of the population and that little appears to be necessary to permit social cohesion, as long as some consensus does exist among the elites, which occurs in the United States more than in France (McClosky, "Consensus and Ideology," pp. 365–90; Philip E. Converse, "The Nature of Belief Systems in Mass Publics," pp. 129–55).

12. François Mauriac, "L'Engagement de l'écrivain." See also René Rémond, "Les Intellectuels et la politique," p. 877; Maurice Merleau-Ponty, *Sense and Non-Sense*, pp. 139–52; Simone de Beauvoir, *The Mandarins*; Sartre, *What Is Literature?*; M. Adereth, *Commitment in Modern French Literature*.

13. The high status of intellectuals in France is described in Aron, *Opium of the Intellectuals*, pp. 218–19; Bodin, *Intellectuels*, pp. 55–59, 79; Louis Bodin and Jean Touchard, "Les Intellectuels dans la société française contemporaine," pp. 849–52; Rémond, "Intellectuels et la politique," p. 861; Kenneth Douglas, "The French Intellectuals," pp. 61–63. According to Rémond (pp. 862–63 n.), however, another reason that French newspapers relied on literary figures and academics instead of on journalists was the papers' poverty. Contrast the descriptions of English intellectuals in T. R. Fyvel, *Intellectuals Today*, pp. 15–65, and of American intellectuals in Sandy Vogelgesang, *The Long Dark Night of the Soul*, pp. 23–24.

14. See the figures given in Bodin and Touchard, "Intellectuels dans la société française," pp. 845–46.

15. Gerbet, "Influence de l'opinion publique," p. 89, although Michel Crouzet, "La Bataille des intellectuels français," p. 51, contends that the *militants* of the parties and trade unions did not read the writings of the intellectuals during the war in Algeria. Bernard C. Cohen, *The Press and Foreign Policy*, comes to similar conclusions about the role of the "prestige" newspapers in the formulation of American foreign policy. Although only a small minority of the American public reads seriously the news of foreign affairs, it includes the political elite. Moreover, the policymakers themselves have attested in interviews to the press's complex and important impact on American foreign policy. As Cohen underlines in his subsequent book, *The Public's Impact on Foreign Policy*, pp. 106–13, however, the papers are read for their information rather than for their editorial opinion.

16. *Sondages* 8 (16 June 1946): 146.

17. I am grateful to Tom Cassilly, "The Anticolonial Tradition in France," for stressing

the importance of the distinction between the anticolonialist and the anti-imperialist (which he labels "anticolonial") positions. See also Henri Brunschwig, "Colonisation-décolonisation."

18. The imperialist position is described with sensitivity and sympathy in Raoul Girardet, *L'Idée coloniale en France de 1871 à 1962*, chap. 12.

19. Jean-Marie Domenach, interview with the author, 21 April 1970. Rous also was singled out by Claude Bourdet, interview with the author, 28 Feb. 1970; by Jean-Paul Sartre, interview with the author, 11 June 1970; and by the introduction to Jean Rous, *Chronique de la décolonisation*, p. 7.

20. Note that the meaning of "humanism" and "humanist," as used in France at this time, was different from and broader than the meaning of these terms during the Renaissance, although the contemporary meaning clearly developed out of the Renaissance one. Édouard Morot-Sir, *La Pensée française d'aujourd'hui*, p. 9, points to "humanism" as the password common to French writers of all persuasions in the period between the two world wars.

NOTES TO CHAPTER TWO

1. The information in this section is derived largely from Raoul Girardet, *L'Idée coloniale en France de 1871 à 1962*, chaps. 1–9; Hubert Deschamps, *Les Méthodes et les doctrines coloniales de la France*, pp. 9–176; Henri Brunschwig, *Mythes et réalités de l'impérialisme colonial français, 1871–1914*; Manuela Semidei, "De l'empire à la décolonisation à travers les manuels scolaires français," pp. 56–71.

2. Girardet, *Idée coloniale*, p. 23. Contrast the Germans' justifications for imperial conquest, as described in Woodruff D. Smith, "The Ideology of German Colonialism, 1840–1906."

3. Jean–Marie Domenach, interview with the author, 21 April 1970. The same assertion is made by Girardet, *Idée coloniale*, pp. 265–66; and by Alfred Grosser, *Au nom de quoi?* p. 155.

4. A notorious example of racism is Ernest Renan, *La Réforme intellectuelle et morale*, pp. 142–43; note, however, the response to Jules Ferry's racist affirmation, quoted in Brunschwig, *Mythes et réalités*, p. 75. The social theorists are described in Deschamps, *Méthodes et doctrines*, pp. 143–47; see, in particular, Lucien Lévy-Bruhl, *Primitive Mentality*.

5. *Sondages*, no. 3 (Aug. 1939), pp. 11–12, cited by Girardet, *Idée coloniale*, p. 134. Girardet is impressed more by the 43 percent who did not judge it as painful than by the 53 percent who did (with 4 percent giving no response).

6. The key works on the morality of colonization are Joseph Folliet, *Le Droit de colonisation* (Paris: Blond et Gay, 1933), and Albert Sarraut, *Grandeur et servitude coloniales* (Paris: Éditions Sagittaire, 1931). The 1930 session of the Catholics' Semaines Sociales de France and the 1931 congress of the anticlerical Ligue des Droits de l'Homme were devoted to colonization and reached similar conclusions. On the Socialists, see Manuela Semidei, "Les Socialistes français et le problème colonial entre les deux guerres."

7. Jacques J. Maquet, "Objectivity in Anthropology," pp. 49–50; Gérard Leclerc, *Anthropologie et colonialisme*, pp. 57–143.

8. Robert Delavignette, *Freedom and Authority in French West Africa*, p. 150. The contents of the book indicate that it was written before the end of the war even though the French original, *Service africain*, was not published until 1946.

9. Charles de Gaulle, *Discours et messages*, 1:293–95, 372–73, 418–19, 533, 553, 605–6.

10. Ibid, 1:372.

11. *Projet de réformes faisant suite au Manifeste du peuple algérien musulman*, 26 May 1943, quoted in Roger Le Tourneau, *Évolution politique de l'Afrique du Nord musulmane, 1920–1961*, p. 342.

12. Compare the assessments of the Brazzaville conference in D. Bruce Marshall, *The French Colonial Myth and Constitution-Making in the Fourth Republic*, pp. 102–15; William B.

Cohen, *Rulers of Empire*, pp. 163–69; and Deschamps, *Méthodes et doctrines*, pp. 180–82. The English term "self-government" did not imply as complete a severance of ties as did "independence."

13. Raymond Aron, *De l'armistice à l'insurrection nationale*, p. 245; de Gaulle, *Discours*, 1:297, 316, 347, 353, 375, 403, 419, 485, 509, 534; *Le Figaro*, 8–9, 14 Oct. 1944, 20 Jan., 14 March 1945; Colonel F. Bernard, "Le Problème colonial et l'avenir de l'Indochine," pp. 274–75; note 20, below.

14. See Jean Sainteny, *Histoire d'une paix manquée*, pp. 46–49. H. Stuart Hughes, *The Obstructed Path*, pp. 7–9, has pointed to a more general intellectual isolation during this decade; but note also Édouard Morot-Sir, *La Pensée française d'aujourd'hui*, pp. 9–10.

15. Claude Bourdet, interview with the author, 28 Feb. 1970; Claude Bourdet, *L'Aventure incertaine*, pp. 443–44; Jean-Marie Domenach, in *Esprit*, no. 222 (Jan. 1955), p. 172.

16. Domenach, interview; René Hostache, *Le Conseil National de la Résistance*, p. 463. Also Marie Granet and Henri Michel, *Combat*, pp. 121–22, 166, 288, 320, 322.

17. Robert Delavignette, "L'Union française," pp. 230–33, 236.

18. Herbert Luethy, *France against Herself*, p. 220; *Sondages* 8 (1 April 1946): 84.

19. *Le Monde*, 20 Jan. 1945; *Le Figaro*, 20 Jan. 1945. See also the speech of the minister of colonies, reported in *Le Figaro*, 21 March 1945, and *Le Monde*, 22 March 1945; de Gaulle, *Discours*, 1:508–9.

20. *Le Monde*, 1 Feb. 1945; also 21–22 Jan. 1945. On *Le Monde*, see Abel Chatelain, *"Le Monde" et ses lecteurs sous la IVe république*; Alfred Grosser, *La IVe République et sa politique extérieure*, pp. 167–70.

21. *Combat*, 21–22 Jan. 1945, also 28 Oct. 1944, 17 Feb., 14 March, 31 May 1945.

22. *Le Monde*, 14 June 1945, also 28 July 1945. Contrast Walter La Feber, "Roosevelt, Churchill, and Indochina."

23. Communiqué of the government general of Algeria, quoted in *Le Monde*, 12 May 1945; *L'Humanité*, 30 June 1945, quoted in Jacob Moneta, *La Politique du parti communiste français dans la question coloniale, 1920–1965*, pp. 154–55; *Le Monde*, 8–9, 10 July 1945, also 24 May 1945.

24. *Combat*, 13–23 May, 15 June 1945, reprinted in Albert Camus, *Actuelles, III*, pp. 93–122.

25. *Le Monde*, 31 Jan. 1945; also *Combat*, 5 Nov. 1944; *Le Figaro*, 26 Jan. 1945.

26. *Combat*, 22, 27–28 May, 3–4, 6 June 1945; *Le Monde*, 23 May, 2 June 1945; Institut Français d'Opinion Publique, *Bulletin d'Informations*, 16 July 1945, p. 141. Note de Gaulle, *Discours*, 1:462–63, 507–8, 558–80.

27. *Le Monde*, 21 Aug. 1945; Albert Camus, *Le "Combat" d'Albert Camus*, pp. 283–85, 291–95; Colonel F. Bernard, in *Combat*, 14, 18, 22–23, 24 April, 5 Sept., 2 Nov. 1945.

28. *Sondages* 9 (1 March 1947): 59.

29. The discussion of the constituent assemblies is derived largely from Marshall, *French Colonial Myth*, chaps. 5–9, and Gordon Wright, *The Reshaping of French Democracy*.

30. Marshall, *French Colonial Myth*, pp. 216–17. The description of the legislatures is Marshall's.

31. Ibid, p. 241.

32. De Gaulle, *Discours*, 2:5–11.

33. Ibid., p. 19.

34. Wright, *Reshaping of French Democracy*, p. 215. Another stormy session is described in Luethy, *France against Herself*, pp. 222–24.

35. Grosser, *IVe République*, pp. 257–58.

36. *Sondages*, 9 (1 March 1947): 59; Alexander Werth, *France 1940–1955*, pp. 340, 345.

37. The evolution of public opinion on the war is summarized in *Sondages* 16, no. 4 (1954): 10, and is reproduced in table 2. Omitted from the summary are the results of a poll taken in February 1947, before the fury of the Cold War, in which 55 percent wanted to negotiate with the government of Vietnam rather than to continue the war (*Sondages* 9 [1 May 1947]: 90).

38. *Sondages*, 9 (1 Aug. 1947): 160. This account of the revolt is based on Virginia Thompson and Richard Adloff, *The Malagasy Republic*, pp. 54–66; Pierre Stibbe, *Justice pour les Malgaches*.

39. Le Tourneau, *Afrique du Nord*, p. 221.

40. Jacques Arnault, *Procès du colonialisme*, pp. 228–29. Arnault's book was recommended by Jean Suret-Canale, director of the Centre d'Études et de Recherches Marxistes, in an interview with the author, 5 June 1970. This account of the Communist position is a synthesis of Arnault, *Procès du colonialisme*; Suret-Canale, interview; Jean Suret-Canale, "De la libération à la guerre d'Indochine"; Moneta, *Politique du parti communiste*; Jean Baby, *Critique de base*, pp. 105–8; Alfred J. Rieber, *Stalin and the French Communist Party, 1941–1947*, pp. 313–30, 343–46; Hélène Carrère d'Encausse, "Le Parti communiste français et le mouvement de libération nationale algérien"; Marshall, *French Colonial Myth*, pp. 53–61, 98, 236–45, 281–83, 304–6; Bernard B. Fall, "Tribulations of a Party Line"; Aimé Césaire, *Lettre à Maurice Thorez*.

41. *L'Humanité*, 30 June 1945, quoted in Moneta, *Politique du parti communiste*, p. 155.

42. Moneta, *Politique du parti communiste*, pp. 145, 169.

43. Suret-Canale, "De la libération," p. 40; Moneta, *Politique du parti communiste*, pp. 164–65. Other possible motives of the Communists are discussed by Marshall, *French Colonial Myth*, pp. 282–83, 305.

44. T. M., "Ce n'est pas une émeute . . . ," p. 1543; *Sondages* 9 (1 April 1947): 64; 10 (15 Sept. 1948): 168.

NOTES TO CHAPTER THREE

1. See especially *Esprit*, no. 130 (Feb. 1947), no. 132 (April 1947), no. 135 (July 1947), no. 142 (Feb. 1948); *Les Temps Modernes*, no. 15 (Dec. 1946), no. 18 (March 1947); *Chemins du Monde*, no. 5 (1948); Semaines Sociales de France, *Peuples d'outre-mer et civilisation occidentale*. The foresightedness of *Esprit* is noted by Alfred Grosser, *La IVe République et sa politique extérieure*, pp. 177–79; and Raoul Girardet, *L'Idée coloniale en France de 1871 á 1962*, p. 320.

2. Many of Rous's articles are collected in Jean Rous, *Chronique de la décolonisation*.

3. Colonel F. Bernard, "Les Destins de l'Union française," pp. 49, 48, 40. See also chap. 2, n. 27, above; *Combat*, 17–18 March, 24 April, 8 June, 7–8, 9 July, 26 Nov., 15–16 Dec. 1946, 28, 29 May 1947; *Cahiers du Monde Nouveau* 1, nos. 1–2 (1945): 168–75; 1, no. 3 (1945): 264–79; 2, no. 5 (May 1946): 46–61; 2, no. 10 (Dec. 1946): 22–33.

4. J.-M. Sédès, "L'Union française et sa politique," p. 43. Also *Cahiers du Monde Nouveau* 3, no. 1 (Jan. 1947): 70–74; 4, no. 5 (May 1948): 49–61; 4, no. 8 (Oct. 1948): 1–17, 42–52; 4, no. 10 (Dec. 1948): 47–61.

5. Jean-Marie Domenach, *Esprit*, no. 157 (July 1949): 918. See also *Esprit*, no. 149 (Oct. 1948); no. 166 (April 1950). A striking illustration of most intellectuals' neglect of overseas issues is the lack of activity by Daniel Guérin, one of the foremost anticolonialist militants of the late 1930s while a member of the left-wing faction of the Socialist party. His collected writings on colonialism, *Ci-gît le colonialisme*, contain only one article between 1939 and 1953, and that was merely an interview for *Combat* in 1946 with the Algerian leader Messali Hadj.

6. Roger Le Tourneau, *Évolution politique de l'Afrique du Nord musulmane, 1920–1961*, p. 118.

7. Grosser, *IVe République*, p. 266.

8. The judgment of Jean Lacouture, *Cinq Hommes et la France*, p. 217.

9. *Le Monde*, 19 April 1950, 11–12, 15 March 1951; *Esprit*, especially no. 176 (Feb. 1951), no. 192 (July 1952), no. 199 (Feb. 1953); Rous, *Chronique*, pp. 45–50, 69–86, 125–31; *Combat*, 7 Aug. 1947; *L'Observateur*, 15 June 1950, pp. 1–2; 12 Oct. 1950, pp. 1–3; 19 Oct. 1950, pp. 12–13, 24; 26 Oct. 1950, pp. 12–13, 24; 1 Feb. 1951, p. 2; 1 March 1951, pp. 1–2; 15 Nov. 1951, pp. 6–8; 17 Jan. 1952, pp. 5–6; 15 May 1952, pp. 5–6; 24 July 1952, pp. 5–6; 2 Oct. 1952, pp. 5–7; 11 Dec. 1952; *Les Temps Modernes*, no. 64 (Feb. 1951), p. 1491; no. 66

(April 1951), p. 1896; no. 71 (Sept. 1951), pp. 537–48; no. 80 (June 1952), pp. 2247–64; no. 90 (May 1953), pp. 1810–25; no. 92 (July 1953), pp. 129–38. See also *Les Temps Modernes*, no. 66 (April 1951), no. 77 (March 1952), no. 80 (June 1952), no. 87 (Jan.-Feb. 1953). Lacouture, *Cinq Hommes*, p. 214, notes that few newspapers reported the maneuvers of Juin against the sultan in early 1951.

10. Françoise Kempf, "Les Catholiques français," p. 155; "Connaissez-vous la France d'outre-mer?" pp. 30–38.

11. T. M., "Et bourreaux, et victimes . . . "; François Mauriac, "Le Philosophe et l'Indochine"; [Maurice Merleau-Ponty], "Indochine S.O.S.," pp. 1039–52; François Mauriac, "Ici et maintenant." See also *Le Figaro*, 23, 30 Jan., 6 Feb. 1950, 21 Oct. 1952.

12. Mauriac gave different versions of his Stockholm experience in his *Bloc-Notes, 1952–1957*, pp. 200–201; his *Le Nouveau Bloc-Notes, 1958–1960*, p. 11; and his *Mémoires politiques*, pp. 26–27. See Mauriac's articles in 1953 in *Le Figaro*, 13 Jan., 10 Feb., 24 March, 8 April, 5, 13 May, 30 June, 21 July, 24 Aug.; and in *Témoignage Chrétien*, 27 March, 19 June, 17, 24 July, 7, 28 Aug. His "Bloc-Notes" in *La Table Ronde* and *L'Express* are reprinted in Mauriac, *Bloc-Notes*. On the reaction in Morocco to Mauriac's articles, see Alexander Werth, *France 1940–1955*, pp. 618–20.

13. Charles-André Julien, *L'Afrique du Nord en marche*, p. 393; Jean-Marie Domenach, interview with the author, 21 April 1970; Stéphane Bernard, *The Franco-Moroccan Conflict, 1943–1956*, pp. 119–22, 128; Guérin, *Ci-gît le colonialisme*, pp. 27–34, 41–43, 63–64.

14. Grosser, *IVe République*, p. 167, calls the role of *Le Figaro* "almost avant-garde." See Bernard, *Franco-Moroccan Conflict*, pp. 183–85.

15. *Sondages* 16, no. 4 (1954): 12–14. The results for Tunisia are reproduced in table 1; the results for Morocco were almost identical. Only the Communists supported independence.

16. See Lacouture, *Cinq Hommes*, pp. 232–33; *Esprit*, no. 206 (Sept. 1953); Charles-André Julien, "Perdrons-nous le Maroc comme l'Indochine?"; *Preuves*, Oct. 1953, pp. 14–17.

17. Bernard, *Franco-Moroccan Conflict*, pp. 203, 229–30, 245–46, discusses the efforts of these intellectuals.

18. *Sondages* 13, no. 2 (1951): 48–49; 15, no. 3 (1953): 3–4. These issues give not only the polls reproduced in table 2, but a somewhat different poll taken in April 1951.

19. Philippe Devillers, *Histoire du Viêt-Nam de 1940 à 1952*, pp. 472–73; *Sondages* 16, no. 4 (1954): 8–10; Ellen Hammer, *The Struggle for Indochina, 1940–1955*, pp. 299–300. The slow rise of opposition to the war, after an initial jump, was paralleled by the reaction of the American public to its wars in Korea and Vietnam; see John E. Mueller, *War, Presidents and Public Opinion*, especially p. 62.

20. Madeleine Meyer-Spiegler, "Antimilitarisme et refus de service militaire dans la France contemporaine," pp. 295–306; Claude Estier, *La Gauche hebdomadaire, 1914–1962*, pp. 182–85; *Les Temps Modernes*, no. 41 (March 1949), pp. 502–24; Pierre-Henri Simon, "La France est-elle en état de péché?"; Philip M. Williams, *Wars, Plots and Scandals in Post-War France*, pp. 37–48.

21. *Le Figaro*, 30 Nov. 1953.

22. *Sondages* 16, no. 4 (1954): 7–11.

23. See also Rous, *Chronique*, pp. 403–13; Jean Charlot and Monica Charlot, "Un Rassemblement d'intellectuels," p. 1025; Paul Mus, *Le Destin de l'Union française*.

24. Mauriac, *Bloc-Notes*, pp. 73, 74–75, 81, 104; Pierre Stibbe, *Justice pour les Malgaches*, pp. 138–40; *Pour l'amnistie dans les pays d'outre-mer*; *L'Observateur*, 11 Feb. 1954, pp. 8–10; *France-Observateur*, 11 Aug. 1955, pp. 18–19, 24 Oct. 1957, p. 2.

25. The public's new preoccupation with problems in the overseas lands is revealed in *Sondages* 16, no. 4 (1954): 5–8; 17, no. 1 (1955): 4, 6; 17, no. 4 (1955): 6, 8; 18, no. 3 (1956): 3.

26. "Connaissez-vous la France d'outre-mer?" pp. 20, 33, 37; *Sondages* 19, no. 2 (1957): 48–49; Jules Roy, *Autour du drame*, pp. 24–25.

27. Racques Berque, interview with the author, 16 March 1970; Jacques Berque, *Dépossession du monde*, p. 92; Léopold Sédar Senghor, "Un Humanisme de l'Union fran-

çaise," p. 1020; André de Peretti, "Premières Approches d'une psychologie de la colonisation," p. 120.

28. Germaine Tillion, *L'Algérie en 1957*. See Georges Balandier, "La Situation coloniale."

29. Rous, *Chronique*, pp. 284–89. Also Claude Bourdet, "Madagascar-Dreyfus"; Claude Bourdet, "L'Affaire."

30. Claude Bourdet, "Changer le statut et l'esprit"; Francis Jeanson, "Logique du colonialisme."

31. See chapter 4, n. 4, below.

32. Albert Camus, *Essais*, pp. 52–88.

33. Albert Camus, *The Myth of Sisyphus and Other Essays*, especially p. 46; Albert Camus, "Misère de la Kabylie," *Alger-Républicain*, 5–15 June 1939, mostly reprinted in Albert Camus, *Actuelles, III*, pp. 31–90.

34. Camus, *Actuelles, III*, p. 103; also p. 97.

35. Ibid., pp. 121–22.

36. Ibid., p. 112.

37. See Marie Granet and Henri Michel, *Combat*, p. 221; chapter 8, n. 2, below; *Preuves*, Aug.-Sept. 1953, pp. 123–25; and the following pages.

38. Robert Schuman, "Nécessité d'une politique," p. 9. Also, Maurice Dupont, "Les intérêts français contre l'intérêt de la France en Afrique du Nord."

39. Claude Bourdet, "Les Maîtres de l'Afrique du Nord," p. 2256. The following paragraphs are based mostly on this article; for Bourdet's other articles, see n. 9, above.

40. The phrase is from ibid., p. 2250.

41. Note the similar implication in Schuman, "Nécessité d'une politique," p. 7; Rous, *Chronique*, p. 406.

42. Julien, *Afrique du Nord*, p. 36. Similarly, Julien's letter to *Le Monde*, 19 April 1950; François Mitterrand, "La Politique française en Afrique du Nord," p. 6. The conclusion of incompatibility is apparently reached by Rous, *Chronique*, p. 405; but he writes on p. 406 that Paris should train new administrators "capable of the greatest authority" to join with overseas elites "to impose, by way of authority, with the greatest energy and suppleness, the new reforms." The case for the impossibility of justice in the colonies is made more vigorously by Francis Jeanson in "Cette Algérie, conquise et pacifiée," pp. 625, 634; and in Jeanson, "Logique du colonialisme"; but even he does not yet take the final step of calling for independence. By the mid-fifties Jeanson and many others took this step; see, in particular, Sartre's position described in chapter 4.

43. Claude Lefort, "Les Pays coloniaux," pp. 1069–70; Rous, *Chronique*, pp. 405, 407–8; also pp. 414–18, 423. Tom Cassilly, "The Anticolonial Tradition in France," discusses Rous and Césaire as well as other French anticolonialists and severely criticizes their hesitation to call for independence.

44. Domenach, interview with the author. Also Simone de Beauvoir, *Force of Circumstance*, p. 339.

45. Note, for example, the reactions of the editors of *Esprit* to extreme condemnation of European colonization: Albert Béguin, "La Révolte de l'Asie et la conscience européenne"; Jean-Marie Domenach, "Les Damnés de la terre." On the prewar period, see Girardet, *Idée coloniale*, especially pp. 111–12, 143–50; Manuela Semidei, "Les Socialistes français et le problème colonial entre les deux guerres"; Cassilly, "Anticolonial Tradition."

46. Semaines Sociales, *Peuples d'outre-mer*, pp. 162–63, also pp. 18, 22–25, 167–69, 297–98, 348–49; Centre Catholique des Intellectuels Français, *Colonisation et conscience chrétienne*, pp. 9–10, 15–16, 33–34; *Chemins du Monde*, no. 5 (1948), pp. 87–88.

47. Semaines Sociales, *Peuples d'outre-mer*, pp. 18, 349. The French term *éduquer* has a broader meaning than "to educate."

48. Joseph Rovan, "La France devant l'Indochine," p. 835; [Emmanuel Mounier], "Prévenons la guerre d'Afrique du Nord," p. 545; Emmanuel Mounier, *L'Éveil de l'Afrique noire*, p. 249. Also André de Peretti, "L'Indépendance marocaine et la France," pp. 547–50; Esprit, "Une Affaire intérieure," p. 1644.

49. Jean-Marie Domenach, "L'Union française, pour quoi faire?" p. 181; Domenach, interview. Also, *Esprit*, no. 157 (July 1949), p. 918; nos. 230–31 (Sept.-Oct. 1955), p. 1619.

50. Rous, *Chronique*, pp. 423–24, condemns this "revolutionary paternalism"; yet his article exemplifies a mild form of it.

51. Maurice Merleau-Ponty, *Signs*, p. 325; Aimé Césaire, "La Mort des colonies," p. 1367.

NOTES TO CHAPTER FOUR

1. Jean-Marie Domenach, "Algérie, propositions raisonnables," p. 785.

2. Jean-Baptiste Duroselle also wondered about this in his preface to *Sondages* 23, nos. 1–2 (1958): xi–xii.

3. Xavier Yacono, *Histoire de la colonisation française*, p. 112.

4. *Octobre*, 28 Dec. 1946; [Maurice Merleau-Ponty], "Indochine S.O.S.," p. 1040. Also *Octobre*, 7 Dec. 1946; T. M., "Et bourreaux et victimes . . ."; Bertrand d'Astorg, "Pour un Lyautey socialiste," p. 195; Jean-Marie Domenach, *Esprit*, no. 132 (April 1947), p. 65.

5. The first point was suggested by Stanley Hoffmann; the second by Claude Bourdet, interview with the author, 28 Feb. 1970. See Merleau-Ponty, "Indochine S.O.S.," pp. 1041–42, 1047; and, more generally, Maurice Merleau-Ponty, *Humanism and Terror*.

6. Alfred Grosser, *La IVe République et sa politique extérieure*, pp. 256, 258, and 260.

7. Bertrand de Jouvenel, "Reflections on Colonialism," p. 256; François Mitterrand, quoted in Philippe Émery, "Mythes et réalités du dossier algérien," p. 79.

8. Jean-Marie Domenach, "De l'empire à la communauté des peuples," p. 1094.

9. Joseph Rovan, "La France devant l'Indochine," p. 835; Maurice Duverger, "Une Course contre la montre," p. 218. Also Albert Camus, *Le "Combat" d'Albert Camus*, pp. 292–93; Raymond Aron, "Le Courage d'innover"; Tibor Mende, "Bilan de la décolonisation," p. 45.

10. Paul Alduy, "Pour une structure politique de l'Union française," p. 996; André Mandouze, "Le Dilemme algérien," p. 566. See also André de Peretti, "L'Indépendance marocaine et la France," pp. 547–50; Michel Crozier, "The Cultural Revolution," pp. 530–34. The similar position of the Communists is noted in chapter 2.

11. *Octobre*, 7 Dec. 1946; *Combat*, 25 July, 5 Aug. 1947; *L'Observateur*, 24 July 1952, p. 6.

12. Raymond Aron, "Le Refus du choix est la pire solution"; Jules Roy, "Dialogue avec le vaincu"; Maurice Merleau-Ponty, *Signs*, p. 326; Jean-Paul Sartre, *Situations*, p. 66.

13. *Combat*, 21 Dec. 1948; *L'Observateur*, 2 Nov. 1950, p. 1; 28 Feb. 1952, pp. 8–9; 17 Dec. 1953, pp. 6–7; Jean Rous, *Chronique de la décolonisation*, pp. 14–15, 34–35, 39, 389–90; Philippe Devillers, *Histoire du Viêt-Nam de 1940 à 1952*, pp. 460–62; *Preuves*, July 1953, pp. 71–72.

14. Esprit, "Une Affaire intérieure," p. 1646. Also Robert Montagne, "Le Nationalisme nord-africain," p. 10; François Mitterrand, *Présence française et abandon*, p. 227; Roger Barberot, *Malaventure en Algérie, avec le général Paris de Bollardière*, p. 238.

15. Examples of defense of the nationalists are T. M., "Ce n'est pas une émeute . . . ," p. 1539; François Mauriac,"Pour une nouvelle alliance entre la France et l'Islam"; Georges Izard, "De l'usage des aphrodisiaques en politique," p. 67; Claude Bourdet, "Qui sont les chefs du F.L.N.?". The public's opinion is indicated in *Sondages* 18, no. 4 (1956): 11; 19, no. 2 (1957): 39; 21, no. 2 (1959): 30.

16. Albert Camus, *Resistance, Rebellion, and Death*, p. 109; Jacques Soustelle, *Le Drame algérien et la décadence française*, pp. 55–56. See also Raoul Girardet, *L'Idée coloniale en France de 1871 à 1962*, pp. 239–41; Thierry Maulnier, "L'Afrique est à faire," p. 43; Charles Anthony Smith, "French Extremism in Response to the Algerian Revolution," pp. 165–82; *Sondages* 19, no. 2 (1957): 39.

17. Michel Berveiller, "L'Europe d'outre-mer," p. 49. Similarly, J.-M. Sédès, "L'Union française et sa politique," p. 38.

18. See Michel Crouzet, "La Bataille des intellectuels français," pp. 49–50; Claude Lefort, "Les Pays coloniaux," pp. 1069–71.

19. J.-M. Hertrich, "La Crise tunisienne," p. 17. Also Peretti, "Indépendance marocaine," p. 552; Emmanuel Mounier, *L'Éveil de l'Afrique noire*, p. 306; Berveiller, "Europe d'outre-mer," pp. 50–51.

20. O. Mannoni, "The Decolonisation of Myself," p. 329.

21. The quoted phrases are from O. Mannoni, *Prospero and Caliban*, pp. 175, 171, 66. See also O. Mannoni, "Colonisation et psychanalyse"; O. Mannoni, "Psychologie de la révolte malgache"; Maurice Duverger, "La Maladie infantile du nationalisme," pp. 58–59.

22. Georges Balandier, "La Situation coloniale," pp. 46, 71; Georges Balandier, in *Cahiers Internationaux de Sociologie* 9 (1950): 185–86; H. Stuart Hughes, *The Obstructed Path*, pp. 9–10. Note, however, Francis Jeanson's defense of Mannoni in *Les Temps Modernes*, no. 57 (July 1950), pp. 161–65.

23. Aimé Césaire, *Discours sur le colonialisme*, pp. 39–42; *Présence Africaine*, nos. 10–11 (1951), p. 217.

24. Mannoni, *Prospero and Caliban*, pp. 85–86; Frantz Fanon, *Black Skin, White Masks*, p. 99. Also André de Peretti, "Premières approches d'une psychologie de la colonisation," pp. 99–101; R. Codjo, "Colonisation et conscience chrétienne," pp. 14–15.

25. Charles Flory, "Les Conditions nouvelles des rapports de l'Occident et des peuples d'outre-mer," pp. 16–25; Georges Hardy, "Psychologie et tutelle," pp. 41–49; Georges Le Brun Keris, "L'Afrique entre deux civilisations."

26. Marie Granet and Henri Michel, *Combat*, p. 309; Paul Rivet, "Indépendance et liberté"; Barberot, *Malaventure en Algérie*, p. 238; Rous, *Chronique*, p. 416; Lefort, "Pays coloniaux," pp. 1082–89; Albert Memmi, *L'Homme dominé*, pp. 69–70; Tom Cassilly, "The Anticolonial Tradition in France," on Daniel Guérin, in particular.

27. Berveiller, "Europe d'outre-mer," p. 48; Duverger, "Maladie infantile du nationalisme"; Jean Daniel, "Un Français d'Algérie," p. 29; Joseph Folliet, *Guerre et paix en Algérie*, pp. 27–28; François Luchaire, "Les Grandes Tendances de l'évolution politique en Afrique noire," pp. 593–97.

28. Jean–Marie Domenach, *Esprit*, no. 142 (Feb. 1948), p. 186; Y. Lacoste, "Le Sous-développement," pp. 247–50; Alfred Sauvy, "Introduction à l'étude des pays sous-développés," p. 601; Gaston Leduc, "Le Sous-développement et ses problèmes," p. 137; Georges Balandier, "Déséquilibres socio-culturels et modernisation des 'pays sous-développés,' " p. 30.

29. Germaine Tillion, *L'Algérie en 1957*, p. 27, reprinted as part of Germaine Tillion, *L'Afrique bascule vers l'avenir*.

30. Tillion, *Algérie en 1957*, pp. 52–53.

31. Germaine Tillion, *Les Ennemis complémentaires*, pp. 42–43, 50, 63; Albert Camus, *Actuelles, III*, pp. 150–51; Camus, *Resistance, Rebellion, and Death*, p. 109. Also Folliet, *Guerre et paix*, pp. 22, 53–55, 57, 69–75, 162–63. Lower figures for the number of Algerians in France are cited by Vernon Waughray, "The French Racial Scene," pp. 62–64.

32. Merleau-Ponty, *Signs*, pp. 328–36.

33. Jacques Soustelle, *Aimée et Souffrante Algérie*, pp. 55, 79; Michel Massenet, *Contrepoison, ou la morale en Algérie*, p. 49; Girardet, *Idée coloniale*, pp. 259–63. Also Maulnier, "Afrique est à faire," pp. 43–44.

34. Girardet, *Idée coloniale*, pp. 250–57; John Steward Ambler, *Soldiers against the State*, pp. 264, 308–10.

35. Claude Bourdet, "A qui l'Indochine?"; Claude Bourdet, "L'Incorrigible Paternalisme persiste en Afrique du Nord." Also Rous, *Chronique*, p. 423.

36. Frantz Fanon, *Toward the African Revolution*, p. 88. Also Aimé Césaire, *Lettre à Maurice Thorez*, pp. 10–13.

37. See, however, his speeches in 1948: Jean-Paul Sartre, "La Faim au ventre, la liberté au coeur"; Jean-Paul Sartre, "Ceux qui vous oppriment, nous oppriment pour les mêmes raisons."

38. Sartre's articles on colonialism in the fifties and early sixties are collected in Jean-Paul Sartre, *Situations, V*. See also Jean-Paul Sartre, interview in *Vérités Pour*, no. 9 (2 June 1959); Jean-Paul Sartre, *Critique de la raison dialectique*, pp. 344–47 n., 671–87; Jean-

Paul Sartre, "Le Génocide," p. 957. Much of his analysis is supported by XXX, "La Balance des comptes de l'Algérie."

39. Sartre, *Situations, V,* p. 30.

40. Ibid., p. 40. Compare Francis Jeanson, "Logique du colonialisme"; Jean Cohen, "Colonialisme et racisme en Algérie."

41. Compare Merleau-Ponty, *Signs,* pp. 332–33; Tony Smith, "Idealism and People's War," pp. 430–33.

42. Rous, *Chronique,* pp. 290–91; see also pp. 386–87, but contrast pp. 283–89, 414–24.

43. Maurice Duverger, "Les Deux Stades du nationalisme."

44. Jean-Paul Sartre, "Ouragon sur le sucre"; Jacob Moneta, *La Politique du parti communiste français dans la question coloniale, 1920–1965,* pp. 162–63; Raymond Aron, *La Tragédie algérienne,* pp. 42–43; Raymond Aron, *L'Algérie et la république,* pp. 43–44; Raymond Aron, "Conséquences économiques de l'évolution politique en Afrique noire," pp. 617–18; Raymond Aron, *The Industrial Society,* pp. 23–29. See also Georges Oved and Robert Vaez-Olivera, "Conditions économiques d'un renouveau," pp. 127–28; XXX, "Balance des comptes.".

45. Lacoste, "Sous-développement"; Aron, *Tragédie algérienne,* p. 42; Alfred Sauvy, "Le Sous-développement économique et les conditions de développement," pp. 117–20; Charles Bettelheim, "Planification et croissance économique," p. 35; André Philip, "Les Conditions politiques de l'expansion des pays sous-développés," pp. 37, 40.

46. Aron, *Tragédie algérienne,* pp. 22–23, 51; Aron, *Algérie et la république,* pp. 40–47; Lacoste, "Sous-développement," p. 276. Contrast Paul Legatte, "Doit et avoir de l'Union française," p. 31.

47. Georges Balandier, ed., *Le "Tiers Monde,"* pp. 373–75; Bettelheim, "Planification," p. 35; Aron, "Conséquences économiques," p. 627; Lacoste, "Sous-développement," p. 276.

48. Robert Delavignette, "Les Transformations politiques et sociales impliquées par le développement," p. 301; Claude Bourdet, "La Fuite vers l'économique." Also Sauvy, "Sous-développement," p. 116; Philip, "Conditions politiques," pp. 40–41; Pierre Moussa, *Les Nations prolétaires,* p. 161.

49. Balandier, ed., *"Tiers Monde,"* pp. 291–94, 378.

50. Albert Memmi, *The Colonizer and the Colonized,* pp. 128–35, 141, 151–53. The importance of Memmi's study was stressed by Jacques Berque, interview with the author, 16 March 1970.

51. Frantz Fanon, *A Dying Colonialism,* pp. 179, 30, 144–45.

52. Delavignette, "Transformations," p. 299; Pierre-Henri Teitgen, "La Participation de la France à la montée des peuples," p. 315. Also Alain Savary, *Nationalisme algérien et grandeur français,* pp. 109–11; Club Jean Moulin, "Une Algérie viable," pp. 551–52.

53. Rous, *Chronique,* p. 290; Merleau-Ponty, *Signs,* p. 332. Skepticism also is apparent in Georges Balandier, *Ambiguous Africa,* pp. 144–45, 244, 251–53.

54. Tillion, *Algérie en 1957,* p. 113; Aron, *Tragédie algérienne,* p. 22.

55. Aron, *Algérie et la république,* pp. 40–42, 45–46, 74–75; Tillion, *Algérie en 1957,* p. 41. Similarly, the Socialist leader Philip, "Conditions politiques," p. 41.

56. Christine Alix, "Le Vatican et la décolonisation."

57. Françoise Kempf, "Les Catholiques français," pp. 202, 168.

58. See Girardet, *Idée coloniale,* pp. 266–74; René Rémond, ed., *Forces religieuses et attitudes politiques dans la France contemporaine,* pp. 331–37.

59. Rous, *Chronique,* pp. 391, 405.

60. Jean Rous, *Tunisie . . . Attention!,* p. 32.

61. Girardet, *Idée coloniale,* pp. 242–43.

62. Julien is quoted in Claude Estier, *La Gauche hebdomadaire, 1914–1962,* p. 209; the Moslem deputies, in Grosser, *IVe République,* p. 378.

63. *Esprit,* nos. 230–31 (Sept.-Oct. 1955), p. 1630, and no. 239 (June 1956), pp. 941–42; *Les Temps Modernes,* no. 118 (Oct. 1955), p. 386; *France-Observateur,* 22 March 1956, pp. 4–5 (in contrast, 26 May 1955, p. 7); 13 Dec. 1956, p. 4; Jules Roy, *Autour du drame,* pp. 23,

26–27; *Preuves*, Oct. 1955, pp. 50–53; Nov. 1955, pp. 96–98; July 1956, pp. 20–21 (but also March 1956, pp. 10–17); *La Nef*, Dec. 1956, pp. 60–81, 93; Henri Marrou, "France, ma patrie . . ."; Jean-Jacques Servan-Schreiber, *Lieutenant in Algeria*, p. 51; Raymond Aron, *Espoir et peur du siècle*, p. 205; Aron, *Tragédie algérienne*, pp. 24–25, 63–64; Tillion, *Ennemis complémentaires*, pp. 15–21.

64. *Les Temps Modernes*, no. 119 (Nov. 1955), pp. 577–78, and no. 123 (March-April 1956), p. 1347; *France-Observateur*, 29 Sept. 1955, pp. 16–17; 6 Oct. 1955, pp. 6–7; 14 June 1956, pp. 10–11; 25 July 1957, p. 5; 29 Aug. 1957, p. 3; *Esprit*, no. 232 (Nov. 1955), pp. 1647, 1681–90; no. 236 (March 1956), p. 322; no. 243 (Oct. 1956), p. 560; no. 248 (March 1957), pp. 574–76; no. 249 (April 1957), p. 579; no. 250 (May 1957), p. 785. Also Jacques Berque, "L'Algérie ou les faux dilemmes."

65. Jacques Le Prévost, *Défense de l'Algérie*, p. 195; Association Ceux d'Algérie, *Ceux d'Algérie*, pp. 22, 24–25, 38; Marc Lauriol, *L'Intégration fédéraliste*; Serge Bromberger, *Les Rebelles algériens*, p. 271; Jean Servier, *Demain en Algérie*, p. 167; *Sondages* 19, no. 2 (1957): 39; 21, no. 2 (1959): 30. For an intermediate position, see Folliet, *Guerre et paix*, pp. 28, 31–33.

66. Claude Bourdet, "Loi-cadre: Un Bao-Dai moléculaire." Appeals to this right were made in T. M., "Pouvoirs 'spéciaux,'" p. 1347; Émery, "Mythes et réalités," p. 85; Jacques Duquesne, *L'Algérie ou la guerre des mythes*, p. 180; *Algérie et la république*, p. 130; n. 1, above.

67. *Sondages* 21, no. 2 (1959): 40.

68. Jean Lacouture, *Cinq Hommes et la France*, p. 323.

69. André Passeron, *De Gaulle parle*, pp. 225, 288, 456–59, 465–67, 471, 473.

70. See chapter 2, sec. 5, note 40; Estier, *Gauche hebdomadaire*, pp. 209–10; Elie Mignot, "La Guerre coloniale d'Algérie," pp. 59, 61.

NOTES TO CHAPTER FIVE

1. *Sondages* 19, no. 2 (1957): 6.

2. Ibid.; Maurice Duverger, et al., *Les Élections du 2 janvier 1956*, pp. 89–91; Alfred Grosser, *La IVe République et sa politique extérieure*, p. 379. But William G. Andrews, *French Politics and Algeria*, p. 47, sees Algeria as the main electoral issue.

3. *Sondages* 18, no. 4 (1956): 14.

4. Andrews, *French Politics and Algeria*, pp. 25–28; *Sondages* 19, no. 2 (1957): 6.

5. Andrews, *French Politics and Algeria*, pp. 38, 41; Jacob Moneta, *La Politique du parti communiste français dans la question coloniale, 1920–1965*, pp. 231, 240, 248; Hélène Carrère d'Encausse, "Le Parti communiste français et le mouvement de libération nationale algérien," p. 13.

6. *Sondages* 19, no. 2 (1957): 41–42. Note the larger support for independence among the university students in Aix-en-Provence, reported by Jean Barale, "Les Étudiants d'Aix-en-Provence et la politique en mai 1957," p. 973. Compare the somewhat different interpretation of John Talbott, "French Public Opinion and the Algerian War."

7. *Sondages* 22, no. 3 (1960): 56–57.

8. *Sondages* 19, no. 2 (1957): 43; 20, no. 4 (1958): 20.

9. *Sondages* 16, no. 4 (1954): 11; 17, no. 4 (1955): 21 (in contrast to 16, no. 4 [1954]: 12); 25, no. 2 (1963): 32, 54.

10. Compare Raoul Girardet, *L'Idée coloniale en France de 1871 à 1962*, p. 249; Tony Smith, "The French Colonial Consensus and People's War, 1946–58."

11. Jean-Marie Domenach, interview with the author, 21 April 1970. Also S. [Hubert Beuve-Méry], "Sommes-nous les 'vaincus de Hitler'? . . ."; Jean-Paul Sartre, *Situations, V*, pp. 72–73.

12. The phrase comes from Jean Bloch-Michel, "La Discipline des généraux," p. 5. See *L'Observateur*, 6 Dec. 1951, pp. 5–7; *France-Observateur*, 13 Jan. 1955, pp. 6–7; François Mauriac, *Bloc-Notes, 1952–1957*, pp. 151–54; *L'Express*, 29 Dec. 1955–1 Jan. 1956. Madeleine Meyer-Spiegler, "Antimilitarisme et refus de service militaire dans la France

contemporaine," p. 369, points out a few revelations in 1955 of army atrocities.

13. Henri Marrou, "France, ma patrie . . ."; Pierre Vidal-Naquet, *La Raison d'état*, pp. 93–94; Claude Bourdet, "Tortures en Oranie?"

14. Jean-Marie Domenach, "Démoralisation de la nation," p. 577; Comité de Résistance Spirituelle, *Des Rappelés témoignent*, introduction; Joseph Folliet, *Guerre et paix en Algérie*, p. 174.

15. Françoise Kempf, "Les Catholiques français," p. 175.

16. *Le Monde*, 16 March 1957.

17. *Le Monde*, 15 March 1957; John Steward Ambler, *Soldiers against the State*, p. 115.

18. Folliet, *Guerre et paix*, pp. 173–76; Comité de Résistance Spirituelle, *Des Rappelés témoignent*, introduction.

19. *Le Monde*, 26 March 1957.

20. *L'Express*, 29 March 1957.

21. Union Nationale des Étudiants de France, *Le Syndicalisme étudiant et le problème algérien*, p. 31. The membership figure is given by A. Belden Fields, *Student Politics in France*, p. 102.

22. Vidal-Naquet, *Raison d'état*, p. 130.

23. Louis Martin-Chauffier, "L'Éxigence de vérité"; Louis Martin-Chauffier, "Journal de voyage en marge d'une enquête."

24. T. M., "La Réponse d'Henri Alleg."

25. Petition at the end of the American edition of Henri Alleg, *The Question*. Sartre's essay, "Une Victoire," is reprinted in *Situations, V*, pp. 72–88.

26. Claude Bourdet, "Les Racines de l'enfer." See also Michel Crouzet, "La Bataille des intellectuels français," pp. 47–48.

27. Albert Palle, "Crier, mais avec qui?"

28. Pierre Vidal-Naquet, *Torture*, p. 147; Sartre, *Situations, V*, pp. 57–67; Mauriac, *Bloc-Notes*, p. 153.

29. Bourdet, "Tortures en Oranie?"; Claude Bourdet, "Mauriac, l'action politique et nous."

30. The story is told in Alfred Fabre-Luce, *Demain en Algérie*, pp. 92–93; also *Saturne* 3, no. 14 (Aug.-Sept. 1957): 116, 121; 4, no. 17 (Jan.-Feb.-March 1958): 20 n.; *Preuves*, no. 83 (Jan. 1958), p. 56; Roger Barberot, *Malaventure en Algérie, avec le général Paris de Bollardière*, pp. 179–80; Jean-Paul Sartre, *Théâtre*, p. 850. The chaplain is quoted in Vidal-Naquet, *Raison d'état*, p. 109, see also pp. 116–18, 120–21; *Preuves*, no. 83 (Jan. 1958), pp. 52–54.

31. *Preuves*, no. 83 (Jan. 1958), p. 51; also no. 80 (Oct. 1957), p. 91.

32. Bollardière, cited in Barberot, *Malaventure en Algérie*, pp. 116, 180–81; Albert Camus, *Resistance, Rebellion, and Death*, p. 84; Pierre-Henri Simon, *Contre la torture*, p. 116; Billotte, quoted in *Preuves*, no. 80 (Oct. 1957), p. 91; *Saturne* 4, no. 17 (Jan.-Feb.-March 1958): 14. See also Folliet, *Guerre et paix*, pp. 104, 107, 110; *La Nef*, May 1957, pp. 6–8, and April 1958, p. 10.

33. *Preuves*, no. 83 (Jan. 1958), pp. 51–52; Vidal-Naquet, *Raison d'état*, p. 122; Fabre-Luce, *Demain en Algérie*, p. 91; Jean Daniel, "Un Français d'Algérie," p. 25.

34. The quotations in the preceding three paragraphs are from Simon, *Contre la torture*, pp. 64, 48–52, 121–23. See also Marrou, "France, ma patrie"; Bloch-Michel, "Discipline des généraux," pp. 5–8; Martin-Chauffier, "Éxigence de vérité"; Folliet, *Guerre et paix*, p. 175.

35. Domenach, "Démoralisation de la nation," p. 578. Also Louis Martin-Chauffier, "Toute la vérité, rien que la vérité," pp. 4, 7; *La Nef*, "Les Bases nécessaires d'une solution en Algérie," p. 6; Jacques Carat, "Sur trois saisies"; Mauriac, *Bloc-Notes*, p. 310; François Mauriac, *Le Nouveau Bloc-Notes, 1958–1960*, pp. 32, 46–47.

36. Association Ceux d'Algérie, *Ceux d'Algérie*, p. 30.

37. Jean-Jacques Servan-Schreiber, *Lieutenant in Algeria*, pp. 154, 135, 199. Also Barberot, *Malaventure en Algérie*, pp. 108–17, although he blamed the military and political leaders more than the colonial system.

38. Domenach, "Démoralisation de la nation"; Jean-Marie Domenach, "Algérie,

propositions raisonnables," pp. 777–79; *Esprit*, no. 249 (April 1957), p. 582; no. 250 (May 1957), p. 814; no. 261 (May 1958), pp. 830–31. Also, eventually, Jean-Jacques Servan-Schreiber, "Le Sang qui coule."

39. Sartre, *Situations, V*, pp. 84, 86. Compare T. M., "Réponse d'Henri Alleg"; Jean-Paul Sartre, "Le Génocide," p. 969; Sartre, *Théâtre*, p. 862.

40. Simon, *Contre la torture*, pp. 67–71, 96–99; Fabre-Luce, *Demain en Algérie*, p. 92.

41. Pierre-Henri Simon, quoted and criticized by Bloch-Michel, "Discipline des généraux," p. 6; Pierre-Henri Simon, *Portrait d'un officier*, p. 67.

42. Mauriac, *Nouveau Bloc-Notes, 1958–1960*, pp. 72, 127, also pp. 217–18; François Mauriac, *Le Nouveau Bloc-Notes, 1961–1964*, p. 120.

43. Claude Bourdet, interview with the author, 28 Feb. 1970, agreed that such demoralization was the effect.

44. Bloch-Michel, "Discipline des généraux," p. 8; *Preuves*, supplement to no. 118 (Dec. 1960), pp. 3–4; n. 18, above; Marrou, "France, ma partie"; Maurice Duverger, "Absence française."

45. [Maurice Merleau-Ponty], "Indochine S.O.S.," pp. 1047–48; Maurice Merleau-Ponty, *Signs*, pp. 328–36.

46. Domenach, interview. Also *Esprit*, no. 417 (Oct. 1972), p. 402. The continued loyalty to Messali Hadj is illustrated by Daniel Guérin, *Ci-gît le colonialisme*, pp. 40–167, 312–28.

47. Camus, *Resistance, Rebellion, and Death*, p. 95. The statements about Camus are based particularly on Albert Camus, *Essais*, pp. 1531–33, 1535–37, 1840–47, 1862–77; Albert Camus, *The Myth of Sisyphus*, pp. 38–48; Albert Camus, *Le "Combat" d'Albert Camus*, pp. 183–95; Albert Camus, *The Plague*, pp. 192–97, 222–30; Albert Camus, *The Rebel*, pp. 13–22, 279–82; Albert Camus, *Actuelles, III*. A similar concern for reestablishing limits is found in Domenach, "Algérie, propositions raisonnables," p. 782; Jean Bloch-Michel, "Une Morale du succès?" p. 55; Germaine Tillion, *Les Ennemis complémentaires*, pp. 51–64, 171–73.

48. Tillion, *Ennemis complémentaires*, pp. 49–66.

49. See Michel Massenet, *Contrepoison, ou la morale en Algérie*, p. 51; Vidal-Naquet, *Raison d'état*, pp. 111, 118, 134–35, 169 n. 3; Jean Cassou, "Lettre à Paul Rivet"; Jacques Soustelle, *Aimée et Souffrante Algérie*, pp. 215–21. Note in table 4 that the public's desire to crush the rebellion apparently increased between July 1956 and July 1957.

50. Comité de Résistance Spirituelle, quoted in *L'Express*, 7 June 1957, p. 5; *Esprit*, no. 252 (July 1957), pp. 104–6; *France-Observateur*, 6 June 1957. Also Mauriac, *Bloc-Notes*, p. 325; Folliet, *Guerre et paix*, pp. 182–83; *Esprit*, no. 258 (Feb. 1958), p. 248; no. 262 (June 1958), pp. 930–31; Jean-Marie Domenach, in *Arguments* 2, no. 10 (Nov. 1958): 21–22.

51. Pierre-Henri Simon, "Opération bonne conscience," p. 245; Bloch-Michel, "Une Morale du succès?" pp. 55–56; Folliet, *Guerre et paix*, pp. 175–76; Mauriac, *Nouveau Bloc-Notes, 1958–1960*, p. 29.

52. Tillion, *Ennemis complémentaires*, pp. 47, 49–50; Claude Roy, "La Gauche française à l'oeil nu"; Jules Roy, *La Guerre d'Algérie*, p. 122; Frantz Fanon, *A Dying Colonialism*, pp. 23–26, 54–58; Frantz Fanon, *The Wretched of the Earth*, pp. 43–50; Sartre, *Situations, V*, pp. 82–83; Jean-Paul Sartre, *Plaidoyer pour les intellectuels*, p. 49.

53. T. M., "L'Algérie n'est pas la France"; Sartre, *Situations, V*, pp. 46–47, 54–56, 84–86, 177–79; Jean-Paul Sartre, *Critique de la raison dialectique*, p. 687; Jean Cohen, "Colonialisme et racisme en Algérie," pp. 588–89; Colette Jeanson and Francis Jeanson, *L'Algérie hors la loi*, p. 274; *Esprit*, no. 251 (June 1957), pp. 1004–7; Fanon, *Wretched of the Earth*, pp. 40, 84.

54. Jean-Paul Sartre, preface to Fanon, *Wretched of the Earth*, pp. 24–25; Sartre, *Plaidoyer pour les intellectuels*, p. 74; Jean-Paul Sartre, quoted in *Le Monde*, 13 Dec. 1969, p. 15. See also Maurice Merleau-Ponty, *Humanism and Terror*, pp. 101–12; Jean-Paul Sartre, *Situations*, pp. 64–78; Sartre, *Situations, V*, pp. 55–56; Jean-Paul Sartre, "Le Crime," p. 13; Simone de Beauvoir, *Force of Circumstance*, pp. 340–41; Tony Smith, "Idealism and People's War," pp. 436–43.

55. Fanon, *Wretched of the Earth*, pp. 93–94; Sartre, preface to ibid., pp. 21, 24.

Fanon's first chapter, "De la violence," was published in *Les Temps Modernes*, no. 181 (May 1961), pp. 1453–93. Also Frantz Fanon, *Black Skin, White Masks*, pp. 219–22; Sartre, *Situations, V*, pp. 46–47, 85, 181–86, 226–31.

56. See Jean-Marie Domenach, "'Les Damnés de la terre'"; Philippe Ivernel, "Violence d'hier et d'aujourd'hui." Fanon discusses Hegel's dialectic of master and slave in *Black Skin*, pp. 216–22.

57. Girardet, *Idée coloniale*, pp. 251, 261; Ambler, *Soldiers against the State*, pp. 310–16; Jean-Yves Alquier, *Nous avons pacifié Tazalt*, pp. 270–71; Jacques Soustelle, *Le Drame algérien et la décadence française*, p. 22; Mauriac, *Nouveau Bloc-Notes, 1958–1960*, p. 326; Jacques Duquesne, *L'Algérie ou la guerre des mythes*, p. 181.

58. Camus, *Essais*, pp. 1072, 1882; Camus, *Resistance, Rebellion, and Death*, p. 83. Also Albert Camus, letter to *Encounter* 8, no. 6 (June 1957): 68.

59. Maurice Duverger, "La Maladie infantile du nationalisme," pp. 52–53.

60. "Connaissez-vous la France d'outre-mer?" pp. 23–24; Raymond Aron, *La Tragédie algérienne*, p. 26; T. M., "Pouvoirs 'spéciaux,'" p. 1351. Some examples of this attitude are Georges Lavau, "L'Algérie avec la France," p. 859; Jean-Jacques Servan-Schreiber, "Rappelés pour quoi?"; Jacques Ellul, quoted in *La Nouvelle Nouvelle Revue Française*, no. 36 (Dec. 1955), p. 1181; Mauriac, *Nouveau Bloc-Notes, 1958–1960*, p. 326; *Preuves*, no. 99 (May 1959), pp. 16–17; Maurice Duverger, "Les Deux Trahisons."

61. Camus, *Actuelles, III*, pp. 89–90, 95; Renée Quinn, "Albert Camus devant le problème algérien"; Camus, *Essais*, pp. 1840, 1844–46.

62. Albert Camus, *L'Exil et le royaume*, pp. 101–24; Conor Cruise O'Brien, *Albert Camus of Europe and Africa*.

63. Camus, *Actuelles, III*, pp. 127, 139–47. Also Camus, *Le "Combat" de Camus*, p. 288; Germaine Tillion, *L'Algérie en 1957*, p. 16; Tillion, *Ennemis complémentaires*, pp. 108–35; *Preuves*, supplement to no. 118 (Dec. 1960), pp. 3–4.

64. Camus, *Actuelles, III*, p. 122.

65. Camus, "L'Avenir algérien," *L'Express*, 23 July 1955, reprinted in *Essais*, pp. 1874–76, but not in *Actuelles, III*; Andrews, *French Politics and Algeria*, p. 36; Camus, *Actuelles, III*, pp. 207–10; Marc Lauriol, *L'Intégration fédéraliste*.

66. Roger Le Tourneau, *Évolution politique de l'Afrique du Nord musulmane, 1920–1961*, pp. 428–32; *Sondages* 20, no. 4 (1958): 20–23.

67. Albert Memmi, "Camus ou le colonisateur de bonne volonté"; Camus, *Resistance, Rebellion, and Death*, p. 90. See also Raymond Aron, *L'Algérie et la république*, pp. 107–8; Soustelle, *Aimée et Souffrante Algérie*, p. 221; Jean Servier, *Demain en Algérie*, pp. 171–72.

68. Roy, *Guerre d'Algérie*, pp. 13–14. The article, "Dans une juste guerre," *L'Express*, 24 Sept. 1955, is reprinted in Jules Roy, *Autour du drame*, pp. 21–30. The following quotations from Roy are in *Autour du drame*, p. 14; *Guerre d'Algérie*, pp. 172–73, 215.

69. Bloch-Michel, "Discipline des généraux," pp. 6–7; Girardet, *Idée coloniale*, pp. 256–57. Note, for example, even Francis Jeanson, *Notre Guerre*, pp. 62–68; Moneta, *Politique de parti communiste*, pp. 211, 217, 246, 248, 249.

70. Aron, *Tragédie algérienne*, p. 20; Soustelle, *Drame algérien*, p. 24. Compare Folliet, *Guerre et paix*, p. 23.

71. Sartre, *Critique de la raison dialectique*, pp. 683–84, 687.

72. Sartre, *Situations, V*, pp. 27 n., 53; Moneta, *Politique du parti communiste*, p. 249; Jean Baby, *Critique de base*, pp. 109–12; Frantz Fanon, *Toward the African Revolution*, pp. 81, 82; Jeanson and Jeanson, *Algérie hors la loi*, p. 229; Marcel Péju, "Fin du mythe gaulliste," p. 1161.

73. Compare the critiques by Merleau-Ponty, *Signs*, pp. 332–33; and by Domenach, "'Les Damnés de la terre,'" pp. 459–61.

74. See *Sondages* 22, no. 3 (1960): 50–53. The referendum was approved by 75 percent of those voting and 55.6 percent of the total electorate. These percentages were reduced by the Communist party's decision to appeal for a negative vote out of opposition to de Gaulle and to his particular plan.

75. *Sondages* 25, no. 2 (1963): 51.

76. Association Ceux d'Algérie, *Ceux d'Algérie*, pp. 5, 14–32; Xavier Grall, *La Génération du djebel*, pp. 17–18; but also Paul-Marie de La Gorce, *The French Army*, p. 460.

77. *Sondages* 25, no. 2 (1963): 51–54; Jane Kramer, "Les Pieds Noirs."

78. Claude Estier, *La Gauche hebdomadaire, 1914–1962*, pp. 196, 256; P.-M. Dessinges, "Les Atteintes à la liberté de la presse en France."

79. Bourdet, interview; Elie Mignot, "La Guerre coloniale d'Algérie," p. 52; Claude Bourdet, "Notre liberté est la vôtre."

80. N. 31, above; Mauriac, *Bloc-Notes*, pp. 154–55, 157–58, 352, 384; Carat, "Sur trois saisies."

81. Jean-Jacques Servan-Schreiber, "Rendez-vous au retour!"; Servan-Schreiber, *Lieutenant in Algeria*, pp. 55–56, 92–93, 180, 196–97; Jean-Marie Domenach, quoted in UNEF, *Syndicalisme étudiant*, p. 68. Also Bourdet, "Racines de l'enfer"; *Esprit*, no. 249 (April 1957), p. 586; *Les Temps Modernes*, nos. 143–44 (Jan.–Feb. 1958), p. 1147; Folliet, *Guerre et paix*, pp. 145–47; *Preuves*, no. 83 (Jan. 1958), p. 53.

82. Jean Rous, *Tunisie . . . Attention!* p. 99; *L'Observateur*, 26 June 1952, pp. 6–7; 20 Aug. 1953, pp. 5–6; *France-Observateur*, 16 June 1955, pp. 6–7.

83. *Sondages* 20, no. 3 (1958): 49–50.

84. *Sondages* 20, no. 4 (1958): 25–27; 21, no. 2 (1959): 43–44; 22, no. 3 (1960): 51; 25, no. 2 (1963): 39–50.

85. Soustelle, *Aimée et Souffrante Algérie*, p. 241; Massenet, *Contrepoison*, pp. 24–25, 63–64; Servan-Schreiber, *Lieutenant in Algeria*, pp. 189–91; Pierre-Henri Simon, "La Tradition jacobine"; Duquesne, *Guerre des mythes*, p. 181. Such a hesitation was noted by Germaine Tillion, interview with the author, 1 July 1972.

86. Jean-Jacques Servan-Schreiber, "Quel est votre choix?" Compare Servan-Schreiber, "Rappelés pour quoi?"; Jean-Jacques Servan-Schreiber, "L'Indépendance."

NOTES TO CHAPTER SIX

1. Compare on this whole chapter Madeleine Meyer-Spiegler, "Antimilitarisme et refus de service militaire dans la France contemporaine"; Charles Anthony Smith, "French Extremism in Response to the Algerian Revolution," pp. 293–315; and, on the American leftists' similar debates on forms of action against the war in Vietnam, Sandy Vogelgesang, *The Long Dark Night of the Soul*, pp. 93–102, 123–40.

2. *Combat*, 27, 31 Jan., 4–5 Feb. 1950; *Le Figaro*, 30 Jan., also 23 Jan., 6 Feb. 1950, 21 Oct. 1952.

3. Domenach, in Jean-Paul Sartre, ed., *L'Affaire Henri Martin*, pp. 247–48.

4. Sartre, ed., *Affaire Henri Martin*, pp. 7–8, 28, 76, 137–38, 214–17, 245; Raymond Aron, "De la trahison"; Alfred Grosser, *La IVe République et sa politique extérieure*, pp. 185–89.

5. Jean Bloch-Michel, "La Discipline des généraux"; Jean-Jacques Servan-Schreiber, "Avec nos soldats"; *Preuves*, supplement to no. 118 (Dec. 1960), pp. 3–4.

6. *Esprit*, no. 279 (Dec. 1959), p. 685.

7. T. M., "Refus d'obéissance"; Jean-Jacques Servan-Schreiber, "Rappelés pour quoi?"; *Esprit*, no. 222 (Nov. 1955), p. 1766.

8. *L'Express*, 8 June 1956, p. 3; 15 June 1956, p. 3; 13 July 1956, p. 3.

9. François Maspero, ed., *Le Droit à l'insoumission*, p. 209.

10. Maurice Maschino, "Le Refus," pp. 709–11; Henri Marrou, "France, ma patrie . . ."; Maurice Maschino, *L'Engagement*, pp. 82–93.

11. Maspero, *Droit à l'insoumission*, p. 84.

12. Maschino, *Engagement*, pp. 92–131.

13. Francis Jeanson, interview with the author, 9–10 July 1972; Francis Jeanson, *Notre Guerre*, pp. 50–53; Francis Jeanson, "Plus loin avec Francis Jeanson," p. 80.

14. Maspero, *Droit à l'insoumission*, pp. 68, 71, 82–84.

15. Supplement to *Esprit*, no. 289 (Nov. 1960), p. 13; *Esprit*, no. 259 (March 1958), p. 451.

16. *Esprit*, no. 279 (Dec. 1959), p. 675; Jean-Marie Domenach, "Résistances," p. 801; Jean-Marie Domenach, "Mise au point"; Paul Ricoeur, "L'Insoumission"; Maspero, *Droit à l'insoumission*, pp. 139, 141–47; Maurice Duverger, "Les Deux Trahisons."

17. Simone de Beauvoir, *Force of Circumstance*, pp. 340, 368, 408.

18. Jeanson, interview; de Beauvoir, *Force of Circumstance*, pp. 370–71; Francis Jeanson, *Sartre dans sa vie*, pp. 213–14.

19. The quotations are from Francis Jeanson, press conference, Paris, 15 April 1960; Francis Jeanson, "Lettre à Jean-Paul Sartre," pp. 1536–37. Also Jeanson, *Notre Guerre*, pp. 13–15, 31–33, 39–41, 45–47, 81; Francis Jeanson, "Letter à J.-M. Domenach," p. 21; *Vérités Pour*, prepublication announcement; no. 1 (29 Sept. 1958), p. 22; no. 16 (13 June 1960), pp. 6, 7; Maspero, *Droit à l'insoumission*, pp. 65–67, 83, 93, 94.

20. Jean-Marie Domenach, "Sauve-qui-peut?" p. 710; Claude Bourdet, "Pourquoi aident-ils le F.L.N.?"

21. Marcel Péju, "De l'affaire des avocats' au 'réseau des intellectuels'"; Francis Jeanson, "Lettre à Claude Bourdet"; Maurice Maschino, *Le Refus*, pp. 7–8, 181–85; Maschino, *Engagement*, pp. 9, 28–30, 33–38; *Vérités Pour*, no. 18 (26 Sept. 1960), p. 4.

22. Mendès-France, quoted in Grosser, *IVe République*, p. 381.

23. The discussion of Communist policy on Algeria is based on Jacob Moneta, *La Politique du parti communiste française dans la question coloniale, 1920–1965*, pp. 210–71; Hélène Carrère d'Encausse, "Le Parti communiste française et le mouvement de libération nationale algérien"; Jacques Fauvet, *Histoire du parti communiste française*, 2:273–77; François Fejtö, *The French Communist Party and the Crisis of International Communism*, pp. 35–49, 102–3; Jean Baby, *Critique de base*, pp. 99–125; Michel Crouzet, "La Bataille des intellectuels français," pp. 52–56; Daniel Guérin, *Ci-gît le colonialisme*, pp. 101, 116–17; Elie Mignot, "La Guerre coloniale d'Algérie"; Jean Suret-Canale, interview with the author, 5 June 1970. The quotations are from Moneta, *Politique du parti communiste*, pp. 243, 214, 239, 218.

24. The quotations are from Jeanson, "Lettre à Jean-Paul Sartre," pp. 1537–39; Jeanson, press conference. The term is from Marcel Péju, "Une Gauche respectueuse."

25. The quotation is from Jeanson, "Lettre à Jean-Paul Sartre," p. 1540. Also Jeanson, *Notre Guerre*, pp. 19–25, 50–51, 70–71, 77–80; *Vérités Pour*, no. 4 (Dec. 1958), pp. 3–4; no. 9 (2 June 1959), pp. 3–4; no. 16 (13 June 1960), pp. 2–3; Marcel Péju, "Mourir pour de Gaulle?" p. 494; Tony Smith, "Idealism and People's War," p. 445.

26. François Mauriac, *Le Nouveau Bloc-Notes, 1961–1964*, p. 105. See François Mauriac, *Le Nouveau Bloc-Notes, 1958–1960*, especially pp. 205–6, 217, 219, 295, 331, 377; Mauriac, *Nouveau Bloc-Notes, 1961–1964*, especially pp. 84–87; *La Nef*, supplement to June 1958, p. iii; July–Aug. 1958, pp. 4–5, 19–21; Sept. 1958, p. 6; May 1959, p. 9.

27. See Servan-Schreiber's editorials in *L'Express*, 29 May, 5 June, 4 Sept., 16 Oct. 1958, 13 Aug., 22 Oct. 1959, 26 Jan., 4 Feb., 10 March, 15 Dec. 1960, 15 June, 2, 9 Nov. 1961, 26 April, 31 May 1962; Bourdet's editorials in *France-Observateur*, 22 May, 10, 17 July, 28 Aug. 1958, 28 May, 16 July 1959, 28 Jan. 4 Feb., 23 June, 8, 15 Dec. 1960, 12 Jan., 9 Feb., 27 April, 14 Sept., 30 Nov., 7 Dec. 1961, 25 Jan., 31 May 1962. Domenach began in this second group: *Esprit*, no. 262 (June 1958), p. 1005; no. 265 (Sept. 1958), pp. 296–300. But, as de Gaulle's intention to end the war became apparent, he shifted to the first group: *Esprit*, no. 277 (Oct. 1959), pp. 392–94; no. 278 (Nov. 1959), pp. 469–70.

28. *Jeune Résistance/Vérités Pour*, no. 1 (Dec. 1960), p. 8.

29. *Vérités Pour*, no. 14 (15 Feb. 1960), p. 2. Jeanson and his colleagues expounded their ideas in *Vérités Pour*; see especially no. 1 (20 Sept. 1958), pp. 7–11; no. 3 (13 Nov. 1958), pp. 2–4; no. 7 (12 March 1959), p. 20; no. 8 (2 May 1959), pp. 8–9; no. 15 (24 March (1960), p. 2; no. 16 (13 June 1960), p. 21. Note that in Sartre's articles for *L'Express* in 1958 he was closer to the position of Bourdet and Servan-Schreiber, arguing that the real power in the Gaullist regime lay with the army in Algeria: Jean-Paul Sartre, *Situations, V*, pp. 96–98, 111, 143, though also 108. Sartre would continue to focus more on the army than on French capitalism: ibid., pp. 154–56, 163–66. But he agreed with Jeanson's rejection of the Gaullist regime: Maspero, *Droit à l'insoumission*, p. 86; Jean-Paul Sartre et al., "Répondre à la violence par la violence?" Similarly, Marcel Péju stressed de Gaulle's de-

sire to placate the army in "Fin du mythe gaulliste," but subsequently shifted toward Jeanson, in "Mourir pour de Gaulle?" pp. 486–89, 493–95.

30. See the criticisms of Bourdet, "Pourquoi aident-ils le F.L.N.?"; Domenach, "Résistances," p. 800; Aron, "De la trahison," pp. 13–14; General Pierre Billotte, "Réflexions sur l'État et la solidarité nationale," pp. 13–15. In reply, Sartre, *Situations, V*, pp. 152–53; *Vérités Pour*, no. 3 (13 Nov. 1958), pp. 2–4; no. 8 (2 May 1959), pp. 8–9; no. 16 (13 June 1960), p. 3; Jeanson, *Notre Guerre*, p. 34; Jeanson, "Lettre à Jean-Paul Sartre," pp. 1542–43; Francis Jeanson, "Lettre à J.-J. Servan-Schreiber"; Péju, "Gauche respectueuse," p. 1515 n.; Sartre et al., "Répondre à la violence."

31. *Vérités Pour*, no. 3 (13 Nov. 1958), p. 2; no. 4 (Dec. 1958), p. 3; no. 9 (2 June 1959), pp. 3–4; no. 16 (13 June 1960), p. 2; no. 18 (26 Sept. 1960), pp. 1, 4; Jeanson, press conference; Jeanson, *Notre Guerre*, pp. 20–21; T. M., "Réponse à Jean Daniel"; de Beauvoir, *Force of Circumstance*, pp. 614–15; Maspero, *Droit à l'insoumission*, pp. 85–86, 204 (although Sartre, *Situations, V*, pp. 151–59).

32. [Maurice Merleau-Ponty], "Indochine S.O.S.," pp. 1048–52.

33. Jeanson, press conference; Jeanson, "Lettre à Jean-Paul Sartre," p. 1543; *Vérités Pour*, prepublication announcement, p. 1; T. M., "La Gauche française et le F.L.N.," p. 1173; Péju, "De l''affaire des avocats,'" p. 1439; Sartre, *Situations, V*, p. 163; *Vérités Pour*, no. 1 (20 Sept. 1958), pp. 18–19; no. 15 (24 March 1960), p. 2; no. 16 (13 June 1960), p. 8. This orthodox Marxist position had been asserted already by Jean-Paul Sartre, "Ceux qui vous oppriment, nous oppriment pour les mêmes raisons"; Michel Leiris, "L'Ethnographe devant le colonialisme," p. 374. The French Communists, of course, subscribed to the same principle, but were reluctant to put it into practice: Baby, *Critique de base*, pp. 101–5; Carrère d'Encausse, "Parti communiste français," p. 8.

34. Colette Jeanson and Francis Jeanson, *L'Algérie hors la loi*, pp. 264–65; Jeanson, *Notre Guerre*, pp. 75–77; *Vérités Pour*, no. 1 (20 Sept. 1958), p. 19; Maschino, *Engagement*, pp. 125–29; Péju, "Mourir pour de Gaulle?" pp. 500–501.

35. Bourdet, "Pourquoi aident-ils le F.L.N.?"; Claude Bourdet, "Sabotages et grèves"; Domenach, "Sauve-qui-peut?" p. 709; Domenach, "Résistances," p. 804; Jean-Jacques Servan-Schreiber, "Les Étudiants arrêtés"; Jean-Jacques Servan-Schreiber, "Une Lettre d'un non-déserteur"; Maspero, *Droit à l'insoumission*, pp. 128, 140, 146–47.

36. Jeanson, "Lettre à J.-M. Domenach," p. 22; *Jeune Résistance/Vérités Pour*, no. 1 (Dec. 1960), p. 8; Jeanson, "Lettre à Claude Bourdet."

37. Jeanson, interview; *Vérités Pour*, no. 16 (13 June 1960), p. 3.

38. Jeanson, "Lettre à Jean-Paul Sartre," p. 1543.

39. Jean-Paul Sartre, *Black Orpheus*, pp. 11, 55–65; Péju, "Mourir pour de Gaulle?" p. 499; Frantz Fanon, *The Wretched of the Earth*, p. 61; chapter 5, n. 52, above; Sartre, *Situations, V*, pp. 189, 192–93; Jeune Résistance, manifesto, April 1961. Sartre, however, in an interview with the author, 11 June 1970, agreed that a humanist, democratic socialism was unlikely to emerge in the impoverished Third World until revolution had occurred in the developed countries as well.

40. The quotation is from Crouzet, "Bataille des intellectuels," p. 54. Also Smith, "Idealism and People's War," pp. 442–46; Jean Daniel, "Socialisme et anti-colonialisme"; Jean-Marie Domenach, " 'Les Damnés de la terre' "; Leszek Kolakowski, "Intellectuals against Intellect," p. 12; *Esprit*, no. 417 (Oct. 1972), p. 411. But René Dumont and Marcel Mazoyer, *Développement et socialismes*, p. 318.

41. Jean-Paul Sartre, *Search for a Method*, pp. 90, 31.

42. See *France-Observateur*, 21 April 1960, p. 2; 28 April 1960, p. 2; *L'Express*, 21 April 1960, pp. 10–11; 28 April 1960, p. 9.

43. Maspero, *Droit à l'insoumission*, pp. 15–20.

44. Ibid., pp. 22–61, 157; Jean-Jacques Servan-Schreiber, "Le Scalpel"; Billotte, "Réflexions sur l'État," p. 15.

45. Maspero, *Droit à l'insoumission*, pp. 155–58.

46. Bourdet, "Pourquoi aident-ils le F.L.N.?"; Claude Bourdet, "Fini de rêver"; Domenach, "Résistances," pp. 798, 807–8.

47. Duverger, "Deux Trahisons"; Servan-Schreiber, "Avec nos soldats"; Maspero,

Droit à l'insoumission, p. 134; Guy Nania, *Un Parti de la gauche*, pp. 214–15; *L'Express*, 27 April 1961, p. 52; Mignon, "Guerre coloniale d'Algérie," p. 65.

48. Domenach, "Résistances"; Claude Bourdet, "'Action directe' et 'non-violence'"; *Esprit*, no. 285 (June 1960), pp. 1142–45.

49. Claude Bourdet, "Le 27 Octobre: Un Tournant et un début!"; Nania, *Parti de la gauche*, pp. 226–27.

50. Union Nationale des Étudiants de France, *Le Syndicalisme étudiant et le problème algérien*; A. Belden Fields, *Student Politics in France*, pp. 30–40; Maspero, *Droit à l'insoumission*, pp. 149–51; Claude Bourdet, "Les Étudiants donnent l'exemple"; *Esprit*, no. 286 (July–Aug. 1960), pp. 1277–78; Jean-Jacques Servan-Schreiber, "L'Appel"; de Beauvoir, *Force of Circumstance*, p. 575.

51. Louis Terrenoire, *De Gaulle et l'Algérie*, pp. 194–95, 215–17. On the unpopularity of American war protesters, see John E. Mueller, *War, Presidents and Public Opinion*, p. 164.

52. De Beauvoir, *Force of Circumstance*, pp. 586–90, 598–618, 622–24; Sartre et al., "Répondre à la violence"; Philip M. Williams and Martin Harrison, *Politics and Society in de Gaulle's Republic*, p. 43.

53. Raoul Girardet, *L'Idée coloniale en France de 1871 à 1962*, pp. 241, 248–55, 261–62.

NOTES TO CHAPTER SEVEN

1. Claude Bourdet, interview with the author, 28 Feb. 1970. See Claude Bourdet, "Politique d'abord"; Marie Granet and Henri Michel, *Combat*, pp. 65–66; Claude Bourdet, *L'Aventure incertaine*, p. 382.

2. Maurice Duverger, "Défendre Hanoi ou défendre Paris?" p. 181. See Bourdet's articles in *Combat*, 14 Jan. 1949; *L'Observateur*, 11 May 1950, pp. 2–3; 3 Jan. 1952, pp. 5–6; 19 March 1953, pp. 5–7; 22 April 1954, p. 7. Also "Pour le paix au Viet-nam,"pp. 122–25; *Esprit*, no. 152 (Jan. 1949), pp. 114–18; *L'Express*, 16 May 1953, p. 1; 23 May 1953, p. 1; 28 May 1954; Alexander Werth, *France 1940–1955*, p. 469.

3. *Sondages* 13, no. 1 (1951): 17; *Octobre*, 7 Dec. 1946; *Combat*, 1, 22 Aug. 1947, 25 May, 14 Aug. 1948, 8 March, 13–14 Aug. 1949, 30 Jan. 1950; *L'Observateur*, 19 March 1953, p. 6; 9 July 1953, pp. 5–7; 22 Oct. 1953, pp. 5–6. Also "Pour le paix au Viet-Nam"; Claudine Chonez, "Vu et entendu en Indochine," p. 45; Duverger, "Défendre Hanoi," p. 177; Alain Savary, "Paix en Indochine," pp. 127–29; Raymond Aron, "La Décomposition des empires coloniaux."

4. "Pour le paix au Viet-nam," p. 122; Duverger, "Défendre Hanoi," pp. 178–79; Hubert Beuve-Méry, *Réflexions politiques, 1932–1952*, p. 227; *L'Observateur*, 23 Nov. 1951, p. 8; 25 Dec. 1952, pp. 5–6; 19 March 1953, p. 5; *Sondages* 16, no. 1 (1954): 8, 10; Pierre Gerbet, "L'Influence de l'opinion publique et des partis sur la politique étrangère de la France," p. 88.

5. *Octobre*, 7 Dec. 1946; *Combat*, 13 March, 29–30 Oct., 7 Nov. 1949; *L'Observateur*, 2 Nov. 1950, p. 1; 5 July 1951, pp. 1–2; *France-Observateur*, 22 April 1954, pp. 6–7; Chonez, "Vu et entendu," p. 54; Philippe Devillers, *Histoire de Viêt-Nam de 1940 à 1952*, pp. 441–65; Paul Mus, *Viêt-Nam, sociologie d'une guerre*, pp. 354–74.

6. *Le Figaro*, 4 Dec. 1953. Also *Le Figaro*, 24 Oct. 1952; but Raymond Aron, *The Century of Total War*, p. 232.

7. Duverger, "Défendre Hanoi," pp. 180–83; Raymond Aron, "La Revanche militaire de l'Asie," p. 19.

8. See, for example, Raymond Aron, *Le Grand Schisme*, pp. 13, 56; *Combat*, 1, 20 Aug. 1947; Duverger, "Défendre Hanoi," p. 178; *La Nef*, n.s., no. 2 (March 1953), pp. 53, 59, 167–69, 220; Jean Rous, *Tunisie . . . Attention!* pp. 7–9.

9. Raymond Aron, *Espoir et peur du siècle*, p. 191, also pp. 200–202, 235; Maurice Duverger, "Une Course contre la montre," p. 219. Also *La Nef*, n.s., no. 9 (June 1955), pp. 146–47; *Esprit*, no. 232 (Nov. 1955), pp. 1689–90; François Mitterrand, *Présence française et abandon*, pp. 103–8, 158, 161–62, 222, 228–30, 235–36.

10. The phrase is from Paul Alduy, "Pour une structure politique de l'Union fran-çaise," p. 1001. Also *Combat*, 20 May, 29 Dec. 1949; *L'Observateur*, 7 Jan. 1954, pp. 12–14; Jean Rous, *Chronique de la décolonisation*, pp. 412–13; Joseph Folliet, *Guerre et paix en Algérie*, pp. 157–58.

11. Colonel F. Bernard, "L'Union française," p. 47; Bourdet, "Politique d'abord"; *Esprit*, no. 157 (July 1949), pp. 1071–80, 1093; Beuve-Méry, *Réflexions politiques*, p. 229; Rous, *Chronique*, p. 408; Rous, *Tunisie*, pp. 36, 73–74, 96; Charles-André Julien, "Perdrons-nous le Maroc comme l'Indochine?"

12. Raymond Aron, *L'Algérie et la république*, pp. 114–15; Raymond Aron, "De la politique de grandeur," pp. 11–12.

13. Jean-Marie Domenach, "Dernières chances de l'Union française," p. 917; Alfred Grosser, *French Foreign Policy under de Gaulle*, p. 54.

14. Jean-Baptiste Duroselle, introduction to *Sondages* 20, nos. 1–2 (1958): xi; Hubert Deschamps, *La Fin des empires coloniaux*, p. 104.

15. See Laurence Wylie, "Youth in France and the United States"; Michel Crozier, *The Bureaucratic Phenomenon*; Stanley Hoffmann et al., *In Search of France*.

16. Hoffmann et al., *In Search of France*, pp. 75, 341; *Bulletin d'informations*, 1 July 1945, p. 134.

17. Charles de Gaulle, *Discours et messages*, 2:81; Raoul Girardet, *L'Idée coloniale en France de 1871 à 1962*, pp. 84, 125–27, 197–99.

18. This is an aspect of the "functional" theory of attitudes, as described in Bernard C. Hennessy, *Public Opinion*, pp. 367–70, 391–92.

19. See Girardet, *Idée coloniale*, pp. 244–48, 290–91; Alfred Grosser, *La IVe République et sa politique extérieure*, p. 392; *Sondages* 18, no. 3 (1956): 32–33; Claude Bourdet, "L'Im-périalisme des pauvres"; André de Peretti, "Psychologie française et pays d'outre-mer," pp. 70–75; Raymond Aron, *France: The New Republic*, pp. 44–46; Raymond Aron, *France: Steadfast and Changing*, pp. 148–55; Jacques Duquesne, *L'Algérie ou la guerre des mythes*, p. 177; René de Lacharrière, "Pour une révision de la doctrine politique," p. 60; Arend Lijphart, *The Trauma of Decolonization*, pp. 288–90; A. P. Thornton, *The Imperial Idea and Its Enemies*, pp. 398–403.

20. Albert Camus, *Actuelles, III*, pp. 86–87, 119, 122; *Le Figaro*, 10 Feb., 13 May, 21 July 1953; François Mauriac, *Bloc-Notes, 1952–1957*, pp. 153–54; *Esprit*, no. 130 (Feb. 1947), p. 201; no. 142 (Feb. 1948), pp. 213, 220; no. 149 (Oct. 1948), pp. 535, 556; no. 157 (July 1949), pp. 1001, 1092–94; Jean-Marie Domenach, "L'Union française, pour quoi faire?" pp. 184–86.

21. Mitterrand, *Présence française*, pp. 210, 237. See also François Mitterrand, "Condi-tions d'une négociation"; François Mitterrand, "La Politique française en Afrique du Nord"; François Mitterrand, "Paradoxes et promesses de l'Union française"; *La Nef*, Jan. 1958, p. 7; Folliet, *Guerre et paix*, pp. 154–62; Girardet, *Idée coloniale*, pp. 225–27, 256–57.

22. The quotations are from *L'Express*, 25 May 1956, p. 3; 31 Oct. 1957, p. 3. Also *L'Express*, 16 Oct. 1954, p. 8; 18 May 1956, p. 3; 8 June 1956, p. 3; 23 Feb. 1961, pp. 5–6; 18 May 1961, p. 48.

23. Rous, *Tunisie*, pp. 8–9; Francis Jeanson, *Notre Guerre*, p. 33. Also *La Nef*, May 1958, p. 8; Jean Baby, *Critique de base*, pp. 103–4; Jacob Moneta, *La Politique du parti com-muniste dans la question coloniale, 1920–1965*, pp. 237, 240, 247, 253.

24. Examples of criticisms are Colonel F. Bernard, "L'Union francaise"; Herriot, quoted in Grosser, *IVe République*, p. 250; Aron, *Grand Schisme*, p. 264; *Cahiers du Monde Nouveau* 2, no. 10 (Dec. 1946): 30–31; Lacharrière, "Pour une révision," p. 52; Duverger, "Course contre la montre," pp. 213–14; Domenach, "Union française," p. 182; Alain Savary, *Nationalisme algérien et grandeur française*, p. 109.

25. *La Nef*, n.s., no. 9 (June 1955), pp. 53, 58, 147, 148–61, 177–86, 223–31.

26. *Esprit*, no. 226 (May 1955), p. 862; nos. 230–31 (Sept.–Oct. 1955), p. 1630; no. 232 (Nov. 1955), pp. 1647–48, 1681–90; Maurice Duverger, "La Politique de Metternich"; *La Nef*, March 1957, p. 14; May 1957, p. 9; July–Aug. 1957, p. 15; Sept. 1957, pp. 5–8; Jan. 1958, p. 7; March 1958, p. 9; May 1958, pp. 8–9; July–Aug. 1958, p. 7; Sept. 1958, p. 6; Nov. 1958, pp. 8–9; Dec. 1958, p. 9. Similarly, *Preuves*, Nov. 1955, pp. 97–98; Aug. 1958, pp. 56–58; Oct. 1958, pp. 3–6; Nov. 1958, pp. 23–24.

27. P. F. Gonidec, *Droit d'outre-mer*, 1:346–48; Léopold Sédar Senghor, *Liberté 2*, p. 197; Folliet, *Guerre et paix*, p. 21.

28. Duverger, "Politique de Metternich," p. 95; Raymond Aron, "Après le coup d'état, avant la négociation," pp. 8–9; *L'Observateur*, 28 Feb. 1952, p. 5; 7 May 1953, p. 7; Claude Bourdet, "C'est la France qui est indispensable à l'Algérie"; *Preuves*, no. 84 (Feb. 1958), p. 65; Chonez, "Vu et entendu," p. 54; Domenach, "Union française," pp. 184–86; Jacques Berque, "L'Algérie ou les faux dilemmes," pp. 709–10; Mitterrand, *Présence française*, pp. 230, 239; *La Nef*, March 1957, p. 12; Jan. 1958, p. 8.

29. Independents, quoted in William G. Andrews, *French Politics and Algeria*, p. 50; Jacques Soustelle, *Aimée et Souffrante Algérie*, p. 93; Marc Lauriol, *L'Intégration fédéraliste*; *Sondages* 22, no. 3 (1960): 57 (in contrast to chapter 5, n. 8, above).

30. *Sondages* 16, no. 4 (1954): 11; 18, no. 3 (1956): 32; 22, no. 3 (1960): 61; 25, no. 2 (1963): 55; 26, no. 3 (1964): 52; Aron, "De la politique de grandeur," p. 11. Also Raymond Aron, "Conséquences économiques de l'évolution politique en Afrique noire," pp. 613–14; François Sengat-Kuo, "La France fait son examen de conscience ou 'Le Fédéralisme sauvera-t-il l'Union française?' " p. 94; Alain Berger, "L'Algérie et la gauche française," pp. 472–78; Frantz Fanon, *Toward the African Revolution*, p. 88; Pierre Alexandre, "Les Voies de l'indépendance," pp. 35, 43.

31. Roy Pierce, *Contemporary French Political Thought*, chap. 8; Raymond Aron, "La Planète vue par un des cerveaux les plus lucides de notre temps: Raymond Aron"; Raymond Aron, interviews with the author, 12 May 1970 and 9 June 1972.

32. Raymond Aron, *L'Age des empires et l'avenir de la France*, p. 47; also pp. 44–48, 349.

33. Aron, *Age des empires*, p. 350; Raymond Aron, "Le Courage d'innover"; Aron, *Grand Schisme*, pp. 13, 56; Raymond Aron, "Les Désillusions de la liberté," pp. 99–101; *Combat*, 22–23 Dec. 1946; Aron, *Algérie et la république*, pp. 5–6.

34. The quotations are from Aron, *Age des empires*, pp. 65, 48. Also Domenach, "Union française," p. 185; Aron, *Algérie et la république*, p. 129; Aron, "De la politique de grandeur," pp. 10–12; Aron, "Après le coup d'état," pp. 5–6; Raymond Aron, *The Industrial Society*, p. 67. Aron explained in his second interview with the author that he used the language of *grandeur* quite often in his wartime writings because of his alliance with the Gaullists. Jean-Baptiste Duroselle describes a postwar "mystique of realism" in Hoffmann et al., *In Search of France*, p. 337.

35. Aron, *Algérie et la république*, p. 6; Aron, second interview.

36. Aron, *Espoir et peur*, p. 200.

37. Raymond Aron, *La Tragédie algérienne*, pp. 24, 44–46, 63–64; Aron, *Algérie et la république*, pp. 16–25, 32, 34–36, 109; Raymond Aron, "Un An après," p. 11; Aron, "De la politique de grandeur," p. 8.

38. Raymond Aron, *On War*, pp. 61–71; Aron, *Century of Total War*, p. 158; Aron, "Décomposition des empires coloniaux"; *Preuves*, no. 95 (Jan. 1959), pp. 11–12; no. 100 (June 1959), p. 8; no. 117 (Nov. 1960), pp. 3, 8; no. 119 (Jan. 1961), p. 5. Also *La Nef*, May 1957, p. 6.

39. Aron, *Tragédie algérienne*, pp. 22–23, 42–43, 51; Aron, *Algérie et la république*, pp. 31–32. Also Savary, *Nationalisme algérien*, pp. 92–104. Popular opinion was that the burden of developing Algeria was "heavy but bearable": *Sondages* 21, no. 2 (1959): 32.

40. Aron, *Tragédie algérienne*, pp. 21, 46–50, 55, 58–61; Aron, *Algérie et la république*, pp. 59–66; Raymond Aron et al., *L'Unification économique de l'Europe*, pp. 29–32. Also *Esprit*, no. 232 (Nov. 1955), pp. 1703–9; XXX, "La Balance des comptes de l'Algérie." In contrast, Soustelle, *Aimée et Souffrante Algérie*, pp. 240–41; Lauriol, *Intégration fédéraliste*.

41. Jacques Soustelle, *Le Drame algérien et la décadence française*, pp. 32–33; Alfred Fabre-Luce, *Demain en Algérie*, pp. 76–80; *La Nef*, Nov. 1957, pp. 28–31; Girardet, *Idée coloniale*, pp. 17, 126–27, 132, 311; *Sondages* 19, no. 2 (1957): 47.

42. Aron, *Tragédie algérienne*, pp. 55–56; Aron, *Algérie et la république*, pp. 64, 67–70; Aron, "De la politique de grandeur," pp. 10–11.

43. *La Nef*, June 1959, p. 4; Jan.–March 1960, especially pp. 15, 94, 108, 118, 128.

44. The quotations are from Aron, *Tragédie algérienne*, p. 69, and Aron, *Algérie et la république*, p. 130. See also Aron, *Tragédie algérienne*, pp. 26, 30–33, 92; Aron, *Algérie et la*

république, pp. 4, 45, 92, 103; Aron, "Un An après," p. 12; Aron, "De la politique de grandeur," p. 11; Berque, "Algérie."

45. Raymond Aron, "La Présomption," p. 8. Also Aron, "De la politique de grandeur," p. 9; Raymond Aron et al., "De Gaulle et l'Algérie"; Raymond Aron, "L'Heure de vérité," p. 3; Savary, *Nationalisme algérien*, p. 197.

46. Soustelle, *Drame algérien*, p. 4; Roger Barberot, *Malaventure en Algérie, avec le général Paris de Bollardière*, pp. 238–40; Aron, *Algérie et la république*, p. 85. The partisans of integration are described in *Sondages* 20, no. 4 (1958): 23–24; 22, no. 3 (1960): 45–48, 58.

47. Aron, *Tragédie algérienne*, pp. 49–51; Aron, *Algérie et la république*, pp. 41–42, 64.

48. *Paris-Match*, 14 Nov. 1953, quoted in André Larquier, "L'Idéologie politique de *Paris-Match*," p. 96.

49. Raymond Cartier, "En France noire avec Raymond Cartier," *Paris-Match*, 18 Aug. 1956, p. 35; 1 Sept. 1956, p. 41; Girardet, *Idée coloniale*, pp. 228–330.

50. Compare the opinion polls in "Connaissez-vous la France d'outre mer?" pp. 18–19, 35–36; *Sondages*, 18 no. 3 (1956): 32; 21, no. 2 (1959): 41. Also Aron, *France: Steadfast and Changing*, pp. 130–31.

51. Centre Catholique des Intellectuels Français, *Colonisation et conscience chrétienne*, pp. 129–35; Raymond Aron, "Les Colonies: Une Mauvaise Affaire?" p. 4; Girardet, *Idée coloniale*, pp. 7, 55, 325; Gonidec, *Droit d'outre-mer*, 1:103–7, 238.

52. *Sondages* 22, no. 3 (1960): 61–62; Gilles Martinet, in Raymond Aron, "Que deviendra la France après la décolonisation?"; Jean-Paul Sartre, *Situations, V*, pp. 194–253.

53. De Gaulle, *Discours*, 3:140–42, 288–89; Larquier, "Idéologie politique de *Paris-Match*," pp. 117–27; Aron, "Après le coup d'état," p. 8.

54. Aron, *Tragédie algérienne*, pp. 20, 33; Raymond Aron, "Un Seul Homme, un homme seul," pp. 11–12; Aron, "La Présomption," p. 8. Also Club Jean Moulin, "Une Algérie viable," p. 556.

55. See Pierre Fougeyrollas, *La Conscience politique dans la France contemporaine*, pp. 223–24.

56. The debate is discussed in Girardet, *Idée coloniale*, pp. 43–66, and in Henri Brunschwig, *Mythes et réalités de l'impérialisme colonial français, 1871–1914*, pp. 73–77. The quotations are from the former, pp. 57, 49–50.

57. Soustelle, *Drame algérien*, pp. 3, 69, also pp. 10–16, 37–38, 64–70; Thierry Maulnier, "Confort et inconfort intellectuels devant le 'colonialisme,'" pp. 9–13; Girardet, *Idée coloniale*, pp. 237–39, 244–48, 290–92.

58. Pierre-Henri Simon, *Contre la torture*, p. 20; *Esprit*, no. 305 (April 1962), p. 514; no. 311 (Nov. 1962), p. 563. Also Domenach, "Union française," pp. 178, 184–86; *Esprit*, no. 282 (March 1960), pp. 585–86; Barberot, *Malaventure en Algérie*, pp. 237–40; Maurice Merleau-Ponty, *Signs*, p. 336; *Chemins du Monde* 5 (1948): 12; Duquesne, *Guerre des mythes*, pp. 177–80.

59. The quotation is from Aron, *Algérie et la république*, p. 85. Also Aron, *Espoir et peur*, pp. 216, 230–37; Aron, *Tragédie algérienne*, p. 72; Aron "De la politique de grandeur," pp. 10–12; Aron, "Colonies," p. 4. Compare Aron, *Age des empires*, pp. 43–44; Savary, *Nationalisme algérien*, pp. 153–64.

60. W. W. Kulski, *De Gaulle and the World*, pp. 1, 5–10; André Passeron, *De Gaulle parle*, pp. 227–28, 326; Aron, *France: Steadfast and Changing*, p. 187; Centre d'Études des Relations Internationales, "La Politique des puissances devant la décolonisation," p. 6.

61. Charles de Gaulle, *Mémoires de guerre*, 1:5; de Gaulle, *Discours*, 2:18–19.

62. Passeron, *De Gaulle parle*, p. 456; de Gaulle, *Discours*, 3:291. Also Passeron, *De Gaulle parle*, pp. 303, 306, 324, 339–40, 346, 465–66, 470–73, 481–82.

63. The quotation is from de Gaulle, *Discours*, 4:155, see also 3:140–41; Kulski, *De Gaulle and the World*, pp. 25, 335–40, 348–66; Girardet, *Idée coloniale*, pp. 282–84; Hoffmann et al., *In Search of France*, p. 75; *Sondages* 26, no. 3 (1964): 73–74; 29, no. 4 (1967): 86; and, in contrast, 22, no. 3 (1960): 61; Manuela Semidei, "De l'empire à la décolonisation à travers les manuels scolaires français," pp. 79–83, 86.

64. Compare Kulski, *De Gaulle and the World*, p. 37; *Esprit*, no. 417 (Oct. 1972), pp. 389–90.

1. André Siegfried, "Approaches to an Understanding of Modern France," p. 6. Also, for example, Emmanuel Mounier, *L'Éveil de l'Afrique noire*, pp. 273, 293, 335; Hubert Deschamps, *Les Méthodes et doctrines coloniales de la France*, pp. 16, 197; Henri Brunschwig, *L'Avènement de l'Afrique noire*, pp. 189–91; Manuela Semidei, "De l'empire à la décolonisation à travers les manuels scolaires français," p. 71.

2. O. Mannoni, *Prospero and Caliban*, especially pp. 32–33, 97–121, 197–204; Francis Jeanson, "Cette Algérie, conquise et pacifiée," pp. 619–26; Francis Jeanson, "Logique du colonialisme," pp. 2225–26; Jean-Paul Sartre, *Situations, V*, pp. 44, 49–56, 84–86; Jean-Paul Sartre, *Critique de la raison dialectique*, pp. 344–47 n.; Albert Memmi, *The Colonizer and the Colonized*, pp. xii–xiii, 4–76. Also Michel Leiris, *Cinq Études d'ethnologie*, pp. 75–80; Jean Cohen, "Colonialisme et racisme en Algérie"; Frantz Fanon, *Toward the African Revolution*, pp. 31–44.

3. See, on the one hand, Frantz Fanon, *Black Skin, White Masks*, pp. 109–22, and Paul H. Maucorps, Albert Memmi, and Jean-Francis Held, *Les Français et le racisme*; on the other hand, Shelby T. McCloy, *The Negro in France*, pp. 2–4, and Vernon Waughray, "The French Racial Scene," pp. 68–70.

4. Charles Morazé, *The French and the Republic*, p. 198; Siegfried, "Approaches to an Understanding," p. 15. Also Stéphane Hessel, "Préface" to *Sondages 23*, no. 3 (1961): 7; Alfred Grosser, *Au nom de quoi?* p. 155; Louis Bodin, *Les Intellectuels*, p. 75; Claude Bourdet, *L'Aventure incertaine*, pp. 446–50.

5. Compare Alioune Diop, "Discours d'ouverture," pp. 11–12; Léopold Sédar Senghor, *Liberté 2*, pp. 216–17; David C. Gordon, *North Africa's French Legacy, 1954–1962*, pp. 8–10. Note that the other colonial power that believed intensely in its civilizing vocation, Portugal, resisted decolonization even more stubbornly than did France.

6. Maurice Duverger, "Une Course contre la montre," p. 217; Herbert Luethy, *France against Herself*, p. 224, also pp. 210–11. See also Bertrand de Jouvenel, "Reflections on Colonialism," pp. 255–58; Colonel F. Bernard, "L'Union française," pp. 58–61; Albert Béguin, "La Révolte de l'Asie et la conscience européenne"; W. W. Kulski, *De Gaulle and the World*, pp. 72–74.

7. The quotation is from Léopold Sédar Senghor, *Liberté 1*, p. 98. See Fanon, *Black Skin*; Memmi, *Colonizer*, pp. 120–27; Gordon, *North Africa's French Legacy*, pp. 55–56; Isaac Yetiv, *Le Thème de l'aliénation dans le roman maghrébin d'expression française de 1952 à 1956*, pp. 11–12, 34–41, 227–28.

8. Senghor, *Liberté 1*, p. 282, also pp. 177, 285; Michael Crowder, *Senegal*, p. 39; Raymond F. Betts, ed., *The Ideology of Blackness*, pp. 78–83.

9. See Senghor, *Liberté 1*, pp. 19, 67, 133, 142, 225–26, 228–29, 358–63, 399; Jean-Paul Sartre, "Orphée noir," pp. xvii–xxi; Fanon, *Black Skin*, pp. 17–40; Frantz Fanon, *A Dying Colonialism*, pp. 89–92; Memmi, *Colonizer*, pp. 104–11; Gordon, *North Africa's French Legacy*, pp. 37–40, 60; Diop, "Discours d'ouverture," pp. 15–16; Michel Leiris, "Martinique, Guadeloupe, Haiti," pp. 1347–48; Jacques Berque, preface to Raoul Makarius, ed., *Anthologie de la littérature arabe contemporaine*, 1:26–29.

10. Albert Memmi, ed., *Anthologie des écrivains maghrébins d'expression française*, p. 15, refers to the first generation of indigenous North African writers as "the generation of 1952"; similarly, Yetiv, *Thème de l'aliénation*, p. 11.

11. The key study of the origins of the negritude movement, on which this and the following paragraphs are based, is Lilyan Kesteloot, *Les Écrivains noirs de langue française*. See also Jacques Louis Hymans, "French Influences on Leopold Senghor's Theory of Négritude, 1928–48"; Lilyan Kesteloot, ed., *Anthologie négro-africaine*; the collections of most of Léopold Sédar Senghor's essays and speeches, *Liberté 1* and *Liberté 2*; Aimé Césaire, "An Interview with Aimé Césaire."

12. Albert Hourani, *Arabic Thought in the Liberal Age, 1789–1939*, pp. 367–73; Berque, preface to Makarius, ed., *Anthologie de la littérature arabe*, pp. 7, 10–12.

13. The quotations in the following three paragraphs are from Aimé Césaire, *Cahier d'un retour au pays natal (Return to My Native Land)*, pp. 73, 97–99, 129, 115–19, 139, and

119. I have altered the translations considerably, with the aid of Craig Williamson.

14. Senghor, *Liberté 1*, pp. 135, 9, also pp. 21, 93, 145. The term "orphic" is from Sartre, "Orphée noir," p. xvii. Albert Memmi, *L'Homme dominé*, pp. 39–46, criticizes aptly the ambiguity of the term "negritude"; compare Senghor's definition with those given by Césaire, quoted in Kesteloot, *Écrivains noirs*, p. 113, and by Sartre, "Orphée noir," p. xxix.

15. The quotations are from Senghor, *Liberté 1*, pp. 139, 23, 211, 24, 136, 141, see also pp. 35–37, 70–71, 80, 150, 202–3, 208, 258–64, 280, 317–18; Senghor, *Liberté 2*, pp. 155, 288–89. A similarity to Rousseau and the English Romantics is noted by Craig Williamson, introduction to Léopold Sédar Senghor, *Selected Poems/Poésies choisies*, p. 13. Senghor utilized Hegelian and phenomenological terminology that was the common currency of French philosophers, but cited the Catholic poet Paul Claudel for his use of *con-naître* (*Liberté 1*, p. 259; *Liberté 2*, p. 289).

16. Senghor, *Liberté 1*, pp. 203, 260; *Liberté 2*, p. 289. On the obvious similarity of Senghor's ideas to Henri Bergson's, see Hymans, "French Influences," p. 367; Sartre, "Orphée noir," p. xxxi, but also p. xxxii; Henri Bergson, *Creative Evolution*, pp. 192–95. Senghor himself does not refer to Bergson.

17. Senghor, *Selected Poems*, p. 41. See Senghor, *Liberté 1*, pp. 22–38, 45, 68–69, 85, 88–89, 95, 101–2, 150, 283–87. Tom Reefe has pointed out to me that the writers of the negritude movement discovered for themselves many of the points already made by earlier black thinkers such as Edward Wilmot Blyden.

18. Senghor, *Liberté 1*, pp. 264–66; Senghor, *Liberté 2*, pp. 285–91. Senghor wrote a book on Teilhard de Chardin: *Pierre Teilhard de Chardin et la politique africaine* (Paris: Éditions du Seuil, 1962).

19. See *Présence Africaine*, n.s., no. 3 (Aug.–Sept. 1955), p. 4; Senghor, *Liberté 1*, pp. 29–30, 49–50, 275, 282–84; Senghor, *Liberté 2*, p. 154.

20. André Breton, preface to Césaire, *Cahier d'un retour*, pp. 26–27. See also Robert Delavignette, "L'Accent africain dans les lettres françaises"; Mounier, *Éveil de l'Afrique noire*; *Les Temps Modernes*, no. 37 (Oct. 1948) and no. 52 (Feb. 1950). Fanon criticized the patronizing, if not racist, tone of praise such as Breton's, in *Black Skin*, pp. 39–40. Diop also organized public meetings in Paris at which Sartre, Camus, Leiris, and Senghor spoke, according to Georges Balandier, *Ambiguous Africa*, p. 247.

21. On the question of the racism of the negritude movement, see Senghor, *Liberté 1*, pp. 8–9, 13, 83–85, 136, 165, 254–57, 316, 400; Senghor, *Liberté 2*, p. 59; Irving Leonard Markovitz, *Léopold Sédar Senghor and the Politics of Negritude*, pp. 49–58; Léon Damas, "Misère noire," p. 340; Alioune Diop, "Le Sens de ce congrès," pp. 42–43, 47–48; Kesteloot, *Écrivains noirs*, pp. 297–302. For concern about such racism, see Mounier, *Éveil de l'Afrique noire*, pp. 268–69, 335–36; Charles-André Julien, "Impérialisme économique et impérialisme colonial," pp. 27–28; Francis Jeanson, "Sartre et le monde noir," pp. 205–6, 214; Balandier, *Ambiguous Africa*, pp. 247–53; Edgar Morin, "La Question nègre," pp. 4–7; André de Peretti, "Premières Approches d'une psychologie de la colonisation," pp. 120–21.

22. See Mounier, *Éveil de l'Afrique noire*, pp. 256–57; O. Mannoni, "La Plainte du noir"; O. Mannoni, "The Decolonisation of Myself," pp. 331–35; Alioune Diop, "Malentendus"; Aimé Césaire, "Culture et colonisation," pp. 195–96, 202–5; Betts, ed., *Ideology of Blackness*, p. 187.

23. Sartre, "Orphée noir," pp. xiv, xl–xli. My translations are based on Jean-Paul Sartre, *Black Orpheus*, pp. 59–60.

24. Morin, "Question nègre," p. 6.

25. Césaire, *Cahier d'un retour*, pp. 139–41; Senghor, *Liberté 1*, pp. 45, 69, 91, 96, 150, 309–11, 363; Senghor, *Liberté 2*, p. 157; Diop, "Discours d'ouverture," p. 17; Diop, "Sens de ce congrès," p. 44; Sartre, "Orphée noir," pp. xiv, xli; Kesteloot, *Écrivains noirs*, pp. 120–23; Memmi, *Homme dominé*, pp. 48–49. Yet see Jeanson, "Sartre et le monde noir," pp. 207–11.

26. Aimé Césaire, *Lettre à Maurice Thorez*, pp. 8–9; also Césaire, "Interview," pp. 69–70.

27. Fanon, *Black Skin*, pp. 133–34, 138. I have altered the translation. This chapter was first published in *Esprit*, no. 179 (May 1951), pp. 657–79.

28. Fanon, *Black Skin*, pp. 16, 197, 231. See also Fanon, *Toward the African Revolution*, p. 27; Césaire, *Cahier d'un retour*, pp. 154–55.

29. Fanon, *Black Skin*, pp. 183–87, 202–3; chap. 6, no. 39, above; Irene L. Gendzier, *Frantz Fanon*, pp. 45–60; Frantz Fanon, *The Wretched of the Earth*.

30. Claude Lévi-Strauss, *Tristes Tropiques*, trans. and slightly abridged by John Russell, p. 381, also pp. 39, 54–62; Claude Lévi-Strauss, *The Scope of Anthropology*, pp. 41–44; Claude Lévi-Strauss, "À contre-courant"; Gérard Leclerc, *Anthropologie et colonialisme*, pp. 59, 67, 80–81.

31. Lévi-Strauss, *Scope of Anthropology*, p. 52. Also Claude Lévi-Strauss, "Diogène couché," p. 1214; Michel Leiris, "L'Ethnographe devant le colonialisme"; Jacques J. Maquet, "Objectivity in Anthropology," pp. 47–51.

32. Claude Lévi-Strauss, *Race and History*, pp. 13–14, 19; Claude Lévi-Strauss, *Structural Anthropology*, pp. 3–10. The UNESCO series was collected and translated as UNESCO, *Race and Science*.

33. Lévi-Strauss, *Race and History*, pp. 24, 26–28. Also Lévi-Strauss, *Structural Anthropology*, pp. 97–98, 110–13; Leiris, *Cinq Études*, pp. 66–71; Léopold Sédar Senghor, "Défense de l'Afrique noire," pp. 240–42; Benoit Verhaegen, "La Perspective historique de sous-développement," pp. 582, 586.

34. Lévi-Strauss, *Race and History*, pp. 42–43; Georges Charbonnier, *Entretiens avec Lévi-Strauss*, p. 29; Leiris, *Cinq Études*, pp. 53–56, 64–65; Georges Balandier, "Le Hasard et les civilisations"; Claude Lévi-Strauss, *Tristes Tropiques*, French edition, pp. 438–39; Senghor, *Liberté 1*, pp. 91, 96, 103. This section in *Tristes Tropiques* is not included in the American edition; all other references, however, will be to the American edition.

35. Roger Caillois, "Illusions à rebours," no. 25, pp. 69–70.

36. Lévi-Strauss, "Diogène couché," especially pp. 1202–20; Lévi-Strauss, *Tristes Tropiques*, pp. 381–98; Aimé Césaire, *Discours sur le colonialisme*, pp. 50–58; *La Nouvelle Nouvelle Revue Française*, no. 29 (May 1955), pp. 934–36.

37. Claude Lévi-Strauss, *The Savage Mind*, pp. 233–34.

38. Charbonnier, *Entretiens avec Lévi-Strauss*, p. 41, also pp. 35–63; Lévi-Strauss, *Race and History*, pp. 46–49; Lévi-Strauss, *Tristes Tropiques*, pp. 300–310, 389–92; Lévi-Strauss, *Structural Anthropology*, pp. 363–65; Lévi-Strauss, *Scope of Anthropology*, pp. 46–49. Compare Caillois, "Illusions à rebours," no. 25, p. 64.

39. Lucien Lévy-Bruhl, *Primitive Mentality*, pp. 5–9, 55, 59–62, 79, 89–96, 144, 442–47, but also 29–33; Jean Cazeneuve, *Lucien Lévy-Bruhl*, pp. 1–23; André Gide, *Le Retour du Tchad* (1929), in *Oeuvres complètes d'André Gide*, 14:48–49 n., 54, 56 n.; Caillois, "Illusions à rebours," no. 24, p. 1023; no. 25, pp. 62–65, 68–69; Senghor, *Liberté 1*, p. 43; Raoul Girardet, *L'Idée coloniale en France de 1871 à 1962*, pp. 158–61.

40. Doctor Pelage, "La Fin d'un mythe scientifique"; Mannoni, *Prospero and Caliban*, p. 189. Also Raymond Aron, *The Industrial Society*, p. 69.

41. Lévi-Strauss, *Structural Anthropology*, p. 227.

42. Lévi-Strauss, *Savage Mind*, pp. 14, 2–3, 10. Also Lévi-Strauss, *Race and History*, pp. 32–35; Charbonnier, *Entretiens avec Lévi-Strauss*, pp. 30–31; Marcel Griaule, "L'Inconnue noire." Contrast Lévy-Bruhl, *Primitive Mentality*, pp. 61, 443–44; Caillois, "Illusions à rebours," no. 25, pp. 62–63.

43. Lévi-Strauss, *Savage Mind*, pp. 1–38. Compare Lévy-Bruhl, *Primitive Mentality*, pp. 22–25, 29–33, 433–34, 445–46; Senghor, *Liberté 1*, p. 73.

44. Lévi-Strauss, *Savage Mind*, p. 219. Also Leiris, *Cinq Études*, pp. 71–73.

45. Lévi-Strauss, *Savage Mind*, p. 21.

46. Lévi-Strauss, "À contre-courant," p. 30. Also Lévi-Strauss, *Tristes Tropiques*, pp. 59–62; Lévi-Strauss, *Structural Anthropology*, pp. 21–22; Claude Lévi-Strauss, "Réponses à quelques questions," p. 631; Claude Lévi-Strauss, *The Raw and the Cooked*, pp. 1, 10–12.

47. Lévi-Strauss, *Savage Mind*, pp. 267–69. Compare n. 18 above.

48. Lévi-Strauss, *Scope of Anthropology*, p. 49; Lévi-Strauss, *Tristes Tropiques*, pp. 39, 397–98; Lévi-Strauss, "Réponses à quelques questions," p. 648; Claude Lévi-Strauss,

interview with the author, 19 March 1970. *La pensée sauvage* can mean "wild pansy"; a picture of pansies was on the dust jacket of the original French edition.

49. Raymond Aron, *Le Grand Schisme*, pp. 341–42; Aron, *Industrial Society*, pp. 67, 89–90; Mounier, *Éveil de l'Afrique noire*, p. 257; Maurice Merleau-Ponty, *Signs*, p. 336; Paul Ricoeur, "Civilisation universelle et cultures nationales," p. 450; Leiris, "Ethnographe devant le colonialisme," pp. 359–71; Georges Balandier, "La Situation coloniale"; Leclerc, *Anthropologie et colonialisme*, pp. 168–69, 195–213; but also Leiris, *Cinq Études*, pp. 139–51.

50. Jacques Berque, *Dépossession du monde*, pp. 59–60. Also Jacques Berque, lectures at the Collège de France, 13 and 20 Dec. 1969.

51. Berque, *Dépossession*, pp. 57–58, 81–82, 96–106, 113–20, 168, 206; Jacques Berque, "L'Afrique du Nord entre les deux guerres mondiales."

52. The quoted phrases are from Jacques Berque, first interview with the author, 16 March 1970. See Berque, *Dépossession*, pp. 36–37, 66, 143, 154, 169–70, 200–201, 206–7; Jacques Berque, Jean-Paul Charnay, et al., *De l'impérialisme à la décolonisation*; Jacques Berque, *Les Arabes d'hier à demain*; Jacques Berque, Jean-Marie Domenach, and Paul Thibaud, "L'Orient et l'avènement de la valeur monde," pp. 323–24, 328–34; Jacques Berque, *L'Orient second*.

53. Berque, et al., "Orient et l'avènement de la valeur monde," p. 326; Berque, *Orient second*, p. 414. Also Berque, *Dépossession*, pp. 174, 208, 212–13; Berque, lectures at the Collège de France, 5, 6, and 12 Dec. 1969.

54. Lévi-Strauss, interview; Jacques Berque, second interview with the author, 12 June 1972.

55. Jean-Marie Domenach, introduction to "De l'assistance à la solidarité," *Esprit*, no. 299 (Oct. 1961), p. 357. Also François Fontaine, "Le Métissage du monde."

56. Jean-Marie Domenach, "L'Union française, pour quoi faire?" p. 178.

57. *Esprit*, no. 311 (Nov. 1962), pp. 809, 571; no. 262 (June 1958), p. 954.

58. Berque, et. al., "Orient et l'avènement de la valeur monde," p. 333. Also *Esprit*, no. 417 (Oct. 1972), pp. 406–7.

NOTES TO CONCLUSION

1. Bernard C. Hennessy, *Public Opinion*, pp. 201–7, 292–98, 364–79, 389–92.

2. Alfred Grosser, *La IVe République et sa politique extérieure*, pp. 178–79. Compare John E. Mueller, *War, Presidents and Public Opinion*, pp. 164–65.

3. Compare René Rémond, "Les Intellectuels et la politique," p. 880; Pierre Gerbet, "L'Influence de l'opinion publique et des partis sur la politique étrangère de la France," p. 91. Manuela Semidei, "De l'empire à la décolonisation à travers les manuels scolaires française," *Revue Française de Science Politique* 16, no. 1 (Feb. 1966): 79–83, 86, points out that in the early 1960s the school textbooks suddenly presented decolonization as inevitable and exalted the idea of cooperation with the former colonies.

4. *New York Times*, 20 Oct. 1974. See also Stéphane Hessel, "De la décolonisation à la coopération."

5. David C. Gordon, *The Passing of French Algeria*, pp. 214–19; Gérard Chaliand and Juliette Minces, *L'Algérie indépendante*.

6. "Retour sur la guerre d'Algérie," pp. 387–412. See, for example, Jacques Massu, *La Vraie Bataille d'Alger*; Jules Roy, *J'accuse le général Massu*; Pierre Vidal-Naquet, *La Torture dans la république*; Jacques Soustelle, *Lettre ouverte aux victimes de la décolonisation*.

7. The quotations are from "French Intellectuals," p. 14.

8. Francis Jeanson, *L'Action culturelle dans la cité*; Jean-Paul Sartre, "What's Jean-Paul Sartre Thinking Lately?" pp. 205–7.

9. Frédéric Bon and Michel-Antoine Burnier, *Les Nouveaux Intellectuels*; Philip Rieff, ed., *On Intellectuals*.

10. Compare Jean-François Revel, *En France*, pp. 59–60.

◦ℕ Bibliography

A. PRIVATE SOURCES

1. Interviews
Aron, Raymond. Paris, 12 May 1970, 9 June 1972.
Berque, Jacques. Paris, 16 March 1970, 12 June 1972.
Bourdet, Claude. Paris, 28 February 1970.
Domenach, Jean-Marie. Paris, 21 April 1970.
Jeanson, Francis. Claouey, 9-10 July 1972.
Julien, Charles-André. Paris, 8, 13, June 1972.
Lévi-Strauss, Claude. Paris, 19 March 1970.
Rous, Jean. Sceaux, 1 May 1970.
Sartre, Jean-Paul. Paris, 11 June 1970.
Suret-Canale, Jean. Paris, 5 June 1970.
Tillion, Germaine. Saint-Mandé, 1 July 1972.

2. Letters to the Author
Malraux, André. 30 March 1970.
Sauvy, Alfred. 14 May 1970.
Simon, Pierre-Henri. June 1972.

B. PUBLIC SOURCES

1. Periodicals
L'Année Politique, 1955, 1956, 1960.
Arguments, Dec. 1956–1962. See especially vol. 2, no. 10 (Nov. 1958); vol. 4, no. 20 (1960).
Cahiers du Monde Nouveau, 1945–49.
Chemins du Monde, 1947–48. See issue no. 5 (1948).
Combat, 1944–March 1950.
Esprit, 1933–76. Of particular importance are the following issues: no. 132 (April 1947); no. 142 (Feb. 1948); no. 157 (July 1949); no. 166 (April 1950); no. 206 (Sept. 1953); no. 232 (Nov. 1955); no. 236 (March 1956); no. 249 (April 1957); no. 251 (June 1957); no. 284 (May 1960); no. 291 (Jan. 1961); no. 299 (Oct. 1961); no. 305 (April 1962); no. 310 (Oct. 1962); no. 311 (Nov. 1962); no. 322 (Nov. 1963); no. 417 (Oct. 1972).

L'Express, May 1953–1963.
Le Figaro, Oct. 1944–May 1945, 1953.
France-Observateur, April 1950–1963. Called *L'Observateur* until April 1954.
La Gauche: Pour une Nouvelle Résistance Internationale, May 1948–May 1949.
Jeune Résistance/Vérités Pour, no. 1 (Dec. 1960).
Le Monde, Dec. 1944–April 1946, Jan.–April 1957.
La Nef, 1944–63. Especially nos. 75–76 (April–May 1951); n.s., no. 2 (March 1953); n.s., no. 9 (June 1955); 2d n.s., no. 1 (Dec. 1956); 3d n.s., nos. 12–13 (Oct. 1962–Jan. 1963).
Octobre, Sept.–Dec. 1946.
Présence Africaine, Oct. 1947–1963. See, in particular, no. 1 (Oct.–Nov. 1947); n.s., nos. 8, 9, 10 (June–Nov. 1956); n.s., no. 20 (Aug.–Sept. 1958); n.s., nos. 24–25 (Feb.–May 1959).
Preuves, March 1951–1963. Especially no. 25 (March 1953); no. 61 (March 1956); no. 83 (Jan. 1958); supplement to no. 88 (June 1958); supplement to no. 118 (Dec. 1960).
Saturne, 1957–58.
Sondages, Oct. 1944–1970. Called *Bulletin d'Informations* until Feb. 1945.
Les Temps Modernes, 1945–70. See especially no. 18 (March 1947); no. 77 (March 1952); no. 80 (June 1952); nos. 93–94 (Aug.–Sept. 1953); no. 119 (Nov. 1955); no. 123 (March–April 1956); nos. 167–68 (Feb.–March 1960); nos. 169–70 (April–May 1960).
Vérité-Liberté: Cahiers d'Information sur la Guerre d'Algérie, May 1960–June 1962.
Vérités Pour, Sept. 1958–Sept. 1960.

2. *Single Titles*
Listed below are the articles, books, and unpublished papers that are cited in the footnotes as well as a few others of particular interest.
Adereth, M. *Commitment in Modern French Literature: Politics and Society in Péguy, Aragon, and Sartre*. New York: Schocken Books, 1967.
Aimé Césaire. Series "Littérature africaine," no. 9. Paris: Fernand Nathan, 1967.
Albertini, Rudolf von. *Decolonization: The Administration and Future of the Colonies, 1919–1960*. Garden City, N.Y.: Doubleday and Co., 1971.
Alduy, Paul. "Pour une structure politique de l'Union française." *Esprit*, no. 157 (July 1949), pp. 983–1001.
Alexandre, Pierre. "Les Voies de l'indépendance." *Preuves*, supplement to no. 88 (June 1958), pp. 33–47.
Alix, Christine. "Le Vatican et la décolonisation." In *Les Églises chrétiennes et la décolonisation*, edited by Marcel Merle, pp. 2–113. Paris: Armand Colin, 1967.
Alleg, Henri. *The Question*. Translated by John Calder. New York: Alfred A. Knopf, 1958.
Alquier, Jean-Yves. *Nous avons pacifié Tazalt: Journal de marche d'un officier parachutiste*. Paris: Robert Laffont, 1957.
Ambler, John Steward. *Soldiers against the State: The French Army in Politics*. Garden City, N.Y.: Doubleday and Co., Anchor Books, 1968.
Andrews, William G. *French Politics and Algeria: The Process of Policy Formation, 1954–1962*. New York: Appleton-Century-Crofts, 1962.
Ardagh, John. *The New French Revolution: A Social and Economic Study of France, 1945–1968*. New York and Evanston: Harper and Row, Harper Colophon Books, 1969.

Arnault, Jacques. *Procès du colonialisme*. Paris: Éditions Sociales, 1958.

Aron, Raymond. *L'Age des empires et l'avenir de la France*. Paris: Éditions Défense de la France, 1945.

———. *L'Algérie et la république*. Tribune Libre, no. 33. Paris: Plon, 1958.

———. "Un An après." *Preuves*, no. 100 (June 1959), pp. 5–13.

———. "Après le coup d'état, avant la négociation." *Preuves*, no. 124 (June 1961), pp. 3–9.

———. *The Century of Total War*. Boston: Beacon Press, 1955.

———. "Les Colonies: Une Mauvaise Affaire?" Interview in *France-Observateur*, 20 April 1961, p. 4.

———. "Conséquences économiques de l'évolution politique en Afrique noire." *Revue Française de Science Politique* 9, no. 3 (Sept. 1959): 610–28.

———. "Le Courage d'innover." *Combat*, 3 April 1947.

———. "La Décomposition des empires coloniaux." *Le Figaro*, 12 Jan. 1950.

———. "De la politique de grandeur." *Preuves*, no. 105 (Nov. 1959), pp. 3–12.

———. *De l'armistice à l'insurrection nationale*. Paris: Gallimard, 1945.

———. "De la trahison." *Preuves*, no. 116 (Oct. 1960), pp. 3–15.

———. "Les Désillusions de la liberté." *Les Temps Modernes*, no. 1 (Oct. 1945), pp. 76–105.

———. *Dimensions de la conscience historique*. Paris: Plon, 1961.

———. *Espoir et peur du siècle*. Paris: Calmann-Lévy, 1957.

———. *France: Steadfast and Changing*. Translated by J. Irwin and Luigi Einaudi. Cambridge: Harvard University Press, 1960.

———. *France: The New Republic*. New York: Oceana Publications, 1960.

———. *Le Grand Schisme*. Paris: Gallimard, 1948.

———. "L'Heure de vérité." *Preuves*, no. 119 (Jan. 1961), pp. 3–7.

———. *L'Homme contre les tyrans*. New York: Éditions de la Maison Française, 1944.

———. *The Industrial Society: Three Essays on Ideology and Development*. New York: Simon and Schuster, 1967.

———. "Industrialisation de l'empire." *Combat*, 24 July 1946.

———. *On War*. Translated by Terence Kilmartin. New York: W. W. Norton, 1968.

———. *The Opium of the Intellectuals*. Translated by Terence Kilmartin. New York: W. W. Norton, 1962.

———. *Peace and War: A Theory of International Relations*. Translated by Richard Howard and Annette Baker Fox. Garden City, N.Y.: Doubleday and Co., 1966.

———. "La Planète vue par un des cerveaux les plus lucides de notre temps: Raymond Aron." Interview in *Réalités*, no. 253 (Feb. 1967), pp. 78–81.

———. *Polémiques*. Paris: Gallimard, 1955.

———. "La Présomption." *Preuves*, no. 117 (Nov. 1960), pp. 3–10.

———. "Que deviendra la France après la décolonisation?" Interview in *France-Observateur*, 27 April 1961, pp. 12–13.

———. "Le Refus du choix est la pire solution." *Le Figaro*, 4 Dec. 1953.

———. "La Revanche militaire de l'Asie." *Preuves*, no. 41 (July 1954), pp. 8–19.

———. "La Révolte asiatique connaît-elle ses limites?" *Preuves*, no. 37 (March 1954), pp. 44–54.

———. "Révolution en Asie." *Le Figaro*, 5, 12, 17 Jan. 1950.

———. "Un Seul Homme, un homme seul." *Preuves*, no. 109 (March 1960), pp. 3–12.

_____. *La Tragédie algérienne*. Tribune Libre, no. 2. Paris: Plon, 1957.
_____, ed. *World Technology and Human Destiny*. Translated by Richard Seaver. Ann Arbor: University of Michigan Press, 1963.
_____; Faure, Edgar; Mitterrand, François; and Martinet, Gilles. "De Gaulle et l'Algérie." *France-Observateur*, 16 June 1960, pp. 3–5.
_____; Malagodi, Giovanni R.; Abs, Hermann J.; La Vallée-Poussin, Étienne de; Cavendish-Bentinck, Victor F. W.; Goes van Naters, M. van der; and Freymond, Jacques. *L'Unification économique de l'Europe*. Neuchatel: Éditions de La Baconnière, 1957.
Association Ceux d'Algérie. *Ceux d'Algérie*. Débats de Tribune Libre, no. 1. Paris: Plon, 1957.
Astorg, Bertrand d'. "Pour un Lyautey socialiste." *Esprit*, no. 130 (Feb. 1947), pp. 193–202.
Auzepy, Véronique. "Le Problème colonial à travers 'L'Humanité,' 1928–1935." Treatise, Institut d'Études Politiques, 1967.
Baby, Jean. *Critique de base*. Paris: François Maspero, 1960.
Balandier, Georges. *Ambiguous Africa*. Translated by Helen Weaver. New York: Random House, 1966.
_____. "Déséquilibres socio-culturels et modernisation des 'pays sous-développés.'" *Cahiers Internationaux de Sociologie* 20 (1956): 30–44.
_____. "Le Hasard et les civilisations." *Cahier du Sud*, no. 319 (1953), pp. 501–6.
_____. "La Situation coloniale: Approche théorique." *Cahiers Internationaux de Sociologie* 11 (1951): 44–79.
_____, ed. *Le "Tiers Monde": Sous-développement et développement*. Paris: Presses Universitaires de France, 1956.
Barale, Jean. "Les Étudiants d'Aix-en-Provence et la politique en mai 1957." *Revue Française de Science Politique* 9, no. 4 (Dec. 1959): 964–82.
Barberot, Roger. *Malaventure en Algérie, avec le général Paris de Bollardière*. Tribune Libre, no. 4. Paris: Plon, 1957.
Barrat, Robert. *Justice pour le Maroc*. Preface by François Mauriac. Paris: Éditions du Seuil, 1953.
Barthes, Roland. "Écrivains et écrivants." *Arguments* 4, no. 20 (1960), pp. 41–44.
Beauvoir, Simone de. *Force of Circumstance*. Translated by Richard Howard. New York: G. P. Putnam's Sons, 1965.
_____. *The Mandarins*. Translated by Leonard M. Friedman. Cleveland and New York: World Publishing Company, 1956.
Béguin, Albert. "La Révolte de l'Asie et la conscience européenne." *Esprit*, no. 223 (Dec. 1955), pp. 1801–19.
Berge, François. "Editorial." *Chemins du Monde* 5 (1948): 5–14.
Berger, Alain. "L'Algérie et la gauche française." *Esprit*, no. 259 (March 1958), pp. 472–78.
Bergson, Henri. *Creative Evolution*. Translated by Arthur Mitchell. New York: Modern Library, 1944.
Bernard, Colonel F. "Les Destins de l'Union française." *Cahiers du Monde Nouveau* 4, no. 1 (Jan. 1948): 39–50.
_____. "Le Problème colonial." *Combat*, 14 April 1945.
_____. "Le Problème colonial et l'avenir de l'Indochine." *Cahiers du Monde Nouveau* 1, no. 3 (1945): 264–79.

————. "L'Union française: Illusions et réalités." *Cahiers du Monde Nouveau* 2, no. 5 (May 1946): 46–61.

Bernard, Stéphane. *The Franco-Moroccan Conflict, 1943–1956*. Translated by Marianna Oliver, Alexander Baden Harrison, Jr., and Bernard Phillips. New Haven and London: Yale University Press, 1968.

Berque, Jacques. "L'Afrique du Nord entre les deux guerres mondiales." *Cahiers Internationaux de Sociologie* 30 (Jan.–June 1961): 3–22.

————. "L'Algérie ou les faux dilemmes." *Politique Étrangère* 21, no. 6 (Dec. 1956): 703–10.

————. *Les Arabes d'hier à demain*. 2d ed. Paris: Éditions du Seuil, 1969.

————. "Au dossier de la négociation." *France-Observateur*, 16 Nov. 1961, p. 4.

————. *Dépossession du monde*. Paris: Éditions du Seuil, 1964.

————. *L'Orient second*. Paris: Gallimard, 1970.

————. "Pour la paix en Algérie." *Esprit*, no. 259 (March 1958), pp. 491–94.

————. "Vers une humanité plénière." *Esprit*, no. 380 (April 1969), pp. 652–57.

————; Charnay, Jean-Paul; et al. *De l'impérialisme à la décolonisation*. Paris: Éditions de Minuit, 1965.

————; Domenach, Jean-Marie; and Thibaud, Paul. "L'Orient et l'avènement de la valeur monde." *Esprit*, no. 395 (Sept. 1970), pp. 323–35.

Berveiller, Michel. "L'Europe d'outre-mer." *Cahiers du Monde Nouveau* 4, no. 7 (Aug.–Sept. 1948): 47–51.

Bettelheim, Charles. "Planification et croissance économique." *Présence Africaine*, n.s., no. 20 (June-July 1958).

Betts, Raymond F. "The French Colonial Frontier." In *From the Ancien Régime to the Popular Front: Essays in the History of Modern France in Honor of Shephard B. Clough*, edited by Charles K. Warner. New York and London: Columbia University Press, 1969.

————, ed. *The Ideology of Blackness*. Lexington, Mass.: D. C. Heath and Co., 1971.

Beuve-Méry, Hubert. *Réflexions politiques, 1932–1952*. Paris: Éditions du Seuil, 1951.

———— [S.]. "Sommes-nous les 'vaincus de Hitler'? . . ." *Le Monde*, 13 March 1957.

———— [Sirius]. *Le Suicide de la IVe république*. Éditions du Cerf, 1958.

Bidault, Georges. *Algérie: L'Oiseau aux ailes coupées*. Paris: La Table Ronde, 1958.

Billotte, General Pierre. "Réflexions sur l'État et la solidarité nationale." *Preuves*, no. 118 (Dec. 1960), pp. 13–15.

Bloch-Michel, Jean. "La Discipline des généraux." *Preuves*, no. 77 (July 1957), pp. 3–8.

————. "Une Morale du succès?" *Preuves*, no. 83 (Jan. 1958), pp. 53–56.

Bodin, Louis. *Les Intellectuels*. "Que sais-je?" no. 1001. Paris: Presses Universitaires de France, 1962.

————, and Touchard, Jean. "Les Intellectuels dans la société française contemporaine: Définitions, statistiques et problèmes." *Revue Française de Science Politique* 9, no. 4 (Dec. 1959): 835–59.

Bon, Frédéric, and Burnier, Michel-Antoine. *Les Nouveaux Intellectuels*. 2d ed. Paris: Éditions du Seuil, 1971.

Borella, Françqis. "Fédéralisme et décolonisation." *Esprit*, no. 258 (Feb. 1958), pp. 229–46.

Bosquet, Alain. *Roger Caillois*. Paris: Éditions Seghers, 1971.

Bosworth, William. *Catholicism and Crisis in Modern France*. Princeton: Princeton University Press, 1962.

Bourdet, Claude. "À qui l'Indochine?" *Octobre*, 7 Dec. 1946, p. 1.

———. "'Action directe' et 'non-violence.'" *France-Observateur*. 2 June 1960. p. 3.

———. "L'Affaire." *Combat*, 5 July 1949.

———. "L'an I du règne." *France-Observateur*, 28 May 1959, pp. 3–4.

———. *L'Aventure incertaine: De la Résistance à la Restauration*. Paris: Stock, 1975.

———. "Bluff sur l'Indochine." *L'Observateur*, 3 Jan. 1952, pp. 5–7; 10 Jan. 1952, pp. 7–9.

———. "Camus et la révolte de Sisyphe." *L'Observateur*, 13 Dec. 1951, pp. 17–18; 20 Dec. 1951, pp. 17–18.

———. "C'est la France qui est indispensable à l'Algérie." *France-Observateur*, 14 June 1956, pp. 10–11.

———. "Changer le statut et l'esprit." *L'Observateur*, 2 Nov. 1950, pp. 12–13.

———. "El Glaoui ou le féodalo-capitalisme." *Les Temps Modernes*, no. 92 (July 1953), pp. 129–38.

———. "L'Équilibre social et le fait colonial." *Les Temps Modernes*, no. 71 (Sept. 1951), pp. 537–48.

———. "Les Étudiants donnent l'exemple." *France-Observateur*, 9 June 1960, p. 2.

———. "Faire la guerre à la moitié du monde." *France-Observateur*, 6 Oct. 1955, pp. 6–7.

———. "Fini de rêver." *France-Observateur*, 10 March 1960, p. 2.

———. "La Fuite vers l'économique." *France-Observateur*, 11 Dec. 1958, p. 5.

———. "L'Impérialisme des pauvres." *Combat*, 25 July 1947.

———. "L'Incorrigible Paternalisme persiste en Afrique du Nord." *France-Observateur*, 7 July 1955, pp. 6–7.

———. "Loi-cadre: Un Bao-Dai moléculaire." *France-Observateur*, 6 Feb. 1958, p. 4.

———. "Lueur sur l'Indochine." *Combat*, 1 Aug. 1947.

———. "Madagascar-Dreyfus." *Combat*, 30 July 1948.

———. "Les Maîtres de l'Afrique du Nord." *Les Temps Modernes*, no. 80 (June 1952), pp. 2247–64.

———. "Le Maroc a deux visages." *L'Observateur*, 19 Oct. 1950, pp. 12–13; 26 Oct. 1950, pp. 12–13; 2 Nov. 1950, pp. 12–13.

———. "Marocains et Français du Maroc." *Les Temps Modernes*, no. 90 (May 1953), pp. 1810–25.

———. "Mauriac, l'action politique et nous." *France-Observateur*, 16 July 1959, p. 5.

———. "Notre Liberté est la vôtre." *France-Observateur*, 15 Sept. 1955, p. 6.

———. "Politique d'abord." *Combat*, 11 Oct. 1947.

———. "Pourquoi aident-ils le F.L.N.?" *France-Observateur*, 3 March 1960, p. 5.

———. "Qui sont les chefs du F.L.N.?" *France-Observateur*, 7 Nov. 1957, pp. 5–6.

———. "Les Racines de l'enfer." *France-Observateur*, 4 April 1957, p. 3.

———. "Sabotages et grèves." *Combat*, 27 Jan. 1950.

———. "Les Silence est de sang." *France-Observateur*, 11 April 1957, p. 3. Reprinted in *Les Temps Modernes*, no. 136 (June 1957), pp. 1897–99.

———. "Le Suicide du général de Gaulle." *France-Observateur*, 25 Jan. 1962, p. 6.

———. "Tortures en Oranie?" *France-Observateur*, 27 Sept. 1956, p. 4.

———. "Trois Continents." *Combat*, 16 June 1948.

———. "Le 27 Octobre: Un Tournant et un début!" *France-Observateur*, 2 Nov. 1960, p. 2.

———. "Vers la guerre d'Algérie?" *France-Observateur*, 26 May 1955, pp. 7–8.

———. "Voici le bilan coloniale de la France." *La Gauche*, Aug. 1948, pp. 1, 4.

———. "Votre Gestapo d'Algérie." *France-Observateur*, 13 Jan. 1955, pp. 6–7.

Brace, Richard, and Brace, Joan. *Ordeal in Algeria*. Princeton: D. Van Nostrand, 1960.

Brogan, D. W. *Citizenship Today: England–France–The United States*. The Weil Lectures on American Citizenship, 1959. Chapel Hill: University of North Carolina Press, 1960.

Bromberger, Serge. *Les Rebelles algériens*. Paris: Plon, 1958.

Bruller, Jean [Vercors]. *Les Pas dans le sable*. Paris: Albin-Michel, 1954.

Brunschwig, Henri. *L'Avènement de l'Afrique noire*. Paris: Armand Colin, 1963.

———. "Colonial Imperialism." *Confluence* 4 (July 1955): 217–28.

———. "Colonisation-décolonisation: Essai sur le vocabulaire usuel de la politique coloniale." *Cahiers d'Études Africaines* 1, no. 1 (Jan. 1960): 44–54.

———. *Mythes et réalités de l'impérialisme colonial français, 1871–1914*. Paris: Armand Colin, 1960.

Burnier, Michel-Antoine. *Les Existentialistes et la politique*. Paris: Gallimard, 1966.

Caillois, Roger. "Illusions à rebours." *La Nouvelle Nouvelle Revue Française*, no. 24 (Dec. 1954), pp. 1010–24; no. 25 (Jan. 1955), pp. 58–70.

Campbell, Peter. *French Electoral Systems and Elections 1789–1957*. New York: Frederick A. Praeger, 1958.

Camus, Albert. *Actuelles, III: Chroniques algériennes, 1939–1958*. Paris: Gallimard, 1958.

———. *Le "Combat" d'Albert Camus*. Edited by Norman Stokle. Québec: Presses de l'Université Laval, 1970.

———. *Essais*. Edited by Roger Quilliot. Bibliothèque de la Pléiade. Paris: Gallimard, 1965.

———. *L'Étranger*. Paris: Gallimard, 1957.

———. *L'Éxil et le royaume*. Paris: Gallimard, 1957.

———. *The Fall*. Translated by Justin O'Brien. New York: Random House, 1956.

———. Letter to *Encounter* 8, no. 6 (June 1957): 68.

———. *The Myth of Sisyphus and Other Essays*. Translated by Justin O'Brien. New York: Random House, Vintage Books, 1958.

———. *Notebooks, 1935–1942*. Translated and annotated by Philip Thody. New York: Alfred A. Knopf, 1963.

———. *The Plague*. Translated by Stuart Gilbert. New York: Modern Library, 1948.

———. *The Rebel*. Translated by Anthony Bower. New York: Random House, 1956.

———. *Resistance, Rebellion, and Death*. Translated by Justin O'Brien. New York: Modern Library, 1960.

Capelle, Russell B. *The MRP and French Foreign Policy*. New York: Frederick A. Praeger, 1963.

Carat, Jacques. "Sur trois saisies." *Preuves*, no. 86 (April 1958), pp. 43–44.

Carmoy, Guy de. *Les Politiques étrangères de la France, 1944–1966*. Paris: Table Ronde, 1967.

Carrère d'Encausse, Hélène. "Le Parti communiste français et le mouvement de libération nationale algérien." In "La Politique des puissances devant la décolonisation," colloquium of the Centre d'Études des Relations Internationales, Paris, 31 March–1 April 1962, mimeographed, report IIb.

Cartey, Wilfred. *Whispers from a Continent*. New York: Random House, 1969.

Cartier, Raymond. "En France noire avec Raymond Cartier." *Paris-Match*, no. 383 (11 Aug. 1956), pp. 38–41; no. 384 (18 Aug. 1956), pp. 34–37; no. 386 (1 Sept. 1956), pp. 38–41.

Cassilly, Tom. "The Anticolonial Tradition in France: The Eighteenth Century to the Fifth Republic." Ph.D. dissertation, Columbia University, 1973.

Cassou, Jean. "Lettre à Paul Rivet." *France-Observateur*, 19 July 1956, p. 4.

Cayrol, Roland. *François Mitterrand, 1945–1967*. Paris: Fondation Nationale des Sciences Politiques, 1967.

Cazeneuve, Jean. *Lucien Lévy-Bruhl*. Translated by Peter Rivière. New York, Evanston, San Francisco, London: Harper and Row, Harper Torchbooks, 1973.

Centre Catholique des Intellectuels Français. *Colonisation et conscience chrétienne*. Recherches et débats, n.s., no. 6 (Dec. 1953). Paris: Arthème Fayard, n.d.

Centre d'Études des Relations Internationales. "La Politique des puissances devant la décolonisation." Colloquium, Paris, 31 March–1 April 1962. Mimeographed.

Césaire, Aimé. *Cahier d'un retour au pays natal (Return to My Native Land)*. Bilingual edition. Translated by Émile Snyder. Preface by André Breton. Paris: Présence Africaine, 1971.

_____. "Culture et colonisation." *Présence Africaine*, n.s., nos. 8–10 (June–Nov. 1956), pp. 190–205.

_____. *Discours sur le colonialisme*. Paris: Présence Africaine, 1955.

_____. "L'Impossible Contact." *Chemins du Monde*, no. 5 (1948), pp. 105–11.

_____. "An Interview with Aimé Césaire." Translated by Maro Riofrancos. In *Discourse on Colonialism*, by Aimé Césaire, translated by Joan Pinkham, pp. 65–79. New York and London: Monthly Review Press, 1972.

_____. *Lettre à Maurice Thorez*. 3d ed. Paris: Présence Africaine, [1956].

_____. "La Mort des colonies." *Les Temps Modernes*, no. 123 (March–April 1956), pp. 1366–70.

Chaliand, Gérard, and Minces, Juliette. *L'Algérie indépendante*. Paris: François Maspero, 1972.

Chapsal, Jacques. "Le Suffrage politique et l'expression de l'opinion publique française depuis 1945." In *L'Opinion publique*, by Gaston Berger et al., pp. 261–303. 2d session, Centre de Sciences Politiques de l'Institut d'Études Juridiques de Nice, 1955. Paris: Presses Universitaires de France, 1957.

Charbonnier, Georges. *Entretiens avec Lévi-Strauss*. Paris: Plon and Julliard, 1961.

Charlot, Jean, and Charlot, Monica. "Un Rassemblement d'intellectuels: La Ligue des Droits de l'Homme." *Revue Française de Science Politique* 9, no. 4 (Dec. 1959): 995–1028.

Chatelain, Abel. *"Le Monde" et ses lecteurs sous la IVe république*. Paris: Armand Colin, 1962.

Chevalier, Louis. *Madagascar: Population et ressources*. Preface by Alfred Sauvy. Paris: Presses Universitaires de France, 1952.

Chonez, Claudine. "Vu et entendu en Indochine." *La Nef*, no. 56 (Aug. 1949). pp. 45–54.

Club Jean Moulin. "Une Algérie viable." *Esprit*, no. 272 (April 1959), pp. 547–61.

Codjo, R. "Colonisation et conscience chrétienne." *Présence Africaine*, n.s., no. 6 (Feb.–March 1956), pp. 9–19.

Cohen, Bernard C. *The Press and Foreign Policy*. Princeton: Princeton University Press, Princeton Paperbacks, 1965.

———. *The Public's Impact on Foreign Policy*. Boston: Little, Brown and Co., 1973.

Cohen, Jean. "Colonialisme et racisme en Algérie." *Les Temps Modernes*, no. 119 (Nov. 1955), pp. 580–90.

Cohen, William B. *Rulers of Empire: The French Colonial Service in Africa*. Stanford: Hoover Institution Press, 1971.

"Colonialism and Decolonisation." *Journal of Contemporary History* 4, no. 1 (Jan. 1969).

Comité de Résistance Spirituelle. *Des Rappelés témoignent*. N.p., 1957.

Congrès des Peuples. *Les Peuples dépendants s'adressent aux Nations Unis*. Paris: Société Nationale des Entreprises de Presse, [1952].

"Connaissez-vous la France d'outre-mer?" *Bulletin Mensuel de Statistique d'Outre-mer*, supplemental series "Études," no. 22 (1 Oct. 1951).

Contat, Michel, and Rybalka, Michel. *Les Écrits de Sartre: Chronologie, bibliographie commentée*. Paris: Gallimard, 1970.

Converse, Philip E. "The Nature of Belief Systems in Mass Politics." In *Public Opinion and Politics: A Reader*, edited by William J. Crotty, pp. 129–55. New York: Holt, Rinehart and Winston, 1970.

———, and Dupeux, Georges. "Politicization of the Electorate in France and the United States." In *Mass Politics in Industrial Societies*, edited by Giuseppe di Palma, pp. 41–63. Chicago: Markham Publishing Co., 1972.

Corbett, Edward M. *French Presence in Black Africa*. Washington, D.C.: Black Orpheus Press, 1972.

Corval, Pierre. "Les Forces en présence." *La Nef*, n.s., no. 2 (March 1953), pp. 68–77.

Coser, Lewis A. *Men of Ideas: A Sociologist's View*. New York: Free Press, 1965.

Cranston, Maurice. "Albert Camus." *Encounter* 28 (Feb. 1967): 43–54.

———. "Sartre and Violence." *Encounter* 29 (July 1967): 18–24.

Crouzet, Michel. "La Bataille des intellectuels français." *La Nef*, 3d n.s., nos. 12–13 (Oct. 1962–Jan. 1963), pp. 47–65.

Crowder, Michael. *Senegal: A Study in French Assimilation Policy*. London: Oxford University Press, 1962.

Crozier, Michel. *The Bureaucratic Phenomenon*. Translated by the author. Chicago: University of Chicago Press, 1964.

———. "The Cultural Revolution: Notes on the Changes in the Intellectual Climate of France." *Daedalus* 93, no. 1 (Winter 1964): 514–42.

Damas, Léon. "Misère noire." *Esprit*, no. 81 (June 1939), pp. 333–54.

Daniel, Jean. "Colonialisme et bonne conscience." *Preuves*, no. 65 (July 1956), pp. 14–21.

———. "Un Français d'Algérie." *Preuves*, no. 79 (Sept. 1957), pp. 25–29.

———. "Socialisme et anti-colonialisme." *Esprit*, no. 284 (May 1960), pp. 809–14.

De Gaulle, Charles. *Discours et messages*. 5 vols. Paris: Plon, 1970.

———. *Mémoires de guerre*. 3 vols. Paris: Plon, 1954, 1956, 1959.

Delavignette, Robert. "L'Accent africain dans les lettres françaises." *La Nef*, no. 12 (Nov. 1945), pp. 62–72.

———. *L'Afrique noire française et son destin*. Paris: Gallimard, 1962.

———. *Freedom and Authority in French West Africa*. Translated by the International African Institute. London: Oxford University Press, 1950.

———. "Les Transformations politiques et sociales impliquées par le développement." In *La Montée des peuples dans la communauté humaine*, by Semaines Sociales de France, 46th session, Angers, 1959, pp. 297–311. Lyon: Chronique Sociale de France, 1959.

———. "L'Union française." *Esprit*, no. 112 (July 1945), pp. 214–36.

Deschamps, Hubert. *La Fin des empires coloniaux*. "Que sais-je?" no. 409. 3d ed. Paris: Presses Universitaires de France, 1963.

———. *Les Méthodes et les doctrines coloniales de la France*. Paris: Armand Colin, 1953.

Dessinges, P.-M. "Les Atteintes à la liberté de la presse en France." *Cahiers de l'I. I. P.: Bulletin Mensuel de l'Institut International de la Presse* 9, no. 3 (July 1960): 3–5.

De Tarr, Francis. *The French Radical Party from Herriot to Mendès-France*. London: Oxford University Press, 1961.

"La Détention en Algérie: La C.I.C.R.C. rend publique ses conclusions." *Saturne* 3, no. 14 (Aug.–Sept. 1957): 110–17.

Devillers, Philippe. *Histoire du Viêt-Nam de 1940 à 1952*. 3d ed. Paris: Éditions du Seuil, 1953.

Diop, Alioune. "Discours d'ouverture." 1st Congrès International des Écrivains et Artistes Noirs, Paris, 1956. *Présence Africaine*, n.s., nos. 8–10 (June–Nov. 1956), pp. 9–18.

———. "Malentendus." *Présence Africaine*, no. 6 (1949), pp. 3–8.

———. "Le Sens de ce congrès." 2d Congrès International des Écrivains et Artistes Noirs, Rome, 1959. *Présence Africaine*, n.s., nos. 24–25 (Feb.–May 1958), pp. 40–48.

Domenach, Jean-Marie. "Algérie, propositions raisonnables." *Esprit*, no. 250 (May 1957), pp. 777–89.

———. "Conditions de la grandeur." *Esprit*, no. 267 (Nov. 1958), pp. 715–20.

———. "'Croyez-vous à la démocratie?'" *L'Express*, 30 April 1959, pp. 9–10.

———. "'Les Damnés de la terre.'" *Esprit*, no. 304 (March 1962), pp. 454–63; no. 305 (April 1962), pp. 634–45.

———. "De l'empire à la communauté des peuples." *Esprit*, no. 157 (July 1949), pp. 1081–96.

———. "Démoralisation de la nation." *Esprit*, no. 249 (April 1957), pp. 577–79.

———. "Dernières Chances de l'Union française." *Esprit*, no. 157 (July 1949), pp. 917–20.

———. "Esprit, nouvelle série." *Esprit*, no. 255 (Nov. 1957), pp. 468–85.

———. "Mise au point." *Vérités-Libertés*, no. 3 (July–Aug. 1960), p. 4.

———. "Politique et action culturelle." *Esprit*, no. 424 (May 1973), pp. 1116–23.

———. "Pour en finir avec l'aliénation." *Esprit*, no. 344 (Dec. 1965), pp. 1058–83.

———. "Pour une reconversion du courage." *L'Express*, 26 July 1957, p. 4.

———. "Résistances." *Esprit*, no. 284 (May 1960), pp. 794–814.

———. "Sauve-qui-peut?" *Esprit*, no. 283 (April 1960), pp. 707–10.

———. "S'entendre contre l'irréparable." *Esprit*, no. 291 (Jan. 1961), pp. 1–6.

———. "L'Union française, pour quoi faire?" *La Nef*, n.s., no. 9 (June 1955), pp. 177–86.

———, and Suffert, Georges. "Algérie et renaissance française." *Esprit*, no. 239 (June 1956), pp. 937–48.

Douglas, Kenneth. "The French Intellectuals: Situation and Outlook." In *Modern France: Problems of the Third and Fourth Republics*, edited by Edward Mead Earle, pp. 61–80. Princeton: Princeton University Press, 1951.

Dresch, Jean; Julien, Charles-André; Marrou, Henri; Sauvy, Alfred; Stibbe, Pierre. *La Question algérienne*. Paris: Éditions de Minuit, 1958.

Dumont, René. *L'Afrique noire est mal partie*. Paris: Éditions du Seuil, 1962.

———, and Mazoyer, Marcel. *Développement et socialismes*. Paris: Éditions du Seuil, 1969.

Dupont, Maurice. "Les Intérêts français contre l'intérêt de la France en Afrique du Nord." *Esprit*, no. 192 (July 1952), pp. 45–65; nos. 193–94 (Aug.–Sept. 1952), pp. 321–52.

Duquesne, Jacques. *L'Algérie ou la guerre des mythes*. N.p.: Desclée de Brouwer, 1958.

Duroselle, Jean-Baptiste, ed. *La Politique étrangère et ses fondements*. Cahiers de la Fondation Nationale des Sciences Politiques, no. 55. Paris: Armand Colin, 1954.

Duverger, Maurice. "Absence française." *Le Monde*, 22 March 1957.

———. "Aid Given by the Mother Country to Colonized Peoples: The Example of France." *Confluence* 4 (Jan. 1956): 421–31.

———. "Une Course contre la montre." *La Nef*, n.s., no. 9 (June 1955), pp. 212–22.

———. "Défendre Hanoi ou défendre Paris?" *La Nef*, nos. 75–76 (April–May 1951), pp. 177–83.

———. "Les Deux Stades du nationalisme." *Le Monde*, 16 March 1957.

———. "Les Deux Trahisons." *Le Monde*, 27 April 1960.

———. *The French Political System*. Translated by Barbara North and Robert North. Chicago: University of Chicago Press, 1958.

———. "Un Homme a remplacé l'état." *La Nef*, May 1959, pp. 5–11.

———. "La Maladie infantile du nationalisme." *La Nef*, n.s., no. 2 (March 1953), pp. 51–59.

———. "La Politique de Metternich." *La Nef*, Dec. 1956, pp. 93–96.

———. "Préparer la paix." *Le Monde*, 7 April 1956.

———; Goguel, François; Touchard, Jean; et al. *Les Élections du 2 janvier 1956*. Cahiers de la Fondation Nationale des Sciences Politiques, no. 82. Paris: Armand Colin, 1957.

Ehrmann, Henry W. *Politics in France*. 2d ed. Boston: Little, Brown and Co., 1971.

Émery, Philippe. "Mythes et réalités du dossier algérien." *La Nef*, Dec. 1956, pp. 78–85.

Esprit. "Une Affaire intérieure." *Esprit*, no. 232 (Nov. 1955), pp. 1641–48.

Estier, Claude. *La Gauche hebdomadaire, 1914–1962*. Paris: Armand Colin, n.d.

Fabre-Luce, Alfred. *Demain en Algérie*. Tribune Libre, no. 19. Paris: Plon, 1958.

Fall, Bernard B. "Tribulations of a Party Line: The French Communists and Indo-China." *Foreign Affairs* 33, no. 4 (April 1955): 499–510.

Fanon, Frantz. *Black Skin, White Masks*. Translated by Charles Lam Markmann. New York: Grove Press, 1967.

_____. *A Dying Colonialism*. Translated by Haakon Chevalier. New York: Grove Press, 1965.

_____. *Peau noire, masques blancs*. Preface by Francis Jeanson. Paris: Éditions du Seuil, 1952.

_____. *Toward the African Revolution*. Translated by Haaken Chevalier. New York: Grove Press, 1967.

_____. *The Wretched of the Earth*. Preface by Jean-Paul Sartre. Translated by Constance Farrington. New York: Grove Press, 1968.

Fatouros, A. A. "Sartre on Colonialism." *World Politics* 17, no. 4 (July 1965): 703–19.

Fauvet, Jacques. *Histoire du parti communiste français*. Vol. 2. Paris: Arthème Fayard, 1965.

_____. *La IVe République*. Paris: Arthème Fayard, Livre de Poche, 1959.

Fejtö, François. *The French Communist Party and the Crisis of International Communism*. Cambridge, Mass., and London: M.I.T. Press, 1967.

Fields, A. Belden. *Student Politics in France: A Study of the Union Nationale des Étudiants de France*. New York and London: Basic Books, 1970.

Flory, Charles. "Les Conditions nouvelles des rapports de l'Occident et des peuples d'outre-mer." In *Peuples d'outre-mer et civilisation occidentale*, by Semaines Sociales de France, 35th session, Lyon, 1948, pp. 15–34. Lyon: Chronique Sociale de France, 1948.

Folliet, Joseph. *Guerre et paix en Algérie: Réflexions d'un homme libre*. N.p.: Chronique Sociale, 1958.

Fontaine, François. "Le Métissage du monde." *Preuves*, Oct. 1956, pp. 20–23.

Fougeyrollas, Pierre. *La Conscience politique dans la France contemporaine*. Paris: Éditions Denoël, 1963.

Fournier, Christiane. *Nous avons encore des héroes*. Preface by Maréchal Alphonse Juin. Paris: Plon, 1957.

"French Intellectuals: Do They Serve a Purpose?" *Manchester Guardian*, 22 Feb. 1975, p. 14.

Fyvel, T. R. *Intellectuals Today: Problems in a Changing Society*. New York: Schocken Books, 1968.

Gault, Jean-Pierre. *Histoire d'une fidelité: Témoignage Chrétien, 1944–1956*. N.p.: Éditions Témoignage Chrétien, n.d.

Geertz, Clifford. "The Cerebral Savage." *Encounter* 28 (April 1967): 25–32.

Gendzier, Irene L. *Frantz Fanon: A Critical Study*. New York: Random House, Pantheon Books, 1973.

Gerbet, Pierre. "L'Influence de l'opinion publique et des partis sur la politique étrangère de la France." In *La Politique étrangère et ses fondements*, edited by Jean-Baptiste Duroselle, pp. 83–106. Cahiers de la Fondation Nationale des Sciences Politiques, no. 55. Paris: Armand Colin, 1954.

Gide, André. *Oeuvres complètes d'André Gide*. Edited by Louis Martin-Chauffier. Vols. 13, 14. Paris: NRF, n.d.

Gifford, Prosser, and Louis, William Roger, eds. *France and Britain in Africa: Imperial Rivalry and Colonial Rule*. New Haven and London: Yale University Press, 1971.

Girardet, Raoul. "L'Idée coloniale devant l'opinion française (1930–1935)." *Revue Française de Science Politique* 18 (Dec. 1968): 1085–1113.

————. "L'Idée coloniale en France de 1871 à 1962." Course given at the Institut d'Études Politiques, 1965–66. Mimeographed by the Amicale des Élèves.

————. *L'Idée coloniale en France de 1871 à 1962.* Paris: Table Ronde, 1972.

Gonidec, P. F. *Droit d'outre-mer.* 2 vols. Paris: Éditions Montchrestien, 1959.

Gordon, David C. *North Africa's French Legacy, 1954–1962.* Harvard Middle Eastern Monograph no. 9. Cambridge: Harvard University Press, 1962.

————. *The Passing of French Algeria.* London: Oxford University Press, 1966.

Grall, Xavier. *François Mauriac journaliste.* Paris: Éditions du Cerf, 1960.

————. *La Génération du djebel.* Paris: Éditions du Cerf, 1962.

Granet, Marie, and Michel, Henri. *Combat: Histoire d'un mouvement de résistance de juillet 1940 à juillet 1943.* Paris: Presses Universitaires de France, 1957.

Griaule, Marcel. "L'Inconnue noire." *Présence Africaine,* no. 1 (Oct.–Nov. 1947), pp. 21–27.

Grimal, Henri. *La Décolonisation, 1919–1963.* Paris: Armand Colin, 1965.

Grosser, Alfred. *Au nom de quoi?* Paris: Éditions du Seuil, 1969.

————. *French Foreign Policy under De Gaulle.* Translated by Lois Ames Pattison. Boston and Toronto: Little, Brown and Co., 1967.

————. *La IVe République et sa politique extérieure.* 2d ed. Paris: Armand Colin, 1967.

Grunebaum, G. E. von. *French African Literature: Some Cultural Implications.* The Hague: Mouton and Co., 1964.

Guérin, Daniel. *Ci-gît le colonialisme.* Paris and The Hague: Mouton and Co., 1973.

Hammer, Ellen. *The Struggle for Indochina, 1940–1955.* Stanford: Stanford University Press, 1955.

Hardy, Georges. "Psychologie et tutelle." *Chemins du Monde,* no. 5 (1948), pp. 41–49.

Hellman, John William. "Emmanuel Mounier and *Esprit.*" Ph.D. dissertation, Harvard University, 1969.

Hennessy, Bernard C. *Public Opinion.* 2d ed. Belmont, Cal.: Wadsworth Publishing Co., 1970.

Henri, Comte de Paris. "La Dernière Chance." *L'Express,* 29 Jan. 1955, p. 6.

Hertrich, J.-M. "La Crise tunisienne." *Preuves,* Jan. 1953, pp. 15–21.

Hessel, Stéphane. "De la décolonisation à la coopération." *Esprit,* July–Aug. 1970, pp. 5–12.

Hoffmann, Stanley. "Protest in Modern France." In *The Revolution in World Politics,* edited by Morton A. Kaplan. New York: John Wiley and Sons, 1962.

————. "Vietnam: An Algerian Solution?" *Foreign Policy,* no. 2 (Spring 1971), pp. 3–37.

————; Kindleberger, Charles P.; Wylie, Laurence; Pitts, Jesse R.; Duroselle, Jean-Baptiste; and Goguel, François. *In Search of France.* New York: Harper and Row, Harper Torchbooks, 1965.

Hostache, René. *Le Conseil National de la Résistance.* Paris: Presses Universitaires de France, 1958.

Hourani, Albert. *Arabic Thought in the Liberal Age, 1789–1939.* London: Oxford University Press, 1962.

Hughes, H. Stuart. *The Obstructed Path: French Social Thought in the Years of Desperation, 1930–1960.* New York and Evanston: Harper and Row, 1968.

Hymans, Jacques Louis. "French Influences on Leopold Senghor's Theory of Négritude, 1928–48." *Race* 7, no. 4 (April 1966): 365–70.

"Intellectuals and Change." *Daedalus* 101, no. 3 (Summer 1972).
"Intellectuals and Tradition." *Daedalus* 101, no. 2 (Spring 1972).
"Les Intellectuels." *Arguments* 4, no. 20 (1960).
"Les Intellectuels dans la société française contemporaine." *Revue Française de Science Politique* 9, no. 4 (Dec. 1959).
Ivernel, Philippe. "Violence d'hier et d'aujourd'hui." *Esprit*, no. 310 (Oct. 1962), pp. 386–98.
Izard, Georges. "De l'usage des aphrodisiaques en politique." *La Nef*, Dec. 1956, pp. 65–67.
Jeanson, Colette, and Jeanson, Francis. *L'Algérie hors la loi*. 2d ed. Paris: Éditions du Seuil, 1955.
Jeanson, Francis. *L'Action culturelle dans la cité*. Paris: Éditions du Seuil, 1973.
_____. "Cette Algérie, conquise et pacifiée." *Esprit*, no. 166 (April 1950), pp. 613–34; no. 167 (May 1950), pp. 841–61.
_____. Interview for a Swiss journal, May 1960. Typed transcript. Private papers of Francis Jeanson.
_____. Interview in *Vérités Pour*, no. 18 (26 Sept. 1960), pp. 2–3.
_____. "Lettre à Claude Bourdet." Mimeographed, March 1960. Private papers of Francis Jeanson.
_____. "Lettre à J. J. Servan-Schreiber." *Vérités Pour*, no. 17 (26 July 1960), pp. 4–7.
_____. "Lettre à J.-M. Domenach." *Vérités Pour*, no. 16 (13 June 1960), pp. 19–22.
_____. "Lettre à Jean-Paul Sartre." *Les Temps Modernes*, nos. 169–70 (April–May 1960), pp. 1535–49.
_____. "Logique du colonialisme." *Les Temps Modernes*, no. 80 (June 1952), pp. 2213–29.
_____. *Notre Guerre*. Paris: Éditions de Minuit, 1960.
_____. "Plus loin avec Francis Jeanson." Interview in *L'Express Rhône-Alpes*, Dec. 1970, pp. 80–113.
_____. Press conference, Paris, 15 April 1960. Typed transcript. Private papers of Francis Jeanson.
_____. *La Révolution algérienne*. Milan: Feltrinelli, 1962.
_____. *Sartre dans sa vie*. Paris: Éditions du Seuil, 1974.
_____. "Sartre et le monde noir." *Présence Africaine*, no. 7 (1949), pp. 189–214.
Jeune Résistance. *"Jeune Résistance" s'explique* . . . Paris: N.p., 1960.
_____. Manifesto, April 1961. Mimeographed. Private papers of Francis Jeanson.
Jouvenel, Bertrand de. "Reflections on Colonialism." *Confluence* 4, no. 3 (1955): 249–65.
Julien, Charles-André. *L'Afrique du Nord en marche: Nationalismes musulmans et souveraineté française*. 2d ed. Paris: René Julliard, 1952.
_____. "Impérialisme économique et impérialisme colonial." *Chemins du Monde*, no. 5 (1948), pp. 25–40.
_____. "Perdrons-nous le Maroc comme l'Indochine?" *Le Monde*, 26 July 1954.
Kempf, Françoise. "Les Catholiques français." In *Les Églises chrétiennes et la décolonisation*, edited by Marcel Merle, pp. 147–215. Paris: Armand Colin, 1967.

Kent, Raymond K. *From Madagascar to the Malagasy Republic*. New York: Frederick A. Praeger, 1962.

Kesteloot, Lilyan. *Les Écrivains noirs de langue française: Naissance d'une littérature*. Brussels: Université Libre de Bruxelles, 1963.

———, ed. *Anthologie négro-africaine*. Verviers, Belgium: Gérard & Co., 1967.

Kolakowski, Leszek. "Intellectuals against Intellect." *Daedalus* 101, no. 3 (Summer 1972): 1–15.

Kramer, Jane. "Les Pieds Noirs." *The New Yorker*, 25 Nov. 1972, pp. 52–108.

Kristol, Irving. "American Intellectuals and Foreign Policy." *Foreign Affairs* 45 (July 1967): 594–609.

Kulski, W. W. *De Gaulle and the World: The Foreign Policy of the Fifth Republic*. Syracuse: Syracuse University Press, 1966.

Lacharrière, René de. "Pour une révision de la doctrine politique." *La Nef*, n.s., no. 9 (June 1955), pp. 46–61.

Lacoste, Y. "Le Sous-développement: Quelques Ouvrages significatifs parus depuis dix ans." *Annales de Géographie* 71, no. 385 (May–June 1962): 247–78; no. 386 (July–Aug. 1962): 387–414.

Lacouture, Jean. *Cinq Hommes et la France*. Paris: Éditions du Seuil, 1961.

———. *De Gaulle*. Translated by Francis K. Price. New York: Avon, 1968.

La Feber, Walter. "Roosevelt, Churchill, and Indochina: 1942–45." *American Historical Review* 80, no. 5 (Dec. 1975): 1277–95.

Lafon, Monique, ed. *Le Parti communiste français dans la lutte contre le colonialisme*. Paris: Éditions Sociales, 1962.

La Gorce, Paul-Marie de. *The French Army: A Military-Political History*. Translated by Kenneth Douglas. New York: George Braziller, 1963.

La Nef. "Les Bases nécessaires d'une solution en Algérie." *La Nef*, May 1957, pp. 5–10.

La Nef. "1958: Paix en Algérie?" *La Nef*, Jan. 1958, pp. 4–8.

Larquier, André. "L'Idéologie politique de *Paris-Match*." Treatise, Institut d'Études Politiques, 1960.

Latreille, André, and Rémond, René. *Histoire du Catholicisme en France*. Vol. 3. 2d ed. Paris: Éditions Spes, 1965.

Lauriol, Marc. *L'Intégration fédéraliste*. Edited by Jacques Bassot. N.p., [1958].

Lavau, Georges. "L'Algérie avec la France." *Esprit*, no. 226 (May 1955), pp. 852–63.

Leach, Edmund. *Claude Lévi-Strauss*. New York: Viking Press, 1970.

Le Brun Keris, Georges. "L'Afrique entre deux civilisations." *Preuves*, no. 83 (Jan. 1958), pp. 3–15.

Leclerc, Gérard. *Anthropologie et colonialisme*. Paris: Arthème Fayard, 1972.

Leduc, Gaston. "Les Sous-développement et ses problèmes." *Revue d'Economie Politique* 62 (March–April 1952): 133–89.

Lefort, Claude. "Les Pays coloniaux: Analyse structurelle et stretégie révolutionnaire," *Les Temps Modernes*, no. 18 (March 1947), pp. 1068–94.

Legatte, Paul. "Doit et avoir de l'Union française." *Preuves*, no. 86 (April 1958), pp. 22–31.

Leiris, Michel. *Cinq Études d'ethnologie*. Paris: Gonthier, 1969.

———. "L'Ethnographe devant le colonialisme." *Les Temps Modernes*, no. 58 (Aug. 1950), pp. 357–74.

———. "Martinique, Guadeloupe, Haiti." *Les Temps Modernes*, no. 52 (Feb. 1950), pp. 1345–68.

Le Prévost, Jacques. *Défense de l'Algérie*. Algiers: Librairie Dominique, 1957.

Le Tourneau, Roger. *Évolution politique de l'Afrique du Nord musulmane, 1920– 1961*. Paris: Armand Colin, 1962.

Levine, Eric. "The French Intellectuals and the Algerian War." Undergraduate thesis, Columbia College, 1962.

Lévi-Strauss, Claude. "À contre-courant." Interview in *Le Nouvel Observateur*, 25 Jan. 1967, pp. 30–32.

———. "Diogène couché." *Les Temps Modernes*, no. 110 (March 1955), pp. 1187–1220.

———. "L'Humanité, c'est quoi?" Interview in *L'Express*, 20 Oct. 1960, pp. 32–33.

———. *Race and History*. Paris: UNESCO, 1952.

———. *The Raw and the Cooked: Introduction to a Science of Mythology: I*. Translated by John Weightman and Doreen Weightman. New York and Evanston: Harper and Row, Harper Torchbooks, 1970.

———. "Réponses à quelques questions." Interview in *Esprit*, no. 322 (Nov. 1963), pp. 628–53.

———. *The Savage Mind*. Chicago: University of Chicago Press, 1966.

———. *The Scope of Anthropology*. Translated by Sherry Ortner Paul and Robert A. Paul. London: Jonathan Cape, 1967.

———. *Structural Anthropology*. Translated by Claire Jacobson and Brooke Grundfest Schoepf. Garden City, N.Y.: Doubleday and Co., Anchor Books, 1967.

———. *Les Structures élémentaires de la parenté*. Paris: Presses Universitaires de France, 1949.

———. *Totemism*. Translated by Rodney Needham. Boston: Beacon Press, 1963.

———. *Tristes Tropiques*. Paris: Plon, 1955.

———. *Tristes Tropiques*. Translated and slightly abridged by John Russell. New York: Atheneum, 1967.

Lévy-Bruhl, Lucien. *Primitive Mentality*. Translated by Lilian A. Clare. Boston: Beacon Press, 1966.

Lijphart, Arend. *The Trauma of Decolonization: The Dutch and West New Guinea*. New Haven and London: Yale University Press, 1966.

Luchaire, François. "Les Grandes Tendances de l'évolution politique en Afrique noire." *Revue Française de Science Politique* 9, no. 3 (Sept. 1959): 578–97.

Luethy, Herbert. *France against Herself*. Translated by Eric Mosbacher. New York: Meridian Books, 1962.

McCloskey, Herbert. "Consensus and Ideology in American Politics." In *Public Opinion and Public Policy: Models of Political Linkage*, edited by Norman R. Luttbeg, pp. 365–90. Homewood, Ill.: Dorsey Press, 1968.

McCloy, Shelby T. *The Negro in France*. Lexington: University of Kentucky Press, 1961.

MacRae, Duncan, Jr. *Parliament, Parties, and Society in France, 1946–1958*. New York: St. Martin's Press, 1967.

Makarius, Raoul, ed. *Anthologie de la littérature arabe contemporaine*. Vol. 1. Preface by Jacques Berque. Paris: Éditions du Seuil, 1964.

Mandouze, André. "Le Dilemme algérien: Suicide ou salut public." *Esprit*, no. 149 (Oct. 1948), pp. 535–66.

Mannoni, O. "Colonisation et psychanalyse." *Chemins du Monde*, no. 5 (1948), pp. 89–96.

————. "The Decolonisation of Myself." *Race* 7, no. 4 (April 1966): 327–35.

————. "La Plainte du noir." *Esprit*, no. 179 (May 1951), pp. 734–49.

————. *Prospero and Caliban*. Translated by Pamela Powesland. 2d ed. New York and Washington: Frederick A. Praeger, 1964.

————. "Psychologie de la révolte malgache." *Esprit*, no. 166 (April 1950), pp. 581–96.

Maquet, Jacques J. "Objectivity in Anthropology." *Current Anthropology* 5, no. 1 (Feb. 1964): 47–55.

————. "Le Relativisme culturel." *Présence Africaine*, n.s., no. 22 (Oct.–Nov. 1958), pp. 63–73; no. 23 (Dec. 1958–Jan. 1959), pp. 59–68.

Marcus, John T. *Neutralism and Nationalism in France: A Case Study*. New York: Bookman Associates, 1958.

Markowitz, Irving Leonard. *Léopold Sédar Senghor and the Politics of Negritude*. New York: Atheneum, 1969.

Marrou, Henri. "France, ma patrie. . . ." *Le Monde*, 5 April 1956.

Marshall, D. Bruce. *The French Colonial Myth and Constitution-Making in the Fourth Republic*. New Haven and London: Yale University Press, 1973.

Martin, Claude. *Histoire de l'Algérie française, 1830–1962*. Paris: 4 Fils Aymon, 1963.

Martin-Chauffier, Louis. *L'Examen des consciences: Algérie an VII*. Paris: René Julliard, 1961.

————. "L'Exigence de vérité." *Le Figaro*, 13 Aug. 1957. Reprinted in *Saturne* 3, no. 14 (Aug.–Sept. 1957): 118–22.

————. "Journal de voyage en marge d'une enquête." *Saturne* 3, no. 15 (Oct.–Nov. 1957): 5–10; 3, no. 16 (Dec. 1957): 7–16; 4, no. 17 (Jan.–Feb.–March 1958): 8–23.

————. "Toute la vérité, rien que la vérité." *Saturne* 3, no. 12 (March–April 1957): 3–13.

Martinet, Gilles. "L'Indépendance condition nécessaire mais non suffisante." *France-Observateur*, 16 Jan. 1958, pp. 12–13.

————, "Qui sont les traîtres?" *France-Observateur*, 28 April 1960, p. 2.

Maschino, Maurice. *L'Engagement*. Paris: François Maspero, 1961.

————. *Le Refus*. 2d ed. Paris: François Maspero, 1960.

————. "Le Refus." *Les Temps Modernes*, no. 152 (Oct. 1958), pp. 701–16.

Maspero, François, ed. *Le Droit à l'insoumission*. Paris: François Maspero, 1961.

Massenet, Michel. *Contrepoison, ou la morale en Algérie*. Paris: Bernard Grasset, 1957.

Massu, Jacques. *La Vraie Bataille d'Alger*. Paris: Plon, 1972.

Maucorps, Paul H.; Memmi, Albert; Held, Jean-Francis. *Les Français et le racisme*. Paris: Payot, 1965.

Maulnier, Thierry. "L'Afrique est à faire." *Preuves*, no. 63 (May 1956), pp. 39–46.

————. "Confort et inconfort intellectuels devant le 'colonialisme.'" *Preuves*, no. 65 (July 1956), pp. 5–13.

————. "Crise de conscience française." *Preuves*, no. 61 (March 1956), pp. 29–35.

Mauriac, François. "L'Âme de l'Église." *Témoignage Chrétien*, 19 June 1953, p. 1.

———. *Bloc-Notes, 1952–1957*. Paris: Flammarion, 1958.

———. "L'Engagement de l'écrivain." *Le Figaro*, 8 April 1953.

———. "Les Faux Justes." *Le Figaro*, 23 Jan. 1950.

———. "Le Fond du problème." *Le Figaro*, 21 July 1953.

———. "Ici et maintenant." *Le Figaro*, 3 May 1947.

———. "La Justice est une politique." *Le Figaro*, 10 Feb. 1953.

———. *Mémoires politiques*. Paris: Bernard Grasset, 1967.

———. *Le Nouveau Bloc-Notes, 1958–1960*. Paris: Flammarion, 1961.

———. *Le Nouveau Bloc-Notes, 1961–1964*. Paris: Flammarion, 1968.

———. "Le Philosophe et l'Indochine." *Le Figaro*, 4 Feb. 1947.

———. "Pour une nouvelle alliance entre la France et l'Islam." *Le Figaro*, 24 March 1953.

———. *Le Sagouin*. Paris: Plon, 1951.

———. "La Vocation des chrétiens dans l'Union française," *Le Figaro*, 13 Jan. 1953.

Memmi, Albert. "Camus ou le colonisateur de bonne volonté." *La Nef*, Dec. 1957, pp. 95–96.

———. *The Colonizer and the Colonized*. Translated by Howard Greenfeld. Boston: Beacon Press, 1965.

———. *L'Homme dominé*. Paris: Gallimard, 1968.

———, ed. *Anthologie des écrivains maghrébins d'expression française*. 2d ed. Paris: Présence Africaine, 1965.

Mende, Tibor. "Bilan de la décolonisation." *La Nef*, July–Aug. 1957, pp. 44–47.

———. *L'Inde devant l'orage*. Translated from English by Jeanne N. Mathieu. Paris: Éditions du Seuil, 1952.

———. *La Révolte de l'Asie*. Translated from English by Jeanne N. Mathieu. Paris: Presses Universitaires de France, 1951.

Merle, Marcel, ed. *Les Églises chrétiennes et la décolonisation*. Cahiers de la Fondation Nationale des Sciences Politiques, no. 151. Paris: Armand Colin, 1967.

Merleau-Ponty, Maurice. *Humanism and Terror: An Essay on the Communist Problem*. Translated by John O'Neill. Boston: Beacon Press, 1969.

[———]. "Indochine S.O.S." *Les Temps Modernes*, no. 18 (March 1947), pp. 1039–52.

———. *Sense and Non-Sense*. Translated by Hubert L. Dreyfus and Patricia Allen Dreyfus. Evanston: Northwestern University Press, 1964.

———. *Signs*. Translated by Richard C. McCleary. Evanston: Northwestern University Press, 1964.

Messud, G. *Autour du statut de l'Algérie*. Paris: Éditions du "Monde," 1947.

Meyer-Spiegler, Madeleine. "Antimilitarisme et refus de service militaire dans la France contemporaine." Doctoral dissertation, Fondation Nationale des Sciences Politiques, 1968.

Meynaud, Jean, and Lancelot, Alain. *La Participation des Français à la politique*. "Que sais-je?" no. 911. 2d ed. Paris: Presses Universitaires de France, 1965.

Mézu, S. Okechukwu. *Léopold Sédar Senghor et la défense et illustration de la civilisation noire*. Paris: Marcel Didier, 1968.

Michel, Henri. *Les Courants de pensée de la Résistance*. Paris: Presses Universitaires de France, 1962.

Mignot, Elie. "La Guerre coloniale d'Algérie." *Cahiers de l'Institut Maurice Thorez* 6, no. 26 (March–April 1972): 48–66.

Mitterrand, François. "Conditions d'une négociation." *La Nef*, n.s., no. 2 (March 1953), pp. 200–217.

———. "Paradoxes et promesses de l'Union française." *La Nef*, n.s., no. 9 (June 1955), pp. 223–31.

———. "La Politique française en Afrique du Nord." *Preuves*, Nov. 1953, pp. 3–8.

———. *Présence française et abandon*. Tribune Libre, no. 12. Paris: Plon, 1957.

Moneta, Jacob. *La Politique du parti communiste français dans la question coloniale, 1920–1965*. Paris: François Maspero, 1971.

Montagne, Robert. "Le Nationalisme nord-africain." *La Nef*, n.s., no. 2 (March 1953), pp. 10–28.

Morin, Edgar. "Intellectuels: Critique du mythe et mythe de la critique." *Arguments* 4, no. 20 (1960): 35–40.

———. "Le Péril jaune." *Arguments* 1, no. 2 (Feb.–March 1957): 12–16.

———. "La Question nègre." *Arguments* 1, no. 1 (Dec. 1956–Jan. 1957): 1–7.

———. "L Révolution coloniale." *Arguments* 2, no. 10 (Nov. 1958): 27–31.

Morazé, Charles. *The French and the Republic*. Translated by Jean-Jacques Demorest. Ithaca: Cornell University Press, 1958.

Morot-Sir, Édouard. *La Pensée française d'aujourd'hui*. Paris: Presses Universitaires de France, 1971.

Mottin, Jean. *Histoire politique de la presse, 1944–1949*. Paris: Éditions "Bilans Hebdomadaires," 1949.

Mounier, Emmanuel. *L'Éveil de l'Afrique noire*. In *Oeuvres*, vol. 3: *1944–1950*, pp. 248–338. Paris: Éditions du Seuil, 1962.

[———]. "Prévenons la guerre d'Afrique du Nord." *Esprit*, no. 132 (April 1947), p. 545.

Moussa, Pierre. *Les Nations prolétaires*. Paris: Presses Universitaires de France, 1959.

Mueller, John E. *War, Presidents and Public Opinion*. New York: John Wiley and Sons, 1973.

Mus, Paul. *Le Destin de l'Union française: De l'Indochine à l'Afrique*. Paris: Éditions du Seuil, 1954.

———. *Viêt-Nam, sociologie d'une guerre*. Paris: Éditions du Seuil, 1952.

Nania, Guy. *Un Parti de la gauche: Le PSU*. N.p.: Librairie Gedalge, 1966.

O'Ballance, Edgar. *The Algerian Insurrection, 1954–62*. London: Faber and Faber, 1967.

O'Brien, Conor Cruise. *Albert Camus of Europe and Africa*. New York: Viking Press, 1970.

Olson, Charles William. "Decolonization in French Politics (1950–1956): Indochina, Tunisia, Morocco." Ph.D. dissertation, Northern Illinois University, 1966.

Oppermann, Thomas. *Le Problème algérien*. Translated from German by J. Lecerf. Paris: François Maspero, 1961.

Ottaway, David, and Ottaway, Marina. *Algeria: The Politics of a Socialist Revolution*. Berkeley and Los Angeles: University of California Press, 1970.

Oved, Georges, and Vaez-Olivera, Robert. "Conditions économiques d'un renouveau." *La Nef*, n.s., no. 9 (June 1955), pp. 94–137.

P. "'L'Algérie n'existe pas. . . .'" *Preuves*, Oct. 1955, pp. 50–53.

Palle, Albert. "Crier, mais avec qui?" *La Nef*, April 1958, pp. 20–23.

Parker, Emmett. *Albert Camus: The Artist in the Arena*. Madison: University of Wisconsin Press, 1965.

Passeron, André. *De Gaulle parle*. Paris: Plon, 1962.

Patri, Aimé. "Problèmes de la 'décolonisation.'" *Preuves*, Aug. 1957, pp. 82–88.

Paxton, Robert O. *Vichy France: Old Guard and New Order, 1940–1944*. New York: Alfred A. Knopf, 1972.

Péju, Marcel. "De l"affaire des avocats' au 'réseau des intellectuels.'" *Les Temps Modernes*, nos. 167–68 (Feb.–March 1960), pp. 1435–40.

————. "Fin du mythe gaulliste." *Les Temps Modernes*, nos. 167–68 (Feb.–March 1960), pp. 1153–66.

————. "Une Gauche respectueuse." *Les Temps Modernes*, nos. 169–70 (April–May 1960), pp. 1512–29.

————. "L'Illusionniste." *Les Temps Modernes*, nos. 153–54 (Nov.–Dec. 1958), pp. i–viii, 769–74.

————. "Mourir pour de Gaulle?" *Les Temps Modernes*, nos. 175–76 (Oct.–Nov. 1960), pp. 481–502.

Pelage, Doctor. "La Fin d'un mythe scientifique." *Présence Africaine*, no. 1 (Oct.–Nov. 1947), pp. 158–61.

Peretti, André de. "L'Indépendance marocaine et la France." *Esprit*, no. 132 (April 1947), pp. 546–76.

————. "Premières Approches d'une psychologie de la colonisation." In *Colonisation et conscience chrétienne*, by the Centre Catholique des Intellectuels Français, Recherches et débats, n.s., no. 6, Dec. 1953, pp. 95–128. Paris: Arthème Fayard, n.d.

————. "Psychologie française et pays d'outre-mer." *La Nef*, n.s., no. 9 (June 1955), pp. 62–76.

Philip, André. "Les Conditions politiques de l'expansion des pays sous-développés." *Présence Africaine*, n.s., no. 20 (June–July 1958), pp. 36–41.

Pickles, Dorothy. *French Politics: The First Years of the Fourth Republic*. London: Royal Institute of International Affairs, 1953.

Pierce, Roy. *Contemporary French Political Thought*. London and New York: Oxford University Press, 1966.

Planck, Russell E. "Public Opinion in France after the Liberation, 1944–1949." In *Common Frontiers of the Social Sciences*, edited by Mirra Komarovsky. Glencoe, Ill.: Free Press, 1957.

Poirier, Jean. "Histoire de la pensée ethnologique." In *Ethnologie générale*. Encyclopédie de la Pléiade. Paris: Gallimard, 1968.

"La Politique anticolonialiste dans l'histoire du parti communiste français." *Cahiers de l'Institut Maurice Thorez* 6, no. 26 (March–April 1972).

Pour l'amnistie dans les pays d'outre-mer: L'Action du groupe socialiste à l'Assemblée de l'Union française. Paris: Librairie des Municipalités, 1955.

"Pour la paix au Viet-nam." *Les Temps Modernes*, no. 39 (Jan. 1949), pp. 122–25.

Priestley, Herbert Ingram. *France Overseas: A Study of Modern Imperialism*. New York: D. Appleton-Century, 1938.

Quinn, Renée. "Albert Camus devant le problème algérien." *Revue des Sciences Humaines* 128 (Oct.–Dec. 1967): 613–31.

Rémond, René. "Les Intellectuels et la politique." *Revue Française de Science Politique* 9, no. 4 (Dec. 1959): 860–80.

————, ed. *Forces religieuses et attitudes politiques dans la France contemporaine*. Cahiers de la Fondation Nationale des Sciences Politiques, no. 130. Paris: Armand Colin, 1965.

Renan, Ernest. *La Réforme intellectuelle et morale*. Paris: Union Générale d'Éditions, n.d.

"Retour sur la guerre d'Algérie." *Esprit*, no. 417 (Oct. 1972), pp. 387–412.

Revel, Jean-François. *En France: La Fin de l'opposition*. Paris: Union Générale d'Éditions, 1968.

Richard-Molard, Jacques. "Propositions pour l'Afrique." *Esprit*, no. 192 (July 1952), pp. 26–44.

Ricoeur, Paul. "Civilisation universelle et cultures nationales." *Esprit*, no. 299 (Oct. 1961), pp. 439–53.

————. "L'Insoumission." *Esprit*, no. 288 (Oct. 1960), pp. 1601–4.

Rieber, Alfred J. *Stalin and the French Communist Party, 1941–1947*. New York and London: Columbia University Press, 1962.

Rieff, Philip, ed. *On Intellectuals*. Garden City, N.Y.: Doubleday and Co., Anchor Books, 1970.

Rivet, Paul. "Indépendance et liberté." *Le Monde*, 1 Feb. 1957.

Rosenau, James N. *Public Opinion and Foreign Policy*. New York: Random House, 1961.

Rous, Jean. *Chronique de la décolonisation*. Paris: Éditions Présence Africaine, 1965.

————. *Le Congrès des Peuples s'adresse aux démocrates de France*. Paris: Société Nationale des Entreprises de Presse, [1950].

————. *Itinéraire d'un militant*. Paris: Jeune Afrique, 1968.

————. *Léopold Sédar Senghor: Un Président de l'Afrique nouvelle*. Paris: Jean Didier, 1967.

————. *Tunisie. . . Attention!* Paris: Deux Rives, 1952.

Rovan, Joseph. "La France devant l'Indochine." *Esprit*, no. 116 (Nov. 1945), pp. 830–35.

Roy, Claude. "La Gauche française à l'oeil nu." *La Nef*, Feb. 1958, pp. 15–18.

Roy, Jules. *Autour du drame*. Paris: René Julliard, 1961.

————. "Dialogue avec le vaincu." *Preuves*, April 1953, pp. 29–34.

————. *La Guerre d'Algérie*. Paris: René Julliard, 1960.

————. *J'accuse le général Massu*. Paris: Éditions du Seuil, 1972.

Sainteny, Jean. *Histoire d'une paix manquée: Indochine 1945–1947*. Paris: Amiot-Dumont, 1953.

Sartre, Jean-Paul. "L'Alibi." Interview in *Le Nouvel Observateur*, 19 Nov. 1964, pp. 1–5.

————. *Being and Nothingness: An Essay on Phenomenological Ontology*. Translated by Hazel E. Barnes. New York: Philosophical Library, 1956.

————. *Black Orpheus*. Translated by S. W. Allen. Paris: Présence Africaine, n.d.

————. "Ceux que vous opprimez, nous opprimant pour les mêmes raisons." *La Gauche*, 15–30 Nov. 1948, pp. 1, 3.

————. "Le Crime." *Le Nouvel Observateur*, 30 Nov. 1966, pp. 12–14.

————. *Critique de la raison dialectique*. Paris: Gallimard, 1960.

————. "La Faim au ventre, la liberté au coeur." *La Gauche*, 15–30 May 1948, p. 1.

————. "Le Génocide." *Les Temps Modernes*, no. 259 (Dec. 1967), pp. 953–71.

———. Interview in *Vérités Pour*, no. 9 (2 June 1959), pp. 14–17.

———. *Nausea*. Translated by Lloyd Alexander. Norfolk, Conn.: New Directions, 1959.

———. *No Exit and Three Other Plays*. Translated by Stuart Gilbert and Lionel Abel. New York: Random House, Vintage Books, n.d.

———. "Orphée noir." Introduction to *Anthologie de la nouvelle poésie nègre et malgache de langue française*, edited by Léopold Sédar Senghor, pp. ix–xliv. 2d ed. Paris: Presses Universitaires de France, 1969.

———. "Ouragan sur le sucre." *France-Soir*, 28 June–15 July 1960.

———. *Plaidoyer pour les intellectuels*. Paris: Gallimard, 1972.

———. "Présence noire." *Présence Africaine*, no. 1 (Oct.–Nov. 1947), pp. 28–29.

———. *Réflexions sur la question juive*. Paris: Gallimard, 1954.

———. "Sartre Looks at the M.E. Again." Interview with Arturo Schwartz, in *New Outlook* 12 (March–April 1969): 35–49.

———. "Sartre par Sartre." Interview with the *New Left Review*, in *Le Nouvel Observateur*, 26 Jan. 1970, pp. 40–50.

———. *Search for a Method*. Translated by Hazel E. Barnes. New York: Random House, 1963.

———. "Le Silence de ceux qui reviennent. . . ." Interview with Maria Craipeau, in *France-Observateur*, 10 Sept. 1959, pp. 12–13.

———. *Situations*. Translated by Benita Eisler. Greenwich, Conn.: Fawcett Publications, 1965.

———. *Situations, V: Colonialisme et néo-colonialisme*. Paris: Gallimard, 1964.

———. *Théâtre*. Paris: Gallimard, 1962.

———. *What Is Literature?* Translated by Bernard Frechtman. New York: Washington Square Press, 1949.

———. "What's Jean-Paul Sartre Thinking Lately?" Interview with Pierre Bénichou, translated by Patricia Southgate, in *Esquire*, Dec. 1972, pp. 204–8, 280–86.

———, ed. *L'Affaire Henri Martin*. Paris: Gallimard, 1953.

———; Schwartz, Laurent; Barrat, Robert; Pouillon, Jean; Martinet, Gilles; Mallet, Serge. "Répondre à la violence par la violence?" *France-Observateur*, 1 Feb. 1962, pp. 7–9.

Sauvy, Alfred. "Introduction à l'étude des pays sous-développés." *Population* 6, no. 4 (Oct.–Dec. 1951): 601–8.

———. *Malthus et les deux Marx*. Paris: Gonthier, 1963.

———. *L'Opinion publique*. "Que sais-je?" no. 701. 5th ed. Paris: Presses Universitaires de France, 1967.

———. "Le Sous-développement économique et les conditions de développement." In *La Question algérienne*, by Jean Dresch et al., pp. 97–120. Paris: Éditions de Minuit, 1958.

Savary, Alain. *Nationalisme algérien et grandeur française*. Tribune Libre, no. 54. Paris: Plon, 1960.

———. "Paix en Indochine." *La Nef*, n.s., no. 4 (July 1953), pp. 125–31.

Schuman, Robert. "Nécessité d'une politique." *La Nef*, n.s., no. 2 (March 1953), pp. 7–9.

Schumann, Maurice. *Le Vrai Malaise des intellectuels de gauche*. Tribune Libre, no. 11. Paris: Plon, 1957.

Sédès, J. M. "L'Union française et sa politique." *Cahiers du Monde Nouveau* 5, no. 1 (Jan. 1949): 37–47.

Semaines Sociales de France. *La Montée des peuples dans la communauté humaine*. 46th session, Angers, 1959. Lyon: Chronique Sociale de France, 1959.

──────. *Peuples d'outre-mer et civilisation occidentale*. 35th session, Lyon, 1948. Lyon: Chronique Sociale de France, 1948.

Semidei, Manuela. "De l'empire à la décolonisation à travers les manuels scolaires français." *Revue Française de Science Politique* 16, no. 1 (Feb. 1966): 56–86.

──────. "Les Socialistes français et le problème colonial entre les deux guerres." *Revue Française de Science Politique* 18, no. 6 (Dec. 1968): 1115–53.

Sengat-Kuo, François. "La France fait son examen de conscience ou 'Le Fédéralisme sauvera-t-il l'Union française?' " *Présence Africaine*, n.s., no. 3 (Aug.–Sept. 1955), pp. 86–95.

Senghor, Léopold Sédar. "Défense de l'Afrique noire." *Esprit*, no. 112 (July 1945), pp. 237–48.

──────. "Un Humanisme de l'Union française." *Esprit*, no. 157 (July 1949), pp. 1019–34.

──────. *Liberté 1: Négritude et humanisme*. Paris: Éditions du Seuil, 1964.

──────. *Liberté 2: Nation et voie africaine du socialisme*. Paris: Éditions du Seuil, 1971.

──────. "Pour une solution fédéraliste." *La Nef*, June 1955, pp. 148–61.

──────. *Selected Poems/Poésies Choisies*. Translations and Introduction by Craig Williamson. London: Rex Collings, 1976.

──────, ed. *Anthologie de la nouvelle poésie nègre et malgache de langue française*. Preceded by "Orphée noir," by Jean-Paul Sartre. Paris: Presses Universitaires de France, 1948.

Servan-Schreiber, Jean-Jacques. "L'Appel." *L'Express*, 6 Oct. 1960, pp. 7–8.

──────. "Au service de qui?" *L'Express*, 13 April 1956, p. 3.

──────. "Avec nos soldats." *L'Express*, 22 Sept. 1960, pp. 5–6.

──────. "Le Bilan." *L'Express*, 15 Dec. 1960, pp. 7–8.

──────. "Les Étudiants arrêtés." *L'Express*, 16 June 1960, pp. 7–8.

──────. "L'Indépendance." *L'Express*, 28 Aug. 1958, p. 3.

──────. "Une Lettre d'un non-deserteur." *L'Express*, 15 Sept. 1960, pp. 5–6.

──────. *Lieutenant in Algeria*. Translated by Ronald Matthews. New York: Alfred A. Knopf, 1957.

──────. "Que veut Mendès-France?" *L'Express*, 25 May 1956, p. 3.

──────. "Quel est votre choix?" *L'Express*, 2 Nov. 1961, p. 48.

──────. "Rappelés pour quoi?" *L'Express*, 10 Sept. 1955, p. 3.

──────. "Rendez-vous au retour!" *L'Express*, 13 July 1956, p. 3.

──────. "Le Sang qui coule." *L'Express*, 18 Sept. 1958, p. 3.

──────. "Le Scalpel." *L'Express*, 13 Oct. 1960, p. 7.

Servier, Jean. *Demain en Algérie*. Paris: Robert Laffont, 1959.

Sheehan, Neil, et al. *The Pentagon Papers*. Toronto, New York, and London: Bantam Books, 1971.

Siegfried, André. "Approaches to an Understanding of Modern France." In *Modern France: Problems of the Third and Fourth Republics*, edited by Edward Mead Earle, pp. 3–16. Princeton: Princeton University Press, 1951.

Simmons, Harvey G. *French Socialists in Search of a Role, 1956–1967*. Ithaca and London: Cornell University Press, 1970.

Simon, Pierre-Henri. *Contre la torture*. Paris. Éditions du Seuil, 1957.

———. "La France est-elle en état de péché?" *Esprit*, no. 157 (July 1949), pp. 1099–1102.

———. *Mauriac par lui-même* . Paris: Éditions du Seuil, [1953].

———. "Opération bonne conscience." *Esprit*, no. 253 (Sept. 1957). pp. 244–246.

———. *Portrait d'un officier*. Paris: Éditions du Seuil, 1958.

———. "La Tradition jacobine." *Le Monde*, 29 March 1956.

Smith, Charles Anthony. "French Extremism in Response to the Algerian Revolution." Ph.D. dissertation, Harvard University, 1970.

Smith, Tony [Charles Anthony]. "The French Colonial Consensus and People's War, 1946–58." *Journal of Contemporary History* 9, no. 4 (Oct. 1974): 217–47.

———. "The French Economic Stake in Colonial Algeria." *French Historical Studies* 9, no. 1 (Spring 1975): 184–89.

———. "Idealism and People's War: Sartre on Algeria." *Political Theory* 1, no. 4 (Nov. 1973): 426–49.

Smith, Woodruff D. "The Ideology of German Colonialism, 1840–1906." *Journal of Modern History* 46, no. 4 (Dec. 1974): 641–62.

Soustelle, Jacques. *Aimée et Souffrante Algérie*. Paris: Plon, 1956.

———. *Le Drame algérien et la décadence française: Réponse à Raymond Aron*. Tribune Libre, no. 6. Paris: Plon, 1957.

———. *L'Espérance trahie (1958–1961)*. Paris: Éditions de l'Alma, 1962.

———. *Lettre ouverte aux victimes de la décolonisation*. Paris: Albin Michel, 1973.

Southworth, Constant. *The French Colonial Venture*. London: P. S. King & Son, 1931.

Steiner, Georges. "A Conversation with Claude Lévi-Strauss." *Encounter* 26 (April 1966): 32–38.

Stibbe, Pierre. *Justice pour les Malgaches*. Preface by Claude Bourdet. Paris: Éditions du Seuil, 1954.

Suret-Canale, Jean. "De la libération à la guerre d'Indochine." *Cahiers de l'Institut Maurice Thorez* 6, no. 26 (March–April 1972): 37–47.

T. M. "L'Algérie n'est pas la France." *Les Temps Modernes*, no. 119 (Nov. 1955), pp. 577–79.

———. "Algérie: Ouverture ou échappatoire?" *Les Temps Modernes*, no. 164 (Oct. 1959), pp. 577–83.

———. "Ce n'est pas une émeute. . . ." *Les Temps Modernes*, no. 77 (March 1952), pp. 1537–43.

———. "Demain comme hier." *Les Temps Modernes*, no. 194 (July 1962), pp. 1–3.

———. "Et bourreaux, et victimes. . . ." *Les Temps Modernes*, no. 15 (Dec. 1946).

———. "La Gauche française et le F.L.N." *Les Temps Modernes*, nos. 167–68 (Feb.–March 1960), pp. 1169–73.

———. "Pouvoirs 'spéciaux.'" *Les Temps Modernes*, no. 123 (March–April 1956), pp. 1345–53.

———. "Refus d'obéissance." *Les Temps Modernes*, no. 118 (Oct. 1955), pp. 385–88.

———. "Réponse à Jean Daniel." *Les Temps Modernes*, nos. 169–70 (April–May 1960), pp. 1530–34.

———. "La Réponse d'Henri Alleg." *Les Temps Modernes*, no. 145 (March 1958), pp. 1529–30.

Talbott, John. "French Public Opinion and the Algerian War: A Research Note." *French Historical Studies* 9, no. 2 (Fall 1975): 354–61.

Teitgen, Pierre-Henri. "La Participation de la France à la montée des peuples." In *La Montée des peuples dans la communauté humaine*, by Semaines Sociales de France, 46th session, Angers, 1959, pp. 313–36. Lyon: Chronique Sociale de France, 1959.

Terrenoire, Louis. *De Gaulle et l'Algérie: Témoignage pour l'Histoire*. Paris: Arthème Fayard, 1964.

Thibaud, Paul. "'La Dépossession du monde.'" *Esprit*, no. 331 (Oct. 1964), pp. 679–88.

Thompson, Virginia, and Adloff, Richard. *The Malagasy Republic*. Stanford: Stanford University Press, 1965.

Thornton, A. P. *The Imperial Idea and Its Enemies: A Study in British Power*. Garden City, N.Y.: Doubleday and Co., Anchor Books, 1968.

Tillion, Germaine. *L'Afrique bascule vers l'avenir*. Paris: Éditions de Minuit, 1961.

———. "Albert Camus et l'Algérie." *Preuves*, Sept. 1958, pp. 69–72.

———. *L'Algérie en 1957*. Paris: Éditions de Minuit, 1957.

———. *Les Ennemis complémentaires*. Paris: Éditions de Minuit, 1960.

Touchard, Jean; Girardet, Raoul; and Rémond, René. "Le Mouvement des idées politiques dans la France contemporaine." Course given at the Institut d'Études Politiques, 1958–59. Mimeographed by the Amicale des Élèves.

UNESCO. *Race and Science*. New York: Columbia University Press, 1961.

Union Nationale des Étudiants de France. *Le Syndicalisme étudiant et le problème algérien*. N.p., 1960.

Verhaegen, Benoit. "La Perspective historique de sous-développement." *Esprit*, no. 272 (April 1959), pp. 569–88.

Vidal-Naquet, Pierre. *La Raison d'état*. Paris: Éditions de Minuit, 1962.

———. *Torture: Cancer of Democracy*. Harmondsworth, Middlesex: Penguin, 1963.

———. *La Torture dans la république*. Paris: Éditions de Minuit, 1972.

Vogelgesang, Sandy. *The Long Dark Night of the Soul: The American Intellectual Left and the Vietnam War*. New York, Evanston, San Francisco, London: Harper and Row, 1974.

Waughray, Vernon. "The French Racial Scene: North African Immigrants in France." *Race* 2, no. 1 (Nov. 1960): 60–70.

Weber, Max. *From Max Weber: Essays in Sociology*. Edited by H. H. Gerth and C. Wright Mills. New York: Oxford University Press, 1946.

Werth, Alexander. *France 1940–1955*. 1956; reprint ed., Boston: Beacon Press, 1966.

Williams, Philip M. *Politics in Post-War France*. 2d ed. London: Longmans, Green and Co., 1958.

———. *Wars, Plots and Scandals in Post-War France*. Cambridge: At the University Press, 1970.

———, and Harrison, Martin. *Politics and Society in de Gaulle's Republic*. Garden City, N.Y.: Doubleday and Co., Anchor Books, 1973.

Winks, Robin W. "On Decolonization and Informal Empire." *American Historical Review* 81, no. 3 (June 1976): 540–56.

Wright, Gordon. "The Dreyfus Echo: Justice and Politics in the Fourth Republic." *Yale Review* 48, no. 3 (Spring 1957): 354–73.

———. *The Reshaping of French Democracy*. 1948; reprint ed., Boston: Beacon Press, 1970.

Wylie, Laurence. *Village in the Vaucluse*. New York: Harper and Row, 1964.

———. "Youth in France and the United States." In Erik Erikson, ed., *The Challenge of Youth*, pp. 291–311. Garden City, N.Y.: Doubleday and Co., Anchor Books, 1965.

XXX. "La Balance des comptes de l'Algérie." *Politique Étrangère* 21, no. 3 (May–June 1956): 313–22.

Yacono, Xavier. *Histoire de la colonisation française*. "Que sais-je?" no. 452. Paris: Presses Universitaires de France, 1969.

Yetiv, Isaac. *Le Thème de l'aliénation dans le roman maghrébin d'expression française de 1952 à 1956*. Sherbrooke, Québec: CELEF (Centre d'Étude des Littératures d'Expression Française), Université de Sherbrooke, 1972.

ᨀ Index

A

Abbas, Ferhat, 28, 34, 37–38, 40, 63–64, 103, 130, 131

Actuelles, III (Albert Camus), 137, 141

Affaire Henri Martin, L' (Jean-Paul Sartre), 56

African, sub-Saharan: French paternalism toward, 26, 69, 75, 86–87; in the constitution of the Fourth Republic, 39; transition to independence, 112, 189, 202–3; civilization of, 217–19. *See also* Brazzaville conference; Cartier, Raymond; Negritude

Afrique du Nord en marche, L' (Charles-André Julien), 51

Algeria: insurrection of May 1945, 28, 33–34, 35, 62–64; statute of 1947, 39, 60; juridical status of, 39, 74–75; fixing of elections in, 60; Algerian war, 75, 103, 105–8, 145–46; Sartre's analysis of, 89–90; reasons for French attachment to, 111–12; Saharan oil and gas of, 112, 198–99; French atrocities in, 113–29; "battle of Algiers," 114, 120, 124, 131–32; Aron's analysis of, 197–201, 204. *See also* Abbas, Ferhat; Front de Libération Nationale; Hadj, Messali; Integration, plan of; Nationalism, colonial; Settlers, European

Algérie en 1957, L' (Germaine Tillion), 84–86, 113

Algérie et la république, L' (Raymond Aron), 197

Algérie hors la loi, L' (Francis Jeanson and Colette Jeanson), 100, 157, 170

Alleg, Henri, 119; *La Question*, 119–20

Americans. *See* United States

An cinq de la révolution algérienne, L' (Frantz Fanon), 95

Anthologie de la nouvelle poésie nègre et malgache de langue française (Léopold Sédar Senghor), 214, 220

Anthropologists: and colonization, 24, 26, 224–28, 232. *See also* Balandier, Georges; Leiris, Michel; Lévi-Strauss, Claude; Lévy-Bruhl, Lucien; Soustelle, Jacques; Tillion, Germaine

"Anticolonialism": definition of, 15–16

"Anti-imperialism": definition of, 15–16

Army, French: colonial mission of, 23–24, 87; atrocities committed by, 55, 61, 113–29; in Algeria, 108, 137, 145–46. *See also* "Fascism," threat of

Aron, Raymond, 20, 195–201; on Indochina, 41, 77, 181, 182; on underdevelopment, 92–93, 96; on Algeria, 92–93, 96, 101, 113, 142–43, 197–201, 204; *La Tragédie algérienne*, 113, 142, 197, 201, 204; on empire, 183, 195–96; on the French mind, 185; on economic modernization and *grandeur*, 195–96, 206–7, 264 (n. 34); *Espoir et peur du siècle*, 196–97; *L'Algérie et la république*, 197

Assimilation, policy of, 29, 31, 34, 63–64, 185, 211, 212–13; definition of, 23; criticisms of, 26, 191

Audin, Maurice, 119

Audry, Colette, 175

Auriol, Vincent, 50

B

Balandier, Georges, 232

Bandung conference, 70, 79, 183

Bao Dai, 55, 74, 180–81

Barberot, Roger, 126, 127; *Malaventure en Algérie*, 117

Barrat, Robert, 174; *Justice pour le Maroc*, 52–53

Barrault, Jean-Louis, 179
Barthes, Roland, 175
Beauvoir, Simone de, 158–59, 174, 179
Béguin, Albert, 18
Berque, Jacques, 113, 200, 232–37, 242; *Dé-possession du monde*, 233–35
Bidault, Georges, 37, 38, 54, 56, 178
Bernard, Colonel F., 35, 48, 179
Beuve-Méry, Hubert, 19, 52, 115, 117, 181
Billotte, Pierre, 122–23
Blanchot, Maurice, 174
Bloch-Michel, Jean, 129, 134
Blum, Léon, 40–41, 43
Bollardière, Paris de, 117, 123, 126, 127, 128, 154
Boulez, Pierre, 174
Boumendjel, Ali: "suicide" of, 116, 117
Bourdet, Claude, 17, 18, 49, 57, 65, 67, 77, 87, 94, 102, 147, 189; realism of, 20, 180, 183, 190; on North Africa, 51, 65–66; on Indochina, 77–78, 179, 180–81; on Algeria, 101, 113, 121, 122, 133; on the threat of fascism, 148, 149, 168; on types of disobedience, 151–52, 154, 155, 160, 167, 170, 175–76; on de Gaulle, 165, 166
Bourguiba, Habib, 28, 49, 50, 51, 94, 120
Brazzaville conference, 27, 29, 31, 32–33, 48
Breton, André, 174, 179, 219
British. *See* Great Britain
Bruller, Jean [pseud. Vercors], 56, 157, 174, 179
Bugeaud, Thomas Robert, 24
Butor, Michel, 174

C
Cahiers du Monde Nouveau, 48–49, 69
Cahier d'un retour au pays natal (Aimé Césaire), 214, 215–17, 219, 223
Callois, Roger, 226–27, 228
"Call to Opinion for a Negotiated Peace in Algeria," 175
Camus, Albert, 18, 19, 53, 65, 77, 188–89, 219, 243; on overseas troubles in 1945, 32, 34, 35; on Algeria, 34, 61–64, 78–79, 86, 128, 138–42; against atrocities, 125–26, 130–31, 132, 133, 135, 137; *L'Homme révolté*, 130; *Le Mythe de Sisyphe*, 130; *Ré-flexions sur la guillotine*, 130; *La Peste*, 130–31, 139; *Actuelles, III*, 137, 141; *L'Ét-ranger*, 139
Capitant, René, 116
Cartier, Raymond, 195, 201–2, 204
"Cartierism," 202, 203, 204, 208, 242
Catholics, French, 18, 51–52, 115; colonial proselytism, 21–22, 23, 24; doctrine on

colonization, 25–26, 68, 95, 97–98. *See also* Intellectuals, Catholic; Mouvement Républicain Populaire
Centre Catholique des Intellectuels Fran-çaise, 53, 57, 68
Centre d'Études et de Documentation, 54
Césaire, Aimé, 36–37, 67, 70, 82, 219, 220, 222; *Discours sur le colonialisme*, 67; *Cahier d'un retour au pays natal*, 214, 215–27, 219, 223. *See also* Negritude
Chemins du Monde, 47, 49
Clemenceau, Georges, 205
Cocteau, Jean, 179
Cold War: and decolonization, 41, 45–46, 76, 77, 79, 147; and intellectuals, 49, 195. *See also* Communism, threat of; Com-munists, French; United States, im-perialist threat of
Colonial interests: power of, 64–66, 89–90, 126
"Colonialism": definition of, 15–16
Combat, 15, 32, 34–35, 41, 48, 195. *See* Bourdet, Claude; Camus, Albert
Comité de Résistance Spirituelle, 116, 133
Comité France-Maghreb, 53, 54
Comité Maurice Audin, 119
Comité pour l'Amnestie aux Condamnés Politiques d'Outre-mer, 57
Commission de Sauvegarde des Droits et Libertés Individuels, 118, 120, 122
Communism, threat of, 41, 54, 76–79, 181–82, 196, 201. *See also* Cold War
Communists, French: political isolation of, 6, 7, 8, 9, 18, 45–46, 110, 111; colonial policy of, 25, 29, 33, 43–46, 69, 72, 83, 88, 92, 103–4, 172, 190, 222; in the constitu-tent assemblies, 36–38; support for the Malagasy deputies, 42, 73; actions against the war in Indochina, 45–46, 55, 151; policy on Algeria, 108, 121, 144, 147, 160–63; opposition to radical actions, 163, 168, 170, 175, 176, 177, 178. *See also* Césaire, Aimé; Cold War; *Humanité, L'*; Thorez, Maurice
Congress for Cultural Freedom. See *Preuves*
Congress of Peoples against Imperialism, 48, 98–99. *See also* Rous, Jean
Conscientious objection, 152, 155. *See also* Disobedience, morality of
Constituent Assembly, first, 23, 31, 36–37, 209
Constituent Assembly, second, 37–40, 191
Contre la torture (Pierre-Henri Simon), 115, 124–26, 127

"Cosovereignty": in the protectorates, 50, 74, 99
Cot, Pierre, 31
Critique de la raison dialectique (Jean-Paul Sartre), 143–44
Cultural relativism, 224–27, 232
Cultures, non-Western: French appreciation of, 26, 213, 219–20, 236–37; literary revival in North Africa, 213, 215. *See also* Anthropologists; Berque, Jacques; Ethnocentrism, French; Lévi-Strauss, Claude; Negritude

D

Damas, Léon, 213–14
Damnés de la terre, Les (Frantz Fanon), 136, 172
"Declaration of the Right to Draft Evasion in the Algerian War." *See* "Manifesto of the 121"
Decolonization, French, compared to Portuguese, 5, 188, 242–42, 266 (n. 5); compared to British, 183, 188, 198, 207, 239, 243; compared to Dutch, 183, 188, 198, 202, 207; compared to Spanish, 183; compared to Japanese, 207. *See also* Great Britain
de Gaulle, Charles, 103, 153; belief in the importance of empire, 27, 34, 187; humanist reforms made by, 28–29, 32; concept of a French community, 37, 38–39, 191, 192; Algerian policy of, 109, 120, 128, 177, 200–201, 204; attitude of leftists toward, 164–67; on France's *grandeur*, 207–8, 242
Delafosse, Maurice, 214
Delavignette, Robert, 26, 30–31, 53, 94, 95, 118
Dépossession du monde (Jacques Berque), 233–35
Déroulède, Paul, 205, 206
Deschamps, Hubert, 186
Devillers, Philippe, 78; *Histoire du Viêt-Nam de 1940 à 1952*, 56
Diop, Alioune, 82, 214, 219, 220
Discours sur le colonialisme (Aimé Césaire), 67
Disobedience, morality of, 151–60, 175–76
Domenach, Jean-Marie, 18, 19, 52, 71, 188–89; idea of France, 23, 185; vision of the French Union, 49, 69, 191; anticolonialist activities of, 53, 56, 67, 116, 175, 179; concern for the overseas peoples, 84, 236–37; against atrocities, 113, 114, 116, 125, 127, 133, 148; on legitimate disobedience, 152–53, 157–

58, 159, 160, 170–71, 175; on the Gaullist regime, 166, 168, 260 (n. 27); for a French-speaking community, 206, 208, 237
Dresch, Jean, 175
Dumont, René, 174
Duras, Marguerite, 174
Duroselle, Jean-Baptiste, 186
Duverger, Maurice, 18, 19, 20, 192, 211; on colonial nationalism, 76, 91–92; against French abuses in Algeria, 116, 129, 146; on legitimate means to oppose the war, 158, 175; for de Gaulle, 165, 166; on the lack of realism, 180, 181, 182, 183

E

Electorate, French. *See* Public opinion
El Glaoui, 50, 53, 54, 64, 65
Elite, political, 5, 7, 11, 15, 36, 53, 108, 110, 201, 203
Espoir et peur du siècle (Raymond Aron), 196–97
Esprit, 15, 17, 18, 95, 156–57; for a humanist French Union, 30–31, 68–69; criticism of overseas policy, 47, 49, 51, 52, 53, 55, 179; for the Vietminh, 72–73; doubts about colonial independence, 76, 77, 78, 83; for Algerian independence, 100, 101, 112, 192; against atrocities, 117–18, 121, 127, 129, 134; on the morality of disobedience, 154, 157–58; for an association of peoples, 193, 206, 236–37. *See also* Domenach, Jean-Marie; Mounier, Emmanuel
Ethnocentrism, French, 209, 224–25, 232, 241; definition of, 210–12; challenges to, 212–36; Marxist version of, 222; revision of, 237
Etiemble, René, 175
Étranger, L' (Albert Camus), 139
Être et le néant, L' (Jean-Paul Sartre), 135, 144, 221
Éveil de l'Afrique noire, L' (Emmanuel Mounier), 69
Évolués, 211, 212–214
"Evolutionism," 24, 224–26, 228, 232
Express, L', 15, 19, 56, 188; on Algeria, 100, 112–13, 114, 116, 121, 139–40; seizures of, 119, 147, 148, 173. *See also* Mauriac, François; Servan-Schreiber, Jean-Jacques

F

Fanon, Frantz, 82, 87–88, 95, 144, 222–23, 234, 236; *L'An cinq de la révolution algérienne*, 95; *Les Damnés de la terre*, 136, 172; *Peau noire, masques blancs*, 223

Melouza: massacre of, 133
Memmi, Albert, 96, 141, 210, 234; *Portrait du colonisé, précédé du portrait du colonisateur*, 94–95, 113, 144
Mendès-France, Pierre, 4–5, 19, 54, 56, 105, 160, 190
Mercier, Paul, 219
Merleau-Ponty, Maurice, 18, 70, 88, 135, 168–69; on independence for the colonies, 73, 87, 96, 129, 175
Middle East, 33–35
Mind, nature of the: Mannoni on, 80–81, 228–29; Senghor on, 217–18, 228, 230; Lévy-Bruhl on, 228; Lévi-Strauss on, 229–31
Mission, overseas (civilizing, colonial, humanist), 20; sources of, 21–26, 224; army's belief in, 23–24, 87, 112; Marxist version of, 44, 69, 83; reaffirmation of, 48–49, 68–70, 96, 125, 193, 195–96, 201, 206, 232, 242; problem of fulfillment of, 70, 79, 83–84, 85–88, 95–97, 99–100. *See also* Assimilation, policy of; Ethnocentrism, French; Vocation, colonial
Mitterrand, François, 19, 75, 100, 190, 191; *Présence française et abandon*, 189
Mohammed ben Youssef, 42–43, 51–54
Mollet, Guy, 7, 106–8, 117, 160, 161–62
Monde, Le, 15, 19, 51, 69, 91, 107, 146, 147, 158; on overseas events in 1945, 32–35, 62; on French atrocities in Algeria, 114–18, 121; on de Gaulle, 165, 166. *See also* Beuve-Méry, Hubert
Monnerville, Gaston, 209
Monod, Théodore, 219
Montaron, Georges, 116
"Moralism": of the anticolonialists, 20, 209, 239–40
Morazé, Charles, 211
Morin, Edgar, 175, 221
Morocco, 24, 25, 28: status as a "protectorate," 23, 39–40, 73–74; crisis of the early 1950s, 50–54, 61. *See also* "Cosovereignty"; El Glaoui; Istiqlal; Mohammed ben Youssef
Mounier, Emmanuel, 18, 51–52, 69, 73, 179, 219
Mouvement Démocratique de Rénovation Malgache (MDRM), 42
Mouvement National Algérien (MNA), 130, 133, 134
Mouvement Républicain Populaire (MRP), 6–7, 9, 37, 52, 108, 111, 117, 118. *See also* Bidault, Georges
Muller, Jean, 114

Mus, Paul, 78, 233; *Viêt-Nam, sociologie d'une guerre*, 56
Mythe de Sisyphe, Le (Albert Camus), 130

N
Nadeau, Maurice, 174
National Council of the Resistance, 30
Nationalism, colonial: growth of, 25, 27–28, 37–38, 69–70, 100–101, 183, 197, 234; French criticism of, 40, 44, 49, 76, 83; defense of, 77–78, 91, 94; as the criterion for independence, 99–102
Nausée, La (Jean-Paul Sartre), 135
Nef, La, 15, 19, 53, 57, 65, 67, 73, 95, 99; on Algeria, 101, 121, 165, 199, 200; federalism of, 191–93. *See also* Duverger, Maurice
Negritude, 214–24, 267 (n. 20)
"Neocolonialism": threat of, 203–4
Notre Guerre (Francis Jeanson), 170
Nouvelle Nouvelle Revue Française, La, 226–27

O
Observateur, L'. See *France-Observateur*
Octobre, 65, 72–73, 180
Ollivier, Albert, 41
Organisation de l'Armée Secrète (OAS), 145–46, 149–50, 165, 166, 177–78
"Orphée noir" (Jean-Paul Sartre), 219–23

P
Pan-Arabism: threat of, 76–79, 129
Paris-Match, 201–2
Paris-Presse, 173
Parti Socialiste Unifié (PSU), 175, 176
Passy, Frédéric, 205, 207
Peau noire, masques blancs (Frantz Fanon), 223
Péju, Marcel, 144, 163, 170, 172, 174, 177, 260–61 (n. 29)
Pensée sauvage, La (Claude Lévi-Strauss), 229–31
"Personalism," 18, 73
Peste, La (Albert Camus), 130–31, 139
Philip, André, 116, 119, 179
Piastre: traffic in, 59, 61
Political system: of the Fourth Republic, 6–7, 10–11, 46, 66–67, 161. *See also* Elite, political
Popular sovereignty, principle of, 99–100. *See also* Self-determination, right of
Portrait du colonisé, précédé du portrait du colonisateur (Albert Memmi), 94–95, 113, 144